"No matter where we are in our .... rom this man, who does it well. Listen to A.. ...., ... you will be blessed with fresh insights and clear applications. You will also take note of his ability to pay careful attention to the text all the while showing its relevance to today's audience. In this book, he uses illustrations to help us understand how he gets from text to sermon, from two thousand years ago to today."

—**Erwin W. Lutzer**, pastor emeritus, The Moody Church

"Abraham Kuruvilla is the E. F. Hutton of the homiletical world. When he writes, professors and preachers read! I have been greatly helped and wonderfully blessed through his other volumes on preaching, *Privilege the Text!* and *A Vision for Preaching*. This newest volume is exactly what its title suggests: a manual for preaching. In this wonderfully readable volume, Dr. Kuruvilla takes us on the homiletical journey from getting ready to preach to the final step of delivering a sermon. Professors will find this volume filled with transferable concepts to share with their students. Preachers will find it to be invaluable as we all learn to preach God's word more effectively. Dr. Kuruvilla has written. We should now read and apply!"

—**Jerry Vines**, pastor emeritus, First Baptist Church, Jacksonville, Florida; former president of the Southern Baptist Convention

"Abe Kuruvilla is one of my favorite preachers and homileticians because he consistently and beautifully blends meaty exegesis and engaging exposition better than anyone I know. Whenever Kuruvilla opens the word—whether in the classroom or in the pulpit—biblical authors live and breathe. His *Manual for Preaching* is an opportunity for a generation of preachers to learn how to preach from a master as they make the journey with him from the sacred text to a contemporary setting."

—**Hershael W. York**, Southern Baptist Theological Seminary

"Abe Kuruvilla knows that the journey from text to sermon is not a straight line. Each week the preacher faces a brand-new challenge: How exactly do we get from this particular text to a sermon that is biblically faithful, theologically accurate, and life changing in its impact? This book offers a reliable guide that will encourage preachers by showing them it can be done. *A Manual for Preaching* is exactly what its name implies. Here you will find practical help that will enable you to enter the pulpit with confidence week after week. Read it! Study it! Share it with a friend!"

—**Ray Pritchard**, president, Keep Believing Ministries

"Homileticians and expositors are getting accustomed to expecting solid work from Dr. Abe Kuruvilla, and this new manuscript will not disappoint them in the least. Therefore, I am happy to recommend this new title—*A Manual for Preaching: The Journey from Text to Sermon*. Ever since I read Dr. Kuruvilla's book *Privilege the Text!*, I have been one of his fans. This volume fits right in line with that previous volume. I think pastors, students, and laypersons will enjoy this new work just as well. I give it my highest commendation."

—**Walter C. Kaiser Jr.**, president emeritus, Gordon-Conwell
Theological Seminary

A
MANUAL
FOR
PREACHING

A MANUAL FOR PREACHING

THE JOURNEY FROM TEXT TO SERMON

ABRAHAM KURUVILLA

Baker Academic
a division of Baker Publishing Group
Grand Rapids, Michigan

© 2019 by Abraham Kuruvilla

Published by Baker Academic
a division of Baker Publishing Group
PO Box 6287, Grand Rapids, MI 49516-6287
www.bakeracademic.com

Printed in the United States of America

Library of Congress Cataloging-in-Publication Data
Names: Kuruvilla, Abraham., author.
Title: A manual for preaching : the journey from text to sermon / Abraham Kuruvilla.
Description: Grand Rapids : Baker Academic, a division of Baker Publishing Group, 2019. |
    Includes bibliographical references and index.
Identifiers: LCCN 2018061706 | ISBN 9780801098635 (pbk.)
Subjects: LCSH: Preaching.
Classification: LCC BV4211.3 .K865 2019 | DDC 251—dc23
LC record available at https://lccn.loc.gov/2018061706

ISBN 978-1-5409-6237-9 (casebound)

Baker Publishing Group publications use paper produced from sustainable forestry practices and postconsumer waste whenever possible.

To those who weekly submit themselves to sermons
—the people of God—
desiring to experience the word of God
facilitated by the preachers of God:

may your lives be transformed thereby into the likeness
of the Son of God
by the wondrous power of the Spirit of God
for the glory of God!

Contents

Contents

Acknowledgments

In J. K. Rowling's magnificent seven-part series that recounts the adventures of Harry Potter and his coterie at Hogwarts School of Witchcraft and Wizardry, there are a number of magical artifacts, none perhaps as fascinating as the Pensieve—the name a play on "pensive" and "sieve." This, in Rowling's exquisitely imaginative conception, is a shallow stone basin covered in runes that is used to store, recover, and review memories. Witches and wizards can extract their memories and save them in the Pensieve in a silvery, thread-like form that is neither gas nor liquid. Later, the owner or another can examine those memories, experiencing the remembered events from a third-party, omniscient perspective, a sort of magical virtual reality. In an interview, Rowling confirmed that the Pensieve does not function like a diary, confined to what one remembers. "The Pensieve re-creates a moment for you, so you could go into your own memory and relive things that you didn't notice [at] the time. It's somewhere in your head, which I'm sure it is, in all of our brains. I'm sure if you could access it, things that you don't know you remember are all in there somewhere."[1]

Writing this book was like accessing my personal homiletical Pensieve, digging deep into the foggy sermonic recesses of my brain, extracting all my thoughts and feelings and experiences concerning preaching, some that I was not even conscious of. A marvelous exercise indeed! And putting it all on paper brought into tremendous focus the whats, hows, and whys of the growth and development of my identity as a researcher, teacher, and practitioner of preaching. No doubt, this is a work still in progress, and for God's

---

1. Anelli and Spartz, "*Leaky Cauldron* and *Mugglenet*." All the links in this work have been gathered together at http://www.homiletix.com/preaching2019/links.

providence and grace throughout this process, I am, and will eternally remain, grateful beyond words.

Memories are, of course, not made solo. As I immersed myself in my Pensieve, I saw an entire community of God's people involved in my life, creating those retrievable moments and generating those remembrances: writers of books, keepers of libraries, administrators of schools, teachers of preaching, students of homiletics, expanders of thought, stretchers of horizons, givers of feedback, tenderers of critique, extenders of love, donors of grace, and, most of all, hearers of sermons. These last, God's people, were the ones to whom God's word was given; to them it belongs and to them it is to be preached. May we preachers, servants of the word of God *and* the people of God, be worthy of the trust reposed in us by the body of Christ and the stewardship entrusted to us by God himself. May the Holy Spirit empower us to discharge our responsibility faithfully. And may the ascended and reigning Christ be the one we follow and to whose image we point, sermon by sermon and pericope by pericope, for God's glory!

Abraham Kuruvilla
Dallas, Texas
Ascension Day 2018

Introduction

The notion of putting everything I know about barbecue into a book is a daunting one. Not because I know so much—I'm still learning—but because of the nature of barbecue itself. It's because the printed word—definitive, exacting, permanent—is in many ways antithetical to the process of cooking barbecue, which is, for lack of a better word, loosey-goosey. So many people want to have a recipe, but with all of the variables in barbecue . . . there is no "magic" recipe.[1]

Those words by the pit maestro Aaron Franklin[2] I echo fervently, except that I'm dealing with preaching, not with a Texas culinary institution. As the first-century classical rhetorician Quintilian warns, "No one however should expect from me the sort of rules that most writers of textbooks have handed down, or ask me to lay down for students a set of laws, as it were, bound by immutable necessity . . . , as if to do otherwise was a sin. Rhetoric would be a very easy and trivial affair if it could be comprised in a single short set of precepts." Instead, he says, everything depends on exigency and expediency that call for adjustment on the part of the speaker in many ways.[3] So at the outset, I admit, with Franklin, that there is no magic recipe—for either barbecue or preaching. Therefore, there really is no right and wrong in these endeavors, only wise and unwise (or good, bad, and ugly).

1. Franklin and Mackay, *Franklin Barbecue*, 1.
2. Of Franklin Barbecue fame, 900 E. 11th St., Austin, TX 78702 (hours: Tuesday–Sunday, 11:00 a.m. until sold out).
3. Quintilian, *Orator's Education*, 341 (2.13.1–3).

I will also confess that my intimate knowledge of preaching relates almost exclusively to my own ponderings and practices. In the decades that I've been engaged in the discipline of homiletics, I have heard, read, and examined a lot of sermons, spoken and scripted, delivered across eras and beyond oceans, in churches various and in classrooms galore. But I know myself and my preaching best (or at least I think I do). "In most books, the *I*, or first person, is omitted; in this it will be retained. . . . I should not talk so much about myself if there were anybody else whom I knew as well."[4] But I don't. So what you are about to read is my conception of how preaching should be undertaken (the practice). And that conception is based solidly on my understanding of what preaching ought to be (the vision). I had the chance to expound on this latter aspect of homiletics in *A Manual for Preaching*: "Biblical preaching, by a leader of the church, in a gathering of Christians for worship, is the communication of the thrust of a pericope of Scripture discerned by theological exegesis, and of its application to that specific body of believers, that they may be conformed to the image of Christ, for the glory of God—all in the power of the Holy Spirit."[5]

There I reflected on preaching as being biblical, pastoral, ecclesial, communicational, theological, applicational, conformational, doxological, and spiritual. But at the core of that vision was a hermeneutic, a way of reading Scripture, that influenced how I saw preaching. That same hermeneutic also informs my conception of how preaching ought to be undertaken. In other words, *A Manual for Preaching* continues what was begun in *A Vision for Preaching*.

Here is a summary of what readers will find in this book's chapters. Chapter 1 ("Getting Ready") will deal with preliminaries, setting the stage with sequential long- and short-term plans for preaching. The long-term plan directs the structure of the remainder of the book. Chapter 2 ("Discerning Theology") lays out the core of my preaching philosophy—its hermeneutic: how the text of Scripture is to be read and interpreted. Readers will be guided with examples to discern the thrust of various texts (the theology of those pericopes). Chapter 3 ("Deriving Application") defines and describes application and the move from pericopal theology to application; it discusses the main characteristics and types of application and how to derive application for sermons on particular pericopes. Chapter 4 ("Creating Maps") delineates the process for mapping a sermon into a number of moves, and Chapter 5 ("Fleshing Moves") explains how one can expand those moves—put flesh on

4. Thoreau, *Walden*, 1.
5. Kuruvilla, *Vision for Preaching*, 1.

skeletons, as it were—attending to both revelation (aspects of the text) and relevance (aspects of the audience). Chapter 6 ("Illustrating Ideas") considers the functions and types of illustrations and how to find, organize, and use them in sermons. Chapter 7 ("Crafting Introductions and Conclusions") dissects the structures of those elements that commence and conclude a sermon and provides tips on how best to compose and deploy them. Chapter 8 ("Producing Manuscripts") emphasizes the utility of producing a sermon manuscript, weighs the different kinds of sermons—with and without notes—and gives suggestions for producing and using manuscripts, considering also the employment of electronic devices to manage notes/manuscripts during preaching. This chapter also debates sermon borrowing. The final chapter ("Delivering Sermons") addresses matters pertaining to delivery as well as rehearsing, nervousness, and how to manage one's immediate pre- and post-sermon routines.

Over the course of these nine chapters, readers will also find short commentaries on some of the pericopes of the Letter to the Ephesians and the Jacob Story (Gen. 25:19–36:43), interpretations that derive the statement of each text's thrust and force—its Theological Focus. (Chapter 1 will provide an introduction to Ephesians and the Jacob Story; chapters 2–9 will consider several of their individual pericopes.)[6] Other examples will necessarily be from brief portions of Scripture (and elsewhere), some of them not even complete pericopes, many from Proverbs. The constraint of book size and the desire to depict easily graspable examples dictated those choices. Besides, didactic and narrative genres, as represented by Ephesians and the Jacob Story, compose half the Old Testament and almost all the New Testament.

Most of the examples and preaching tips herein are drawn from real life—tried in class and proven from pulpits, submitted by students and shared by colleagues. I have learned from many, both dead and living, and continue to do so. In turn, I encourage readers also to be avid learners, never ceasing to grow and improve in their preaching. "We'll be at this craft for a lifetime. There's no rush. Slowly, step-by-step, working on one thing at a time—that's how to build a solid preaching style."[7] That is, no doubt, because learning to preach, and learning to preach better, is a commitment for life—and never easy. The French Dominican friar Humbert of Romans, a leader among preachers in the twelfth century, began his *Treatise on Preaching* with these words: "The

6. These interpretations of some of the Ephesians and Jacob Story pericopes, along with interpretations of those pericopes not dealt with in this work, can be found at http://www .homiletix.com/preaching2019/commentaries. For more exhaustive curations of these pericopes, I recommend my full-fledged commentaries: *Ephesians* and *Genesis*.

7. Galli and Larson, *Preaching That Connects*, 144.

first thing to note is how excellent the office [of preaching] is, how necessary, how acceptable to God, how profitable to the preacher himself, how useful to men, [and] *how difficult it is to do well.*"[8] But hang in there; there is no communication genre as enthralling, no Christian service as exciting, and no edifying ministry as rewarding as preaching. For the preacher to be used by God in the transformation of lives into Christlikeness, pericope by pericope, sermon by sermon, is an incredible privilege. Revel in it!

In sum, this work is an attempt to describe my own praxis of preaching and share what I have learned over the decades. I wish I could say that I preach what I teach. Alas! "It is a good divine that follows his own instructions. I can easier teach twenty what were good to be done than be one of the twenty to follow mine own teaching."[9] But here it is anyway. Please take whatever is offered as suggestions that I consider reasonable and expedient for the attainment of the goals propounded in my vision for preaching. The counsels in this book are, therefore, intended to function as guidelines and not as rules (unless they are rules of thumb) and, as such, may be contravened as readers grow in preaching experience and skill. That is to say, *break the rules!* Ferdinand Ries, a friend and pupil of Beethoven, recalled the genius doing exactly that:

> During a walk, I spoke to [Beethoven] of two perfect fifths . . . in his Violin Quartet in C minor [Op. 18, No. 4; such parallel intervallic progressions were taboo in classical harmony]. . . .
>
> He asked: "Well, who has forbidden them?" . . .
>
> Since I did not know how to take the question, he repeated it several times until I finally answered in amazement: "After all, these are fundamental rules."
>
> The question was repeated again, and I answered: "[Friedrich] Marpurg, [Johann] Kirnberger, [Johann] Fux, etc., etc.—all [music] theorists."
>
> [Beethoven] answered: "And *I* allow them."[10]

Lesser mortals may slavishly abide by rules of theorists, but you, preacher, feel free to break them. This book will hopefully help you find your own voice like a Beethoven while sustaining you until then with avuncular comments and beneficent glances over your shoulder.

And now, a final word from that blackbelt of barbecue, Aaron Franklin, before you fire up your grill:

8. Humbert of Romans, "Treatise on Preaching," 375 (my translation and emphasis).
9. Shakespeare, *Merchant of Venice*, act 1, scene 2.
10. Wegeler and Ries, *Biographische Notizen über Ludwig van Beethoven*, 104–5 (my translation and emphasis).

Hopefully, while you read this book, you'll find yourself chomping at the bit to get out there and throw a few racks of ribs or a big, honking brisket onto your smoker. And all I can say is, Go for it! The key to my own development—and it will be to yours—is repetition. Just as with anything, the more you do it, the better you'll get. . . . Ultimately, that's the best advice I can give. Do, and do some more. Drink beer, but not so much that you lose track of what you're doing. And pay attention. Sweat the details and you'll end up producing barbecue that would make the most seasoned of pitmasters proud.[11]

Ditto for preaching, *mutatis mutandis*.

11. Franklin and Mackay, *Franklin Barbecue*, 3.

1

Getting Ready

Ants shape each other's behavior by exchanging chemicals. We do
it by standing in front of each other, peering into each other's eyes,
waving our hands and emitting strange sounds from our mouths.
Human-to-human communication is a true wonder of the world.
We do it unconsciously every day. And it reaches its most intense
form on the public stage.[1]

Yes, belonging to the family *Hominidae* puts our interpersonal communication on a different plane from that engaged in by members of
the family *Formicidae*. But for us who are children of God, the form
of communication we call preaching is located in an even more unique di-
mension and is different from every other kind of public speech, formal or
informal: it is the parade event wherein the word of God is exposited by a
shepherd of God for the people of God to conform them into the image of
the Son of God by the power of the Spirit of God for the glory of God. An
incomparable and momentous occasion, indeed! And for us who have chosen
the vocation of preaching, this form of communication is critically important:
we are handling Scripture to facilitate listeners' conformation to Christlikeness.[2] Preaching is a crucial responsibility, and one fraught with dignity and
distinction. It is undoubtedly a noble task: preachers speak, "as it were, the

1. Anderson, *TED Talks*, ix.
2. For more on these crucial elements of the preaching endeavor, see Kuruvilla, *Vision for Preaching*.

words of God" (1 Pet. 4:11).[3] Those in Ephesus who "labor in the word and in teaching," Paul declares, are "worthy of double honor" (1 Tim. 5:17); the task of an elder—one who was also required to be "able to teach" (3:2)—was commended as "a good work" (3:1). By fulfilling the preaching duty allotted to him, Timothy is reminded that he would be "a good servant of Christ Jesus" (4:6). So as Colossians 1:28 declares, "We proclaim him, instructing all people and teaching all people with all wisdom, that we may present all people mature in Christ." God is glorified as his people thus manifest his holiness (Christlikeness) and represent him to the world, "filled with the fruit of righteousness through Jesus Christ, to the glory and praise of God" (Phil. 1:11).[4] What a privilege it is to partner with God in the execution of his grand plan to consummate all things in Jesus Christ (Eph. 1:9–10)![5]

Preliminaries

Let me address a few important matters before we begin our journey from text to sermon.

Edification versus Evangelism

Preaching is for those already in relationship with God.[6] There is an important corollary to this assertion that preachers must bear in mind.

Because the goal of preaching is to conform humankind to the image of Christ, and because the first step of such conformation is the placing of one's trust in Christ as one's only God and Savior, the proclamation of the good news of salvation has also generally been considered preaching. But in the Bible, evangelistic proclamation is never a formal exposition of a specific biblical text that contextually interprets the authorial thrust/force in that pericope[7] and that draws out relevant application from that particular text. Rather, evangelistic proclamation deals with the announcement to non-

3. All translations of Scripture are my own unless otherwise noted.

4. Also see Matt. 5:16; 1 Pet. 2:12.

5. For this critical partnership with God, the preacher must be a certain kind of person. See Kuruvilla, "Preaching Is Pastoral," in *Vision for Preaching*, 31–49; Kuruvilla, "Preaching Is Spiritual," in *Vision for Preaching*, 167–85. And for the ultimate end of preaching, see Kuruvilla, "Preaching Is Doxological," in *Vision for Preaching*, 149–66.

6. See Kuruvilla, "Preaching Is Ecclesial," in *Vision for Preaching*, 51–69. The issue of where preaching is to be conducted is also addressed there.

7. "Pericope" (pronounced pə-ri-kə-pē, from the Greek *perikopē* = section, passage) refers to a portion of the biblical text that is of manageable size for homiletical and liturgical use in an ecclesial setting. More on pericopes below.

believers of an accomplished act—the atoning work of Christ. Thus the *text* in evangelistic proclamation plays only a supportive role in such proclamation: it simply serves as a springboard to raise an existential angst, to validate the veracity of the resurrection, to depict the benefits of a relationship with God, to delineate the negative consequences of not being in such a relationship, and so on. The core *message* of evangelistic proclamation is identical in every iteration: Jesus Christ, God incarnate, died and rose again, paying the full, final price for the sins of humanity. *Application* in these proclamations also remains the same, no matter what the text used, no matter who the audience is: *Trust Jesus Christ as your only God and Savior!*[8] Of course, the *audience* for evangelistic proclamations is exclusively unbelievers.

Edifying preaching, on the other hand, involves the exposition of a particular biblical pericope, with the *text* playing the major role, all else being subordinate. The sermon discerns the text's thrust/force (i.e., the theology of that particular pericope), making the *message* of such preaching unique in every sermonic event.[9] The derived *application* is also specific for the theology of that text; besides, such application is tailored for a particular audience. The *audience*, which is being conformed to the image of Christ, comprises those already in relationship with God (i.e., believers).

In light of these differences in text use, message thrust, application specificity, and audience identity, it is best to distinguish evangelistic proclamation and edifying preaching. For the rest of this work, such a distinction will be maintained, and our focus will be exclusively on preaching—the pericope-specific, believer-edifying species of Christian communication.

I contend that there is no *hermeneutical* constraint arising from every text of Scripture to mention the gospel of salvation in every sermon.[10] However, there is a *pragmatic* constraint to do so, for one does not know if every listener in one's audience is saved. Therefore, even though the sermon is primarily for the people of God, the gospel *should* be presented in every worship service, though there is no imperative that such a proclamation be confined to the sermon. It is far more appropriate and prudent to think in terms of presenting the good news *somewhere* in the worship service (not necessarily in the sermon), by *someone* (not necessarily by the preacher), *somehow* (not

8. In this work, application will always be in italics and end with an exclamation mark.

9. For more on the theology of pericopes, see Kuruvilla, "Preaching Is Communicational," in *Vision for Preaching*, 71–89; Kuruvilla, "Preaching Is Theological," in *Vision for Preaching*, 91–109; and also chap. 2 below, "Discerning Theology."

10. See Kuruvilla, *Privilege the Text!*, 238–69; Kuruvilla, *Vision for Preaching*, 42–52; and my contribution, "Christiconic View," as well as my responses to other contributors in *Homiletics and Hermeneutics*.

necessarily in any set format). Discussing the inclusion of this critical element of worship with your team is helpful—be creative.

Choosing a Text: Book and Pericope

Now that you have decided to preach, the first item on the agenda is the selection of a text to preach from. Again, let's assume you are in this for the long run. In that case, my strong recommendation is that you "read continuously" (i.e., *lectio continua*), going from pericope to pericope in a given book, respecting the trajectory of its author's thought and the progression of his ideas. This I shall simply refer to as "preaching," without any qualifying adjectives like textual, topical, expository, and so on.[11] Such preaching alone gives listeners the sense of what the author is *doing* in each pericope and how these *doings* are sequenced and linked together in a given book to further the author's theological agenda for life change unto Christlikeness.[12]

Even when you preach *lectio continua*, you'll need to figure out which book of the Bible to tackle.[13] This will be contingent on your audience. Where are they in their spiritual walk? Are there any particular issues of concern or problems within the flock you are shepherding? Are you reorienting the momentum of the group and the trajectory of its life growth in a new direction? If so, you might consider whether a particular book of the Bible meets the need or situation of your listeners. This is perhaps the only time in *lectio continua* preaching that the need of the audience comes *before* the choice of

11. Walter C. Kaiser once recommended to his students that they "preach a topical sermon only once every five years—and then immediately to repent and ask God's forgiveness" (*Toward an Exegetical Theology*, 19). My sentiments exactly! I am not a fan at all of topical preaching that takes entailments from a variety of texts (not necessarily thrusts/forces that the author intended—e.g., the Trinity from Matt. 28:19–20) and puts them all together to create an exposition of a topic of interest: *lectio selecta* ("reading selectively"). It is "the seduction of the concordance" that produces unity that is "only apparent, not real," as Fred B. Craddock put it (*As One without Authority*, 56; also see chap. 5, "Fleshing Moves"). Though useful on occasion, topical preaching, like fast food, ought never to be the staple diet of the children of God. So here's a personal rule of thumb: try not to have more than five special days (including Easter, Thanksgiving, and Christmas) plus up to five more weeks of other kinds of topical sermons every calendar year (i.e., a series on a theological topic, a current issue, or some such, as you deem necessary for your flock). If you add another six or eight weeks when you are on vacation and/or when someone is filling in for you with assorted texts and topics that you may not have much control over, that leaves you with about thirty-six weeks a year to preach through books *lectio continua*.

12. See Kuruvilla, *Vision for Preaching*, 23–25.

13. If you are going to do a one-off sermon, as I am usually called to do since I am not on staff or on the preaching team in any church, then you need to figure out what your audience needs and what you can do reasonably well within the constraints of available preparation time, personal capacity, efficiency, etc. Pick a passage accordingly.

a text (here, book). But once a book is picked, let its A/author have his way with the audience. As we shall see later, the needs of audiences should still be considered, but only *after* the theology of the text has been discerned. Other considerations for choice of books might be your preaching calendar: What book have you just finished preaching through? What season in the church calendar are you going to be preaching in? And so on.[14]

For the rest of this work, I'll assume that you plan to preach through a book, or a sizable portion thereof, week by week. And for illustration purposes, let's also assume that you want to preach through the Letter to the Ephesians or the Jacob Story in Genesis 25:19–36:43; these will be the main texts we'll handle in this work. With you poring over my shoulder, I'll work out the theologies of several of the pericopes of Ephesians and the Jacob Story.[15] That will give you a sense of what a "pearl necklace" looks like, one from the Old Testament (a narrative) and one from the New Testament (an epistle), the pericopal "pearls" of which were deliberately chosen and carefully strung together by the A/author into the "necklace."

A word about pericopes before we go any further. Though *pericope* technically refers to a portion of, or a scene in, the Gospel narratives, I use it here to designate a preaching text, irrespective of genre or size—a practical definition. In my conception, a pericope's boundaries are constrained by the preacher's need to create discrete sequential sermons from contiguous passages. So a pericope is a portion of text from which one can preach a sermon that is distinct in theological thrust/force and application from sermons preached from adjacent pericopes. As an analogy, take the spectrum of visible light, with wavelengths from 400 nm to 700 nm, violet to red. How many different reds are there in the spectrum? And how many can we distinguish? I, being somewhat opaque in these matters, can discern light red, medium red, and dark red. You, however, may find cherry, rose, merlot, crimson, ruby, brick, blood, blush, scarlet, and so on. In the same way, the slicing of your pericopes may differ from mine. You might be able to discern distinct theological thrusts/forces between pericopes divided minutely and finely and be capable of deriving equally distinct applications therefrom. I, on the other hand, might need larger slices of text to be able to discern such theological and applicational

14. For interim preachers, it is helpful to inventory what has been preached in the recent past by the regular preacher and other pulpit guests.

15. Brief commentaries on the pericopes from these texts can be found toward the end of each subsequent chapter (this chapter will introduce Ephesians and the Jacob Story). All of these, as well as commentaries on pericopes not discussed in this work, are available at http://www.homiletix.com/preaching2019/commentaries. We'll also go through a number of brief examples from the book of Proverbs, not to mention other assorted and diverse texts, both sacred and secular.

differences between my adjacent pericopes. But the fact is that too fine a dicing of passages will often yield similar theologies and applications (and so similar sermons) across weeks. One cannot discern a whole lot of difference between adjacent pericopes that are only a verse or two long (or between red at 680 nm and that at 681 nm). You are safer taking larger chunks of text, as I am prone to do these days after almost a quarter century of preaching. Check out the sizes of the pericopes from Ephesians and the Jacob Story that we will be dealing with in coming chapters—they are not small.

Tools and Resources

Much has been made of the preacher's library, whether in ink and on paper or in 1s and 0s. Libraries are, no doubt, important. The Spirit of God has spoken through many in the past (mostly dead) and continues to do so through many in the present (mostly [!] alive). And we preachers need to listen to what the Author has said through these others and not just proceed by the light of our personal illumination. But there is an obsession with books and electronic resources—the fancier, the better, it seems—that is not based on actual need.

As preachers, our primary task is to lay out what the biblical author is *doing* with what he is saying in each pericope—the theology of the pericope. With this primary task in mind, the most helpful resources for preachers, who facilitate listeners' discerning of theology, are those tomes that enable our own discernment of the theology of the pericope. That is what we preachers need help with—interpretation that discerns pericopal theology: *theological* interpretation. Regrettably, such text-to-theology analyses of biblical books are sorely lacking. And so we lament with Karl Barth:

> My complaint is that recent commentators confine themselves to an interpretation of the text which seems to me to be no commentary at all, but merely the first step toward a commentary. Recent commentaries contain no more than a reconstruction of the text, a rendering of the Greek words and phrases by their precise equivalents, a number of additional notes in which archaeological and philological material is gathered together, and a more or less plausible arrangement of the subject-matter in such a manner that it may be made historically and psychologically intelligible from the standpoint of pure pragmatism.[16]

It is as if, when a patient comes to see me, a dermatologist (my other job), for a rash on the face, I begin to make a list of observations: a fifty-nine-year-old

16. Barth, "Preface to the Second Edition," 6.

gentleman, tortoise-shell-rimmed glasses, thinning hair on the frontal scalp, two ears, blue tie, 170 pounds, and so on. But these observations will not necessarily bring me closer to an accurate diagnosis. I also notice that my patient has red papules and macules on the malar cheeks, and general erythema (redness) in that area—ah, now *those* are significant observations. I am not saying that the patient's weight and hair loss and glasses and tie have no bearing on his facial rash—they might. And so also might the various histories that I elicit from my patient: a family history (of kinship diseases and genetic predilections), a social history (of prevailing habits and unrecognized behaviors), a personal history (of occupation and demographics), and a medical history (of previous illnesses and earlier maladies). But all of these have utility only insofar as they influence the current problem: the facial rash. Histories and backgrounds and cultures and idioms are perhaps necessary but, in and of themselves, are not sufficient for arriving at a diagnosis and moving to treatment (= discerning the theology and deriving application). The immediate physical exam, current imaging, lab work, and so on are of primary importance in the diagnostic process of getting to the cause of the disorder, helped though they are—to some degree—by the assorted histories that are, again, necessary but not sufficient. Without privileging the text, without discerning what the author is *doing*, without arriving at the theology of the pericope, valid application is impossible.

Instead, we preachers are consumed with what is best labeled a "hermeneutic of excavation" and have been trained to shovel up loads of dirt, boulders, potsherds, arrowheads, and fishhooks. We dump it all on our desks. Everything in the text, it seems, is equally important and crucial, and there is hardly any discriminating inference or integration that leads to an understanding of what the author is *doing*—the theology of the pericope. Like cows at pasture, we munch on every available blade of grass, and commentaries abundantly furnish those pieces of herbage for our consumption.[17] The overestimation of the values of all these bits and bytes of information that we have unearthed (or that are served to us by commentators) oft leads the interpretive enterprise astray. And so, on Saturday night we ask in desperation, "What on earth do we do with this mass of material come Sunday morning? What's the author *doing* here? What's important and what's not? And how do we create a sermon and get to valid application?"

It is in the discovery of authorial *doings*—the discernment of the pericopal theology—that commentaries have let preachers down: "Commentaries often provide no theological reflection at all or do not move beyond a summation

17. Paraphrasing Medawar, *Induction and Intuition*, 29.

of the exegesis into true theological reflection."[18] Again, what we preachers need is *theological* exegesis to discern the *doings* of the author of the text (i.e., the theology of the pericope) so that we and our listeners, the people of God, can move to valid application. No wonder the sage of the twentieth century, singer Johnny Cash, after exploring numerous commentaries on Paul's letters, quipped, "Tons of material has been written . . . but I discovered that the Bible can shed a lot of light on commentaries."[19] It can. A careful reading of the text will enlighten our minds and elucidate its theology, as we shall find.

I, therefore, cast a dim eye on the plethora of resources currently available to preachers. I would caution that you be discerning too. Carefully pick a commentary or two on a given book, especially those that seek to clarify what the author of the book is *doing* with what he is saying, pericope by pericope.[20] Needless to say, Bible scholars who write commentaries are rarely ever preachers, and so you are probably going to have to search long and hard to find commentaries suitable for helping you preach in the fashion I recommend.[21] But all is not lost. We can accomplish a great deal ourselves by learning to read better. More on that in the next chapter ("Discerning Theology"), but for now, let me just say this: don't get carried away with books and the accumulation of massive libraries. Save your hard-earned money. Pick a few good tomes, checking them constantly against Scripture as you study them, and learn to do your own work.[22]

18. Watson, "Why We Need Socio-Rhetorical Commentary," 138.

19. Cash, *Man in White*, xvi.

20. For over a decade now, I have been attempting to produce commentaries for this purpose, curating the text for preachers, pericope by pericope. The commentaries on Genesis, Judges, Mark, and Ephesians are in print. Another hundred-odd years and I will be done with the remaining sixty-two books! In the meantime, check out free chapter downloads from every book I've written at http://www.homiletix.com. A quick note if you use my commentaries: they are written for you, the sermon preparer, not the sermon listener. In other words, 80 to 85 percent of what is in those books ought not to show up in the sermon. The extra detail there is simply to validate my interpretive stance for the sermon preparer. In any case, feel free to use whatever you want from my commentaries, even verbatim—I wrote them for you (but do peruse my thoughts on plagiarism in chap. 8, "Producing Manuscripts"). As far as other traditional commentaries are concerned (that deal, for the most part, with authorial sayings and not with authorial *doings*), check out their ratings at https://www.bestcommentaries.com/. (Again, all the links in this book can also be found on http://www.homiletix.com/preaching2019/links.)

21. I'd recommend anything written by Daniel Block, Robert Chisholm, Dale Ralph Davis, Timothy Gombis, John Paul Heil, Kenneth Mathews, John Walton, and Gordon Wenham. On a more technical level, the writings of Robert Alter, Adele Berlin, Jan Fokkelman, Meir Sternberg, and Gregory Wong are among those that I've found useful (particularly with regard to the Old Testament).

22. One of the goals of this book, particularly its illustrative portions dealing with the pericopes of Ephesians and the Jacob Story (and indeed, the goal of all my commentaries), is to guide you through a gallery of pictures (pericopes) with me as the docent/curator. A crucial

What you *will* need is a good Bible software program that handles Hebrew and Greek well, though you don't necessarily need to be an ancient language whiz (see below). My recommendation is Logos, Accordance, or BibleWorks.[23] But watch out: bells and whistles are useful if you are a steam engine driver but not if you are a preacher. What I look for in a software program is instantaneous parsing, access to lexicons and translations (and the occasional grammars), and the ability to see other instances of word roots in the book I am studying or in the entire canon (Old Testament, New Testament, and the Septuagint). Of course, multiple English translations are integral to most common Bible software programs; an added plus are the Targums and the works of Josephus and Philo. If your Bible software package can do this much, you are well on your way. The rest is icing, and not very tasty icing at that.[24]

How much Hebrew and Greek do you need? I am quite countercultural, and at the risk of dismaying my language colleagues, I'll declare here that a couple of semesters each of Hebrew and Greek—that enable one to handle the exceedingly good language tools available *in silico*—is sufficient. Language scholars will argue (they have, and I, in turn, have argued with them)[25] that computer resources, or even commentaries that provide exegesis for us, are not infallible. They try to make a case for preachers doing their own exegesis. But I reply: the chances of a computer (or of a scholar writing a commentary on a book he or she has spent decades studying) making a mistake are far, far less than my own by potentially misleading myself with a few paltry semesters of Greek and Hebrew.

---

way of learning how to discern the thrust/force of the text, the theology of the pericope, is by "catching" it—it is more caught than taught.

23. See https://www.logos.com/; https://www.accordancebible.com/; https://bibleworks.com/ (BibleWorks, the company, has ceased operation as of mid-2018; the software, if you already have it, is still viable, but support will no longer be forthcoming). Logos makes it easy to procure a library of searchable books, though the value of scrolling through works of unclear value—and there are many of those in the Logos suite—is dubious. Distractions are a curse, and frequently such red herrings, goose chases, and rabbit trails are detrimental to any study of the text that attempts to discern what the author is *doing*.

24. Another worthwhile acquisition is a membership in the American Theological Library Association (ATLA; http://www.atla.com) and its databases of journals and articles, many of which are full text in pdf. You can search for articles by keyword, author, or Scripture passage, and these are extremely helpful, particularly for tough texts that you will, no doubt, encounter. If you are an alumnus/a of a theological institution, that school will in all likelihood provide access to ATLA for its grads (here's what my institution, Dallas Theological Seminary, provides for its alumni in terms of library resources: http://library.dts.edu/Pages/ER/alum_menu.shtml). Getting your employers to pay for it is a good perk too, if you can persuade them to do so. Don't forget the obvious Google searches or even Google Scholar searches (https://scholar.google.com/).

25. See Kuruvilla, "'What Is the Author *Doing* with What He Is *Saying*?'" This article and a response by one of my New Testament colleagues, along with my rejoinder, are available for download at http://www.homiletix.com/KuruvillaJETS2017.

Having said that and offended all the Greek and Hebrew scholars on this planet and elsewhere, let me delineate three areas in which standard commentaries are useful.

Textual Criticism. This is not a major issue for preachers, but getting the opinion of experts on possible variant manuscript readings and why one should/could/may choose a reading that differs from the accepted composite version of Greek and Hebrew documents (Nestle-Aland and *Biblia Hebraica Stuttgartensia*, respectively) might be helpful on occasion (though not always). But keep in mind that it is easy to get lost in the weeds of textual criticism. And let us preachers not be cavalier in throwing shade on the English translations that God's people utilize, lest we diminish their faith in their own ability to study Scripture sans the original languages.

Background Material. The better commentaries will give preachers enough (and more) background—histories, biographical details of characters, cultural factors, idioms, and so on—that may be necessary to catch what an author is *doing* with what he is saying. Such elements could therefore aid one in discerning the theology of the pericope (though not always), just as personal and social and familial histories may help a physician arrive at a diagnosis (though not always). However, it is easy to get lost in the forest of background material. For the most part, the overdone detail offered by standard commentaries on these matters is unnecessary for preachers.[26]

Exegetical Detail. Good commentaries will provide enough exegetical detail to validate the conclusions of their authors as to what the biblical writers are *doing* with what they are saying. But since that species of commentary hardly exists, preachers must be careful with the ones commonly available. A random, unselective, and undiscriminating exegesis of every word and sentence (a hermeneutic of excavation), as is usually found in these works, is fruitless. Therefore, it is easy to get lost in the tares and chaff of such analyses. Preachers must learn to be selective, employing a *theological* exegesis that yields clues to the author's *doing* in the text (the theology of the pericope). It is detective work: not everything in the crime scene is significant. We gumshoes must teach ourselves the art of theological detection, and the best way to learn is probably by apprenticing ourselves to those who do it well—either in person or through their writings. Remember, learning to discern the theology of the pericope is more caught than taught.

In any case, establish, sufficiently early on, the translation you want to use in the pulpit. Personally, I use the New American Standard Bible

---

26. I claim that the introductions to Ephesians and the Jacob Story in my commentaries, both in my books and in this chapter, provide sufficient background material for preaching purposes.

(NASB). Occasionally I find that standard translations do not do justice to particular wordplays in the original text, and so I tweak the NASB as I see fit and print out the product for the congregation. I prefer to preach with as close to a literal translation as I can find. Remember, you are not preaching an event behind the text or something abstracted from the text but *the text itself*. To catch what the author is *doing*, one must attend carefully to the way the text is written, the way the story is told, the way the poem is constructed, and so on. For this, a literal translation is invaluable. Interlinears may help you out here: the Blue Letter Bible is an excellent one that also parses (and pronounces) each Hebrew/Greek word; the Lumina Bible, with a click, will highlight all the roots of the word that occur in the passage. Both are free.[27]

Now that you have, hopefully, been persuaded to preach through Ephesians or the Jacob Story, how do you divide your time for sermon preparation?

Managing Time: Long-Term and Short-Term Sermon Preparation

Sermon preparation is hard work, but the word of God and the fruit God produces through preaching are worthy of the labor invested. Therefore, prioritize time spent in preparation and guard quality time whenever that may be for you.[28] It is probably advisable to block off regular times for study, when you are not seeing any walk-ins for counseling or consultation and when you are not attending any committee meetings. Sit down to work and put your humming, chirping, and buzzing devices on airplane mode. You may also want to find a regular place to work, be it office or coffee shop, where you have everything necessary within reach.[29] Someone once said that the three best friends of a sermon preparer are custom, habit, and routine. Indeed! Develop and cultivate the customs, habits, and routines of long-term sermon preparation (what you do long before you preach) and short-term sermon preparation (what you do the week of your preaching), and I guarantee that the majority of your homiletical problems will be solved.

27. See https://www.blueletterbible.org/ and https://lumina.bible.org/. Also be sure to glance at the excellent notes of the NET Bible in Lumina (its notes are of greater value than its translation).
28. For me, this is whenever I can find an available time slot of at least an hour.
29. Home, sweet home, works best for me. I need absolute quiet and a couple of large monitors hooked up to my laptop (Bible software on one; Microsoft Word on the other). I don't have more than one book open on my desk at any given time. Check out the practices of a number of preachers at http://homiletix.com/how-i-preach-archives/ in a series of interviews titled "How I Preach."

If you are a full-time preacher in a church setting, it is fair to assume that you have a number of things to do other than preach and prepare to preach. The demands of pastoral ministry are many and variegated, and I hope you are giving adequate time for all that God calls you to do. In addition, there are family responsibilities. And the cultivation of hobbies. And personal development. Preaching is only one of several plates you are juggling. Don't drop any, please, and the way to keep them all successfully spinning in the air is this: plan ahead in long-term preparation for preaching. If you fail to plan, you are, without a doubt, planning to fail. Starting early keeps you unhurried and unfrazzled and obviates the necessity of taking shortcuts with the text at the last minute. Long-term preparation also gives you sufficient time to live with the text and its message for maximal internalization and, importantly, optimal personal involvement, giving you the time to apply its thrust/force into your own life before preaching it to others. "Time *with* a message is as important as time *for* a message."[30] Simmering sermons are the stock of creativity. Let them brew. Give your inchoate sermons plenty of time to mature. Needless to say, planning ahead will also help you enjoy the preparation process, reduce your stress, and probably keep you from burning out.[31]

For a twelve-sermon series, like the one on Ephesians (or the Jacob Story), begin to work at least three months in advance. A good rule of thumb is this: do one week of long-term preparation for every week of preaching. So long-term preparation for twelve sermons means twelve weeks of preparation *before* you commence the preaching of that twelve-sermon series.[32] Let me

---

30. Olford and Olford, *Anointed Expository Preaching*, 106 (emphasis in original).

31. A well-thought-out calendar created in advance helps you with an overview of biblical books (and topics) you'd like to cover over a long period of time, lists vacations and conference trips, reminds you of special days and ordinance Sundays, demarcates space for guest preachers, and so on. Planning ahead also aids the development of meaningful, intentional, and cohesive worship services—the worship team can collaborate with you only if you give them sufficient notice of your designs. See Rummage, *Planning Your Preaching*, 25–32.

32. A word about the length of a sermon series. The late James Montgomery Boice, erstwhile minister of the Tenth Presbyterian Church in Philadelphia, confessed it took him eight years to preach through Romans—in 239 sermons (see the various prefaces in his anthology of sermons, *Romans*). John F. MacArthur preached through the Gospel of Matthew over an eight-year period and "rarely felt the need to take a break" ("Frequently Asked Questions about Expository Preaching," 340). I wouldn't recommend following in their footsteps. Over the years I have found that dealing with larger chunks is the best way to catch and reflect the overall trajectory of a given book (the "necklace"), pericope by pericope ("pearl by pearl"). Of course, if there are natural breaks within a book, between, say, the major sections of Genesis (Gen. 1:1–11:26 [primeval history]; 11:27–25:18 [the Abraham story]; 25:19–36:43 [the Jacob Story]; and 37:1–50:26 [the Joseph story]), doing another series or a few topical sermons at these seams is not a bad idea.

show you *a* method of long-term preparation, one that has worked for me and the one I know best.[33]

If you are planning ahead, here is what you need to do in terms of managing time: set aside twelve hours a week for long-term preparation. That's it—that's all you need to do each week: twelve hours. For the sake of discussion, let's say you choose to spend Mondays from eight o'clock in the morning to noon and one o'clock to five o'clock in the afternoon, and Tuesdays from eight o'clock in the morning to noon (twelve hours total) on long-term preparation. You can, of course, spread those twelve hours through the week differently. In any case, plan on twelve hours of work a week for twelve weeks (for a twelve-week series of sermons).[34] Now let me add an extra week—we'll call it week −1 (minus one)—to those twelve weeks, a week taken up with the preliminary tasks of sermon preparation (also a twelve-hour week). Here is a breakdown.

Long-Term Preparation Week −1: Getting Ready

Week −1 happens sometime *before* you start long-term preparation, though not too far away from those twelve weeks, perhaps during a sabbatical, a retreat, or a week off. The twelve hours of week −1 may also be spread out over that week. Of course, depending on your time and inclination (and the book you plan to preach through), you could take more or fewer than twelve hours and apportion them over more than a single week.

Here's what you do in week −1:

Assemble resources (see above).

Read the entire book (or the large chunk of the book you are planning to preach on) multiple times.

Delineate pericopes.

33. A variation of this is taught in Dallas Theological Seminary's preaching curriculum. Of course, you should feel free to tweak anything to your own level of comfort, capacity, and heart's content.

34. Needless to say, every aspect of sermon preparation should be bathed in prayer, for yourself (even for wisdom in the choice of a book to preach through or a series to engage in) and your listeners. Engage in sermon preparation as a spiritual exercise and, without a doubt, it will profit your relationship with God immensely, even in the relative mundanities of poring over Hebrew and Greek, creating sermon maps, and worrying over application. And by the way, is there anyone praying regularly for you—for your preaching, your life, and your preparation? If not, find a few trusted people to do so. It's amazing what that commitment of praying friends (and the faithfulness of a God who answers their prayers) can do for you and your preaching.

Start taking notes.

Glance at introductory material in a trusted commentary (or two).

Prayerfully, slowly, and carefully read the text of Scripture or book you are
planning to preach from at least four times and in a variety of translations.[35]
If your facility in the original languages is up to snuff, make sure at least one
of those readings is of the Hebrew or Greek text. Even reading out loud on
occasion in whatever language you prefer, or listening to it being read, perhaps
in a recording you made yourself, is profitable. In these multiple readings you
are simply familiarizing yourself with the text and its contours and cadences,
trying to get a feeling for the whole and a sense of the text's "center of gravity,"
where pericopes begin and end, and how preaching sections may be divided.[36]
Wallow in the text. Soak in it. Absorb it. Think about it even when you are
not reading it—on the treadmill, while taking a walk, in the shower, while
driving. Let it incubate!

And make notes as you go along. Begin writing things down even in
week −1. Start a text file on the first chapter, say Ephesians 1. (Later you will
likely decide to preach 1:1–14 as the first pericope; you can break up your
Ephesians 1 file then.)[37] I usually create a text file for each pericope, adding in

35. Try to do each iteration in a single sitting; it takes roughly thirty minutes to read Ephesians 1–6 and about sixty minutes to read Genesis 25–36 (in English).
36. Long, *Witness of Preaching*, 97. I've already broken down Ephesians and the Jacob Story
for you into twelve pericopes each.
37. I use Microsoft Word 2016 on my Mac, labeling the file, e.g., "Eph 1 180101." The
last six digits are integral to my idiosyncratic file naming: yymmdd. So 2018 January 1 is
the date that file was created. I keep adding to that same file over my preparation period,
only changing the file name (1) if I'm breaking up the file on 2018 February 1 into, say, "Eph
1_1–14 180201" and "Eph 1_15–23 180201"; or (2) if I am deleting portions of the original
file on 2018 March 15 to yield a shorter document, "Eph 1 180315." The reason for this latter
change of name following a significant deletion is so that I can always go back to the older
and longer file if necessary to retrieve what I erased. This is a form of "versioning"—thus
I never get rid of *anything* I've written. As another said long ago, *gegrapha, gegrapha*, or
"What I have written, I have written!" (John 19:22). You'll appreciate that only when you are
looking for something that you realize, too late, you have deleted. On that note, I hope you
are making redundant backups of all your files, and even of your entire computer. CrashPlan
is a worthy investment (https://www.crashplan.com/en-us/), as are Time Machine (https://
support.apple.com/en-us/HT201250) and Carbon Copy Cloner for Mac (https://bombich
.com/) or Acronis for Windows (https://www.acronis.com/en-us/). You will thank me one
day. Did I mention redundant? I use CrashPlan and Time Machine and Carbon Copy Cloner,
and all my important files get launched into the cloud via Dropbox (https://www.dropbox
.com). Dropbox Plus gives you 1 TB of cloud storage space at $99 a year; there is inbuilt
versioning in that app too (other options include Apple's iCloud, Amazon Cloud Drive, and
Google Drive). Paranoia is healthy, for the crash cometh; it's only a matter of *when* it doth,
not if.

anything I want to remember from my reading, studying, and thinking. Any insight, observation on the text, random but related thought, and potential illustration are recorded—nothing is insignificant at this moment. Any questions arise in your reading? Note them. Things that look out of place? Jot them down. Look for repetitions of words, clauses, ideas (if necessary, do a quick check of the Hebrew/Greek). You will get into more detail in subsequent weeks, so don't sweat the difficult bits.

Glancing at a good commentary at this point may be helpful, just to get an initial sense of the boundaries of the pericopes. Create a breakdown of the book/section into preachable pericopes, fine-tuning the seams as you go along.[38] A fair grasp of the introductory material of a biblical book—the author and audience, date and setting, and other related matters—can also be valuable, though treatments of such elements in traditional commentaries give one an overdose. Keep asking, as you read such works, whether you really need to know what those scholars are telling you in order to arrive at what the biblical author is *doing*. In most cases, you will not. (In the commentaries I have written, I've tried to be more discriminating.) At any rate, keep on writing. Making notes is an activity that ought to continue for as long as your preparation is ongoing, not just for week −1 but for the remaining twelve weeks of long-term preparation as well.

I'll deal with those twelve weeks (preparation for the twelve pericopes of Ephesians or the Jacob Story) briefly here. Each preparation routine listed will be expounded in greater detail in the following chapters.

Long-Term Preparation Weeks 1–8: Discerning Theology

During weeks 1–8,[39] you will continue the same schedule: twelve hours a week. In these weeks of long-term preparation, I find it most convenient to spread the twelve hours over two consecutive days (Mondays and Tuesdays, with breaks as needed), though, of course, you could choose otherwise. In those twelve hours each week, continue reading through the text of Scripture in your translation of choice (so eight weeks of twelve hours a week for the twelve pericopes of Ephesians or the Jacob Story). But now you are reading with more intent—to catch the thrust of the text, the author's *doing* (i.e., the theology of the pericope). This is arguably the most difficult part of your work with the text. Never, ever give up until the text has yielded its fruit. No

---

38. For bigger books, grasping the large sections and smaller subsections may be helpful as you try to narrow down a pericope. As was noted, in Genesis, for instance, one discovers four major sections: Gen. 1–11, 12–25, 25–36, and 37–50.

39. See chap. 2.

doubt, some pericopes will take more time and attention than others; it is your call how you allocate the ninety-six hours of weeks 1–8 among your twelve pericopes (roughly eight hours per pericope).

Long-Term Preparation Weeks 9–12: Deriving Application, Creating Maps, Fleshing Moves

Now that you've discerned the theology of the text, you are beginning to ponder application and how to create sermon maps and flesh them out (see chaps. 3, 4, and 5, respectively). This is done in weeks 9–12, again for twelve hours a week. If you work on three pericopes per week, at four hours each, preferably on the same days you did your work in weeks 1–8, you will give long-term preparation a consistency of approach and inculcate a habit. You are essentially asking, Based on this theology of the pericope, where am I (and where is my flock) deficient? How can we begin the process of moving toward fulfilling the call of the text? At the same time, you will also be tentatively thinking of sermon moves (i.e., mapping the sermon) and how to flesh out those moves. Keep writing.

Here's my scheme for the twelve weeks and week −1 (for week 0, see below).

Long-Term Sermon Preparation

Week −1 (12 hours)	Weeks 1–8 (96 hours)	Weeks 9–12 (48 hours)	Week 0
Getting Ready (chap. 1)	Discerning Theology (chap. 2)	Deriving Application (chap. 3)	Short-Term Preparation
		Creating Maps (chap. 4)	
		Fleshing Moves (chap. 5)	

Soon, those twelve weeks of long-term gestation are up, and labor pains are upon you. You've arrived at week 0—the week you are beginning your series with the first pericope. The first Sunday of preaching is here: week 0—your short-term preparation week.

Short-Term Preparation Week 0: Illustrating Ideas, Crafting Introductions and Conclusions, Producing Manuscripts

Week 0, short-term preparation,[40] is when you finalize the sermon you are going to preach at the end of that week. This plan allots eight hours spread

40. See chaps. 6, 7, and 8, respectively.

throughout the final week (week 0) for those tasks. But you are also continuing long-term preparation for the future, even in week 0, with the standard twelve hours on, say, Monday and Tuesday, investing in a future series of sermons.[41] This means, of course, that there is always a short-term preparation week 0 operating concurrently with long-term preparation (week −1 through week 12); each week is a week 0 for a sermon in the current series *as well as* a numbered week in the long-term preparation for an upcoming series of sermons. Here's a day-by-day breakdown of week 0.

Monday–Tuesday (Twelve Hours for the Next Series of Sermons)

You are back to long-term preparation for the next round of sermons: twelve hours allotted between Monday and Tuesday, for instance, are to be reserved for long-term preparation, as we have already seen. Don't even think about the sermon that is due the Sunday of each week as you work on long-term preparation during these sessions.

Wednesday–Friday (Six Hours for the Current Sermon)

Reserve about six hours, split however you like, between Wednesday and Friday for the short-term preparation of the sermon you have to preach this coming Sunday. These six hours will be taken up by hunting for illustrations (but you will likely have been on the lookout in past weeks and may have already discovered a few), formulating an introduction and a conclusion (again, you'll no doubt already have some idea how your introduction and conclusion should look), and finalizing the sermon manuscript that has been embryonically taking shape during its gestation. All the writing you've been doing will help here.

Saturday (Two Hours for the Current Sermon)

Between chores at home and playtime with the kids and shopping and lawn mowing and cooking and Netflix, find time for the last two hours of short-term preparation. This is when you internalize the manuscript and reduce it down to a précis of sufficient detail or otherwise format it into a preachable document—whatever makes you comfortable (see chap. 8, "Producing Manuscripts"). This should take a couple hours. Then relax. And pray a lot.[42]

---

41. I'm assuming a Monday–Sunday week, with you preaching on Sunday. If otherwise, adjust accordingly.

42. Also see chap. 9, "Delivering Sermons," for pre- and post-sermon routines.

Here is what week 0 looks like (short-term preparation):

Short-Term Sermon Preparation (Week 0)

Monday–Tuesday (12 hours)	Wednesday–Friday (6 hours)	Saturday (2 hours)	Sunday
Long-Term Preparation	Illustrating Ideas (chap. 6)	Work. Relax. Pray.	Delivering Sermons (chap. 9)
	Crafting Introductions and Conclusions (chap. 7)		
	Producing Manuscripts (chap. 8)		

Thus you will have spent twenty-one hours total on a single sermon.[43] Congratulations, you have worked hard! You are now on the labor and delivery floor and ready to preach!

Of course, feel free to scale things up or down as you desire. You may want to spend ten hours a week for twelve weeks (instead of twelve hours for twelve weeks). Or you may decide to break that twelve-hour weekly slot into three four-hour periods spread over three days. Of course, if your chosen text or book is of larger or smaller size, you will want to adjust everything accordingly. And as your facility grows, you will, no doubt, get more things done in less time. But the bottom line is this: plan ahead and work ahead, or you'll crash and burn.[44]

Now, if you are called to do more than a single sermon a week, say, on Sunday mornings, Sunday evenings, and Wednesday evenings, let me give you

43. Here is the breakdown for a twelve-part sermon series as described above: week −1 = 12 hours; weeks 1–12 = 144 hours; week 0 = 96 hours (8 hours × 12 sermons). Twenty-one hours per sermon is above average, but you will only get more efficient with experience and be able to whittle this down. The average sermon length these days is roughly thirty minutes—I would recommend not going over that allotment. This means forty-two minutes of preparation for every minute of preaching.

44. Also, remember my counsel to preach only thirty-six weeks of *lectio continua* sermons, the rest of the year being given to a few weeks of topical sermons, vacations, guest preachers substituting for you, etc. (see note 11 above). So there is some room to be flexible, and you are likely to get a few extra weeks to catch up on sermon preparation. My recommendation assigns twenty hours a week for sermon preparation, assuming you are preaching weekly. However, I am well aware of the incessant and burdensome demands on the time of a pastor that may not afford you the luxury of such preparation time for sermons. Treat my recommendation as an ideal, a launching pad for you to take off from. I am confident that you will quickly understand your own strengths and limitations and hone your preparation skills, enabling you to become more efficient and make adjustments on the fly, series by series and book by book. Come up with a system that works for you and stick with it. Hopefully, I've given you enough ideas to spur you into action.

a word of warning: don't! It is impossible for *anyone* to sustain the level of work I am talking about to produce more than one high-quality sermon a week. Besides, listeners cannot digest more than one powerful weekly sermon with an equally potent application that is to be put into practice right away. So I'd make the Sunday morning worship the venue of *the* sermon. For Sunday evening, I'd do something in the nature of a Bible study, perhaps showcasing some exegetical work on the text for next Sunday morning's sermon, leading the congregation through some biblical history, doing a series on living the spiritual life, or addressing a topic you see appropriate for your flock (topical sermons will work here). It might even be worthwhile indulging in some Q&A about that morning's sermon with those who show up in the evening. For Wednesday evening, a compendium of systematic theology culled from your favorite textbook (for about twenty minutes, perhaps even with a handout with verses and an outline) followed by discussion and ending with prayer for shared requests should suffice.

Ephesians and the Jacob Story

Let's go back and put ourselves in week −1. You have read Ephesians (or the Jacob Story) at least four times. You've peeked at my commentary on Ephesians (or Genesis) and gotten a sense of the pericope demarcations. Here is some introductory material for both sermon series that should help you get a sense of the whole.[45]

Introduction to Ephesians

Briefly, I will deal with the purpose of the letter and summarize its various pericopes.

Purpose

The theme of this letter is clearly established early on in Ephesians 1:9–10: "the consummation of all things in Christ—the things in the heavens and the things on the earth in him." God's plan encompasses the entirety of the cosmos. And perhaps no less striking is the fact that God's people are part of this vast and glorious drama. Human history, particularly of the people of God, is the arena for a cosmic battle: God versus the forces of evil opposed to his consummation of all things in Christ. If the children of God ever feel their lives are insignificant, they need to take note of Ephesians: they are the agents of the manifestation of divine victory in the cosmos. Indeed, their victories in spiritual battles redound to God's victory and thereby his glory. This makes the canvas of Ephesians as capacious as the cosmos, on which is being painted the grand masterpiece of divine action. It is because the universe is fractured as a result of sin that a consummation of all things in Christ is a necessary plan of God: a re-creation in which Jesus Christ is the singular head over all and in whom all things are filled with the divine fullness by the Spirit.

Summaries of Pericopes[46]

1. *Ephesians 1:1–14*. The first pericope raises the curtain on God's grand and glorious plan for the cosmos—the consummation of all things in Christ. Into this grand and glorious plan, all (believing) humans have been recruited, God's scheme for them extending

---

45. For a slightly expanded version of these introductions, see http://www.homiletix.com /preaching2019/commentaries, and for an even fuller recital, see Kuruvilla, *Ephesians*, 7–19; and Kuruvilla, *Genesis*, 1–26. As you consume this, and/or other commentaries, make sure you look up verse references and make judicious decisions as to whether what is being said in these works makes sense.

46. Getting a sense of the whole trajectory of the larger block of text is helpful before diving into individual pericopes.

from eternity past to eternity future. A blessed God blesses his people in his Son with grace, love, and delight.

2. *Ephesians 1:15–23.* In co-opting them into his grand scheme, Paul assures believers that divine power—involved in the raising and exaltation of Christ over death and every inimical power in the universe—is working on their behalf, for those who are the body and fullness of Christ and the expression of his divine rule in the cosmos.

3. *Ephesians 2:1–10.* Once lost in sin, influenced for the worse by the world, by evil powers, and by their own flesh, and deserving only of the wrath of God, Christians have now been saved by grace through faith. They now share their Savior's exaltation, proclaiming to the universe the mercy, love, grace, and kindness of God by their salvation from sin and their sanctification in good works.

4. *Ephesians 2:11–22.* Those who were once unbelievers and far from God have been brought near, into the community of God's people, as believers reconciled to God. Now God's people comprises all humanity—all those who have believed in Christ, the personification and producer of peace. Christ removed the condemnation of the law (for sin) on humankind and made possible their access to God and their becoming a holy temple, a dwelling of God in the Spirit.

5. *Ephesians 3:1–13.* Paul's own divinely empowered role in God's administration of the hitherto unknown mystery of the universality of the church was to serve the co-opting of all (believing) humanity into the community of God's people. This grand role of the apostle—howbeit paradoxical, for he was but a prisoner and one who was "less than the least of all the saints"—becomes the paradigm for the ministry of all believers, as God accomplishes his eternal and glorious plan through those who are seemingly insignificant, uninfluential, and unimportant.

6. *Ephesians 3:14–21.* The accomplishment of God's plan through believers involves their being strengthened by the Spirit and thereby being conformed, more and more, to Christ by faith. Not just individually but corporately as well, God's plan is being worked out as believers in community comprehend the magnitude of Christ's love for them. This enables them to become filled to the fullness of God (i.e., God glorified in the church and dwelling in it)—the church increasingly becoming the holy temple of God and bringing him glory.

7. *Ephesians 4:1–16.* Christians are called to selfless love that leads to unity in the body reflecting the unity of the Godhead, and they are to exercise the grace gifts given to them by Christ. These grace gifts, appropriately granted to church leaders and to every believer, enable the former to facilitate the ministry of the latter so that the church may be built up in unity to the full, mature stature of its head, Christ.

8. *Ephesians 4:17–32.* Believers, no longer living licentiously, ignorant, and devoid of divine life, have learned Christ and are being divinely renewed in the likeness of God. Now they are to manifest his divine character as they engage in activities that build up

one another and are conducive to the development of community: eschewing anger, sharing resources, speaking grace, controlling temper, and forgiving divinely.

9. *Ephesians 5:1–20*. This brings us to the imitation of God and of Christ's selfless love, which calls for the abandonment of illicit worldly "love" (i.e., sexual immorality in word and in deed), eliciting only the wrath of God. Believers, being filled by the Spirit with the divine fullness of God in Christ, are to adopt a lifestyle that is wise and worshipful, inviting the pleasure of God.

10. *Ephesians 5:21–33*. The fullness of God in the church is manifested in the mutual submission of believers in the fear of Christ and in the modeling of the relationship between husband and wife after the relationship between Christ and the church—sacrificial love on the part of the husband and submission to delegated authority on the part of the wife.

11. *Ephesians 6:1–9*. The responsibilities of those in authority and those under authority involve children being obedient to parents, and parents gently instructing their children. In addition, slaves and masters treat each other with sincerity of heart, doing God's will and serving him, the divine Master of all humankind. All are appropriately rewarded in the future on the day of reckoning.

12. *Ephesians 6:10–24*. Victory against supernatural foes, always arrayed against God and the people of God, can be achieved only by divine empowerment. Such empowerment is granted to the believer in the form of God's own armor—relating to the attributes (belt-truth, breastplate-righteousness), deeds (shoe-peace, shield-faith, helmet-salvation), and utterances of God (sword-word). This comprehensive view of life as a battle fought with divine enablement calls for utter dependence of the believer on God for everything, expressed in constant, alert, Spirit-driven prayer for all the saints.

The broad theological thrust of Ephesians may be summarized this way in a single (and long) sentence:

A blessed God blesses his people graciously and lovingly in his beloved Son, redeeming them as his own possession to undertake divinely empowered good works so that they may manifest his power and glory as a united body of all (believing) humanity, exercising grace gifts for edification to Christlikeness, with selfless love abandoning all activities not conducive to community, adopting a wise and worshipful lifestyle pleasing to God—filled by the Spirit with the divine fullness of God in Christ, submitting to one another, modeling marital relationships after the Christ–church relationship, and maintaining household relationships in accordance with God's plan—and gaining victory over supernatural foes by divine empowerment: all of this is integral to God's grand and glorious plan to consummate all things in the cosmos in Christ.

And thus God is glorified. This is the goal of preaching and of preaching the Letter to the Ephesians in particular. What a noble task!

Introduction to the Jacob Story

Genesis may be broadly conceived of as the inauguration of God's work to bring about blessing to humankind. The four major sections of the book, then, deal with different facets of divine blessing.

Text	Section	Theme
Genesis 1:1–11:26	Primeval History	Creating for Blessing
Genesis 11:27–25:18	Abraham Story	Moving toward Blessing
Genesis 25:19–36:43	Jacob Story	Experiencing the Blessing
Genesis 37:1–50:26	Joseph Story	Becoming a Blessing

Purpose

The Jacob Story (Gen. 25:19–36:43)—our focus in this book—tells us how one goes about experiencing the blessing. This cycle of narratives depicts one who is constantly chasing blessing in all the wrong places and in all the wrong ways until he comes to the realization that only God can bless him. Jacob's incapacity to bless himself by his devices and stratagems, and his subsequent recognition of what, instead, he must do to experience divine blessing, is the dynamo of the Jacob Story. Each pericope details a facet of the diamond (or serves as a single pearl in the necklace), describing how God's people ought to live in order to experience (and enjoy) God's promised blessings.

Summaries of Pericopes

1. *Genesis 25:19–34.* The first pericope commences the Jacob Story with Rebekah's twin pregnancy and the oracle detailing the prominence of the younger over the older—a sovereignly ordained hierarchy. The subsequent strife between the twins at their birth and later in life describes the struggle for divine blessing. All told, the story tells of a failure to recognize God's sovereignty in the disposition of his blessings as well as a despising of one's own blessings.

2. *Genesis 26:1–33.* This pericope, a seemingly digressive chapter, details Isaac's response to God's unequivocal promise of descendants and prosperity. The first half of the pericope paints a negative picture of the patriarch who, rather than trusting God, resorts to subterfuge, passing his wife off to Abimelech as his sister. The second half, however, pictures Isaac, though besieged by opposition to his well-digging enterprises, trusting God to provide for him and moving away from his opponents with no thought of retaliation. God can be trusted to keep his promises of blessing.

3. *Genesis 26:34–28:9.* This section constitutes the extended account of the passing of the blessing of the firstborn to Jacob, who obtains it by deception. The narrative clearly portrays each of the characters as culpable—Isaac, Esau, Rebekah, and Jacob

himself—all trying to divert/subvert divine blessings into directions and destinations of their own choices. The result of such a frenetic chase for blessing, with deception and manipulation, is catastrophic fragmentation of family/community.

4. *Genesis 28:10–22*. Here we have Jacob, a fugitive, escaping from his brother and making his way to his uncle's place in Paddan-Aram. He encounters God in a dream, and God reaffirms to Jacob the patriarchal promise, upon which Jacob, rather impertinently, sets conditions on his allegiance to God. God's guaranteed promises for the future should, instead, impel one to worship unconditionally, even before the fulfillment of those promises.

5. *Genesis 29:1–30*. Jacob arrives at his uncle's house in Paddan-Aram. He works for seven years for the hand of Rachel, his uncle's daughter, but is deceived by Laban, who substitutes the older Leah for the younger Rachel on his wedding night. The many parallels between the narrative here and that of the deception of Isaac earlier make it clear that Jacob is now receiving his just deserts. Despite unconditional blessing, discipline for misdeeds is a distinct possibility for God's people in his economy.

6. *Genesis 29:31–30:24*. The next pericope depicts the struggle between Leah and Rachel: one for her husband's love, the other for her husband's children. Rachel does all she can to gain a child, even engaging in deceptive practices, jealous manipulations, and obscure therapies, all in vain. However, the moment she gives up her stratagems, God opens her womb. The blessings of God are experienced by those who maintain not a posture of high-handedness (hubristic manipulation) but one of openhandedness (humble dependence).

7. *Genesis 30:25–31:16*. Jacob now decides to return to Canaan. His request for appropriate compensation from Laban, his employer, is met with insidious tactics on the latter's part to deprive Jacob of his due. Jacob engages in the creative toil of animal husbandry, and his flocks greatly increase in number. Later, he attributes this prosperity to God's sovereign work, thus pointing to the fact that divine sovereignty works in tandem with the faithful discharge of human responsibility.

8. *Genesis 31:17–55*. Jacob and his caravan are on their way back to the promised land. They are pursued by Laban, who accuses Jacob of abruptly decamping with his wives and children; moreover, Laban's household gods are missing as well, stolen by Rachel, unbeknown to others. Rachel's theft is undetected, and Laban departs after striking a peace pact with Jacob. God's protection covers the faithful Jacob (and all believers) even from the dangerous consequences of sin within his (and their) own camp(s).

9. *Genesis 32:1–32*. This pericope describes Jacob preparing to meet Esau, who is approaching with a large company. Not unexpectedly, Jacob is afraid and seeks protection from God, but he also attempts to appease his brother with extravagant gifts. In a desperate moment of his life, he encounters God in a nocturnal wrestling match, recognizes deity, and acknowledges God as the true and sole source of blessing. And for the first time in the Jacob Story, Jacob is said to be blessed! With this dramatic

expression of his transformation, Jacob's name is changed to "Israel," and he realizes he will not have to fight any more, for God will do the fighting for him, as God does for all his children.

10. *Genesis 33:1–20*. The long-awaited encounter between the battling brothers, Jacob and Esau, occurs in this pericope. Jacob (literarily) returns the stolen blessing to Esau, who seems surprisingly content with what God has given him and seeks no more. The brothers are reconciled and go their own ways in peace. The full enjoyment of promised blessings calls for restoration of relationships between alienated members of God's community.

11. *Genesis 34:1–31*. The rape of Dinah, Jacob's daughter, by a Shechemite and its aftermath are described in this pericope. Dinah's siblings, the sons of Jacob, retaliate with an incommensurately violent rampage, slaughtering and pillaging. Jacob's silence throughout the pericope, except for a concern for his own standing in the community, is striking. Apathy toward evil only perpetuates more evil, forfeiting the blessings of peace.

12. *Genesis 35:1–36:43*. In this final pericope of the Jacob Story, God prompts Jacob to keep his promise made in Genesis 28 that he would worship following his safe return to his homeland. Jacob complies. God then reaffirms the patriarchal blessings. In all, the pericope moves God's people to worship him for his blessings; this continues the cycle of future divine blessing.

So here is the "necklace" with its "pearls"—the broad theological thrust of the Jacob Story assembled pericope by pericope, summarized in another long sentence:

> The way to enjoy God's promised blessings is by recognizing that he sovereignly blesses individuals differently and by not despising one's own blessings; by trusting God to secure the promised blessings; by eschewing guile to obtain blessings in one's own way and at one's own time; by worshiping God for his blessings even before their fulfillment; by acknowledging that divine blessings do not preclude divine discipline for misdeeds; by putting away high-handedness; by trusting him to bless even as one works responsibly and faithfully in adverse situations; by remaining in God's will and thereby ensuring divine protection; by remembering that God is the only source of blessing; by making restitution and seeking forgiveness of those one has wronged; by maintaining moral standards in the face of worldly evil; and, once blessings have been fulfilled, by worshiping in gratitude, thus continuing the cycle of divine blessing into the future.

2

Discerning Theology

Theology is, and always has been, an activity of what I call the
"imaginative construction" of a comprehensive and coherent picture of humanity in the world under God.[1]

A few years ago, in a church I was visiting, I found a copy of a popular
daily devotional that is often stacked in the foyer of many churches.
Skimming through its pages in an idle moment, I spotted a homily on Acts 28. Paul is shipwrecked on Malta, and he joins everyone else in
helping out, picking up sticks for a fire. So, the writer recommended, we too
should be willing to do menial jobs in churches and always be willing to do
even the lowliest job. Of course, the devotional conveniently failed to mention the viper that came out of the cord and bit the hapless apostle. Now I,
being the clever guy that I am, could use that part of Acts 28 to recommend
exactly the opposite: never, *ever* do menial tasks, because—who knows?—a
venomous beast, usually of the two-legged variety, may sink its fangs into you.
The Bible, it appears, can be read for application any which way one wants,
manipulated according to the capricious whims of the preacher.

How does one go about this task of finding valid application for an ancient text? The complex and critical issue of how the preacher moves from
text to sermon—from then to now—has remained somewhat of a black box.
One homiletics scholar observed wryly that "we move from the Bible to a

1. Kaufman, *Essay on Theological Method*, ix.

contemporary sermon by some inexplicable magic!"[2] I propose a less mysti-
cal solution.[3]

Take the case of the narrative in 1 Samuel 15, where the prophet Samuel
delivers God's message to King Saul that he should annihilate the Amalekites.
This is how Samuel prefaces his remarks to Saul: "Now listen to the *voice*
[*qol*] of the word of Yahweh" (15:1). Unfortunately, we do not find "voice"
in most of our English Bibles. Such a literal translation of the Hebrew is
found only in the King James Version and its heirs. The seeming redundancy
of "voice" is swept under the rug in all other major English translations,
which essentially say, "Listen to the word of Yahweh." I'll come back to the
significance of this in a bit.

Saul, as you know, does not obey. Rather than eliminate all the animals and
humans as commanded, he saves the good ones of the former and the chief
of the latter. Soon after, Samuel confronts Saul. The king declares that he has
done everything God told him to do, whereupon Samuel issues a memorable
indictment: "What then is this bleating of the sheep in my ears, and the lowing of the oxen which I hear?" (1 Sam. 15:14 NASB; similar in most other
English translations). But it's not "bleating" and "lowing" in the Hebrew.
Can you guess what it is?

Yes, it's "voice" (again *qol*): "What then is this *voice* of sheep in my ears,
and the *voice* of oxen which I hear?" (1 Sam. 15:14). The author is *doing* something here, telling readers that the one committed to God listens to the voice
of God, not the voice of worldly seductions. With English translations reading
"bleating" and "lowing" in 15:14 and with the omission of "voice" from 15:1,
the force of the text is almost completely negated. These translational missteps
are a clear indication that Bible translators and scholars don't think in terms of
what biblical authors are *doing* with what they are saying. Here in 1 Samuel 15,
the thrust/force of the text is clearly related to listening/obedience to God.[4]

Pericopal Theology and Christiconic Interpretation

One might interpret the Bible in many ways depending on one's goal for that
interpretation. But when we interpret the text for *preaching*—and I want to
emphasize that preaching is the sole concern of this work—in order to elicit
valid application for listeners, we must focus on what the author is *doing*
with what he is saying in that particular text. In fact, communication of

2. Buttrick, *Captive Voice*, 89.
3. See Kuruvilla, "Preaching Is Theological," in *Vision for Preaching*, 91–109.
4. In Hebrew, *shama'* means both "to hear/listen" and "to obey."

any kind—sacred or secular, spoken or scripted—is now being recognized in language philosophy as a communicator *doing* something with what is being communicated. "Texts are no longer viewed as inert containers, jars with theological ideas inside, but as poetic expressions displaying rhetorical and literary artistry," *doing* things, intending effects in readers.[5] The discerning of the *doing* of the author (i.e., the pragmatics of the text), as opposed to determining the saying of the author (i.e., the semantics of the text), ought to be the goal of preachers if they want to arrive at valid application and have the text experienced in its fullness by their listeners.[6]

Here is another way to look at this: what an author is *doing* is projecting a transcending vision—what Paul Ricoeur called the *world in front of the text*.[7] For Scripture, this *world in front of the text* is God's ideal world, individual segments of which are portrayed by individual pericopes. So each pericope is God's gracious invitation to humankind to live in his ideal world by abiding by the thrust/force of that pericope—that is, the requirements of God's ideal world as called for in that pericopal world segment (e.g., listening to / obeying only God's voice, from 1 Sam. 15). And as humankind accepts that divine invitation and applies the thrust/force of the pericope, week by week and pericope by pericope God's people are progressively and increasingly inhabiting this ideal world and adopting its values.

Because this projected world depicts how God relates to his creation, the characteristics of that world may rightly be called "theology." Thus the ideal world that each pericope projects becomes the theology of that pericope. To live by pericopal theology, then, is to accept God's gracious invitation to inhabit his ideal world by aligning ourselves with the requirements of that ideal world (i.e., the will of God in that pericope). This is the vision of the *world in front of the text*, God's ideal world, painted by Scripture—a glimpse of and an invitation to the divine kingdom—a vision unveiled by faithful preaching.[8] Without a discernment of pericopal theology, it is impossible to derive valid application. (See fig. 2.1.)

Since only one Man, the Lord Jesus Christ, perfectly met all God's demands, being without sin (2 Cor. 5:21; Heb. 4:15; 7:26), one can say that this

5. Long, "Use of Scripture in Contemporary Preaching," 350.
6. See a series of my articles: "Pericopal Theology"; "Christiconic Interpretation"; "Theological Exegesis"; and "Applicational Preaching." My commentaries on Genesis, Judges, Mark, and Ephesians analyze the authorial *doing* of each pericope therein sequentially. Of course, understanding authorial saying is indispensable for arriving at authorial *doing*. But too often interpreters stop at the former and never reach the latter.
7. Ricoeur, *Hermeneutics and the Human Sciences*, 141–42.
8. For all practical purposes, pericopal theology, the *world in front of the text*, and what its author is *doing* (pragmatics) may be considered equivalent.

Figure 2.1

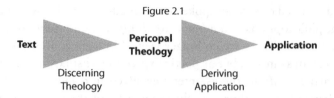

Text | Pericopal Theology | Application

Discerning Theology   Deriving Application

Person, and this Person alone, has perfectly inhabited the *world in front of the text*, living by all its requirements. Jesus Christ alone has comprehensively abided by the theology of every pericope of Scripture. That is to say, each pericope of the Bible is actually portraying a characteristic of Christ, showing us what it means to perfectly fulfill, as he did, the particular call of that pericope. The Bible as a whole, the collection of all its pericopes, images a perfect human, exemplified by Jesus Christ, God incarnate. By him alone is God's world perfectly inhabited, and by him alone are God's requirements perfectly met.

Thus sermon by sermon, through application, God's people become progressively more Christlike as they align themselves with the image of Christ displayed in each pericope. Preaching, therefore, facilitates the conformation of the children of God into the image of the Son of God. After all, God's ultimate goal for believers is that they look like his Son, Jesus Christ, in his humanity—"conformed to the image [*eikōn*] of his Son" (Rom. 8:29). Therefore, I call this model of interpretation for preaching "christiconic."[9] I submit that Scripture is geared primarily for this glorious purpose of God, to restore the *imago Dei* in humankind, by offering a theological description of Christlikeness, pericope by pericope, with which God's people are to be aligned. And so, week by week, sermon by sermon, habits are changed, dispositions are created, character is built, and the image of Christ is gradually formed—in the power of the Holy Spirit, through the instrumentality of Scripture, by the agency of the preacher. "We proclaim him . . . that we may present every person mature in Christ" (Col. 1:28).[10]

The text and its theology are inseparable. For instance, if I am next to you in an elevator and you protest, "Hey, you're standing on my foot!" the

9. See Kuruvilla, *Privilege the Text!*, 211–69; and Kuruvilla, "Preaching Is Conformational," in *Vision for Preaching*, 131–48.
10. These basic elements of the christiconic hermeneutic need not be recited in each preaching event. At most, a one- or two-minute statement of the importance of conformation to Christ would be sufficient, perhaps in every other sermon. I would rather use my precious in-the-pulpit minutes to focus on the uniqueness and specificity of each pericope preached than rehash weekly the unchanging foundations of the hermeneutic.

thrust/force ("theology") of this utterance is that you object to my foot's current location and expect me to remove my foot from the top of yours (the pragmatics: authorial *doing*), even though the content of your complaint only indicated the location of my foot on top of yours (the semantics: authorial saying). Now where exactly is the "theology" of that utterance—under the text, over it, in it, with it? Wherever it is, the theology is integral to the text and inseparable from it. It is discerned from the text, it comes with the text, it is part of the text. In a sense, it *is* the text, for the theology of a pericope is what the text (i.e., its author) is *doing*. For Scripture, the theology of the pericope is the thrust and force of the text that its author wants us to catch, the experience of the text to which its author wants us to respond. So text and theology are virtually inseparable. One rides on the other.[11] I will therefore frequently employ "text + theology" to designate this unified entity.

To catch the pericopal theology (authorial *doing*) is to experience the text with all of its power and pathos. And that is what the preacher is attempting to do in the sermon: demonstrate and point out the crucial elements of the text so that the hearer experiences the text fully and faithfully. This is why I see the sermon primarily as curating the text for listeners.[12] Why else should a preacher be interposed between God's word and God's people? Such a person would have been entirely unnecessary had it been possible for listeners to catch the theological thrust or force of a pericope on their own. But because congregations are far from the origins of the text—in language, culture, forms, values, beliefs, and so on—and because they have forgotten how to read texts to catch their thrusts, a mediator between God's word and God's people is needed: the preacher. This person's role is to do what a curator or a docent does during a museum tour: guide visitors (sermon listeners) through an art gallery, pointing out the color scheme, or a background shape, or the play of light in a particular painting (the textual clues in a particular pericope) so that they may catch the force of the painting (the pericopal theology of the text), experiencing it in its fullness.

It is evident, in this discussion, that the theology of the pericope functions as the crucial intermediary in the move from text to application (see fig. 2.1), showing us the requirements of the ideal world of God and what it means to fulfill those requirements, as did the perfect Man, Christ. It is equally evident that pericopal theology should be the primary interpretive goal of the one

---

11. Perhaps the best way to put this is that pericopal theology supervenes on the text, the one integrated with the other, just as the mind supervenes on and is integrated with the brain.

12. See Kuruvilla, "Preaching Is Communicational," in *Vision for Preaching*, 71–89. A secondary role of the sermon is to provide specific application of the pericopal theology for particular listeners—see chap. 3, "Deriving Application."

who plans to preach a biblical text. The question, then, is this: How do we discern the theology of a particular pericope (its author's *doing*)?

Sayings and *Doings*

You have by now, after week −1, familiarized yourself with the text you plan to preach (chap. 1, "Getting Ready"). Now is the time to start digging deeper. We are attempting in weeks 1–8 to catch the theology of the pericope, the author's *doing* with what he is saying. Let's break up the task into two parts: first, we determine the author's saying, and second, we discern the author's *doing* (pericopal theology).[13]

Determining Saying

We first need to determine the saying of the author in the text. Let me emphasize the importance of determining authorial saying, without which there is no moving toward discerning the *doing* of the author. And without discerning authorial *doing*, there can be no valid application. So the determination of authorial saying is an important part of interpreting the text for preaching purposes. Authorial saying is determined by finding answers to questions and distinguishing between the significant and the insignificant.

Questions and Answers

A good way to begin is to list every question you have about the text: words you don't understand, grammar that you struggle with, clauses that are not straightforward, textual concepts you have questions about, backgrounds that are vague, text-critical issues that are thorny, and whatever looks out of place and puzzling in the pericope. On your own, try to come up with answers to the questions you have raised (always giving the inspired author the benefit of the doubt). However, while I would definitely do my own work first—and I strongly urge you to do so as well—I am not so starry-eyed to consider myself an expert. Without wasting too much time in unceasing struggles

---

13. Proponents of the Big Idea popularized by Haddon W. Robinson (*Biblical Preaching*) would instead look for the subject (What is the author talking about?) and the complement (What is the author saying about what he is talking about?) of the passage. I do not recommend making this subject-complement distinction, because it does not make the distinction that really matters—between the author's saying and the author's *doing*. At best, the Big Idea questions lead one only to authorial sayings. For a couple more important reasons for discarding the Big Idea concept, see Kuruvilla, "Time to Kill the Big Idea?" (available at http://homiletix.com /kill-the-big-idea/); and app. A below, "Big Idea versus Theological Focus."

with the text and after exhausting my meager personal resources, I seek help from those scholars and sages well versed in the languages, deeply immersed in the backgrounds, and who have spent decades, if not a lifetime, studying a particular biblical book.[14] It is in the determination of authorial sayings that standard works excel: the lexicon in your Bible software and traditional commentaries on the book.[15] Needless to say, whatever commentary you peruse, whatever resource you mine, evaluate the arguments carefully, checking with Scripture and going back and forth between those tools and the pericope you are studying. Keep that Bible open!

As you locate the answers to your questions—utilizing your own work and that of others—write them down in your file on that pericope (so you won't have to look them up again), creating a compendium of information on the text that you think is essential for determining the authorial saying (so that you can then discern the authorial *doing*). I note only items that are not obvious to me, things I didn't know until now, elements that someone else has insight about, and anything I fear I may forget. I don't write down the things that I already know and that I'm unlikely to forget.

To get you started on this interrogation of the text, here are some questions that may come up when you look through the first six pericopes of Ephesians (Eph. 1–3).

Ephesians 1:1–14
> Why are there three forms of "bless" in 1:3? What is "heavenlies" (1:3)? Why is there a Trinitarian focus in 1:1–14? What is the "mystery" (1:9)? What do "administration of the fullness of times" and "the consummation of all things in Christ" (1:10) mean? What does it mean to be "claimed [by God] as an inheritance" (1:11)? What is "sealed with the Holy Spirit of promise" (1:13), and why is this "a pledge of our inheritance" (1:14)?

Ephesians 1:15–23
> What exactly is Paul praying for in 1:15–19? What do "rule" and "authority" and "power" and "dominion" indicate (1:21)? What does it mean for the church to be "the fullness of him who fills all things in all ways" (1:23)?

---

14. Among those scholars and sages, I include those who have put together some exceedingly helpful Bible software: the geniuses and geeks. Could those scholars and sages and geniuses and geeks be wrong? Of course. But have we weighed the chances of *their* being wrong against the chances of the rest of us being wrong? Follow their lead, by all means.

15. Since these standard commentaries help mostly with matters related to authorial sayings (semantics) and not authorial *doings* (pragmatics), I don't purchase such commentaries. I check them out from a library, use them, make notes, and return them. I'd recommend you save your hard-earned money as well.

Ephesians 2:1–10
Who are "the ruler of the authority of the air" and "[the ruler] of the spirit" (2:2)? What does "by nature children of wrath" (2:3) mean? Whom is God demonstrating "the surpassing riches of his grace" to (2:7)? What does the "this" in 2:8 stand for—grace, faith, gift, or something else?

Ephesians 2:11–22
Who are "the ones called 'circumcision' in the flesh, hand-done" (2:11)? Who are the "far," and who are the "near" (2:13)? What are "the middle wall of partition—the enmity" (2:14), "the law of commandments in decrees" (2:15), and "enmity" again (2:16)? And how did Christ "destroy," "nullify," and "kill" them, respectively?

Ephesians 3:1–13
What is "the administration of God's grace" (3:2) and "the administration of the mystery" (3:9; "mystery" also shows up in 3:3, 4)? What does "less than the least of all the saints" indicate (3:8)?

Ephesians 3:14–21
"For this reason" (3:14)—what reason? What is the relationship between "the Father" (3:14) and "every family" (3:15)? What exactly is Paul praying for in 3:16–19? What does it mean for Christ to "dwell in your hearts through faith" (3:17), and why is this being prayed for? How do we become "filled to all the fullness of God" (3:19)?

Try to get at the answers yourself. Some of them involve digging through grammar, others require a careful reading of the text, and several call for expert opinion very generously granted to us in traditional commentaries.

Significant and Insignificant

Do not chase every conceivable rabbit in the text; that will get you only into burrows and warrens whence there is no escape. Not everything is important. I realize that discriminating between what is significant and what is not is a skill cultivated over time. The development of your sensibilities in this regard is the genius of becoming a good textual detective. Be discriminatory. Keep asking, right from the start, Will knowing this help me discern the *doing* of the author? Do I need to know this in order to apply this text?[16] Then you will be well on your way to honing your powers of observation.

16. One commentary takes over five dozen pages to discuss the issue of authorship of Ephesians (Hoehner, *Ephesians*, 1–61). No doubt this is an important issue, but not for preaching the theology of each of the pericopes of a text the church has accepted as canonical. For preaching

What makes a textual element significant is the purpose for its inclusion. For example, why did the author of 1 Samuel use "voice" in 15:1, "the *voice* of the word of Yahweh"? If you suspect that it is purposeful—and it is—then it is significant. Make a note of it. At this stage of determining authorial saying, you might not know exactly why it was said, but mark it as something to follow in the next stage of discerning authorial *doing*. Of course, on occasion you might have to go back to exploring in greater depth a particular word or a syntactical element that you did not pay attention to at first. But I want you to be ruthless about abandoning semantic pursuits that do not lead to the goal of figuring out pericopal theology. Do not do word studies just for the sake of doing word studies. Do not track histories and geographies just for the delight of doing so. Do not translate every verse from the Hebrew or the Greek just to give your linguistic muscles a workout. If a verse is reasonably clear as to its saying, leave it alone; you've gotten it.[17] Do not be compelled to slice, dice, dissect, and atomize. Save yourself precious time and energy.

In Ephesians 1, for instance, you don't need to dig deep into what "apostle" (1:1) means or the different nuances of Paul's greeting—"grace" versus "peace" (1:2). If you get the general drift, you're good, as far as preaching is concerned. "Blessed," being an important term in 1:1–14, may need some digging into. Tough verbiage, such as "the administration of the fullness of times" (1:10) may need some explication. In the first pericope of the Jacob Story (Gen. 25:19–34), it might help to figure out if the descriptions of Jacob and Esau in 25:27 are negative or positive, what "birthright" (25:31–34) means, and so on. Not everything in the saying is significant for discerning the *doing*/theology.

Permit me to affirm here that the study of biblical languages in seminaries is essential for the determination of authorial sayings. Unless one comprehends what "f-o-o-t" and "s-t-a-n-d-i-n-g" mean and how they are connected with the pronouns "my" and "you," respectively, and the role of the verb "are" and the interjection "hey," one can never arrive at the pragmatic understanding (*doing*) of your exclamation to me in that elevator: "Hey, you're standing on my foot!" And at determining what the author is saying, traditional scholars and standard commentaries are unbeatable. And

---

purposes, some things just aren't that important. I would say that the five-page disquisition in my own Ephesians commentary on the matter of authorship is sufficient (see Kuruvilla, *Ephesians*, 9–13) or even the briefer discussion in the introduction to Ephesians at http://www.homiletix .com/preaching2019/commentaries.

17. Diagramming is touted by traditional exegetes, one and all. I'm not a big fan of that exercise. If there is a convoluted sentence with long clauses that never seem to end, perhaps there is a place for it. Ephesians has a few of those, but I don't think even they have ever forced me to diagram a sentence. Standard commentaries on Ephesians ably help me through those tortuosities.

they, those writers of commentaries with years of experience, can do—and have already done—this kind of exegesis to determine authorial sayings far more accurately and efficiently than can the frazzled pastor-preacher in the midst of baptisms, funerals, dinners on the ground, counseling sessions, elder meetings, extinguishing fires, and cajoling volunteers. But remember: textual interpretation for application is never complete until the authorial *doing* (pericopal theology) has also been discerned. What preachers need, beyond traditional exegesis that helps determine textual semantics (the author's saying), is *theological* exegesis to discern textual pragmatics (the author's *doing*). Only then can they, and the people of God they shepherd, move to application.

Without a doubt, this step, determination of saying (involving questions and answers and discriminating between significant and insignificant), is already merging into the next step, discernment of *doing*. That's because, right from the get-go, we have an eye on our destination: authorial *doing* that will get us to valid application. Or to put it another way, exegesis is begun with determining the saying, but it is completed only with discerning the *doing*.

Let's go back to my dermatology patient with a facial rash. Even as I, the physician, take a history and conduct an examination (determining "authorial saying"), I am already considering a potential diagnosis (discerning "authorial *doing*") so that I may subsequently prescribe a remedy (deriving "application"). I hazard a guess that my patient may have rosacea, one of the commonest causes of face rash in adults. So to confirm my tentative impression, I investigate further: "Do your eyes itch? Do you tend to get flushing reactions [not unusual for rosacea]?" "Nope," comes the reply. Now my diagnosis is suspect. Examining the rash more carefully, I find it warm to the touch and somewhat indurated (i.e., hard) and shiny. I suspect it might be erysipelas (a bacterial infection). "Any joint pain, headache, or nausea?" "Yes, my head's been aching for the last few days," answers the patient. Symptoms are evaluated, a diagnosis is proposed, local findings are assessed, the diagnosis is readjusted, local findings are reexamined, and the diagnosis is fine-tuned. Now I can prescribe treatment (antibiotics for erysipelas).[18]

All that to say, diagnosis is a focused task with the goal of discerning what's going on so that one may provide treatment. So also exegesis—I call it *theo-*

18. Of course, I'm also distinguishing between the significant (redness, induration, headache) and the insignificant (the patient's receding hairline, his blue tie, and the fact that he wears glasses). Elsewhere I have noted how the medical diagnostic undertaking is quite similar to the operation of textual interpretation: Kuruvilla, "'What Is the Author *Doing* with What He Is *Saying*?'"

logical exegesis—should be focused on "diagnosing"/discerning the theology of the pericope so that one may derive valid application. So on to discerning *doing*.

Discerning Doing

Unfortunately, for discerning authorial *doing* (pericopal theology), you are going to be on your own for the most part. Neither translators nor commentators have latched on to the importance of textual pragmatics, being content to remain submerged in textual semantics.

Discerning *doing* is probably one of the hardest steps in sermon preparation. There is no recipe-driven technique that will automatically output the *doings* of authors when you press the appropriate buttons. In the last decade or so that I have been grappling with this notion, I have come to realize that textual pragmatics—discerning authorial *doing*—is more art than science, less amenable to being codified into steps.[19]

Lists of things to do and items to look for in a text—a common approach to exegesis of any sort—are generally unhelpful. Nonetheless, since they are standard fare in preaching textbooks, in the spirit of collegiality, here is a "Watch for . . ." checklist of my own, with examples of significant clues to discerning *doing* in the first six pericopes of Ephesians (Eph. 1–3).[20]

Structure
 chiasm centering on 1:10; chiasm centering on 1:20; bracketing of 2:1–10 by "walk" (2:2, 10); chiasm centering on 2:15–16; chiasm centering on "love of Christ" (3:19)

Unusual Elements
 1:3–14, the longest sentence in the New Testament; Trinitarian focus of 1:3–14; anatomy (head, hand, feet, body) in 1:20–23; digression of 3:2–13; paradox—Paul's insignificance (prisoner, 3:1; "leaster," 3:8; and passive verbs indicating his ministry, 3:2, 3, 5, 7, 8, 9, 10) in light of his significant role in God's grand plan (3:2–9)

Emphases
 divine plan/purpose (1:5, 9, 11) (multiple words); four synonyms for power (1:19) and four synonyms for hostile agents (1:21); "greatness"

---

19. See Kuruvilla, "Time to Kill the Big Idea?"; this essay is condensed in two appendixes in this work: app. A, "Big Idea versus Theological Focus," and app. B, "Preaching: Argumentation versus Demonstration."

20. For the significance of these clues (symptoms) for discerning authorial *doing* (diagnosis), see the commentaries on these passages in this work and in Kuruvilla, *Ephesians*.

(1:19)—only here in the New Testament; Christ's power over time and
space (1:21)

Contrasts

past (2:1–3) versus present (2:4–9) versus future (2:10); formerly (2:11–
12) versus now (2:16–22)

Links between Pericopes

"all things" (1:10, 22); hostile powers (1:21; 2:2); glory of God filling
temple (1:23; 2:21–22); words containing *oik* (the stem of *oikos*, "house";
2:19, 20, 21, 22; 3:2, 9, 17); "administration" (1:10; 3:2, 9); "power" (1:19–
23; 3:7); hostile agents (1:21; 2:2; 3:10); "purpose" (1:11; 3:11); "fullness"
(1:23; 3:19)

I confess that I am not at all convinced about the utility of such checklists
other than to state that, for discerning *doing*, the interpreter ought to attend
to the text's structure, its unusual elements, its emphases and contrasts, and
links between pericopes, among other things.

Imagine that a patient, Perry Cope, comes in for a skin check. You, a budding
dermatologist, P. R. Eacher, MD, have a checklist to follow, one item of which
is moles. That probably won't be of much help because you see all kinds of
things on Mr. Cope's skin. Which is a mole? Which is a barnacle? Which is a sun
spot? Which is a cyst? Even if you can accurately determine that a given lesion
is a mole, how do you know if it is benign or malignant, a cause for concern
or not? And even with more specific criteria for assessment provided as yet
another checklist—"Look for Asymmetry, Border, Color, Diameter, Evolution"
(the ABCDEs of moles)—how would you decide what degree of asymmetry,
what quality of border, what range of color(s), what length of diameter, and
what manner of evolution are innocuous, worrying, or dangerous?

Checklists are helpful, but there is more to diagnosis than a mechanical
rundown of listed items. There is the history of the patient as well as that of
the patient's family (Any previous skin cancers? How much sun exposure?
Use of sunscreen?), the patient's skin type, the gestalt of this one mole in light
of all the patient's other moles (the "ugly duckling" test), the employment
of the dermatoscope for a better look, and so on. Perhaps most importantly,
even if background and history are unsuspicious, there is the subtle clinical
sense and diagnostic acumen that come only with years of dermatological
experience. For this there can be no substitute. Not different at all is the "diagnosis" of a text's *doing*.

Here is how I approach discerning *doing*. After I have determined authorial
saying, I engage even more deeply with the text, absorbing and assimilating it, and then postulate a first guess of an authorial *doing* that is the best

explanation of all the textual data (abduction—an inferred form of thinking—from textual data to postulated authorial *doing*). Based on this inference, I look for other textual data that might substantiate my first guess (deduction from my initial inference to other data). From these findings I then arrive at a more precise authorial *doing* (induction from other textual data to a more refined understanding of authorial *doing*). Often this cycle/spiral is repeated for a few iterations. There is science involved, but this is mostly art, not to mention the Spirit's work of illumination in those who walk with God.[21]

Learning how to discern *doing* is caught more than it is taught (as is making diagnoses in medical training).[22] Earlier I proposed the analogy of the preacher as a curator of a text for listeners. Let me take this metaphor a step backward. If you are the student, learning how to discern *doing*, you will be greatly helped by a curator who can mediate the text-picture and its theological thrust for you first, before you, in turn, curate it for your listeners in a sermon. This is what I am attempting to do with pericopes from Ephesians and the Jacob Story in each chapter of this book—curate passages for readers and students.[23] Over a period of time, and after experiencing a number of pericopes curated for you, you will get a sense of how this is accomplished. It is a matter of developing your sensibilities to artistic nuance and nicety, to textual hue and shade. Trust me, discerning *doing* will become more natural as you catch it through your reading and as you grow in your experience.[24]

If there's one important piece of advice for discerning *doing*, it's this: do not give up too soon. Read the text multiple times; immerse yourself in it; grapple and wrestle with it; don't let go till it yields its fruit. Keep asking, Why did the author say what he said? What is he *doing*? Come up with reasons ("diagnoses") that explain the *doing*. Do all the determined sayings (the elements of the text, the various "symptoms") fit the discerned *doing* (your "diagnosis")? If not, you may be on the wrong track. Move sideways and try again. This is not a trial-and-error (or seek-and-find) operation; rather,

21. Once again, let this be a reminder that we preachers, young and old, novices and experts, need to be paying close and constant attention to our walk with God. This is a lifetime engagement—we should never, ever give up on growing closer to God and developing and maturing in our spiritual lives. That alone will advance us, in leaps and bounds, toward becoming better interpreters and preachers.

22. While much can be passed on through lectures and books and such, impactful learning in medical education happens primarily through apprenticeship—clerkship, internship, residency, and fellowship. That is when medicine is "caught," as one shadows an expert and practices under that one's aegis, with cases being "curated" for the trainee.

23. That is also what I attempt to do in my commentaries: curate text-picture after text-picture so readers develop responsive eyes and ears, sensitive to authorial *doings*. See Kuruvilla, *Ephesians*; and Kuruvilla, *Genesis*.

24. Likewise, experience in medical practice also builds a physician's diagnostic acuity. In that half of my split life, this has taken me over two decades of patient care.

it involves the assessment of discerned *doing* for its compatibility with determined saying. Some diagnoses are not consistent with symptoms and are
obviously wrong. For instance, 1 Samuel 15, with its intricate wordplays on
"voice," is clearly not about the fate of evil peoples (the Amalekites), a warning to believers that they too may expect severe chastisement from God for
living shoddy Christian lives. Neither is it about divine omnipotence—God's
absolute authority to order what seems to be genocide—exhorting current
readers to submit to God's judgment in every situation.[25]

As you gradually discern *doing*, as it begins to take shape, here is a tip on
proceeding further: find "labels" (or shorthands, titles, or handles) for ideas in
the text to enable you to get your head around those ideas. These labels may be
words, phrases, or sentences that signal what you think the text is about and
what the author is *doing*. Collect them all. Eliminate the ones you think are not
important or are clearly wrong. Rinse and repeat. Then tie those words/phrases/
sentences together and keep going till you get a single integrated sentence (or two
or three, but a single sentence is best because it clarifies in your mind the relationship between those labels). That sentence—I call it the Theological Focus—will
itself be a label for the authorial *doing* in the text, the pericopal theology.[26]

Let's try discerning *doing* with some verses from Proverbs. I'll assume
you have determined the saying and that nothing in these texts—words or
notions—is puzzling.[27]

Proverbs 4:1
> Hear, sons, the instruction of a father,
>   and be attentive to gain understanding.

Some idea labels here might be hearing, instruction, father, sons, or understanding.[28] Expand those labels a bit: listening to a father's instruction; sons

25. I am not denying the validity of these issues; they need to be addressed, but not in a
sermon. Perhaps another venue, say a Sunday School class, would serve the cause better.
26. The Theological Focus relates to pericopal theology as a label relates to the thing it
names. For instance, "d-o-g" is not a canine; it is simply an English label for one, merely point-
ing/referring to *Canis lupus familiaris* and serving as a label, shorthand, title, or handle for that
species. The label can never be a stand-in for the actual animal. Likewise, the Theological Focus,
a label for the text + theology, can never substitute for the experience of the latter. Rather, it is
simply a tool for the sermon preparer (see app. A).
27. My brief comments will treat determining saying and discerning *doing* without making
much distinction between the two operations. That is usually how theology is discerned and
diagnoses are made: one moves back and forth between symptoms and provisional conclusions
until a final diagnosis is reached.
28. In the initial stages of your preaching career, it is good practice *not* to use words from
the biblical passage as labels, unlike what I've just done. Avoiding biblical words will implicitly
force you to interpret rather than simply describe.

gaining understanding. Now tie everything together into a single sentence: "Listening to a father's instruction gains understanding for sons." Let's go a step further—remember, you are trying to visualize what happens in an ideal *world in front of the text* for all God's people for all time. You could see "father" as "parent" (father or mother), as "elder" (mentor, pastor, church leader, professor), and so on. Of course, "sons" would involve all children, of either gender. With that in mind, you might construct the Theological Focus this way: "Children gain understanding by listening to a parent's instruction" or "God's people gain understanding by listening to their elders." There is plenty of room for flexibility here.

This sentence is the Theological Focus of Proverbs 4:1.[29] There is no reason to phrase this in any particular form as long as (1) it is not an imperative: save imperatives in the sermon for the application, otherwise your listeners will be confused as to what they should be doing (see chap. 3, "Deriving Application"); and (2) it does not have any first- or second-person pronouns: in the ideal world that the text is dealing with, *all* God's people are being addressed by Scripture, so it is best to avoid these constrictive pronouns. So "Listen to your elders to gain understanding"—an imperative with a second-person pronoun—would be unacceptable as a Theological Focus.

It is helpful to write down your first thought and to keep reshaping it until you obtain an acceptable final product. Write, tweak, and repeat till you are satisfied with the final Theological Focus as a summary representation (label) of what happens in the ideal *world in front of the text*.

Imagine you were preaching this proverb at a men's Bible study. You might want to narrow down "children" to "sons." And if you were preaching to male adolescents, you might do well to substitute "parents" for "elders." Now if it happened that all of those male adolescents were sons of single male parents, then, of course, "sons" and "fathers"—as in the proverb—would fit perfectly. All that to say, even as you begin to discern *doing*, you are keeping one eye on your audience and considering where you might be heading in terms of application.

Here's another proverb.

Proverbs 15:23

> A man has joy in an answer from the mouth,
> and how good is a word at the right time.

---

29. Because we are dealing with one-verse "pericopes," it is possible for our Theological Foci to become as long as, if not longer than, the proverb itself. Not to worry; it won't happen with larger pericopes.

Determining Saying. The lines A and B are synonymous (i.e., A = B) but loosely so. Therefore, "an answer from the mouth" must be equivalent to "a word at the right time."

Discerning Doing. The idea labels here include a man's joy and goodness of an apt answer or of a word at the right time. Keeping in mind the parallelism in Proverbs 15:23, you might expand these into joy/goodness experienced by a man on receiving an apt/timely word. In a sentence, "A man is gladdened by a timely word." In the ideal world of God, "man" is likely a metonym for "person." So here's the Theological Focus: "One is gladdened by a timely word."[30]

Let's try another example—this time a narrative, but an uninspired one from Aesop.

Aesop's "The Fox and the Crow"

Once upon a time a crow found a big chunk of cheese. She grabbed it with her beak and settled on a branch of a nearby tree, rejoicing in her good luck. Just then a fox happened to pass by and noticed the crow on the tree and the cheese in her beak. Determined to get the cheese, it hatched a plot.

The fox went to the tree and shouted out to the crow, "What a beautiful bird you are—your shape, your plumage, your eyes! Wow! And you must have a really beautiful voice to match the rest of your beauty. Would you be so gracious as to let me enjoy the beauty of your voice? Would you please sing a song for me?"

The crow's heart swelled with pride. She thought, "Yes, of course, I'm beautiful. And, yes, I have a beautiful voice. I'll show this fox how marvelous my singing is." She forgot the cheese in her mouth and began to caw.

The cheese fell out. The fox had a good meal.

From this Aesop's fable, you might collect a number of idea labels: pride (crow's); greed (fox's); gullibility (crow's); slyness and flattery (fox's); loss (crow's); gain (fox's). Let's try expanding those words into phrases/sentences: the sly fox flatters; the prideful crow gullibly succumbs to flattery; the crow loses its booty; the fox gains. Now ligate those ideas together into a single sentence: "The prideful crow gullibly succumbs to the flattery of the sly fox and loses its booty to the fox." That's a good start, but all you have done is summarize the story: that's what the author is saying. Try moving away from animal and bird and what happened to them, distancing yourself from cheese and song, beauty and plumage (i.e., the semantics, the saying). Instead, try to catch the picture of the ideal *world in front of the text* that Aesop has

---

30. As a mental exercise, you might want to start considering what the response to this Theological Focus might be—that is, the application. Giving timely/apt words to others in order to bring gladness, perhaps?

painted (i.e., the pragmatics, the *doing*). What is the author *doing*? What is the characteristic of the ideal world he is projecting, or what is the requirement of that world according to the author? "Avoiding prideful gullibility to flattery prevents loss." This is what Aesop sees as happening in the ideal world that he is projecting with this text—an ideal world in which inhabitants, not being prideful and gullible, escape loss.

You may have noticed that I opted to focus on the crow and her attitude and action as a (negative) model. Why did I not focus on the fox instead? To catch authorial *doing* in a narrative, one of the first things one must do is decide on the character with whom the author intends the reader to identify—either negatively (we shouldn't be like him/her/them) or positively (we should be like him/her/them).[31] Of course, in theory Aesop could have been proposing this: "Engaging in flattery, deception, and cheating enables gain."[32] But more likely, he was intending for his readers to identify with the crow: "Avoiding prideful gullibility to flattery prevents loss." That's the "Theological" Focus of the narrative. What we want to arrive at is a characteristic of the ideal *world in front of the text* projected by the author, what he is *doing* with what he is saying.

In sum, delineating words/phrases to serve as labels for textual ideas and organizing these labels into a sentence yield the Theological Focus, a sentence summary (label) of the theology of the pericope—what the author is *doing*. There's nothing wrong with employing two sentences, or even a paragraph, but a single sentence makes the Theological Focus easily graspable since it is intended (1) to help you, the sermon preparer, stay on track as you work through the various parts of the sermon and put it all together—keeping you north oriented; (2) to give focus to the derivation of application (see chap. 3, "Deriving Application"); and (3) to aid you in structuring your sermon (the Theological Focus is particularly useful for this purpose; see chap. 4, "Creating Maps").[33]

An Important Note

We saw earlier that the theology of the pericope is inseparable from the text, so much so the integrated entity may be designated text + theology. By

---

31. There are some who deprecate such "Be like . . ." approaches. But the Bible is replete with such role modeling (negative or positive): Abraham and Rahab (James 2); the prophets, Job, and Elijah (James 5); etc. Indeed, Jesus himself frequently exhorted his listeners to imitate characters in his teaching: the wise builder (Matt. 7), David (Mark 2), and the good Samaritan (Luke 10), which actually concludes with the express injunction, "Go and do likewise," i.e., "Be like the good Samaritan" (10:37). See Kuruvilla, *Privilege the Text!*, 242–47.

32. Or "Avoiding flattery, deception, and cheating precludes gain."

33. I haven't tried creating a Theological Focus with pictures rather than words, but why not? If it helps you and serves these three purposes, by all means draw.

virtue of its inseparability from the text, the theology is inexpressible apart
from the words of the text. All the words of the text are necessary to convey
its theology with power and pathos, fully and faithfully. I could try to distill
the theology of 1 Samuel 15 into words: "The one committed to God listens
to the voice of God, not the voice of worldly seductions" or something to that
effect—a reasonable Theological Focus. But notice what has happened: the
power, pathos, and everything else that the text + theology (1 Sam. 15 and
the authorial *doing*) has is now lost in this rather sterile reduction or distillation. That is to say, we cannot get rid of 1 Samuel 15 and use the Theological
Focus (a label for the pericope's theology) in its place. We would be wrong to
assume that the reduction exhaustively encapsulates the text's *doing* and that
it can now substitute for the text. No reduced Theological Focus can ever be
a "lossless" stand-in for the pericope from which it was obtained. Remember,
our call is to preach the text + theology, not any reduction thereof. Then what
is the role of the reduction, the Theological Focus, in homiletics? As was
noted, first, it helps the sermon preparer—you—get a handle on the text's
theology. The Theological Focus is a reduction of this irreducible (I know,
that's a contradiction) theology into a convenient label (or shorthand, title,
or handle) for that pericopal theology and keeps the preacher focused as the
sermon is prepared. Second, it aids in the specification of application. Third,
it helps the preacher with sermon shaping. All that to say, there is utility in
coming up with a Theological Focus, but do be aware of its limitations: it
can never be a substitute for the text + theology.

Here's another uninspired "pericope."

Johann Sebastian Bach

The musical genius, Johann Sebastian Bach, at the age of ten lived with his
brother Johann Christoph Bach after his parents had died. Though the older
sibling instructed Bach in keyboard playing, for some reason, JC kept JS's
hands off a book he owned that was a compilation of keyboard pieces by the
famous masters of the day. Ravenous for stimulation, Bach apparently took
the rolled-up book out of the locked cabinet it was secured in through the
grate that made its doors and, over several weeks, copied the whole thing out
painstakingly by moonlight!

"We would have to try imitating him to grasp fully what this involved for
an eleven- to thirteen-year-old. Music paper had to be set aside, goose quills
had to be cut, and the calendar and weather had to be taken into account. . . .
Children at such an age need their sleep, but he could not doze off. He had to
stay awake until everybody else in the house had gone to bed, then arrange his
utensils on the windowsill, creep over to the cabinet, and cautiously pull the
book out—all without making a peep. And then he had to write and write by

a wretched light as long as the moon was favorable. It rose an hour later each day, he had to wait for the nights until it was at least halfway visible. You can almost write a text with your eyes shut. Even when the lines run together and the letters are blurred, they still remain legible. But notes have to be placed exactly on and between five lines, precisely on top of each other, with their different values, accidentals, and bar lines. Afterward all traces had to be eliminated, the book put back just as carefully as it had been removed. Then he had to get a bit of sleep, since school required daily achievement, and he also had to keep his big brother from noticing his lack of rest."[34]

Read the text a number of times. Get a sense of the whole. What are the ideas lurking in it? Their labels may include seeking stimulation, learning from other composers, and incredible perseverance. Based on the detailed account of the hardship Bach had to undergo just to learn from other composers (more than two-thirds of the words of the "pericope" are devoted to this), it seems the author is emphasizing the necessity of perseverance for the sake of growth and development, even for a genius like Bach. So what might the "Theological" Focus be? "If you want to get better at something, even to develop and improve already existing talent, you must work hard." But that's an imperative, and it has a second-person pronoun and a lot of words—twenty. Try to get the Theological Focus down to about a dozen words. Here's a possibility in ten words: "Improvement calls for hard work, even if one is gifted."[35]

Validation

How does one know one is right in this discerning of *doing*? How does one know one has accurately discerned the author's *doing*? There are two things to remember here.

1. *Intrapericopal coherence.* Within a given pericope (so *intra*pericopal), there are a number of textual elements/clues ("symptoms"). If your "diagnosis" of the authorial *doing* is accurate, then all of those elements will cohere and point to and support your "diagnosis." You should be able to visualize a tightly knit picture of the author's *doing* from all the various elements/clues within the particular pericope. In other words, your "diagnosis" must be the best explanation of everything in the pericope, consistent with the "symptoms."

2. *Interpericopal coherence.* Between pericopes (so *inter*pericopal), there also should be coherence—that is, a perceptible movement from pericope to pericope ("pearl to pearl") as one reconstructs the overall trajectory of a

34. Eidam, *True Life of Johann Sebastian Bach*, 11.
35. Remember, again, this is only the "Theological" Focus, a condensate of the text's "theology." It cannot substitute for the original text, only point or refer to it, as does a label.

book ("pearl necklace"). There should be discernible design as to the choice of the pearls and how the overall necklace is rendered smooth, shiny, and seamless.[36]

For the Ephesians and Jacob Story examples that follow, I have attempted, both here and in my commentaries, to demonstrate that the textual elements of a given pericope are consistent with its discerned authorial *doing*/theology (intrapericopal coherence). And moreover, I have tried to show how the trajectory of the entire book (Eph. 1–6) or the complete section (Gen. 25–36) also is consistent, showing a recognizable and concatenated movement from pericope to pericope (interpericopal coherence). Such coherence and movement are evident in every genre of Scripture and should be traced as a means of ensuring one is on the right track with the discerning of authorial *doings* in individual pericopes.

Besides intrapericopal and interpericopal coherence, you must also employ, with dexterity, Ockham's razor: when there is seemingly more than one possible theology ("diagnosis") for a given pericope, choose the one that is the simplest consolidation of all the textual elements ("symptoms"). Simplicity always wins. Cut away all unnecessary complexities and convoluted explanations of the data of the text. Employ Ockham's sharp implement liberally.

The Theological Focus may also be useful in running a quick check to see if the pericopal theology from which it is drawn is consistent with the scheme of biblical and systematic theology you subscribe to. If it is not, you might have to rethink your diagnosis of the theology of the pericope. Here's an analogy. Say you are married. Your marital status governs every decision you make, though its influence is not necessarily acknowledged consciously at every moment. Whether you go to Burger King or McDonald's for lunch with your coworkers does not impinge upon, or contravene, that all-important relationship. But if you were to start a bank account for yourself or enter into a close relationship with a person of the opposite sex (without letting your spouse know), that would spell trouble. In other words, there are boundaries in your marriage, but within those boundaries, there is freedom to decide one way or another, to do one thing or another, or to say some things or others without breaking your wedding vows or even consciously thinking about them. Likewise with systematic and biblical theology. Thou shalt not transgress the boundaries drawn by the theological tradition and system you endorse. But within those limits, pericopal theology (being more specific than other species of theology) gives you particular guidelines for life that do not impinge

---

36. Perhaps one might compare this with a diagnosis consistent with the patient's family history, or social history, or elements of his or her life and genetic background that might lend coherence to the present examination conducted in the clinic.

upon or contravene your broader doctrinal fences and guardrails.[37] Blessing God for his grand and glorious plan of consummating all things in Christ, a plan that includes God's people (from Eph. 1:1–14; see below), and not despising what God has blessed you with (from Gen. 25:19–34; see below), for example, are not likely to violate any facet of your biblical or systematic theology grid, no matter what your theological perspective. Thus biblical and systematic theology do not usually or necessarily come directly into play in the discerning of pericopal theology and the derivation of its application to life. For preaching purposes, biblical and systematic theology serve only as cautionary barriers.[38]

Now for some serious practice utilizing larger volumes of text.

---

37. I have differentiated systematic and biblical theology from pericopal theology elsewhere. See Kuruvilla, *Vision for Preaching*, 98–99.

38. Remember that the sermonic goal is the congregation's experience of the text + (pericopal) theology so that lives may be changed. Expositions of biblical and systematic theology, a very different species of Christian communication, are best dealt with as topical sermons or relegated to non-pulpit and Sunday school–type occasions.

Ephesians and the Jacob Story

1. Ephesians 1:1–14

Read the text a number of times until you are familiar with its contours. Remember, don't give up too soon.[39]

This opening pericope of the book of Ephesians, at first blush, seems to be rambling.[40] But one notices that God's grand design is clearly stated in 1:10: "the consummation of all things in Christ." Right now everything is broken, undone, chaotic. But one day, in God's grand design, everything is going to be integrated, harmonized, and aligned with Christ. He becomes the unifying end of the cosmos. This is the purpose of God, and God's grand design has already begun, here and now.

> The grand purpose of God, the consummation of all things in the universe in Christ.[41]

All this clearly has to do with divine intentionality: notice the emphasis here on God's "pleasure," God's "will," God's "purpose," God's "counsel," and God's "predestination" (i.e., his divine appointing) (1:5, 9, 11). This consummation in Christ that God is undertaking is deliberate.

> The deliberate grand purpose of God, the consummation of all things in the universe in Christ.

Though the consummation of all things in Christ involves the cosmos—"things in the heavens and things on the earth"—the many first- and second-person plural pronouns and verbs (see 1:3, 4, 5, 6, 7, 8, 9, 11, 12, 13, 14) demonstrate that this grand design of God involves us, humans. Wonder of wonders—God is co-opting his people into his grand design to consummate all things in Christ. God's choice of believers, we are told, was made "before" (*pro*) the foundation of the world (1:4), and they are said to be

---

39. Again, I will assume you have determined the saying of Eph. 1:1–14: all its words and notions are clear to you.

40. For an expanded curation of this text, see Kuruvilla, *Ephesians*, 20–37; for an annotated manuscript of a sermon on this pericope, see app. C.

41. These shaded phrases are the labels for ideas in the text discussed in the paragraph(s) above the labels. The labels become progressively cumulative, culminating in a single sentence, the Theological Focus of the pericope. It bears reiterating that the Theological Focus is only a reductive label for the theology of the text (text + theology). Essentially, what I am doing here (and elsewhere) is demonstrating clues to the theology of the text and facilitating your discernment of the theology as I curate your experience of the text + theology. In the process, I am simultaneously creating a Theological Focus reduction of the (inexpressible) pericopal theology, not to be a substitute for the text a sermon listener must catch but for the three specific purposes noted earlier that help the sermon preparer.

"predestined/destined-before" (*proorizō*, 1:5), a sovereign choice on the part of God. That they are chosen *to be* "holy and blameless," and this "before him" (1:4), referring to the eschatological presentation of the church on the day of the Lord Jesus Christ (see 5:27), makes the span of God's choice of his people extend from eternity past to the last things—a grand plan, indeed! (The rest of the letter will spell out this responsibility of humans to be "holy and blameless.")

> The deliberate grand purpose of God, the consummation of all things in the universe in Christ, involves believers.

And so, to include us in his purpose, God graciously saves us through Christ (1:6–8). Thus, not only was God gracious in his predestination (1:6), but he was lavishly so in his redemption—commensurate with the wealth of his grace (1:7–8a). Not incidental, grace is integral to God's mission to include his people in his grand design.

> The deliberate grand purpose of God, the consummation of all things in the universe in Christ, involves believers, graciously redeemed by Christ.

All of this is evidence of God's love for his people. Having chosen believers "in love" (1:4), God graced them "in the Beloved" (1:6). An underlying theme of God's overwhelming love is discernible. So not only was this a carefully planned program way back when, but it was also a *loving* plan to include us in his purpose. Accomplished in love, this is a relationship that brings God delight ("good pleasure," 1:5).

> The deliberate grand purpose of God, the consummation of all things in the universe in Christ, involves believers, graciously and delightedly redeemed by Christ in love.

In case we were wondering, the co-optation of humans into God's purpose is a blessing. It is a blessing to be involved in God's grand design (1:3). He blessed us by involving us in his purpose, and the only way we can ever be fulfilled is by taking our place in that purpose—the consummation of all things in Christ. If that wasn't enough, the privilege of being God's children ("predestined," 1:5) will one day become the honor of being God's inheritance (also "predestined," 1:11). "All things"—in heaven and on earth—may be consummated in Christ (1:10), but believers remain at the core of the plan of God, who works "all things" according to his will. And this glorious privilege of believers to become God's possession is guaranteed by the Holy Spirit (1:13–14).

> The deliberate grand purpose of God, the consummation of all things in the universe in Christ, involves believers, graciously and delightedly redeemed by Christ in love—an abundant blessing.

This privilege is so awe-inspiring that the apostle breaks out into a blessing of God in 1:3–14, the longest sentence in the New Testament, composed of 202 words: "Blessed be God . . ."

> The deliberate grand purpose of God, the consummation of all things in the universe in Christ, involving believers, graciously and delightedly redeemed by Christ in love—an abundant blessing—evokes, in return, a blessing of God.

Thirty-six words is too long. Let me condense this a bit, eliminating some of the more obvious elements of the Theological Focus.

> **God, who blesses his people, redeeming them for his grand plan to consummate all things in Christ, is worthy of being blessed.**[42]

What I've done here is collect the idea labels and ligate them into a Theological Focus sentence, which itself becomes an expressible label (or shortcut, title, or handle) for the inexpressible pericopal theology. Tweak and rewrite until you get a satisfactory end product.

Ready to tackle the Old Testament?

1. Genesis 25:19–34

Read the pericope, then read it again, and again, and yet again.[43] Who do you think the author wants us to identify with (negatively: don't be like . . . ; or positively: be like . . .)? Is there a difference in character identification between Genesis 25:19–26 and 25:27–34? Now read on.

The beginning of the story sounds routine. The barrenness of the matriarch is not a first in Genesis. Neither is Yahweh's answering of prayer to open wombs. However, the glaring difference between this initial scene of the Jacob Story and the Abraham Story must be pointed out: "but the *sons* . . ." (25:22). For the first time in biblically narrated human history, there is more than one individual in the same womb at the same time—two equals! The problem is this: Who will be the firstborn, and who will thereby obtain the sovereign blessing?

> Obtaining divine blessing.

At the center of this pericope stands the children's struggle and the divine oracle delineating the line of blessing. Notice the orderly structure:

42. Twenty-two words is the best I can do. I am sure you can do better, though if you think this isn't too unwieldy, keep it as is.
43. For an expanded curation of this text, see Kuruvilla, *Genesis*, 291–303.

Isaac is forty when he takes Rebekah as his wife (25:20)

    Barrenness: Isaac "entreats" (ʿatar) Yahweh because his wife is barren (25:21a)

    Conception: Yahweh "answers" (ʿatar) Isaac, and Rebekah conceives (25:21b)

Children struggle; Rebekah inquires of Yahweh; Yahweh sovereignly ordains (25:22–23)

    Gestation: Her days of pregnancy are fulfilled; twins in the womb (25:24)

    Delivery: Birth, appearance, and naming of children (25:25–26a)

Isaac is sixty when Rebekah gives birth (25:26b)

The fight to be firstborn is the drive to obtain the blessing of God, and the participants slug it out between themselves in a bid for the prize. The verb denoting "struggle"
(ratsats, 25:22) is quite a violent term (used for "smashing/crushing" of skulls in Judg.
9:53); the *hithpolel* form of the Hebrew verb stem denotes the mutually aggressive
action and reciprocity of the tussle. Both are culpable (both Jacob and Esau become
negative examples for our identification, though one might conceivably focus on Jacob's
grasping tendencies that get prominent billing here; Esau's character flaw follows in the
next episode of this pericope). Consider that this is part of a larger document written
for the newly birthed nation of Israel. Will there be intramural conflicts in that community as each member unilaterally seeks the blessing of God at the expense of others?

> Conflicts in the zeal to appropriate divine blessing.

Two decades of prayer, two equals in the womb fighting, but one cannot direct blessing
as one wishes. Divine design can never be overcome by human vigor. Only a sovereign
God can distribute blessing, the centerpiece of this section of the pericope.

> God sovereignly distributes blessing, and conflicts ensue in the zeal to appropriate di-
> vine blessing.

This episode, Genesis 25:19–26, thus projects the potential for human strife when
God sovereignly blesses—in this case, strife between individuals who are equal in the
same womb at the same time.

> God sovereignly distributes blessing, and conflicts ensue among equals in the community
> in the zeal to appropriate divine blessing.

The second episode, 25:27–34, is structured with a concluding emphasis on Esau's
despising of his birthright (he is clearly the negative example we must focus on). The
cascade of five *qal* imperfect Hebrew verbs (*waw*-consecutives) in 25:34b is stunning and
condemning: "and he ate, and he drank, and he rose, and he went, and he despised"—the
brutal staccato of Esau's passions. This final comment from the narrator summarizing

the story and providing a negative editorial assessment of what happened is quite rare in Old Testament narrative. Ultimately, Esau was despising Yahweh's sovereign promises and blessing, a surrendering of valuable long-term blessing for the instant gratification of physical desires.

So in the first episode, one (Jacob) wants the blessing of the other, and each is willing to fight for it;[44] in the second, the other (Esau) despises his own blessing. Putting the ideas together, and moving from individuals to community, we arrive at a Theological Focus.

> God sovereignly distributes blessing, and conflicts ensue among equals in the community in their zeal to appropriate divine blessing, particularly when they despise their own blessing from God—all resulting in loss.

And here's a shortened version.

> **Failing to recognize God's sovereign distribution of blessing and despising one's own blessing can lead to strife and loss.**

Yes, I agree that discerning *doing* seems rather difficult at first, particularly for longer passages. But hang in there. The more you see this being done, the easier it gets. Remember, discerning *doing* is caught. Following along with me here (and in my commentaries) is a good strategy to "catch" it.

Now let's try a couple more pericopes.

2. Ephesians 1:15–23

Make sure you have soaked yourself in this pericope for a while.[45] Let it sink in.[46]

This pericope is essentially a prayer by Paul. At the onset, he asks that the Ephesians might know three things: the hope to which God has called them, the glorious inheritance that God possesses in them, and the great power of God working for them (1:18–19). The first two—hope of divine calling and glory of divine inheritance—have already been dealt with in 1:1–14 (as part of the magnificent privilege of believers incorporated into God's grand plan to consummate all things in Christ: 1:4, 5, 11, 12; and 1:11, 14, respectively). Here the last element, power, stands out, separated from the first two with an "and." The topic of power takes most of the space in 1:15–23.

---

44. We identify negatively with *both* brothers. Or you could focus negatively on Jacob alone, the "heel grabber" (Gen. 25:26).

45. For an expanded curation of this text, see Kuruvilla, *Ephesians*, 38–51.

46. I haven't tried this but have always been tempted to: memorize the text you are preaching on as you commence your preparation. That might help you grapple with it on an intimate level. Of course, you might have to add time for this, and it may be somewhat of a futile expenditure of resources when it comes to narratives. Perhaps key verses thereof?

There is also a shift in this pericope to the use of a first-person plural pronoun in 1:19. This indicates that *all* believers, including Paul himself, benefit from the working of God's incredible power.

All believers. Experiencing the power of God.

Also notice that several of the New Testament words that indicate "power" show up in 1:19 (*dynamis, energeia, kratos, ischys*; "power," "working," "strength," and "might," respectively), emphasizing the incomparability and all-encompassing nature of divine power. The potency of Paul's description is evident in his use in 1:19 of the participle of *hyperballō* ("surpassing," used only five times in the New Testament) and the noun *megethos* ("greatness," employed only here in the New Testament). So power is integral to the thrust of this pericope (intrapericopal coherence).

All believers. Experiencing the incredible power of God.

But why launch into this declamation on power? And why here? (We are searching here for interpericopal coherence—why this pericope is dealing with this issue, and why here, after pericope 1, Eph. 1:1–14.)

Some background information is helpful here. These early Christians in Ephesus lived among pagans who believed in a plentitude of supernatural entities. Therefore, Paul's declaration here is a strong word of comfort as it emphasizes the supremacy of God's power over every other kind of power. Ephesians 1:21 also balances the four synonyms of divine power in 1:19 by labeling four entities of hostile power: *archē, exousia, dynamis, kyriotēs*; "rule," "authority," "power," and "dominion," respectively. Thus the listing of four hostile powers in 1:21 is likely intended to be a contrast to the four specifications of divine power in 1:19.

All believers. Experiencing the incredible power of God. Hostile powers at work.

Now we are getting closer. The first pericope focused on God's grand plan to consummate "all things *in the heavens* and on earth" in Christ, co-opting humans into that glorious scheme. This divine enterprise is going to meet with some significant pushback from certain denizens "in the heavens" who are inimical to God and antithetical to all he is doing. Great plan, grand scheme, no doubt. But guess what? Great will also be the opposition, and that opposition will be directed toward us who have been co-opted into God's plan.

All believers. Experiencing the incredible power of God. Hostile powers at work to oppose God's plan and God's people.

But divine power is far greater than any other power of any other being anywhere in the universe. God demonstrated the magnificence of his might in the resurrection of Christ and his exaltation in heaven, thereby subjugating all hostile powers under Christ's feet and giving him as head to the church (1:20–22). In terms of time, then, the scope of Christ's reign is eternal: "not only in this age but also in the one to come" (1:21b). In terms of space, Christ is seated "at his [God's] right hand," "in the heavenlies," and "far above" every other conceivable power (1:20b–21a). Thus both space and time are encompassed in this depiction: divine power in Christ overrides every opposing power in the universe as he subjugates them all under his feet forever.

> Hostile powers at work to oppose God's plan and God's people are overwhelmed by God's incredible power in and through Christ.

This same incredible power that God "worked in Christ" (1:20) is at work for believers—"for us who believe" (1:19). Thereby, every antagonistic power is subject not only to Christ but also to his body, the church (1:22)[47]—another facet of the saints' marvelously privileged position. In this sense, the church is more powerful (in Christ) than every other anti-God power.

> Hostile powers at work to oppose God's plan and God's people are overwhelmed by God's incredible power in and through Christ—power that is extended toward believers.

It is very likely that the idea of "fullness" (*plērōma*, 1:23) in Ephesians refracts the Old Testament concept of divine presence, akin to God's *shekinah* glory. In the Old Testament, God filled the sanctuary; now in Christ, he fills the church that thereby partakes of divine fullness. Christians are truly empowered beings in Christ. We have nothing to fear, as God involves us in his grand and glorious plan to consummate all things in Christ.

> Hostile powers at work to oppose God's plan and God's people are overwhelmed by God's incredible power in and through Christ—power that is extended toward believers, the body of Christ, his fullness, as Christ reigns.

Here's a more convenient label (or shorthand, title, or handle) for the pericopal theology.[48]

47. This makes good sense. Every other lesser power has been subdued "under his [Christ's] feet" (1:22). So if believers are "his body" (1:23), then all of those powers are under believers' feet as well.
48. Remember, again, that the Theological Focus is a reduction of an irreducible pericopal theology simply to help with sermon preparation: to keep you on the right track, to aid you in deriving application, and to help you create a sermon structure. The Theological Focus (the reduction) is *not* what you want to convey to the audience. It is the pericopal theology that must be experienced by listeners rather than a reduction thereof. Hence, the Theological Focus

> **As the fullness and body of Christ, the church manifests God's incomparable power against supernatural foes.**

Now for the second pericope of the Jacob Story.

2. Genesis 26:1–33

This pericope appears to be a flashback.[49] The events of Genesis 26 likely occur in the two decades of Rebekah's barrenness, for it is inconceivable that Isaac's lie that Rebekah was his sister would have otherwise gone undetected by the men of Gerar for "a long time" (Gen. 26:8); had there been two kids running around in Isaac's camp, the game would have been up. In addition, in 25:11, God is shown blessing Isaac, yet that blessing is only a promise in 26:3, later fulfilled in 26:12. So this pericope is a flashback. But why? And why two discrete episodes in this flashing-back pericope (26:1-11 and 26:12-35)?

God instructs Isaac quite specifically that he is *not* to go to Egypt but is to stay in "this land" (26:1, 3). Since he decreed that Isaac dwell in Gerar (26:3), it would have been appropriate for Isaac to expect God to protect him, especially since God also explicitly promised to be with the patriarch (26:3). Later, even outsiders—Abimelech and Phicol—acknowledge this fact (26:28). And notice that the promise of divine presence, blessing, and land is "to you and to your descendants" (26:3). The word *descendants* (*zera*ʿ) echoes four times in God's utterance to Isaac in 26:3–4. Isaac is assured of divine protection, at least until such descendants are produced.

> Promised blessing—unambiguous and unequivocal.

But it appears that the patriarch does not put much stock in divine promises. In 26:7-11, Isaac passes off his wife, Rebekah, as his sister, fearing for the safety of his own life, even willing to jeopardize the welfare of his spouse. After the divine promise of presence grounded in a divine oath (26:3), one must conclude that Isaac's fear was unjustified. Remember, this episode occurs before the couple had children. Surely, Isaac's life was secure in light of God's fourfold affirmation that Isaac would produce "descendants."

> Promised blessing—unambiguous and unequivocal. Deception manifests distrust in God.

Thus in the first episode we have a man not trusting God and his word. In response to fear and threats to his own life, he falls apart.

---

is primarily for the sermon *preparer*, not necessarily for the sermon *listener* (see chaps. 3 and 4 and apps. A and B).

49. For an expanded curation of this text, see Kuruvilla, *Genesis*, 304–15; for an annotated manuscript of a sermon on this pericope, see app. D.

The second episode of this pericope (26:12-35) begins with a description of God's blessing of Isaac (26:12-14). Not only does he reap a hundredfold—an incredible harvest in any season anywhere, and this was in the patriarch's first year of sowing—but he also grows rich, richer, and even more rich (26:13). No wonder he was being envied by those outside his camp (26:14). And that envy spurs action—inimical action intended to endanger Isaac and his people: his opponents sabotage Isaac's wells or take them away from him (26:15, 18-20). No water meant no survival in the Middle East.

> Promised blessing—unambiguous and unequivocal. Deception manifests distrust in God.
> Blessing leads to opposition.

However, surprisingly (particularly after the first episode), in response to each of the instances of oppression, Isaac refuses to retaliate, instead moving away and digging wells elsewhere (26:17-18, 21, 22). It is not that Isaac was incapable of responding: even his enemies acknowledged that he was "too powerful for us" (26:16). Besides, if Isaac's "great household" (26:14) was anything like that of his father, Abraham, who had raised a homegrown army of 318 soldiers with which he successfully waged wars (Gen. 14), Isaac could surely have fought off any kind of oppression. Indeed, it appears that Abimelech was actually afraid of Isaac (26:29).

> Promised blessing—unambiguous and unequivocal. Deception manifests distrust in God.
> Blessing leads to opposition. No retaliation.

Apparently, by the time of this second episode of this pericope, Isaac had learned his lesson: God was trustworthy and could be relied on to protect and secure Isaac's blessings even from fierce opposition. Hence, the patriarch refrains from retaliation; in fact, he makes peace with his enemies (26:26-31). And why not? In 26:3, God promised to be with Isaac in the future; in 26:24, God assures Isaac that he is with the patriarch in the present; in 26:28, Abimelech recognizes that God has been with Isaac in the past.

> Promised blessing—unambiguous and unequivocal. Deception manifests distrust in God.
> When blessing leads to opposition, not retaliating, but rather reconciling, manifests
> trust in God.

Ultimately this pericope—a two-sided coin, one negative, one positive—exhorts us to trust God that he will secure his blessings to us without our having to fear any loss thereof. So stating this in the positive (and in fewer words), we have:

> **God's promised blessings are sure and obviate any attempt to secure them by
> deception in fear or retaliation against opposition—instead, reconciliation is called
> for.**

3

Deriving Application

Only [the one] who believes is obedient, and only [the one] who is obedient believes.[1]

W̶e have now looked at a text, determined its saying, and then discerned the *doing*—pericopal theology. Now we proceed to derive application from the text. Here is the scheme we discussed in chapter 2, "Discerning Theology."

Figure 3.1

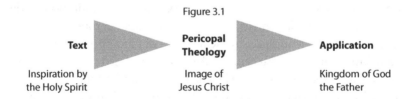

Text	Pericopal Theology	Application
Inspiration by the Holy Spirit	Image of Jesus Christ	Kingdom of God the Father

The Spirit's words (text) depict Christ's image (pericopal theology), and as God's people are aligned with that image, they are inhabiting the Father's kingdom (application)—it is coming to be! A biblical pericope thus is more than informing; it is also transforming. By aligning ourselves with the pericopal theology of each text, we are becoming increasingly Christlike, because Christ is the only one who fulfilled all the theologies of all the pericopes in all the books of Scripture. And this is God's goal for his people, that they may

1. Bonhoeffer, *Cost of Discipleship*, 69.

be "conformed to the image [*eikōn*] of his Son" (Rom. 8:29). Therefore, as mentioned in chapter 2, I call this a christiconic interpretation of Scripture for homiletics. Thus preaching is the means by which we are taught how to be Christlike. In other words, the biblical text is to be preached for growth in godliness, that the church may be "holy and blameless" (Eph. 1:4; 5:27), conformed into the image of Christ, for the glory of God.

Importance of Application

Preaching is not only the explanation of God's word but also its application to life. This was a key value for God's people in every age. When Moses gave the "second law" in the book of Deuteronomy, he constantly placed his audience in Egypt, even the next generation who had not experienced firsthand the bondage under the pharaohs: "The Egyptians treated *us* with evil, and afflicted *us*, and laid upon *us* hard labor; then *we* cried to Yahweh . . . and Yahweh heard *our* voice and he saw *our* distress, and *our* oppression, and Yahweh brought *us* out of Egypt" (Deut. 26:6–8). Likewise, Paul could affirm to his Roman readers that "whatever was written previously was written for *our* instruction" (Rom. 15:4). Such a contemporizing of prior events and writings for current audiences makes Scripture applicable in every age, creating a corporate solidarity of God's people of all time.

This concern for the application of Scripture also dominated Christian communities from very early on. In the early second century, Justin Martyr, describing a worship service in Rome, noted that after the reading of the Gospels, the leader verbally teaches "and exhorts to the imitation of these good things."[2] Later, the Christian apologist Tertullian wrote, "We assemble to read our sacred writings, . . . by inculcations of God's precepts we confirm good habits."[3] In the fourth century, Augustine declared that the aim of an expositor of Scripture was "to be listened to with understanding, with pleasure, and with obedience"—in other words, by application.[4] Throughout church history, the application of Scripture has consistently been considered the culmination of interpretation and the endpoint of preaching.

2. Justin Martyr, *First Apology* 67, in *Ante-Nicene Fathers* (hereafter *ANF*) 1:118.
3. Tertullian, *Apology* 39, in *ANF* 3:65.
4. Augustine, *On Christian Teaching* 141 (4.26.56). This was a key value in early Jewish communities as well. Philo, *On the Special Laws* 2.15.62, observed that "on the seventh day there are spread before the people in every city innumerable lessons of prudence, and temperance, and courage, and justice, and all other virtues; . . . some of those who are very learned explain to them what is of great importance and use, by which the whole of their lives may be improved" (*Works of Philo Judaeus* 3:270).

By application the community of God is progressively and increasingly aligned with the will of God, becoming conformed to the image of the Son of God. And such "instruction in righteousness" (2 Tim. 3:16), leading to the "completion" of the believer in Christ (3:17), is accomplished in the power of the Spirit by the medium of Scripture, the agency of the preacher, and the instrument of the sermon. In other words, application is the theology of the pericope actualized, the appropriate response of listeners to the text, the consummation of their experience of the text + theology.

Application marks the one who loves God, and it promises divine blessing. Jesus says, "The one who has my commandments and obeys them is the one who loves me" (John 14:21).[5] And he declares, "Blessed are those who hear the word of God and obey it" (Luke 11:28).[6] One cannot deny the crucial nature of this aspect of homiletics: if God's people are to be aligned with God's will in obedience, then preaching for application is a necessary responsibility that preachers have to discharge. God's word is intended to be applied, and therefore preaching, which facilitates the experience of God's word by God's people, must be applicational. Application, then, extends the divine call in the theological thrust of a single pericope (pericopal theology) to a particular audience to conform lives to Christlikeness.[7]

Theology to Application

Deriving application is not an easy task, considering that the text is embedded in eras, grounded in localities, scripted in languages, characterized by institutions, and marked by values—all temporally, spatially, and conceptually far from a modern audience.

Let's look at an example. This specific command appears three times in the Old Testament law: "You shall not boil a young goat in its mother's milk" (Exod. 23:19; 34:26; Deut. 14:21). How on earth do we apply this ancient text? Some might assert the inapplicability in the current dispensation of "ceremonial" and "civil" laws such as this one, which directly pertained to Israel's unique situation; only the "moral" law, they would argue, is applicable today. But the fact is that every law of God is moral, reflecting the morality of the Lawgiver. Every law of God is therefore theological. Besides, the Bible sees law

5. Also see John 14:15, 23; 15:10; 1 John 2:3, 5; 3:24; 4:12; 5:2–3; 2 John 6; etc. for the link between loving God and obeying him.

6. After giving his disciples an example of humility, Jesus exhorted, "If you know these things, blessed are you if you do them" (John 13:17).

7. I am grateful to my colleagues in the Department of Pastoral Ministries at Dallas Theological Seminary for their input into this statement of the applicational goal.

as a monolithic unit, without distinctions. "For whoever keeps the whole law, but stumbles in one [law], has become guilty of all" (James 2:10). One cannot pick and choose what Scriptures to apply. "*Every* Scripture . . . is profitable" (2 Tim. 3:16, my emphasis).[8] So it will not do to say that the prohibition of boiling a kid in its mother's milk is not applicable to a modern-day believer. It is applicable; the question is *how*.

Imagine I am helping the saints at my home church in Dallas, Northwest Bible Church, to apply this Old Testament command. Let's say I give my modern audience this application: *Never, ever boil a kid in its mother's milk!* That would have a great deal of authority because it comes directly from the text, but it would have no relevance at all, since Christians in twenty-first-century Dallas are not tempted to boil baby goats in their mothers' milk.

Let's take the same text again, but this time assume I tell my congregation, *Don't eat cheeseburgers!* (Orthodox Judaism employs these verses proscribing the boiling of flesh in milk, among other texts, to develop its kosher stance that meat should never be mixed with dairy [see the Babylonian Talmud, *Hullin* 113a–15b].) Now this application would have a great deal of relevance for contemporary listeners, since most of us love our cheeseburgers. But it wouldn't have much authority since it is difficult to conceive of the ancient text as having anything to do with such modern culinary delicacies.

So if all Scripture is profitable—and it is—how do we go from ancient text to modern audience, or from "then" to "now"? We already know that the leap has to be via pericopal theology: text to pericopal theology to application. The first step, then, is to discern the theology of the text/pericope, what the author is *doing* with what he is saying (see chap. 2). While we are not certain about the thrust of those verses dealing with goats—their context and background are shrouded in the mystery of an age long gone—let's assume, for the sake of discussion, that boiling a young goat in its mother's milk was an ancient Canaanite ritual of some sort. Then the Theological Focus of the text, assuming the accuracy of our interpretation, might be something like, "The holiness of God demands avoidance by his people of the pagan rituals of those around them."

With this Theological Focus as a launching pad, I can now help people at Northwest Bible Church, my modern audience, apply an otherwise obscure and ancient text. Application might be a call not to adopt one's neighbors' New Age practices, dabble in astrology, play with Ouija boards, or some such. The specificity depends, of course, on one's audience and its location on the planet, both in space and time. In other contexts, idolatry, animism,

---

8. See Kuruvilla, *Privilege the Text!*, 157–58, 163–90.

shamanism, voodoo, superstitions, and similar unbiblical engagements might be warned against.

Thus, as shown in figure 3.2, there is a twofold aspect to interpreting Scripture for application: discerning the theology of the pericope (the theological move: text to theology) and deriving application (the applicational move: theology to application). It is in this second step of preaching, theology to application, that the theology of the text is localized into the context and circumstances of the audience. This is how the biblical text maintains its relevance for readers in every generation, sustaining its value across time and space. By so applying the theology of the pericope to the specific situations of believers, the values of the cosmos are gradually undermined, while the values of God's ideal world are increasingly established in the life of the community. This is part of what it means to acknowledge, "Thy kingdom come!"

Figure 3.2

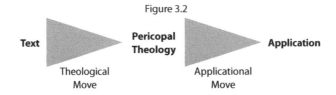

Let me remind you of our earlier discussion of 1 Samuel 15, with the word-plays on "voice." The particulars of that text, dealing with prophet, king, voices, enemies, and animals, bore the theology of that pericope with power and pathos. Now, in application, not only textual elements but also the specific audience and their specific circumstances need to be considered. The "voice" of the 1 Samuel 15 narrative would be muffled if we were simply to view the entire episode as something that happened in the eleventh century BCE between the prophet Samuel and the king Saul and as completely irrelevant for us today. Instead, because 1 Samuel 15 is an integral part of the canon of Scripture, which the church acknowledges as binding for all time and for all God's people, contemporary hearers need to experience the text as providing guidelines for life here and now.[9] So if the primary task of the preacher is to convey the theology of the text to listeners, then the secondary task is to provide them with specific ways of adopting that theology into their lives. And thereby spiritual formation takes place, as the text + theology is applied to listeners' lives.[10]

9. See Kuruvilla, "Preaching Is Biblical," in *Vision for Preaching*, 13–30.
10. Or perhaps as listeners' lives are applied to the text + theology.

Types of Application

In classical rhetoric, speeches fell into one of three categories: an assessment of past events (to induce in listeners a change of cognition; e.g., the speech of a prosecutor: *Think this way!*), an advocacy with regard to future actions (to influence a change of volition; e.g., the speech of a legislator: *Act this way!*), or an appreciation of particular beliefs or values in the present (to inculcate a change of emotion; e.g., the speech of a eulogizer: *Feel this way!*).[11] Sermonic application, in parallel to this threefold shape of rhetorical purpose, may also have one or more of these broad aims: to induce a change of mind (a response of cognition), to influence a change of action (a response of volition), or to inculcate a change of feeling (a response of emotion). And for each of these three facets, application may be an exhortation to start, to continue, or to stop thinking, feeling, or acting in a particular way. Thus application may call the audience to

start, continue, or stop *thinking* in a particular way (response of cognition);

start, continue, or stop *acting* in a particular way (response of volition); or

start, continue, or stop *feeling* in a particular way (response of emotion).[12]

While one may therefore have nine discrete options for application, I would advise treating individuals holistically: application should involve all aspects of our humanity—cognition, volition, and emotion—directly or indirectly. In practice, what generally happens is that the rest of the sermon gets the thinking and feeling parts in place (as the theology of the text is curated) and the application proper endorses the acting part.[13]

Application requires attentiveness to the current context, with the preacher being responsible for, and accountable to, the particular community of God's people to whom sermons are preached. Preaching, therefore, needs to be not only faithful to the text but also, in application, faithful to the audience. This particular facet of the preacher's task calls for an intimate knowledge of the flock, its spiritual state and its growth, so that the theology of the text may be relevantly tailored to the lives of listeners in application.[14] Thereby, the people of God are conformed into Christlikeness.

11. Quintilian, *Orator's Education* 3.7–9; Aristotle, *Art of Rhetoric* 1.3.1; etc.
12. T. Warren, "Purpose, Proposition, and Structures," 95.
13. For shaping sermons to include an application move, see chap. 4, "Creating Maps."
14. More on relevance and audience adaptation in chap. 5, "Fleshing Moves."

Characteristics of Application

There are three main characteristics of application: it should be specific, striking, and singular.[15]

Specific Application

As noted above, application should be directed to listeners so that they think, feel, or act *in a particular way*. That is to say, application must be *specific*, spelling out exactly what the audience is expected to do. Specificity in application—thinking/feeling/acting in a *particular* way—as opposed to a nebulous abstraction, is essential.

In the 1 Samuel 15 pericope we examined earlier, the author was *doing* something, recommending to readers that "the one committed to God listens to the voice of God, not the voice of worldly seductions" (the Theological Focus, a reduction of the pericopal theology into a single sentence). Now what would you do for an application of that text? A possibility is *Listen to the voice of God and not to the voices of the world!* But that is an abstract imperative and will not do at all: What is the voice of God? What are the voices of the world? How does one listen to the former and not to the latter? If application gets no more specific than an abstract imperative, then listening to God's voice (or not listening to the voices of the world) is never going to be actualized in life. Abstractions are impossible to apply, for people need specifics and details to get started doing something. Providing vague generalities as application is like a marriage counselor advising a couple with marital problems, *Love one another!* Of course, it is the responsibility of counselors to encourage that, but they must also show how such mutual love may specifically be practiced in this particular case of marital discord. Likewise, the preacher must not stop at abstractions but offer specific ways to change the lives of a particular congregation of God's people.

If life change is being sought through a sermon, then specificity in sermon application is vital. As popular business writers Chip Heath and Dan Heath observe, "Any successful change [in life/behavior] requires a translation of ambiguous goals into concrete behaviors. In short, to make a switch, you need to *script the critical moves*."[16] This "scripting of the critical moves" is the preacher's task—the detailing of specific application. The goal is to get listeners started on the lifelong journey of aligning their lives with the theology of

15. Another characteristic might well be "simple." However, I will assume that every part of your sermon is geared toward simplicity, including application, because simplicity always wins.
16. Heath and Heath, *Switch*, 53–54 (emphasis in original).

the pericope preached. The responsibility of the preacher is, therefore, to get listeners moving, to take the first step toward that goal: a step that hopefully will become a habit, which will become a disposition, which will become part of their character, instilling Christlikeness in them. Application is spiritual formation commenced and continued, one day to be consummated.

So coming back to 1 Samuel 15, the preacher must ask, What exactly can we (i.e., preacher and listeners) start doing to listen more keenly to God's voice and to shut out the voices of the world? How are we going to realize pericopal theology into specific practice come Monday morning? Listeners need help putting pericopal theology into shoe leather, and it is up to the preacher to render that aid. This is why the preacher has been ordained. That individual is the one who walks with God and knows him, the one who pores over God's word and studies it, the one who loves God's people and prays for them. It is up to the preacher, wise in the ways of God, shrewd in the ways of the world, discerning as to the call of Scripture, and tender in the care of sheep, to help listeners with application, to be their spiritual guide through life and maturity as their parent figure, their elder, and their pastor. As such, the preacher has the responsibility to guide the flock into *specific* application based on the theological thrust/force of the pericope being preached. Karl Barth called this a "translation" of theology into "the language of the newspaper": into the vernacular and idiom of listeners, into the routines of their lives and being, into the specifics of their praxis and behavior.[17] If such translation into specific application does not occur in a sermon, then the goal of gradual conformation to Christlikeness will not begin either.

Know the Audience

Here is a text-less (and uninspired) "Theological" Focus: "Sun exposure is a cause of skin cancer." If you were preaching this, how would you apply it to your audience?

If you have been following along thus far, at this point I expect you to raise a hand and ask me, "But who is my audience?" Great question! Unless you know who your audience is, you are not going to be able to provide specific application. This is one reason why preaching cannot be separated from pastoring. The pastor not only loves God and his word but also loves God's people and knows their spiritual state, their needs, their hungers, their yearnings. Such a person, with a burden for the people of God and a sensitivity to their unique situations, is well qualified to design application fit for listeners,

---

17. Barth, *Dogmatics in Outline*, 32–33.

suited for where they are in their walk with God—specific application.[18] In other words, application is part of making the sermon relevant to listeners by adapting the text + theology to those in the audience in specific ways appropriate for them.

So how might you apply that cutaneous "theology" to a group of high school or college students, knowing their predilection for the outdoors?[19] How about if you were speaking to a group of dermatologists at their annual convention?[20] Or to a melanoma survivors support group (you'd be preaching to the choir here)?[21] If you were the main speaker at a gathering of pharmaceutical company CEOs, where would you go with this "theological" focus?[22] All this to say, know your audience.

Apply the Text Personally

Now consider this passage.

Proverbs 13:20
> The one walking with the wise will become wise,
>> but the one dealing with the foolish will suffer detriment.

Theological Focus: "Those keeping company with the wise become wise, but those keeping company with the foolish suffer."

The general and rather abstract application that comes directly from the text is *Keep company with the wise/godly!* (Since "wisdom" in Proverbs indicates godly wisdom, the "wise" in Proverbs also points to those who are godly.)

Here is a starting tip to find specific application: apply the text personally. Ask yourself what *you* can do, as a first step, to keep company with the wise/godly. Once you find something specific for yourself, be sure to start applying it in your own life, even as you prepare to preach this verse. This ought to be the case with any text you preach. The application you yourself decide to practice will, more often than not, also be perfectly suitable for your listeners. This asking of a first-person application question (What can *I* do?) will not only get us preachers within reach of a specific and doable application for all listeners but will also keep us from being hypocrites who

18. See Kuruvilla, "Preaching Is Pastoral," in *Vision for Preaching*, 31–49; Kuruvilla, "Preaching Is Applicational," in *Vision for Preaching*, 111–29. More on audience adaptation in chap. 5.
19. *Wear sunscreen!* or perhaps *Avoid the sun between 10:00 a.m. and 3:00 p.m.!*
20. *Make sure you counsel your patients regarding sun protection!*
21. *Tell your relatives (and anyone who will listen) to be careful in the sun!*
22. Perhaps *Invest in more research on sunscreens!*

think application is for everyone else. If the text is to be fully and faithfully experienced by preachers first, there certainly ought to be an intake of the theology of the passage into our own lives and a commensurate life-changing output of application. We preachers should never forget that we too are fellow pilgrims with our flocks, all following the same Lord Jesus Christ in discipleship. There is no text that we leaders can have so exhaustively applied that we can now expunge it from our copies of Scripture. That is, there is no text for which application cannot be made to ourselves at any stage of our spiritual growth.[23] So use your sermon as a tool for spiritually forming yourself as well. And when the text stimulates your own spiritual growth, you will be passionate about preaching it to others because you will have seen firsthand the power of its Author working through his word. To repeat, application that works for you will usually also work well for the ones you preach to, so this is a good strategy to derive performable, specific application. In the case of Proverbs 13:20, I might decide to find a wise friend or two to have lunch with every Sunday after church (or once a week). This might work for most of my listeners as well.

Here is another example.

Proverbs 15:8
> The sacrifice of the wicked is abominable to Yahweh,
> but the prayer of the upright his delight.

Theological Focus: "God is disgusted with the worship of the wicked but delighted with the worship of the upright."

The general and abstract application that arises out of the text and its theology is *Delight God with your worship by living uprightly!* In effect, this is a call to delight God by uprightness: it makes a person's worship delightful to God. Perhaps this might first be turned into a personal application that has you setting aside specific time for confession each Sunday morning before leaving home to worship corporately (recognizing that no one is ever perfectly upright). Or you could go in another direction: acknowledging that we have been made (positionally) righteous in Christ, let us delight God in frequent prayer. So *Every time you pray—every time—before you begin,*

---

23. Of course, that is not to say that one should have completely integrated the theology of a given pericope into one's own life in application before preaching it. If that were the case, there would be no one qualified to preach! But determining to apply the call of the text to ourselves ought to be a part of our preaching routine. In fact, I have, on occasion, announced to my listeners that I have *not* applied what the passage calls for and that I am resolving to do so henceforth by doing [fill in the blank]. And then I call on the congregation to join me in undertaking that same application.

remember, for a few brief seconds, that God is being delighted! Maybe you could even voice it out loud: "Lord, I come before you, righteous in Christ, to delight you." Indeed, this could also be the application you suggest to your listeners. Generally, what works for us preachers works quite well for our audiences too.[24]

Ask the Three Hows

We have seen that we must derive specific applications to change lives. The idea is to get God's people started on the lifelong journey of aligning their lives with the theology of the pericope. Our responsibility as preachers and shepherds of our flocks is not just to discern the pericopal theology but also to help our listeners apply it, to take the initial move toward that theology, to embark on the first specific step that will hopefully become a habit, which, as was noted, will become a disposition, which will become character, which will become Christlikeness.

Let's go back to 1 Samuel 15 and its general/abstract application: *Listen to the voice of God and not to the voices of the world!* But generalities, we know, will not suffice. Application must be specific. Here's another tip on getting to the specific from the abstract: ask the "three hows." When you think you have derived a potential application, ask at least three times *how* that application can/should be performed. For instance, *Listen to the voice of God and not to the voices of the world!* is too abstract, so ask of that application, "How [do we do that]?" (the first of the three hows). Your answer might be, *Listen to the Bible!* That's a fine way to listen to God's voice, but the application is still nebulous. So you ask again, "How [do we do that]?" (the second of the three hows). Answer: *Memorize Scripture!* That's good practice for listening to the Bible but, again, not very specific. So you raise yet another "How [do we do that]?" (the third iteration of the three hows). Answer: *Here is a Scripture memory program all of us can engage in. Let's do it together—five verses a week!* Ah, now we're getting somewhere. This application is specific enough to do and meaningful enough to try. All of this serves to force us from abstraction to an application that is specific. You could, of course, go in many different directions with the three hows.[25] You might put reins on your media consumption—internet surfing or perhaps engaging with social media (but specify it by asking, "How? How? How?"); find an accountability partner to

24. There are other reasons to pray, of course, but Prov. 15:8 suggests that delighting God is a wonderful motivation.

25. And for sure, you could do as many iterations of the hows as you wish; the goal is to arrive at something specific. Keep on asking "How?" till you get there.

help you be vigilant about your web browsing (again, "How? How? How?");
repent for not having listened to God's voice ("How? How? How?"); and
other pastoral and creative exhortations. Feel free to brainstorm and generate many potential applications. Then weed out the inferior ones and save
the best of the lot. Linus Pauling, a scientist and humanitarian who won two
Nobel Prizes, is said to have remarked, "The best way to get a good idea is
to get a lot of ideas."[26] He was right.

Let's look at another example using the three hows. In a sermon on Genesis
32:1–32,[27] I wanted my audience to *Trust the God who fights for you!*[28] But
that was too vague. So I asked the first of the three hows. Answer: *Know the
truth that God fights for you!* But that was still operating in the realm of the
abstract. So the second round of the three hows was undertaken. This time
I decided I wanted my listeners to *Remember that God fights for you!* It was
still not specific enough, so I went for the third take: *Make the sign of the
cross every mealtime, saying aloud [or thinking] as you trace its four points,
"God fights for me"!* Finally, this was a specific application.

Determine Significance

Here's something you, no doubt, have already picked up implicitly, but
permit me to put it into words. Returning to 1 Samuel 15, if the congregation I
am preaching to is prone to disregarding God's voice because of a general ad-
diction to internet pornography (a seducing "voice" of the world)—perhaps
I am addressing a group of young people hooked on such activities—I could,
with my pastoral authority, suggest as an application that they install an
internet-filtering software program or that they permit a trusted friend to
inspect their web browser's history folder at any time. Of course, *Install an
internet filter!* or *Permit an accountability partner to inspect your browser's
history folder!* is not a mandate that arises directly from the theological thrust
of 1 Samuel 15; the author of that ancient text would have had no idea what
I was talking about. The only application that can be drawn directly from
the theology of that pericope is the rather abstract *Listen to the voice of
God and not to the voices of the world!* However, installing internet filters
and becoming accountable to another person are certainly prudent activities
that, if heeded, will likely help my listeners accomplish the direct application *Listen to the voice of God . . . !* Installation of filtering software and

26. Cited in Kelley and Littman, *Art of Innovation*, 55.
27. See chap. 7 for a discussion of this pericope.
28. In the sermon map on this text (see chap. 7), I phrased it as *Cling to God alone because
God fights for me!*

establishment of accountability to others can, therefore, be seen as applications that help move God's people toward fully inhabiting God's ideal world, in which, according to the direct call of 1 Samuel 15, God's people listen only to God's voice and not to worldly and deceiving voices. Though not directly commanded by the text, such preemptive strikes, filter installation, and establishment of accountability, enable alignment with the obedience-to-God's-voice-only kind of world projected by 1 Samuel 15. Such applications that do not emerge directly from the text and its theology but nevertheless help one move toward the call of the text are called "significances"—as in significant to us, impacting us/listeners directly.[29] They enable one to arrive at the state (in this case, the state of obedience to God's voice alone) demanded by the text. Therefore, significances rightly belong in the preacher's quiver of homiletical arrows, and when designing application, the preacher should always bear in mind their utility. Here again, knowing well the flock to whom the sermon is directed is critically important: preaching is never to be separated from shepherding.

Let's consider a simple example to illustrate significances.

Ephesians 5:18
Do not get drunk with wine.

Clearly, this fragment of a verse does not constitute a pericope, but it is useful for explaining significances. If you were asked what the direct application of that verse was, it would be pretty straightforward: *Don't get drunk!* Will that be good enough for your audience? It might be, but as your listeners' pastor, elder, spiritual director, or parent figure, you have to be far more specific, telling them how they can start accomplishing this *today*.

Now suppose I am living in Scotland, and every day on my way home from work I drive by a distillery and am tempted to stop and buy a bottle of Scotch. As a result, I get drunk every night. What might be a more specific application for me if I were listening to your sermon on Ephesians 5:18? You might advise me, "From now on, change your driving route when you return from work. Avoid the road that goes by the distillery." This application— *Change your driving route!*—would keep me from passing by the distillery, which would keep me from visiting it, which would keep me from buying Scotch, which would keep me from getting drunk. I would then be abiding by the call of the text and inhabiting the ideal world it projects. Of course, changing my driving route is not part of the meaning of the text; it certainly

29. See Kuruvilla, *Privilege the Text!*, 63–65.

wasn't what Paul meant. But it is a perfectly good response to the text in my particular situation and in my unique context: this one concrete step, changing my driving route, would help me move toward the application called for by Ephesians 5:18. *Change your driving route!* is therefore a significance that would enable me to take the first specific step of application. That's how life change happens, one specific step at a time. Therefore, such significances are important for making application specific.

The derivation of significances is where pastoral wisdom and love come into play. You might wonder what authority such an application has, when it is derived by a preacher for a specific audience, especially if it is a significance that does not arise directly from the text. *Don't get drunk!* would certainly have authority since it surfaces directly from the text + theology. Derivations thereof—that is, significances like *Change your driving route!*—do not seem as authoritative. But they do come from the wealth of the pastor's wisdom and love for the flock, from that leader's discernment about the ways of God and the ways of humankind. And so significances, as application, are not entirely devoid of authority, even though they may only be suggestions for listeners to practice. The words of a wise mentor, spiritual director, elder, pastor, parent figure—one ordained to preach—are always to be taken seriously and applied to the best of one's abilities. We have already considered this in Proverbs 4:1 (see chap. 2; also see Prov. 19:20; 2 Thess. 5:12–13; 1 Tim. 5:17; Heb. 13:7, 17; 1 Pet. 5:5; etc.). So yes, preachers bear the authority of their office, but it must be worn humbly and handled gently, with shepherds "not lording over those entrusted to [them] but being examples to the flock" (1 Pet. 5:3).

Striking Application

The application you suggest might be quite specific, but it can still lack vim, verve, and vitality if it is just a vanilla sort of application: *Read your Bible in the morning after your coffee!* or *Make a note in your journal!* or *Stick a Post-It note on your bathroom mirror about . . . !*[30] or *Give more to church!* or other such banal, albeit specific, applications.[31] We need to derive application that is striking. Unleash that creativity. Let those juices flow. Here's where the burden for your flock intersects with your ingenuity. This is not

30. This one in particular, for some reason, has been so common with student preachers in my classes that, after more than a decade of teaching preaching, my bathroom mirror is covered with Post-Its! (I shave blind.)

31. In a bid to force some creativity, I have banned applications in student sermons that begin with *Trust God . . . !* or *Pray . . . !* I have nothing against trust and prayer, of course, but those can easily be cop-outs, recycled as application for almost any pericope of Scripture.

easy, I confess. It took me days before I came up with *Make the sign of the cross every mealtime, saying aloud [or thinking] as you trace its four points, "God fights for me"!* But you do want to arrive at such striking applications. "Unexpected ideas are more likely to stick because surprise makes us pay attention and think. That extra attention and thinking sears unexpected events into our memories."[32] Even now, years after my sermon that called for making the sign of the cross, whenever I visit that church, people come up to me and confess that they are still crossing themselves. I tell them I am too. The habit that I began with my own sermon has become part of my disposition, so much so that even if I don't actually make the sign of the cross, I hear in my mind, "God fights for me!"

Another unusual one (at least for me) was *Every time you eat bread, remember [or say out loud], "God's word—better than bread"!* (This was for a sermon on Mark 7 that dealt with God's word; the passage also has a number of references to bread.) This application was striking enough to cause surprise and thus to cause it to stick. The element of surprise is vital, though it shouldn't devolve into gimmickry. "To be surprising, an event can't be predictable. Surprise is the opposite of predictability. But, to be satisfying, surprise must be 'post-dictable.' The twist makes sense after you think about it, but it's not something you would have seen coming."[33] While the striking application will immediately raise an eyebrow or two, those appendages will soon relax as people think, "Yes, of course, now that I think about it, that is a natural application for this text." When the application is striking, people will remember it. When they remember it, there is a better chance it will get done, and likely more than once. If it gets done more than once, it is on its way to becoming a habit. And as it becomes a habit, it is getting one step closer to forming a disposition. And dispositions can develop into character. Thus is Christlikeness instilled.

A key part of offering striking application is to build it in at least two steps. First, create a cue, hopefully one that occurs frequently: where and when one performs the application. Second, link it with the specific actionable step/ significance (response). The creative combination of cue + response makes the application striking and the doing of it sticky. Here's one I used in a sermon that dealt with divine power extended toward us (from Eph. 1:15–23): *Every time you pump gas in your car* [cue; likely to happen weekly], *remember the power of God operating in your life* [response]! The striking application puts

32. Heath and Heath, *Made to Stick*, 68.
33. Heath and Heath, *Made to Stick*, 71. The rest of my sermon on Mark 7, which preceded the bread-eating application, implicitly primed listeners for that action. Though unexpected, the application was, after the fact, "post-dictable."

cue and response (or context and action) within easy reach of the listener: it should be unexpected and unpredictable, but once heard, "post-dictable."

To make the application striking (and sticky in the memory bank), you can also frame it as a slogan of, preferably, ten words or fewer. Repeat that slogan often in the application move of the sermon. I would not fret too much about sloganizing, but if the application comes together easily for you in a catchy line, by all means employ it. I once used *Give till you laugh! Give till you cry!* for a sermon on 2 Corinthians 8–9 to indicate that giving should be both "cheerful" (*hilaros*, 2 Cor. 9:7) and sacrificial (8:2–3). For a sermon on Mark 1:21–45, starring Peter's mother-in-law, one of the few who serve Christ in that Gospel (1:31), I stated the application as *Be a mother-in-law!* (I did specify what exactly that should involve.) Sloganizing to produce striking application is another chance to exercise your creativity.[34]

An important facet of deriving striking application is to develop it fully in the application move of the sermon body (see chap. 5, "Fleshing Moves"). Here's what the move of application looks like.

Application	
Tell	Say what to do
Show	Detail how it is done by someone

Tell. Give your listeners the specific and striking application/significance, in a brief sloganized imperative that has a cue and a response.

Show. Develop the application/significance by detailing how it is done, usually by describing someone actually performing, or planning to perform, the application. Here you sketch the steps of application clearly for listeners. Perhaps you began engaging in it yourself. If you did, then take listeners through your own routines of doing the application; such details are always helpful, especially when personal. And you might want to add how performing it is benefiting you. Essentially, the "show" gives more detail and body to the application.[35] To accomplish all this "tell" and "show" of application takes a bit of time in the sermon. Give the application move an adequately

---

34. Conceivably, a decent application may be derived from the Theological Focus of a pericope. But that application, if orphaned and standing apart from the rest of the sermon, is unlikely to be compelling, no matter how striking. In reality, it is the entirety of a sermon curating the theology of the pericope that makes the application compelling. Listeners experience the text + theology (not just a reduction thereof, the Theological Focus), and they are moved and convicted by the Spirit. And when at the very point at which they are asking in their hearts, "So, preacher, what shall we do? How do we put this theology into practice?" you give them a specific and striking application, it cannot but be compelling.

35. E.g., see the application portion of the manuscript for my sermon on Eph. 1:1–14 (app. C).

sized slot in the sermon body; reserve that space exclusively for telling the application and showing it.[36]

Here's another example of a personal application of 1 Samuel 15 to my own life—an application of significance and, for me, a striking one that stuck. Years ago I used to employ an application launcher on my laptop. I would call up this launcher with a hot key, then type in a sequence of predetermined keystrokes, and the launcher would then open the appropriate app. In my quest to acknowledge God's voice more in my life, I designated the letters *H*, *I*, and *A* to open my Bible software program when typed in sequence. HIA stood for "Here I am [ready to listen to your voice, O God]!" Over the years of doing this constantly, I got into a better frame of mind to listen to God's voice as I commenced my Bible study. Obviously, 1 Samuel 15 says nothing about application launchers or hot keys, but this significance helped me take a first actionable step to attend more carefully to God's voice. The goal was to foster a habit that would become second nature—a disposition, character, and Christlikeness—whether I used the application launcher in the future or not.

Singular Application

Application should be specific and striking, and it should also be singular. What do I mean?

One important reason God has placed you as pastor-preacher for a particular congregation in the body of Christ is so you can derive application appropriate for it. It is obvious that the Bible cannot in itself bear the burden of explicitly expressing all possible future applications tailor-made for each and every individual in every time and in every place: "[Any such canonical work], to contain an accurate detail of all the subdivisions of which its great powers will admit, and of all the means by which they may be carried into execution, . . . could scarcely be embraced by the human mind."[37] It is impossible even to conceive of that task, let alone secure enough paper and ink (or digital storage space) to record what would be an unimaginably massive document. In the Christian canon, the theology of the pericope implicitly encompasses every possible legitimate option of application by anyone

36. In the actual sermon, the application move, usually the last move in the sermon body, will likely merge seamlessly with the conclusion, frequently rendering both into a single entity: application + conclusion. See chap. 7, "Crafting Introductions and Conclusions," for an account of this coalition between application and conclusion.

37. Marshall, *McCulloch v. Maryland*, 407. He was writing about the US Constitution, but the analogies between the hermeneutics of law and that of Scripture are obvious—both are canonical texts intended for application in the future. See Kuruvilla, *Vision for Preaching*, 120–22.

anywhere. In other words, pericopal theology governs the faithfulness of an application to the particular portion of Scripture exposited. But it is up to pastor-preachers, drawing from their knowledge of God and his word and their love and care for the flock, to derive specifically tailored application for that particular congregation.

By now you've no doubt figured out that there is a multiplicity of possible applications/significances for any given pericope. And when you preach the same text five years later, you might—you *should*—come up with a totally different application. Rightly so, for the flock will be different, perhaps at a different point in their spiritual pilgrimage than they were before. That is to say, there is an unlimited number of ways in which the pericopal theologies of Scripture may be applied to God's people. In a sermon on 1 Samuel 15, I might go with a Bible-reading/memorizing program for my congregation; you may opt to go with small group accountability for internet surfing; another preacher might lead the congregation in a prayer of repentance. The possibilities are endless. How do you choose? That is between you, the Holy Spirit, and your particular audience. This is where you prayerfully and humbly exercise your pastoral wisdom, love, and authority as you proffer specific and striking application/significance for your flock. That's why you are the pastor-preacher of this congregation, parish, Bible study group, or whatever the flock you have been appointed to shepherd. Acknowledge the multiplicity of applications as a God-ordained blessing. Such a plurality of potential applications is an essential property of Scripture that enables the sacred text to cross the bounds of time and go beyond the needs of any one generation of its readers. And so the Bible's utility in the future is ensured as an abiding, weighty, and binding tome that is profitable for all God's children in all times and in all places, "intended to endure for ages to come, and, consequently, to be adapted to the various *crises* of human affairs."[38]

After all that has been said about the multiplicity of applications/significances, let me offer a word of advice: application should be *singular*, as in one, solo, solitary, and unitary, for a given text-sermon-audience combination. Your sermon will ideally provide *one* application—a singularity. If you can find one that hits the ball home, the nail on the head, one application that is specific and striking *and* singular—one size to fit all—you are in good shape! You've heard it said, "One Lord, one faith, one baptism," but I say unto you, "One text, one sermon, one application." Yes, one! There is something powerful about the members of an entire congregation engaging in the same application together for a week or more. Accountability increases. Responsibility rises.

38. Marshall, *McCulloch v. Maryland*, at 415 (emphasis in original).

Motivation surges. Excitement is high. Community is formed. But when you provide a buffet from which people can choose applications as they wish, there is not only a diversity of practice that tends to disunite but also a significant paralysis of choice that will, very likely, induce them to abandon the whole meal. Stick with one application/significance—one *good* one: specific, striking, and singular.

Of course, it is not easy to derive one application that can fit every one of the tens, hundreds, or thousands you are preaching to in any given event—a variety of individuals from a variety of backgrounds with a variety of experiences and in various stages of spiritual growth. So here is a ballpark number for you to consider: find one application that fits 30 percent of your listeners—one (i.e., singular) application that is specific and striking. What about the remaining 70 percent, you ask? Seeing your passion for Scripture, experiencing the fruit of your labor, and enjoying your enthusiasm and the directness with which you provide specific and striking and singular application—albeit for only a third of your listeners—*all* your listeners are surely going to think, "Well, the preacher sure thinks this is worth doing. Now I don't care for the application that was given; it doesn't fit my situation. But I'm going to tweak it for my own circumstances." To that I would say, more power to those folks who take, tweak, and tackle the application their own way.

Once, at my home church a few years ago, the application I gave in a sermon involved using the Evernote app to create a list/notebook of items for which one was grateful to God.[39] On the monitors behind me, I actually showed my own notebook, titled "Portfolio of Gratitude," with pictures of all kinds of things—cards, people, places, and objects that reminded me of events in my life for which I was grateful to God. I encouraged my listeners to create a "Portfolio of Gratitude" for themselves. A few weeks later, an elderly couple came up to me after the service and said, "We had no idea what you were talking about that day with that 'Nevernote' stuff, so we did something different. We created a '*Basket* of Gratitude,' an actual basket into which, every Sunday, we put in index cards on which we had written reasons for our gratitude to God. We've already accumulated over a hundred cards in that basket since we began!" I suppose I had been a bit too optimistic about the hi-tech savvy of my listeners, but what this couple did is exactly what preachers should hope for. We want our listeners (those in the 70 percent bracket, that is) to take the offered application, tweak it, and tackle it for themselves, adapting it for their own situations. (For the remaining 30 percent, of course, life is a bit easier.) But for this trickle-down application to happen, the sermon

39. See chap. 6, "Illustrating Ideas," for more on Evernote.

as a whole must be convicting and compelling. When listeners are convinced that the theology of the text needs to be applied (the sermon works on their thinking), listeners are moved to the urgency of applying (the sermon works on their feeling), and they actually apply what is suggested, or they take/tweak/tackle what is offered (the sermon works on their acting). All that to say, provide *one* good application in your sermon—singular. Don't give up until you find it, even though deriving that one good application calls for patience and perseverance and prayer.

You may have already noticed that all my applications are in the imperative mood. The application is best stated as an imperative, as the examples in this work show (as was noted, I also italicize those sentences and end them with an exclamation point). There is no magic behind this, but an imperative is the clearest indication to your listeners that *this* is the application. For that reason, it is also useful to go through the rest of the sermon and remove all the faux applications, (the imperatives that you included here and there without intending them to be applicational). Frequently such imperatives creep in, commonly in the form "We must/should/ought to . . ." Removing them—or rephrasing them—keeps the singular application clear to listeners. My personal preference is the hortative or jussive, especially in the first-person plural: *Let us do . . . !* That takes the edge off an imperative that could be misconstrued as a pastoral command. It also reminds listeners (and the preacher) that all of us are part of the same body and that everyone is in need of God's grace and growth in Christlikeness. All of us can profit from this text, its theological force and its application, so that in the power of the Spirit we may all become more like our Lord and Savior Jesus Christ.

One more thing about the singularity of application. There is a strong tendency, particularly in evangelical quarters, to look at application as "singular" in this way: application that involves the individual and his or her God. For example, *I* begin doing something to keep company with the wise/godly (Prov. 13:20), *I* delight God with *my* prayer (Prov. 15:8), *I* draw the sign of the cross for *myself* (Gen. 32), *I* memorize Scripture (1 Sam. 15), *I* type in HIA on *my* laptop in the privacy of *my* study, and so on. Such application is very "singular," in the sense of being performed by each individual without any apparent corporate connection with the community of God's people. While it is certainly true that one's spiritual life, to a great extent, is an individual responsibility, let us not lapse into an isolationism that keeps application individual ("singular" in this sense), as if "Jesus and me" were all that mattered. The corporate nature of application is well attested in the Bible. Here are a few of the "Let us . . ." passages, employing the first-person plural subjunctives in Greek: Romans 13:12–13; 1 Corinthians 5:8; 2 Corinthians 7:1; Galatians

5:25–26; 6:9–10; Philippians 3:15–16; 1 Thessalonians 5:6–8; Hebrews 4:11, 14, 16; 6:1; 10:22–24; 12:1, 28; 13:15; 1 John 3:18; 4:7.[40] Such corporate application is appropriate not only because no single individual goes through the Christian life as a lone ranger but also because, in and through preaching, a community is being created, a household is being formed, a new citizenry is jointly inhabiting God's ideal *world in front of the text*, and thus cometh the divine kingdom! The people of God are being presented collectively to Christ as his bride (2 Cor. 11:2), they are being strengthened en masse until the day of Christ (1 Cor. 1:7–8), and, of course, it is not just the individual Christian who is being conformed to the image of Christ: "Christ is formed in you [plural]" (Gal. 4:19). "We all . . . are being transformed into the same image" (2 Cor. 3:18), for "the word of God," Paul declares in 1 Thessalonians 2:13, "is at work among you [plural] who believe." The body of Christ is jointly being "filled to all the fullness of God" (Eph. 3:19), "until we all attain the unity of faith and the knowledge of the Son of God—a mature person, commensurate with the stature of the fullness of Christ" (Eph. 4:13).[41] In a sermon on Ephesians 1:1–14, I asked the congregation to commit to bless God for his grand plan of consummating all things in Christ: *Blessed be God who . . . !* I suggested they go around the table at Sunday lunch, sharing this blessing in a public and corporate setting.[42] So in this sense, application should not always be "singular"; balance the applications you offer with "plural" responses too.

Needless to say, deriving application that is specific, striking, and singular is hard work. It takes all of one's pastoral sensitivity, discernment, and wisdom, not to mention a significant investment of time, energy, and resources. But the more specific and striking and singular you can get, the greater the chance that the application will actually get done and lives will be changed toward Christlikeness.

Ritual Practices, Radical Passions, Revolutionary Power

What exactly happens with these applications/significances in the course of spiritual formation, the goal of which is our conformation to the image of Christ? Significances, as I have already mentioned, are geared toward the development of habits. "Habits," James K. A. Smith notes, "are inscribed in

---

40. There are, of course, many second-person *plural* imperatives that also indicate a united approach to application.

41. See chap. 5, "Fleshing Moves," for sermon relevance that also helps create a unified community.

42. See app. C for an annotated manuscript of this sermon.

our heart through bodily practices and rituals that train the heart, as it were, to desire certain ends. This is a noncognitive sort of training, a kind of education that is shaping us often without our realization."[43] The ultimate goal of a sermon is for God's people to be aligned with the particular call of the pericope being preached. And a habit, created by application/significance, is the preliminary step toward that goal. Start small, create momentum, move forward, and reach the goal. "Small targets lead to small victories, and small victories can often trigger a positive spiral of behavior."[44] The responsibility of God's people is to take the first actionable step toward that theology, the call of the text—a step that will become a habit, which will become a disposition, which will become part of Christlike character. One of the greatest college basketball coaches of all time, UCLA's John Wooden, puts it this way: "When you improve a little each day, eventually big things occur. . . . Not tomorrow, not the next day, but eventually a big gain is made. Don't look for the quick, big improvement. Seek the small improvement one day at a time. That's the only way it happens—and when it happens, it lasts."[45]

So here's a line to remember as you create applications: ritual practices create radical passions. That is to say, habits (ritual practices) regularly done become second nature, part of who a person is—in disposition, character, and ultimately Christlikeness (radical passions). That's the intention: to start a ritual practice that gradually becomes a radical passion—Christ in me. Such a development of habit to create disposition, to produce character, and to form Christlikeness is not moral striving or behaviorism. It is not an adopted façade, an outward show, or an artifice. This is no pretense or playacting but a participation in the reality of who believers actually are in Christ, a living out in practice of who believers really are in position. "For those who by faith through the Spirit have been united to Christ, putting on Christ is not a fiction (what *if*) but a reality (what *is*). . . . Disciples do not act like Christ in order to approximate an exemplar *outside* them. Rather, disciples put on Christ *from the inside out*."[46] This is a growing up into Christ, into "a mature person, commensurate with the stature of the fullness of Christ" (Eph. 4:13).

But is this all a sort of do-it-yourself lifting up of oneself by one's own theological bootstraps?[47] Not at all! The gradual conformation to the image of Christ in this life (and ultimate conformation in the next) is a matter of

43. Smith, *Desiring the Kingdom*, 58.
44. Heath and Heath, *Switch*, 146.
45. Wooden and Jamison, *Wooden*, 143.
46. Vanhoozer, "Putting on Christ," 161 (emphasis in original).
47. Bryan Chapell labels this "*sola bootstrapsa*" (*Christ-Centered Preaching*, 289).

God's grace—notwithstanding the component of human responsibility to obey divine will. Here I echo N. T. Wright:

> Everything . . . about moral effort, about the conscious shaping of our patterns of behavior, takes place simply and solely within the framework of grace—the grace which was embodied in Jesus and his death and resurrection, the grace which is active in the Spirit-filled preaching of the gospel, the grace which continues to be active by the Spirit in the lives of believers. It is simply not the case that God does some of the work of our salvation and we have to do the rest. It is not the case that we begin by being justified by grace through faith and then have to go to work all by ourselves to complete the job by struggling, unaided, to live a holy life.[48]

No, we need gracious empowerment (through the Spirit) because anything we do with our own resources (our flesh) is not pleasing to God (Rom. 8:8). Let me explain.

In Scripture, relationship to God is always followed by responsibility. That is to say, when we come into relationship with God, he places demands on how we should live—in alignment with the values of his ideal world, in accordance with pericopal theology. This has been true throughout biblical history, even in the Old Testament period. God elected a people; *then* he required of them obedience. In fact, even the Ten Commandments (responsibility) were prefaced by an announcement of relationship: "I am Yahweh your God, who brought you out of the land of Egypt, out of the house of slavery" (Exod. 20:2). Therefore, "Thou shalt . . ." and "Thou shalt not . . ." Relationship always precedes responsibility. *Because* God's people were in relationship with a holy God (a relationship inaugurated prior to the giving of the Mosaic law), they were responsible to be as holy as their God was. Likewise, Leviticus 18:2–4 says, "I am Yahweh your God. . . . You shall do my judgments and keep my statutes, to walk in them. I am Yahweh your God. So you shall keep my statutes and my judgments. . . . I am Yahweh." In other words, obedience is the response of God's people to his already operating (prevenient) grace: relationship (divine grace) *precedes* responsibility (human duty). "First God redeems Israel from Egypt, *and then* he gives the law, so obedience to the law is a response to God's grace, not an attempt to gain righteousness by works."[49] Therefore, a loving relationship with God should result in the keeping of his commandments, as the New Testament is not hesitant to point out (John 14:21; 1 John 2:3; 3:24; 5:3). And it is the role of each pericope of Scripture to

---

48. Wright, *After You Believe*, 60.
49. Schreiner, *Paul, Apostle of God's Glory in Christ*, 117–18 (emphasis in original).

spell out what those commandments of God are so that we might keep them and be holy, as God, our Father, is holy. Pericopal theology thus provides the text's direction for holiness, and the preacher's task is to help God's people apply this theology to the concrete circumstances of their lives by deriving specific, striking, and singular applications for the congregation. And through obedience in application, God is glorified as his people manifest his holiness and represent him to the world.[50] Such obedience, of course, does not accumulate merit toward salvation: it is not justification oriented. Rather, it is sanctification oriented, intended for those *already* in relationship to God.

Besides, it is God himself who empowers us to obey him. Obedience to God can be accomplished only by God's own power. The Holy Spirit now indwells believers, enabling them to overcome the flesh and meet God's "righteous requirement": "By sending his own Son . . . he condemned sin in the flesh, so that the righteous requirement of the law may be fulfilled in us, who do not walk according to the flesh but according to the Spirit" (Rom. 8:3–4). This is an integral part of the new covenant: "I will put my Spirit within you, and I will cause you to walk in my statutes, and you will keep and obey my ordinances" (Ezek. 36:27). This power of God through the Spirit is at work in believers, enabling obedience and a life that pleases God. Colossians 1:10 encourages believers to "walk worthy of the Lord, in everything pleasing [him], bearing fruit in every good work." And, as we have seen, the Bible is clear that there are benefits that accrue from God's pleasure, even though his people's obedience is a consequence of God's own gracious operation in them.[51]

How the development of Christlikeness can be a function of both divine sovereignty and human responsibility is an inscrutable question. That tension is visible in Hebrews 13:20–21: "Now may the God of peace . . . equip you with every good thing to *do* his will [*poieō* = our doing], [he] *doing* in us [*poieō* = God's doing] what is pleasing before him, through Jesus Christ, to whom be glory forever. Amen." The two uses of the verb *poieō*, "to do," depict both parties "doing"—the people of God and God himself. We are doing *and* God is doing! This is equivalent to Ephesians 2:10 ("For we are his workmanship, created in Christ Jesus for good works which God prepared

50. See Kuruvilla, "Preaching Is Doxological," in *Vision for Preaching*, 149–66.
51. The experience of divine blessing is contingent on an obedient walk with God. See John 13:17; 15:10; Luke 11:28; etc. Thus preaching brings about divine blessing—in preachers' lives as they obey and in others' lives as preachers help them obey. On the other hand, there are also consequences for the child of God who disobeys. "For whom the Lord loves he disciplines, and he chastises every son whom he receives" (Heb. 12:6). Of course, there are also eternal rewards for obedience (see Matt. 6:1–4; Rom. 14:10–12; 1 Cor. 3:13; 4:5; 9:24; 2 Cor. 5:10; Col. 3:22–25; 2 Tim. 2:5; James 5:7–11; etc.) and loss thereof for disobedience (see 1 Cor. 3:15; 10:4–5; 1 John 2:28; etc.).

beforehand that we may walk in them"), Philippians 4:13 ("I can do all things in him who strengthens me"), and Galatians 2:20 ("And no longer do I live, but Christ lives in me"). Wright's words are wise: "We are here, as so often in theology, at the borders of language, because we are trying to talk at the same time about 'something God does' and 'something humans do' as if God were simply another character like ourselves, as though (in other words) the interplay of God's work and our work could be imagined on the model of two people collaborating on a project. There are mysteries here."[52] Indeed!

The sum of all this is that the child of God is never to attempt a self-glorifying, flesh-driven, merit-attempting, grace-rejecting, faith-negating obedience to God's demands. That is legalism. Rather, with a faith-filled dependence on the work of Christ and the power of the Spirit, the flesh is defeated, obedience to divine will is achieved, and God is glorified. And so obedience to God is a God-glorifying, Spirit-driven, merit-rejecting, grace-accepting, faith-exercising endeavor. Now we can expand our earlier statement: ritual practices (of application) become radical passions (of Christlikeness) *by the revolutionary power (of the Spirit)*.[53]

---

52. Wright, *After You Believe*, 97.

53. Please remember that all of this about ritual practices, radical passions, and revolutionary power need not—*should* not—be rehashed in every sermon. But a mention of the fact that we are unable, without the Holy Spirit's help and power, to perform any application is not a bad idea. That won't take more than a minute anyway. In fact, this could be achieved even in a prayer following the sermon, à la Augustine: "Father, what you call us to do in this text, we are utterly incapable of accomplishing with our own contrivances and devices. Grant, through your Holy Spirit, the wherewithal to accomplish what you would want us to, that we may be like your Son, for the sake of your glory" (my loose paraphrase of the church father in *Confessions* 10.29.40).

Ephesians and the Jacob Story

Let's dig into our Ephesians and Jacob Story series and examine the third pericopes of each. Don't forget to soak yourself in the pericopes, perhaps even memorizing key verses. Look up anything that is difficult to understand (determine the saying) and then get into this section to discern the theology and to create a Theological Focus for each pericope.

3. Ephesians 2:1–10

Prior to regeneration, the sphere of the Ephesians' lives was controlled by evil influences (Eph. 2:2–3), so much so unbelievers are referred to as "sons of disobedience."[54] These are people characterized by disobedient lives. They are rebels against God, and their fate is divine punishment: the "sons of disobedience" become "children of wrath" (2:3). A total pervasiveness of sin in every aspect of pre-Christian life is characteristic of such people "by nature" (2:3), for humanity is *born* dead to God.

> Utter lostness.

Verses 5–6 contain the three main verbs of the single sentence of 2:1–7, describing three divine operations, each prefixed with *syn-* (the preposition "with," translated as the prefix "co-"): *synezōopoiēsen, synēgeiren,* and *synekathisen* ("co-enlivened," "co-raised," and "co-seated"). All three indicate identification "with" Jesus Christ, with whom believers were made alive, raised, and seated. The point is reinforced by "with Christ" and "in Christ" in 2:5–6. The similarities between the raising up and seating of Christ and that of believers are striking (1:20; 2:6). This is a shared destiny: what is true of Christ is also true of believers.

> Utter lostness contrasted with the privileges of union with Christ.

A number of contrasts are visible within 2:1–10 that develop the pericope's thrust: "dead" in sin (2:1, 5) versus "co-enlivened" (2:5); following the "course of this world" and the dictates of evil entities (2:2) versus being related intimately to Christ and exalted with him in the heavenlies (2:5–6); and God's wrath (2:3) versus God's mercy, love, grace, and kindness (2:4, 5, 7). There has also been a change of lineage: from doomed "by nature" (2:3) to exalted "in Christ" (2:5–6).

> Utter lostness contrasted with privileges of union with Christ—past versus present.

---

54. For an expanded curation of this text, see Kuruvilla, *Ephesians,* 52–65.

The referent of "this" in 2:8 (and implied in 2:9) is best seen as the entire process of God's saving work. God's glorious salvation is, all of it, a gift from God. Paul pointedly makes it clear by a deviation from normal word order: 2:8c literally has "of God the gift," thus juxtaposing "of yourselves" with "of God"—making 2:8bc read, "and this not of yourselves, *of God* the gift."

> Utter lostness contrasted with the privileges of union with Christ—past versus present. Made possible by the gift of God's grace.

This salvation wrought by God was a public demonstration, even proof (*endeiknymi*, "to show/prove," 2:7), of divine grace and kindness—an eternal display on a cosmic scale. Thus God's concern is not restricted to individuals or even to the community of his people; it involves the whole of creation. This is part of the consummation of all things in Christ (1:9–10), for the glory of God (1:6, 12, 14).

> Utter lostness contrasted with the privileges of union with Christ—past versus present. Made possible by the gift of God's grace, a demonstration on a cosmic scale.

"Workmanship" (*poiēma*, 2:10) is used elsewhere by Paul in Romans 1:20 for the creation of the universe. Here, then, is a *second* creation of sorts in Ephesians 2:10. In fact, the verb used here, *ktizō* ("create"), is employed in Ephesians only for the first creation of the universe (3:9) and for this second creation of a new people (here and in 2:15; 4:24)—both works of God.

> Utter lostness contrasted with the privileges of union with Christ—past versus present. Made possible by the gift of God's grace, new creation, a demonstration on a cosmic scale.

This pericope, 2:1–10, is bounded on either side by *peripatein*, "to walk/live" (in 2:2 and 2:10). Thus there is also the contrast in lifestyles between those who once "walked" in the evil way (2:1–2) and those who are now to "walk" in God's way (2:10). Notice the parallels (following the word order in the Greek text): 2:1–2 has "in transgressions and sins . . . in which you formerly walked," and 2:10 has "for good works . . . in them we may walk." Thus though salvation is not "*of* works" (2:9), the outcome is "*for* . . . works" (2:10), already prepared by God for his people to undertake. This is the future role of believers as they participate in God's magnificent scheme for the cosmos in Christ. This is why God acted in grace to save them.

> Utter lostness contrasted with the privileges of union with Christ—past versus present. Made possible by the gift of God's grace, new creation, a demonstration on a cosmic scale: believers doing good works prepared by God.

Here is the Theological Focus.

> **Believers, once in dire straits but now sharing Christ's exaltation, demonstrate to the universe God's mercy, love, grace, and kindness as they undertake good works.**

Application. Clearly, what arises directly from the text is a call to good works, a demonstration of God's mercy, love, grace, and kindness. Now the preacher needs to consider the best application/significance for the particular audience. What is the optimal way to get people started on a habit of good works? *Do good works!* is all well and good. But how? How? How? This might be an appropriate occasion for a more corporately directed application. Perhaps a new program could be introduced into the church that engages the congregation in doing something for others once a week: visiting shut-ins, contributing to the benevolence fund, sending handwritten cards of appreciation (perhaps a stamped postcard could also be distributed after the sermon to further stimulate action), taking on nursery duties, participating in ministry to the disabled, giving rides, helping during the holiday season, and so on.

3. Genesis 26:34–28:9

No more than two members of Isaac's dysfunctional and disharmonious family appear together in this pericope.[55] The various scenes are structured chiastically, with the two central scenes—with Isaac and Jacob/Esau (Gen. 27:18–29, 30–41)—detailing the deception in the narrative.

```
A   Esau (26:34–35)
  B   Isaac and Esau (27:1–4)
    C   Rebekah (and Isaac?) (27:5)
      D   Rebekah and Jacob (27:6–17)
        E   Isaac and Jacob (27:18–29)
        E'  Isaac and Esau (27:30–41)
      D'  Rebekah and Jacob (27:42–45)
    C'  Rebekah and Isaac (27:46)
  B'  Isaac and Jacob (28:1–5)
A'  Esau (28:6–9)
```

> Dysfunctional family.

Isaac is culpable. His summoning of only one of his two sons, Esau, for the patriarchal blessing is a major faux pas, especially since they are twins. And Isaac, no

---

55. For an expanded curation of this text, see Kuruvilla, *Genesis*, 316–29.

doubt, was aware of the oracle received by Rebekah (25:23) as well as of the sale of the birthright (25:29–34). He ought not to have sought to bless Esau—certainly not in the absence of his other son. Moreover, the one Isaac chooses to bless has had little concern for endogamy or monogamy and has thereby caused his parents grief (see below). Isaac's senses are altogether faulty: sight (27:1); touch (27:16, 21, 23); smell (27:15, 27); taste (27:3, 4, 7, 19, 25, 31, 33; also 27:9, 14, 25); and, of course, hearing (27:22).

Rebekah's culpability is no less significant: her initiative in this episode is unique, signi-fied by the only use of the feminine participle of *tsavah* ("command") in the entire Old Testament (27:8), in reference to her "commanding" her son. Rebekah is doubtless the dynamo behind the deception of Isaac; she does everything (27:14–17), while Jacob gets a mere three verbs in that paragraph (27:14).

Esau is culpable in his marital decisions (26:34; 27:46), as was noted. He has appar-ently contracted the marriages on his own initiative, disregarding parental opinion; he opts for exogamy and prefers polygamy. Esau is likely attempting to obtain the patriarchal blessing by producing progeny and forcing Isaac's hand.

Jacob's culpability needs no expatiation. He lies twice, in 27:19, 24: he is neither Esau nor the firstborn, as he claimed to be to his father. In the process, Jacob also takes the name of Yahweh in vain (27:20). The "deceit" (*mirmah*, 27:35) perpetrated by Jacob indicates deliberate planning.

Rather than trust God to disburse his blessings sovereignly to his people, each one in this pericope is conspiring against and cheating others. Each one has his or her own ideas as to whom divine blessings should go, and how and when.

> Dysfunctional family, each member trying to obtain the blessing his or her own way, without trusting God.

And the result is chaos! Isaac's reaction, when he realizes how he has been deceived by Jacob, is emotional and torturous (27:33). And as Esau realizes what has happened, he responds similarly, in anguish (27:34). Later, he declares he will kill Jacob (27:41). Fearing for the life of her favorite son, Rebekah schemes to send Jacob away to her brother, Laban, in Paddan-Aram (27:41–28:5) for "a few *days*" (27:44). But it would be a few *decades* (twenty years, 31:38, 41) before Jacob would return to Canaan. And by then Rebekah would be dead: she would never see this son again. This is her last appearance in Genesis. Deception leads only to catastrophe, and that for the entire family/community.

> Dysfunctional family, each member trying to obtain the blessing his or her own way, without trusting God. The result is breakdown of community.

Here is a single-sentence version.

> **Deception to obtain divine blessing, rather than trusting God to secure it, only results in catastrophic fragmentation of the community.**

Application. One might consider *Don't deceive!* or something of that nature, striving for an application that is specific, striking, and singular, derived by utilizing the three hows. Frequently, students preaching this text to their fellow seminary students decry common deceptive practices like fudging résumés, falsifying reading reports, cheating on take-home tests, and so on, tailor-making application for their particular listeners. Inculcating a habit of rejecting such fraudulent maneuvers is a good start to aligning lives with the call of the text.

Here is where it is important, when preaching *lectio continua*, to have at least a tentative sense of what the application of each pericope might be before the sermon series actually commences—another plug for long-term sermon preparation. The pericope after the next (pericope 5: Gen. 29:1–30; see chap. 4) is where Jacob is disciplined by God for his past misdeeds. What would be the direction of application for that sermon? *Don't deceive!* might fit there too. So some nuanced negotiation is necessary. If one keeps the focus of the application for the current pericope (Gen. 26:34–28:9) on averting *future* misdeeds/deception (*Don't deceive in the future!*), the application for pericope 5 (Gen. 29:1–30) might be repentance for *past* misdeeds/deception (*Repent of deception in the past!*).

4

Creating Maps

To craft a sermon that logically presents the big ideas of the text to hearers is not the same thing as designing a sermon as a piece of drama intended to precipitate a powerful and life-changing experience.[1]

As far back as the fourteenth century, a "three-point sermon" was mentioned by Robert of Basevorn, writing tongue in cheek: "Only three statements, or the equivalent of three, are used in the theme [i.e., exposition] either from respect to the Trinity, or because a threefold cord is not easily broken [Eccles. 4:12], or because this method is mostly followed by Bernard [of Clairvaux, a twelfth-century abbot], or, as I think more likely, because it is more convenient for the set time of the sermon."[2] For most of rhetorical and homiletical history, points in an outline have served to structure the entire sermon as an argument, validating a Big Idea, a distillate of the text. But neither the notion of an argument nor the concept of reducing a text to a Big Idea serves preaching well. First, preaching is a new form of rhetoric, unknown to classical rhetoricians. It is a unique text-based form of address, employing an *inspired* text, and has the goal of enabling listeners to experience the text + theology under the guidance of the preacher. Second, a text can never be reduced to a Big Idea without incurring significant loss.

1. Long, *Witness of Preaching*, 122.
2. Robert of Basevorn, *Form of Preaching*, 138.

Yet traditional homiletics assumes that the distillate is what the text is all about and that preaching that distillate is what the sermon is all about. Such operations implicitly minimize the role of the text, relegating it to providing proofs for the audience that the Big Idea, as the preacher sees it, is the sum and substance of the text. The sermon thus becomes an argument outlined point by point to substantiate a Big Idea.[3]

Instead, I propose the analogy of a curator guiding visitors in an art museum through a series of paintings. Each text is a picture, the preacher is the curator, and the sermon is a curation of the text-picture, enabling the experience of the text + theology by congregants, the gallery visitors. The sermon is thus more a *demonstration* of the thrust of the text than an argument validating a Big Idea. In this sermonic demonstration, a creative exegesis of the text is undertaken in the pulpit with a view to portraying for listeners what the author is *doing* (pericopal theology).[4] The preacher, who is not the chief explainer of the text *to* listeners but a co-explorer of the text *for* listeners, thus facilitates the audience's experience of the text + theology in the sermon.[5]

Mapping Sermons

Sermon shaping is essential in order to succeed in this all-important communicative act of the church, the demonstration (and application) of pericopal theology so that listeners experience the text in its fullness. All sermons—indeed all formal kinds of communication—have the fundamental shape of an introduction, a body, and a conclusion. Right at the outset, let me give you a rule of thumb for sermons: in terms of time, the introduction takes about 15 percent of the time allotted for the sermon, the body about 75 percent, and the conclusion about 10 percent. If you work with word count or page numbers in a manuscript, the same proportions hold. In other words, these ratios work both for time (in the pulpit) and for space (in the manuscript).

Sermon	
Introduction	15%
Body	75%
Conclusion	10%

3. See app. A, "Big Idea versus Theological Focus," and app. B, "Preaching: Demonstration versus Argument," as well as Kuruvilla, "Time to Kill the Big Idea?"

4. This curational discerning of theology for listeners is followed by a pastoral deriving of application for them (see chaps. 2 and 3).

5. In a related effort, see my attempts to curate text-pictures for preachers themselves in my commentaries: *Genesis*; *Judges*; *Mark*; and *Ephesians*.

This chapter deals with how to shape the *body* of the sermon into moves (introductions and conclusions will be considered in chap. 7).

Maps and Moves

It is a fact of life that our nomenclature for things affects how we see them. With the shift in paradigm from preaching as argument to preaching as demonstration, we need to reexamine the terminology we employ in sermon creation. In the traditional approach to homiletics, the sermon is an argumentation of the Big Idea (of the text's saying) and comprises points (with propositions) that are organized into an outline—a blueprint that serves the sermon's goal of establishing the Big Idea of the text for listeners. In contrast, with the fresh approach to homiletics, the sermon is a demonstration of the experience (of the text's *doing*) and comprises moves (with labels) that are shaped into a map—a cheat sheet for the preacher to accomplish the sermon's goal of engaging listeners with the text.[6] We'll adopt this latter set of descriptors for our homiletical undertakings. (See the table below for a comparison of the two approaches.)

	Traditional Approach	Fresh Approach
A sermon is an/a	Argumentation	Demonstration
of the	Big Idea (of the text's saying)	Experience (of the text's *doing*)
and comprises	Points (with propositions)	Moves (with labels)
that are	Organized	Shaped
into an/a	Outline	Map

Elsewhere I offered my vision for preaching: "Biblical preaching, by a leader of the church, in a gathering of Christians for worship, is the communication of the thrust of a pericope of Scripture discerned by theological exegesis, and of its application to that specific body of believers, that they may be

6. See Lowry, *Doing Time in the Pulpit*, 17; Long, "Distance We Have Traveled," 15; and Buttrick, *Homiletic*, 23. An *outline* also has some self-imposed constraints: its points are constructed as full sentences (usually propositions with subjects and complements), with main points subsuming subsidiary points, and so on, all of which pedantries are unnecessary for a *map* that aids the sermonic curation of the text + theology (see below). While not denying that a sermonic demonstration deals with ideas, and even arguments, I deprecate only the dominant metaphor of the traditional approach and its complicit nomenclature. In my opinion, these have stultified the way we think about preaching, especially in light of our fast-advancing understanding of how language works and how the brain works to comprehend texts and speech. See Kuruvilla, "'What Is the Author *Doing* with What He Is *Saying*?'"

conformed to the image of Christ, for the glory of God—all in the power of the Holy Spirit."[7] Notice there are two tasks for the preacher: "the communication of the thrust of a pericope [pericopal theology]" and "[the communication] of its application to [a] specific body of believers." That is, the preacher discerns the theology of the text for listeners and then derives application for them. Taken together, this facilitates the experience of the text + theology by the audience.

These two tasks of the preacher, of course, correspond to the two moves in our preaching paradigm: text to theology and theology to application (see fig. 4.1). Of the two, I believe the first move—text to theology—to be primary and the most important. The reason the preacher stands between the word of God and the people of God is primarily to help listeners discern the theological thrust of the text. Because modern audiences may not be able to do this on their own, this is our main task as preachers—facilitating the discernment of theology by listeners.

Figure 4.1

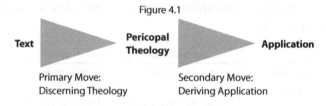

Text   Pericopal   Application
                         Theology

Primary Move: Secondary Move:
Discerning Theology   Deriving Application

Of course, there remains the secondary task the preacher has as pastor, spiritual director, elder, parent figure, and mentor of the congregation: to derive specific application for that particular body of believers. The preacher directs the flock on how the discerned pericopal theology may be made reality, how the people of God may inhabit the ideal world of God, the *world in front of the text*. Because the preacher is the person who walks with God, who knows God, and has devoured God's word, and because this is the one who lives with God's people, loves them, and is burdened for them, this is the one most qualified to lead God's people in life transformation according to the theology of the scriptural pericope preached. Deriving application for listeners is thus the secondary task of the preacher.

With these primary and secondary tasks of the preacher in view, the basics of sermon mapping (of the body, that is) now become clear. The primary move of the body (corresponding to the primary task of the preacher) helps listeners discern the theology of the pericope, and the secondary move (corresponding to the secondary task of the preacher) derives application for them. In the

7. Kuruvilla, *Vision for Preaching*, 1.

sermon, the primary move, text to theology (discerning theology), generally takes about twice as long to develop as the secondary move, theology to application (deriving application). So working with the same proportions of sermon parts that we saw earlier, we now have, in the body of the sermon, a 50:25 ratio of primary moves to secondary moves (both in manuscript space and in sermonic time).

Sermon	
Introduction	15%
Body	75%
Conclusion	10%

Body	
Primary move (discerning theology)	50%
Secondary move (deriving application)	25%

This gives us a somewhat unbalanced body, with one move (discerning theology) taking a lot more space and time than the second (deriving application). And it is also evident that the first and top-heavy theology move is where all the text of Scripture will show up. That in itself is not detrimental to the sermon. But there is a danger, particularly for those who are just embarking on this adventurous ministry of preaching. As you look at the breakdown of the body shown above, where do you think the audience will show up in the sermon? Where will I, the listener, directly be talked about—my life, my spiritual walk, my circumstances, my world, my culture, my cares, my concerns, my victories, my failures? It seems obvious that the audience will be considered only in the secondary move (deriving application) of the sermon. This means that for most of the sermonic body, listeners may not be directly involved. That's a no-no. We will lose our hearers if we leave them out for two-thirds of the body (and for half the sermon). In order not to neglect the audience for most of the sermon body, the preacher should split the primary move into at least two separate moves so as to be able to introduce a submove of relevance at the end of each of those moves that involves the audience more directly.

Body	
Primary move (discerning theology) 1 (including a submove: relevance)	25%
Primary move (discerning theology) 2 (including a submove: relevance)	25%
Secondary move (deriving application)	25%

Such a breakdown of the primary move into two discrete moves gives the sermon body a better balance: a 25:25:25 ratio of the three moves. The preacher should feel free to divide the primary move into even smaller chunks as necessary, with the secondary move of application being correspondingly fungible in space and time. For instance, in the scheme below, the primary move has four parts, and the application has undergone an appropriate condensation so that the body contains five balanced moves.

Body	
Primary move (discerning theology) 1 (including a submove: relevance)	15%
Primary move (discerning theology) 2 (including a submove: relevance)	15%
Primary move (discerning theology) 3 (including a submove: relevance)	15%
Primary move (discerning theology) 4 (including a submove: relevance)	15%
Secondary move (deriving application)	15%

This segmenting of the primary move simply reminds the preacher not to go too far and too long without a direct involvement of the audience by means of the submoves of relevance. For the rest of this work, I'll use a 25:25:25 ratio of moves in the sermon body: primary move 1, primary move 2, and secondary move (application), with each of the primary moves including a submove of relevance.[8] Such a three-part division of the sermon body is more than adequate given the standard window of thirty-five to forty minutes for the sermon in most evangelical circles. In any case, don't forget that *you* are the captain of your ship. You should shape your sermon as you see fit, for your particular text and your particular audience and as your unique personality, capacity, and pastoral wisdom call for.

You will have noticed that in the maps shown above, the secondary move of application always follows the primary move(s) of theology. This reflects the fact that valid application can be derived for listeners only after the theology of the pericope has been discerned by them (facilitated by the preacher). Therefore, the most obvious place for the application move in the sermon is *after* the theology of the text has been curated. Usually this means at the end of the sermon body.[9]

8. More on relevance in chap. 5, "Fleshing Moves." There is no magic in having three moves in the body; however, it is probably the minimum number of moves a sermon body should have to avoid the imbalance discussed earlier.

9. There are other ways of doing this, but the vast majority of my own sermon maps follow this guideline. I suggest yours should too. (For an exception, see my sermon manuscript

Inductive or Deductive Sermons?

Much has been made in homiletical literature of deductive and inductive sermons. On the one hand, "Deductive preaching moves from a general statement of sermon purpose to the more specific facts regarding that purpose. Often it declares the *main idea* for the sermon and then states propositions, points, or spiritual truths concerning that theme." On the other hand, "Inductive sermons move from specific truths, examples, or ideas (particulars) in the text to the *general truth* of the sermon, which is normally revealed at or near the end of each unit in the sermon or at the end of the sermon itself. If based on sound exegesis, the particulars lead to correct assertions or statements of truth."[10] What exactly is this "main idea" or "general truth" that is aimed at—up front in a deductive sermon and downstream in an inductive one? As we have seen, the goal of the sermon is twofold. The primary aim is to enable the audience to discern the theology of the text, and this cannot be reduced into a "main idea" or a "general truth" (i.e., Big Idea). The secondary aim is to derive application for the audience, and neither can the application become a "main idea" or a "general truth."[11] So one is left to wonder what one is deducing or inducing in those traditional operations. In the way I see sermons functioning, such categorizations of sermons into inductive and deductive are unfruitful. Instead, the preacher is to curate the text for the audience so that the theology of the pericope (an irreducible entity) is discerned with all its power and pathos; the preacher then guides listeners into life change by deriving application. The preacher is not inductively helping listeners to arrive at some main point / Big Idea, but rather is curating the text + theology for listeners so that the text (and not a reduction thereof) and its theology may be experienced fully and faithfully.[12]

A big advantage of curating the text + theology for listeners is that they, thereby, enjoy the thrill of discerning theology for themselves, just as the

---

for Gen. 26 in app. D, but even there you will notice that derivation of application follows the discernment of theology, though the former is distributed in three discrete moves.)

10. Carter, Duvall, and Hays, *Preaching God's Word*, 34 (emphasis added).

11. Rather, the application is the finale of the sermon, the intended response of listeners to the text, an integral part of their experience of the text + theology.

12. The primary move(s), from text to theology, might appear to be inductive, in that the preacher curates the textual clues that enable the audience to discern the theology (see below and chap. 5, "Fleshing Moves"). But this theology that listeners are helped to discern is not something that can be expressed in a Big Idea reduction or in any words other than those of the text. Therefore, unlike standard inductive moves intended to arrive at a distilled idea of the text, the curation of the text (a seeming induction) facilitates listeners' experience of the text and its theology, an irreducible entity. As was noted, the Theological Focus is, indeed, a distillate of the pericopal theology, but it simply functions as a label (or shorthand, title, or handle) for the theology for the benefit of sermon preparers (as we will see again); it is not necesssary to derive it inductively in preaching for the benefit of sermon listeners.

preacher did while studying the text and preparing the sermon. It is an attempt on the preacher's part to let the audience persuade itself. As Thomas G. Long notes dryly about traditional homiletics, "On one side of the bridge the preacher has an exciting, freewheeling experience of discovering the text, but the preacher has been trained to leave the exegetical sleuthing in the study, to filter out the zest of that discovery, and to carry only processed propositions across to the other side. The joy of 'Eureka!' becomes, in the sermon, the dull thud of 'My thesis [Big Idea] for this morning is . . .'"[13] Instead, why not let the way the text affected us preachers affect our listeners? Ideally, in a sermon, once the clues to pericopal theology have been put forth, the thrust/force of the text (pericopal theology) will be discerned by the audience.[14] That is how all art forms are curated, whether it be a painting, a poem, a photograph, a piece of music, or even a work of verbal art such as a text. All that to say, the facilitator (preacher) helps others (listeners) discern what the art form (the text) is *doing* by curating it.

But though this task of facilitating the inspired text is important, let us not forget that we preachers are only curators and docents of (or handmaids and midwives to) the text. We are not producing anything new or momentous; we are not creating a piece of art of our own. Instead, we preachers serve God's word, primarily to help God's people discern its pericopal theology and secondarily to derive application for them. Let's keep the interpolation of ourselves between these two entities, God's word and God's people (to whom God's word was written), as unobtrusive as possible. Let's not take on more responsibility than is called for, fellow curators!

Guidelines for Presentation of Maps

If you have to show your sermon map to someone—a professor, a guide or mentor, or fellow members on the preaching team—there are certain standard

---

13. Long, *Witness of Preaching*, 118. Unfortunately, this is true in far too many pulpits on far too many Sundays.

14. Our brains are hardwired to discern the thrust of utterances once we catch the clues to what the author is *doing*. This is how communication works. Because the texts we deal with are ancient, and the originals are in languages our listeners are unfamiliar with, they need help in spying the clues. As these clues are unveiled, the theology is discerned, usually without any recourse to a Theological Focus reduction (or Big Idea). Indeed, neuroscience research has shown that when there is successful communication, the listener's brain activity mirrors the speaker's brain activity—"speaker-listener neural coupling." The same areas of the brain seem to be active in three discrete states: when the *speaker* experiences something, when the *speaker* recalls and recounts that same experience, and when the *listener* hears the speaker's recounting. In other words, preachers enable their listeners to experience the text the way they themselves experienced it first. See Stephens, Silbert, and Hasson, "Speaker-Listener Neural Coupling."

protocols you should employ that may help them comprehend your sermon map more easily. You can safely ignore these guidelines if you are creating maps for yourself.

Numbering. The main parts of the sermon—introduction, body, and conclusion—are themselves not numbered. But in the body, numbering generally follows this scheme: first-level Roman numeral, second-level alphabet upper case, third-level Arabic numeral, fourth-level alphabet lower case—all appropriately indented (see below). While this numbering system technically applies to outlines, it is helpful for the sermon maps recommended in this work too. But never go beyond four levels; more levels are only of academic interest and of no practical use whatsoever (I usually have only two levels, rarely three, in my maps).

Structuring of move labels. Phrases are fine, or even single words (as often in the examples in this work).[15] However, if the person you are showing your map to is not familiar with the text you are preaching or with what the biblical author is *doing* therein, you are better off using full sentences for the labels of moves and submoves. Such sentences should be in the indicative mood at every level, except for the application statement, which should be an imperative. Including the reference of the verse(s) being dealt with (at least for the first-level items) might also be helpful. The application, of course, will have no verse reference.[16] Here is a sample map structure.

Introduction
Body
    I.
        A.
        B.
    II.
        A.
            1.
            2.
            3.
        B.
   III.
        A.

15. Why not pictures, with or without words?

16. Standard outlines also demand that a point at any level subsume all subordinate points below it. This norm can be safely ignored in our mapping enterprises.

1.
   a.
   b.
2.
B.
1.
2.
IV. *Application!*
Conclusion

Again, these standard protocols are not necessary when you do not plan to share your maps with others. When creating maps for my own use, I almost never subscribe to these niceties and particularities.

Canned Maps

Before I explain my preferred way of creating sermon maps, let me offer a couple of what I call "canned" maps that are useful in a pinch. Each has three moves: Problem–Solution–Application and Saying–*Doing*–Application. When you find yourself in a bind—because of lack of time or resources—you can use one of these canned products. But I would strongly recommend that you do not force such maps on a text in other circumstances; that would only make your sermon shape quite artificial and contrived, as we shall see. Not every sardine in a textual stream can be neatly squeezed into a can!

Problem–Solution–Application

While Problem–Solution–Application is a canned map, there is an intuitiveness to it. My suspicion is that there may be some hardwiring in our brains to think in a Problem–Solution–Application sequence even when we are not consciously trying to do so. This map takes the shape of answers to the following questions: What is the problem the text is addressing? What is the solution to that problem? What should we do? Let's try Problem–Solution–Application on a few texts.

Proverbs 13:20
   The one walking with the wise will become wise,
     but the one dealing with the foolish will suffer detriment.

First, let's decide on a Theological Focus. "Those keeping company with the wise become wise, but those keeping company with the foolish suffer."[17]

Notice a couple of things. First, there is a pattern of Hebrew parallelism between line A (13:20a) and line B (13:20b) that renders the two antithetical: A x B. It is therefore fair to see the result noted in line A as countering that mentioned in line B. Second, the paronomasia (wordplay) in the Hebrew is significant (highlighted): *holek 'et-khakamim wekhkam* (13:20a) and *wero'eh kesilim yero'a* (13:20b). In my translation of the verse, I have attempted to retain this parallel somewhat with "wise" and "wise" in 13:20a and the alliteration of "dealing" and "detriment" in 13:20b. The wordplay suggests a deliberate patterning in this verse, as is always the case in poetry in any language. Meanings in this genre are often more dependent on how the parallelism works (here line A is antithetical to line B) than on the precise nuances of the words employed in any given line. Thus "becoming wise" is intended to be antithetical to "the suffering of the foolish."

What's the problem the text is addressing? It's not "foolishness" or "dealing with the foolish." One must isolate the actual deprivation or loss, the specified negative, as the problem. In this case, it is the suffering if one associates with the foolish (13:20b). Now *that's* a problem, because no one wants to suffer. The solution to that problem is, of course, the counterthrust of the verse: the wisdom that comes with associating with the wise precludes suffering (13:20a). Application? Fairly straightforward: *Keep company with the wise!*

I. Problem: Keeping the company of fools leads to suffering (13:20b)

II. Solution: Keeping the company of the wise precludes suffering (13:20a)

III. Application: *Keep company with the wise!*[18]

Notice I switched the order of the text here, putting 13:20b in the first move (Problem) and 13:20a in the second (Solution). There is no constraint on the preacher to follow the textual sequence. The order of the text is something its author determined as best for a particular medium (writing) and for a particular audience. The shape of the sermon is something the preacher determines as best for another medium (speaking) and for another audience. The two media are different, and they function in their unique ways for their respective audiences: readers and listeners. There is nothing magical about having a sermonic shape that parallels the structure of the text. Spoken

---

17. Never mind if the Theological Focus turns out to be longer than the actual text in these examples. That is simply because we are dealing with such short texts.

18. Yes, my applications here and in the following maps are far from specific and striking—and far from ideal.

sermons are a different form of media than scripted texts and address different audiences than the latter, so speech does not necessarily have to follow the order of thought or parallel the sequence of the writing. The kind of sermon map appropriate for the audience is something that must be decided preaching event by preaching event. Of course, there may be something to be said for ease of following along (from a listener's point of view) with a sermon whose sequence closely follows that of the biblical text. Congruence of text and sermon arrangements means fewer leaps around the text by the preacher. The fewer these leaps, the greater the clarity and, hopefully, the firmer the assimilation of the text + theology in the hearts, minds, and lives of listeners.

I also chose to employ parallel wordings for the labels in I. Problem and II. Solution (see above). That kind of uniformity is helpful for clarity and for mental retrieval—both for the preacher and for the listener. Complicated wordings confound, but simplicity always wins.

Let's try another.

Proverbs 10:25
> When the storm passes, the wicked one is no more,
>   but the righteous one [has] a foundation forever.

The problem in 10:25a is the suffering of the wicked (or guilty) when the catastrophes of life hit. The solution in 10:25b is that the righteous one, the person of God, has nothing to fear from passing misfortunes: he or she is secure forever. One could take this in a different direction if the "storm" is seen as a synecdoche for divine judgment (as in Ps. 83:15; Isa. 17:13; 29:6; 66:15; Nah. 1:3). Then the problem in 10:25a is the eternal fate of the unbeliever: away from the presence of God, equivalent, poetically speaking, to annihilation. The solution in 10:25b, on the other hand, is surviving divine judgment (and enjoying eternal bliss) by becoming righteous in God's eyes (by the work of Christ). Let's assume you are a preaching student scheduled to preach this verse to your seminary classmates. It is unlikely that any of them is an unbeliever. What, then, might be an appropriate application for them? (Hint: remember one of the examples in chap. 3 that had us consider application of "Sun exposure is a cause of skin cancer" for those in a melanoma survivors support group.) Think about that for a second and come up with your own application before looking at my suggestion in the footnote below.[19]

---

19. The Theological Focus might be "Unbelievers will be judged by God, but believers, escaping judgment, will be established eternally in relationship to God."
   I. Problem: Unbelievers will not escape God's judgment (10:25a)

Ephesians 1:15–23

Here is the Theological Focus of Ephesians 1:15–23 that we derived in chapter 2: "Hostile powers at work to oppose God's plan and God's people are overwhelmed by God's incredible power in and through Christ—power that is extended toward believers, the body of Christ, his fullness, as Christ reigns." A shorter version reads: "As the fullness and body of Christ, the church manifests God's incomparable power against supernatural foes."

Here's a Problem–Solution–Application sermon map that arises quite naturally from Ephesians 1:15–23. Notice that the Problem of "our fearfulness" (below) is not explicitly stated in the text. It is, however, an assumption of the text, as we saw in the commentary on this pericope in chapter 2, a reasonable implication that is substantiated by context and the flow of thought from 1:1–14 to 1:15–23 (interpericopal coherence). In 1:15–23, there is an extended declamation of divine power that is exercised on behalf of the church and that forms the Solution (God's/Christ's powerfulness) to the implicit Problem.

    I. Problem: Our fearfulness of our powerful supernatural foes

    II. Solution: God's powerfulness against any foe, manifest in and through the reigning Christ for believers (1:15–23)

    III. Application: *Live powerfully!*

Saying–Doing–Application

Saying–*Doing*–Application is another staple preaching map that can be employed for a variety of texts. However, it is best used when the text's saying is difficult to grasp and needs significant explanation. The preacher using this map will therefore see the need to reserve a block of time in the sermon (and space in the manuscript)—I. Saying—simply to explain the passage to listeners so that they comprehend what the author is saying (or, in the case of a narrative text, the story that is being told).[20] In the second move, II. *Doing,* the preacher discerns for listeners what the author is *doing,* the theology of the pericope. These two moves are then followed by III. Application. One might also call this a Text–Theology–Application map.[21]

Let's try some examples of this map.

    II. Solution: Believers will escape God's judgment (being established forever in relationship to God) (10:25b)

    III. Application (for believers): *Tell your unbelieving friends/neighbors . . . !*

20. The disadvantage of a move exclusively dealing with the text is that the audience is left out for this significant chunk of the sermon, which will not have a submove of relevance.

21. For narrative texts, in I. Saying, you would likely explain the lineaments of the narrative that, in these days of biblical illiteracy, may be unfamiliar to your audience.

Proverbs 21:1
> In the hand of Yahweh, the king's heart is [like] channels of water;
> wherever he wishes, he turns it.

Theological Focus: "Yahweh is absolutely sovereign, even controlling a monarch."

   I. Saying: [Explanation of the figures of speech: "hand" for power; "heart" for decision making; "channels of water" for irrigation ditches; etc.]

   II. *Doing*: Even a king is totally controlled by God (21:1)[22]

   III. Application: *Trust in God's absolute sovereignty!*[23]

1 Corinthians 10:23–33
Theological Focus: "Love for others limits the believer's liberty" (or something to that effect).

First Corinthians 10:23–33 is the portion of Paul's letter that talks about the issue of eating meat offered to idols—not something a contemporary reader would easily comprehend; it is not a question that is debated in churches today. The text is therefore somewhat opaque and will need explanation. So I. Saying is a good place to explicate the text's saying. The next move, II. *Doing*, would then discern from textual clues what Paul is *doing*, following which comes III. Application.

   I. Saying: [Explanation of the practice; how it might cause another to stumble; etc.]

   II. *Doing*: Love for others limits the believer's liberty (10:23–33)

   III. Application: *Avoid . . . for the sake of others!*[24]

1 Samuel 15
Theological Focus: "The one committed to God listens to the voice of God, not the voice of worldly seductions."

---

22. This is a modified version of the Theological Focus. Remember, again, that the Theological Focus is *not* the theology (which is inexpressible in words other than those of the text); the Theological Focus is only a label for pericopal theology.

23. It bears repeating yet again: this is an inadequate application. *Trust!* and *Pray!* as applications are best avoided, as I have mentioned before: they are so nonspecific that they can conceivably be used in a sermon on any biblical pericope.

24. Having written "sake" in the application, I acknowledge that the issue of alcohol might be one in which a believer chooses to limit his or her liberty in love.

For the 1 Samuel 15 narrative that we have touched on in previous chapters, a retelling of the story may be necessary, since it is rather obscure. That could be accomplished in the I. Saying move, with the *Doing* and Application following in subsequent moves.

I. Saying: [Brief retelling of the story]

II. *Doing*: The one committed to God listens to the voice of God, not the voice of worldly seductions (1 Sam. 15)

III. Application: *Listen to God's voice!*[25]

Several of the Jacob Story pericopes could also be made to fit this Saying–*Doing*–Application mode of mapping sermons (but see below).

Focus Splitting

We have seen a couple of canned sermon maps. I began this section by saying they are useful when you are in dire homiletical straits and stranded without much time to prepare your sermon (hopefully not because of sloth). In such situations, those two canned maps may come in handy. But please—*please!*—do not take the liberty of employing one of them for every pericope you encounter. Consider them cookie cutters. If you force a cookie cutter (map) on the batter (text), you are going to get a lot of waste—things won't fit precisely. Or you might see them as ready-made clothing. Such clothes may be good as low-budget casual wear, but if you want a perfect fit, then you need to go bespoke. Resist the temptation to take the easy way out by resorting to canned maps.

Then what should you do instead? Come up with your own map for each pericope you preach, one that is unique and specific for that text. This forces you to discern the theology of the pericope, derive the application, and then ask, What is a good map to use, a good sermon shape to employ, that will best enable my listeners to experience the text + theology? I offer a maneuver that can be gainfully employed for this purpose: Focus Splitting. Let me show it to you in action.

Take my favorite "Theological" (Dermatological) Focus: "Sun exposure is a cause of skin cancer." If you, with the authority of a dermatologist, had to give a talk on this, and if you were forced to create a three-move shape for your address, what would you do? Well, the last point is probably going to be

---

25. A more appropriate application would be one of the significances discussed in chap. 3.

the application: *Wear sunscreen!* (or something similar). That's easy enough. What might be the two moves before that? Of course, there is no text on which this "sermon" is based, so you are free to brainstorm and head in whatever direction you want, as long as that path is informed by who your audience is and where they stand in relation to this "Theological" Focus.

Here's the Focus Splitting maneuver: take the "Theological" Focus, split it in half, and use those halves to create the two moves prior to the application. Splitting "Sun exposure is a cause of skin cancer" in the middle creates "Sun exposure" and "is a cause of skin cancer." One of these becomes the label for the first move, and the other becomes the label for the second move. Here is what this might look like.[26]

   I. Sun as a cause of skin cancer [The sun's UV rays produce cancer-causing mutations in skin cells; types and consequences of skin cancer]
   II. Sun exposure [How much is dangerous? On what skin types? At what geographic latitudes? And at what times of the day?]
   III. Application: *Wear sunscreen!*

Notice that I chose to use "Sun as a cause of skin cancer" as the first move and "Sun exposure" as the second move, even though the "Theological" Focus had them in reverse order. That's not a problem; you can choose whatever order you wish. Your communicative burden is to convey the "theology" easily, economically, and efficaciously to your audience (we did this sort of switching earlier for one of the proverbs too).

After looking at this three-move map, you might decide that four (or more) moves are better. Perhaps you feel that the first move might take far more time in the sermon (and space in the manuscript) than the second. In that case, feel free to break up the first move into two discrete moves to make things more equitable in terms of time and space and overall balance. If you also add submoves (see below), the map becomes more organized.[27]

   I. Sun as a cause of skin cancer 1 [The sun's UV rays produce cancer-causing mutations in skin cells]
   II. Sun as a cause of skin cancer 2
      A. Types of skin cancers
      B. Consequences of skin cancer

26. The annotations in brackets, below, help me remember what I intend to say in each of the moves. A map, after all, is a cheat sheet for the preacher.
27. In chap. 5, "Fleshing Moves," we will also add submoves of relevance to each move.

III. Sun exposure

    A. Amount of sun exposure that is dangerous and at what times of the day

    B. Skin types affected and at what geographic latitudes

IV. Application: *Wear sunscreen!*

There is always plenty of room for freedom and creativity.

Let's look at another example. We've seen this story before, one of Aesop's fables (the story of the crow that lost its cheese to the sly fox), in chapter 2.

Aesop's "The Fox and the Crow"

"Theological" Focus: "Avoiding prideful gullibility to flattery prevents loss."

Let's try one of our two canned maps first. The text/story doesn't need much explanation. It is comprehensible at first sight, so let's forget the Saying–Doing–Application map. Is there a Problem here? Yes, of course: the loss the crow incurred. What might the Solution be? Avoiding prideful gullibility to flattery prevents loss.[28] So the application? *Don't be proud(fully gullible and fall for flattery)!*

    I. Problem: Prideful gullibility to flattery leads to [can lead to] loss

    II. Solution: Avoiding prideful gullibility to flattery prevents loss

    III. Application: *Don't be proud(fully gullible and fall for flattery)!*

While this can be made to work—in a pinch—it is really not an ideal sermon shape. The entire story will have to be told in I. Problem. There is nothing wrong with that, but then what will you do in II. Solution? Not a whole lot there would be different from the contents of the previous move. And III. Application would also be quite similar to the Solution. All of this results in a rather unbalanced and redundant map. A better option is to split the "Theological" Focus, "Avoiding prideful gullibility to flattery prevents loss," into two parts: "Prideful gullibility to flattery" and "Causes loss."[29]

    I. Prideful gullibility to flattery [the crow's succumbing to flattery; pride as a common affliction that makes one gullible to flattery]

28. In a Problem–Solution–Application canned map, the Solution is often the Theological Focus.

29. In order for the sermon to better reflect the negative narrative of the crow's loss, I worked with a negative version of the "Theological" Focus: "Prideful gullibility to flattery causes loss."

II. Causes loss [the crow's loss of the cheese; consequences of prideful gullibility]

III. Application: *Don't be proud(fully gullible and fall for flattery)!*

The advantage of this map is that half the story (the crow's succumbing to flattery) can be handled in the first move, and the rest of the fable (the crow's response to flattery and its subsequent loss) can be handled in the second move, providing a fairly even split between the two moves.

Now let's apply Focus Splitting to a couple of proverbs in this idiosyncratic, text-unique fashion.

Proverbs 15:8

> The sacrifice of the wicked is abominable to Yahweh,
>> but the prayer of the upright his delight.

Theological Focus: "God is disgusted with the worship of the wicked but delighted with the worship of the upright."

Is there a Problem here? Perhaps there is an implicit problem that if God finds one's worship abominable, there might be serious consequences—the *felt* Problem. But this has to be supplied from without since the text does not offer it explicitly. So let's not go the canned route but try Focus Splitting instead.

I. God's disgust at the worship of the wicked (15:8a)

II. God's delight at the worship of the upright (15:8b)

III. Application: *Delight God!*

Proverbs 21:16

> A man who wanders from the way of understanding
>> will rest in the congregation of the dead.

"The way of understanding" refers to a life of wisdom, living in God's way. The consequence of not living in God's way is lethal. What is the Theological Focus?[30] Application? Once you get a succinct Theological Focus and Application, try splitting the former into two to create the first two moves of your sermon.[31]

---

30. "Straying from the way of understanding (i.e., God's way of living) has dire consequences."
31. Here's a possibility:
    I. Straying from "the way of understanding" is to abandon God's way of living (21:16a)
    II. Abandoning God's way of living has dire consequences [slaying?] (21:16b)

If you are worrying that this is a one-size-fits-all approach, let me offer you three words of good cheer: you are mistaken! We preachers have the tendency to think we are creating something novel and magnificent in our sermons—a da Vinci painting! But we are not. The *text* is the work of art. You and I, preachers, are merely curators of that objet d'art. Our primary task is to discover the clues in the artwork that help the audience discern what the divine Painter is *doing*. And for this curation, we don't have to sweat over fancy maps to showcase our own sermonic masterpieces. All we need, in order to create a decent sermon map, is a Theological Focus split into two (or more, as we see fit). And by doing it this way, we are letting the text's theology inform the sermon shape and content. But equally significant, notice that with a Focus Splitting transaction, each sermon map created is different from every other. None look alike (except for the fact that application shows up as the last move of the body).[32] In other words, Focus Splitting does not produce maps that are blandly uniform; rather, the maps are unique for the texts employed.

Let's do sermon maps for a couple of texts we examined earlier.

Ephesians 1:1–14
Theological Focus: "God, who blesses his people, redeeming them for his grand plan to consummate all things in Christ, is worthy of being blessed."

This Theological Focus is conducive to being split into two parts. Actually, we could split it into three, with the third part becoming the application.[33]

   I. God's grand plan to consummate all things in Christ (1:9–10)

   II. God's blessing of his people, redeeming them for his grand plan (1:1–8, 11–14)

   III. Application: *Bless God (who is worthy of being blessed)!*

Ephesians 1:15–23
Theological Focus: "Hostile powers at work to oppose God's plan and God's people are overwhelmed by God's incredible power in and through

---

III. Application: *Stay in God's way!*

One might call this a Straying–Slaying–Staying map. Key words, such as "straying" (for I.), "slaying" (for II.), and "staying" (for III.), alliterated or not, will become useful in the sermon introduction (see chap. 7, "Crafting Introductions and Conclusions").

32. Since the theology is curated in the first few moves, it makes sense to place application there.

33. See app. C for the manuscript of a sermon on Eph. 1:1–14 that employs this map.

Christ—power that is extended toward believers, the body of Christ, his fullness, as Christ reigns."[34]

We have already seen a Problem–Solution–Application sermon map for this pericope. Let's try another one by Focus Splitting.

    I. Hostile forces opposing God's plan (1:21)
    II. God's overwhelming power (in and through Christ) (1:15–20)
    III. Believers' power in Christ (as his body) (1:22–23)
    IV. Application: *Live powerfully!*

Ephesians 2:1–10
Theological Focus: "Believers, once in dire straits [in the past] but now sharing Christ's exaltation [in the present], demonstrate to the universe God's mercy, love, grace, and kindness as they undertake good works [in the future]." My annotations in brackets provide a good way to proceed.

    I. The status of sinners (in the past—their dire situation) (2:1–3)
    II. The station of the saved (in the present—the result of God's mercy, love, grace, and kindness) (2:4–9)
    III. The strategy of the stars (in the future—doing good works, God's goal for his redeemed people) (2:10)[35]
    IV. Application: *Do good works!*

I hope this was not too difficult. Practice, however, is what maketh perfect. Try Focus Splitting with other pericopes and with texts you hear preached in church or elsewhere. Determine the saying, discern the *doing,* and come up with a Theological Focus that you can split to create a sermon map.

Preaching Seamlessly

Several years ago I watched a TED2008 Talk given by Benjamin Zander, music director of the Boston Philharmonic and Boston Philharmonic Youth Orchestras, on the (unfortunate) contemporary unpopularity of classical music.[36]

---

34. Sometimes the longer (and pre-final) version of the Theological Focus (as is used here) is more amenable to being split. The shorter (overshortened?) version may not provide the necessary detail in its uncoupled parts for Focus Splitting. Use your discretion.

35. Yes, I got carried away with alliteration. "Stars" is my inelegant attempt to reflect *poiēma,* the divine "workmanship" (Eph. 2:10) that believers growing in Christ are.

36. Benjamin Zander, "The Transformative Power of Classical Music," TED, video, 20:40, accessed May 1, 2018, https://www.ted.com/talks/benjamin_zander_on_music_and_passion /transcript. All the links in this work have been gathered together at http://www.homiletix.com /preaching2019/links.

To speculate on why this might be the case, Zander commenced with an illustration of a child learning to play the piano.[37] Employing the allegro movement of Mozart's Piano Sonata in C Major, K.545, he demonstrated on a piano first how a seven-year-old child might play it, in fits and starts and with every note and every beat being pounded out with heavy emphasis. Then he showed how the same child would play the piece at eight years of age, this time with every *other* beat being emphasized. The nine-year-old reduced the emphases further to every fourth beat, and things began to get smoother. (All along, Zander, with vigorous head nods, depicted which beats were being emphasized.) For the ten-year-old, the emphases were reduced even more, to every eighth beat. Here, Zander, turning to the audience, announced, "At that point, they usually give up! Now if only you had waited one more year, you would have heard this." And he played the entire first motif of the sonata's opening movement with a smooth, suave, svelte, gracile, and limpid articulation that almost sounded like a voice singing: the motif had been performed in a single impulse. Gone were the pounding emphases extracted from the instrument with military regularity. Gone was the jerkiness of intemperate stressing of notes measure after measure. Zander then explained, "Now, what happened was not maybe what you thought, which is, he suddenly became passionate, engaged, involved, got a new teacher, he hit puberty, or whatever it is. What actually happened was the impulses were reduced" progressively, with the eleven-year-old rendering the entire phrase as one unified whole, as the composer intended.

What is interesting is that when Zander played the eleven-year-old, his entire body swayed with the power of Mozart, and he ended the lyrical motif with the upper half of his body leaning precariously to the right on the piano bench, all his weight on his right upper leg. The nuances of the music had captivated the pianist. Zander froze in that unbalanced pose and confessed, "I don't know how we got into this position. I didn't say, 'I'm going to move my shoulder over, move my body.' No, the music pushed me over, which is why I call it 'one-buttock playing'"—the whole thing performed in one impulse, with one move, as one statement, as one song.

After I watched the video, it suddenly hit me why many sermons I heard in classrooms and in churches left me dissatisfied about their shapes. They reminded me of sitting in the passenger seat of a car while its student driver was learning how to drive a stick shift, each switching of gear violently displacing me, the passenger, up and down, back and forth, side to side. What we needed in homiletics, I realized, was "one-buttock *preaching*" (henceforth,

37. You can see this from 1′00″ to 4′12″ in the video.

"one-B preaching"). The whole sermon ought to be one single impulse, one unitary move, not multiple, discrete, jerking spasms that throw listeners into cramps and cricks, giving them pounding heads and shooting pains. One-B preaching is one move—one single move that is not (at least overtly) broken up into a sequence of multiple moves—in which discerning theology blends seamlessly into deriving application.

Body in One-B Preaching
    Single move (discerning theology + deriving application)

This, I believe, is the ideal shape a sermon should take, and I've been trying to create sermons with this shape over the years (with slow but steady improvement).[38] How do we get to this place? We practice and master *multi*-B preaching (the standard model) first, with maps that we learned to create by Focus Splitting.

Body in Multi-B Preaching
    Primary move (discerning theology) 1
    Primary move (discerning theology) 2
    . . .
    Primary move (discerning theology) n
    Secondary move (deriving application)

Once this elementary structure is mastered, we attempt to erase some of the seams that separate the individual moves as we adapt to *one*-B preaching. No need to unduly stress the joints. No need to overemphasize the transitions. With such inordinate stress and emphasis, each move (and each submove?) ends up becoming a sermonette in itself:

> [The preacher] who has had the nerve to cast a critical eye on his old sermons has probably discovered that some sermons were three sermonettes barely glued together. There may have been movement within each point [our "move"], and there may have been some general kinship among the points [moves], but there was not one movement from beginning to end. The points [moves] were as three pegs in a board, equal in height and distance from each other.[39]

38. The sermon manuscript on Eph. 1:1–14 (app. C) is such an attempt.
39. Craddock, *As One without Authority*, 47. "Usually, for the skeleton to be showing, with a sermon as with a person, is a sign of malformation or malnutrition" (145). Only with one-B preaching can the skeleton be kept unobtrusively in the background, without those stresses and emphases accentuating the sermonic bones and joints.

Instead, we need to try to get to one-B preaching. We need to preach sermons like we tell stories—smoothly: "This happened, and then this, and then this." We need to slowly negotiate our way through the sermon in granular fashion, curating the text for listeners.[40] Ultimately, the question is what map best enables the audience to experience the text + theology fully and faithfully, and I would affirm that the one-B shape of sermons is most conducive to that outcome.

In summary, let me urge you, in the early stages of your preaching career, to stick with multi-B preaching that employs Focus Splitting to create sermon maps. What you want your listeners to catch is the theology of the text, and splitting the Theological Focus is an excellent way to shape the sermon and discern pericopal theology for listeners.[41] And as you grow in your experience and develop in your preaching capacity, consider smoothening the seams of the sermon moves and attempting to deliver an almost seamless product—one-B preaching.

40. On making sermons story-like, or narratival, Long observes, "[Sermons] are stories in the sense that the preacher, who has encountered the biblical text in some new way, witnesses to—tells the story of—that encounter. . . . The sermon, then, becomes not an essay, a lawyer's brief, a debater's rebuttal, or a piece of religious rhetoric; it becomes a journey . . . a journey which the preacher has taken once in the study and now guides for the congregation" ("Distance We Have Traveled," 16).

41. I repeat myself, but it is critical to remember that the Theological Focus is but a reduction of the theology of the pericope, serving only as a label for the latter. The two are not equivalent. What you want your listeners to discern is the (inexpressible) pericopal theology, not the (expressible) bare and emaciated reduction thereof. In sermon preparation, we are simply using the Theological Focus as a tool for creating sermon maps and to remind ourselves as we flesh out the moves (see chap. 5, "Fleshing Moves") that north is that way, so as to keep us from going astray (the Theological Focus can also aid in the creation of specific application).

Ephesians and the Jacob Story

Here are two more pericopes from Ephesians and two more from the Jacob Story (pericopes 4 and 5 in each case), with the derivation of their Theological Foci.[42]

4. Ephesians 2:11–22

> **All (believing) humanity has been united in one body, the work of Christ removing the condemnation of the law for sin, winning access to God, and building believers together into a dwelling of God in the Spirit.**

Here is a Focus Splitting map for this pericope:

   I. The work of Christ: humanity united in one body (2:11–15)[43]

  II. The result of the union of humanity in one body (2:16–22)

 III. Application: *Demonstrate the union accomplished by Christ!*

5. Ephesians 3:1–13

> **Paul's divinely empowered role in the administration of God's plan, despite the paradox of his humble circumstances, forms a paradigm for the ministry of all believers, as God is made known to the cosmos through the church.**

Here is a possible sermon map:

   I. Paradox: The humble circumstances of God's people who are part of God's grand plan (3:1–2, 8a, 13)

  II. Paradigm: God's great use of his people, despite their humble circumstances (3:3–7, 8b–12)

 III. Application: *Value God's purpose in you!*

---

42. Beginning in this chapter I will omit commentaries for some pericopes altogether (providing only their Theological Foci), both to give you a chance to do your own work on them and to keep the current work to a manageable size. But you can always look up my thoughts on these texts at http://www.homiletix.com/preaching2019/commentaries. For expanded curations of these texts, see Kuruvilla, *Ephesians*, 66–83, 84–98; and Kuruvilla, *Genesis*, 330–43, 344–54.

43. For convenience, I'm summarizing the Theological Focus splits and using those abbreviated fragments as labels for moves I. and II.

4. Genesis 28:10–22

God's guaranteed promises for the future call for a response of trusting worship.

Here is a possible sermon map:

    I. God's guaranteed promises for the future (28:10–12)
    II. Response of trusting worship (in contrast to Jacob's wrong response) (18:16–22)
    III. Application: *Worship God even before his promises are fulfilled!*

5. Genesis 29:1–30

God's blessings do not preclude the possibility of appropriate discipline for one's misdeeds.

Here is a possible sermon map:

    I. God's blessings (29:1–14)
    II. God's discipline (29:15–30)
    III. Application: *Recognize retribution and repent!*

5

Fleshing Moves

Our people do not so much need to have their heads stored, as to have their hearts touched; and they stand in the greatest need of that sort of preaching, which has the greatest tendency to do this.[1]

You now have a sermon mapped into distinct moves. But with only those moves listed, that map is pretty bare—bones without flesh. Our task in this chapter is to include topographical details in order to make the map more usable—putting flesh on the skeleton.

We've considered the two roles of the preacher: the primary one of discerning for listeners the theology of the text from the clues therein, and the secondary one of deriving for them application that is specific, striking, and singular. On the surface it looks as if the primary task deals exclusively with the text (i.e., revelation) and that only in the secondary task of application is any connection with the audience made (i.e., relevance), as the preacher and the audience grapple with life transformation in their own current circumstances. If this is indeed the case, then a large portion of the sermon, all those moves before application, are not directly relevant to listeners. That would not be optimal. If one wants to keep the attention of listeners, if one wants to carry them along in the sermon, there must be relevance—a link between text + theology and listeners' lives, touching their hearts. Such

1. Edwards, "Part III," I:391.

relevance must be evident in *all* the moves, not just in the last one (application). In other words, the moves in the body of the sermon ought *not* to look like this:[2]

    I. Primary theology move (discerning theology) [only revelation]
   II. Primary theology move (discerning theology) [only revelation]
  III. Secondary application move (deriving application) [relevance]

Rather, they should look like this:

    I. Primary theology move (discerning theology)
      A. Revelation submove
      B. Relevance submove
   II. Primary theology move (discerning theology)
      A. Revelation submove
      B. Relevance submove
  III. Secondary application move (deriving application)

In other words, there should be relevance included in each move. The application move (III.) does not have a separate submove labeled "relevance" simply because application is itself an integral part of making the sermon relevant to listeners (see fig. 5.1, which depicts application as a component of sermon relevance). Of course, there is no revelation (that is, textual exposition) in application (as we discussed in chap. 3).

Figure 5.1

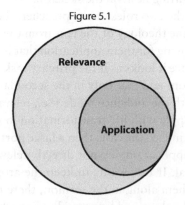

---

2. Your map for a particular text may have more than three moves, but we'll stick with three for ease of depiction.

All that to say, each of the primary theology moves (I. and II. in the maps above) before the secondary application move should include submoves of revelation and relevance (i.e., the preacher should show how the portion of pericopal theology dealt with in that particular move is relevant to listeners). Homiletician Eugene L. Lowry calls such an approach "alternating the story"—engaging the text and engaging the people, a sort of "lateral movement."[3] So let's simplify our map.

I. Theology

    A. Revelation

    B. Relevance

II. Theology

    A. Revelation

    B. Relevance

III. Application

Now let's dig deeper into the revelation and relevance submoves.

Revelation: In the Word

In the map above, the submoves of revelation (I.A. and II.A.) are based on the Theological Focus that is split between moves I. and II. (see chap. 4). So essentially what the preacher is doing in these revelation submoves is discerning for listeners parts of the theology of the pericope (the labels of which are the split portions of the Theological Focus). With each revelation submove, the preacher is curating the text for listeners—performing a creative exegesis of the pericope so that the congregation catches the theology of the text as it is unveiled bit by bit, move by move—a portion in I.A. Revelation and another in II.A. Revelation (and so on, if the sermon has more moves). In sum, here the preacher is facilitating for listeners an encounter with the text similar to what the preacher experienced while studying the pericope (albeit in a more direct and simplified form when preached).

Be careful not to burden listeners with textual explanation that does not help them catch the theology. You need to be ruthless about this: anything that does not further the discernment of the theology by your hearers must be excised

3. Lowry, *How to Preach a Parable*, 40, 133, 136.

from these revelation submoves.[4] So *enough* textual curation is key here—no more, no less. Our modern culture and educational systems are so logocentric and information oriented that we naturally excel in explanation; it is easy to go wildly astray with all kinds of fascinating observations on matters historical, geographical, biographical, and linguistic related to the biblical text that do not have anything at all to do with its theology and what the author is *doing*. Instead, as the preacher (curator), your goal is to help listeners discern the theology of the text for themselves based on clues in the text that you uncover. Therefore, stick with demonstrating the textual clues that point to pericopal theology.[5] If your discernment of that theology is accurate, then every textual element, major and minor, will point to the theology. However, not all of those elements are equally strong clues. Discriminate between essential clues and nonessential ones and curate the former for the audience, mindful of the constraints of time and the uniqueness of the oral-aural route of communication.[6]

Let's look at the map of Ephesians 1:1–14 and its moves and revelation submoves.

Ephesians 1:1–14
Theological Focus: "God, who blesses his people, redeeming them for his grand plan to consummate all things in Christ, is worthy of being blessed."

   I. Theology: God's grand plan to consummate all things in Christ (1:9–10)

     A. Revelation: God's grand plan to consummate all things in Christ[7]

     B. Relevance

---

4. Also, unnecessarily inundating the revelation submoves with Hebrew and Greek will only crush the faith of your listeners in their English Bibles.

5. I have worked out these major clues in the commentaries on Ephesians and the Jacob Story in this work and at http://www.homiletix.com/preaching2019/commentaries.

6. Not everything that a writer has the luxury of expounding in a scriptural pericope (that can be read and reread) needs to be (or can be) expatiated in a spoken sermon (a nonrepeatable, audible event). And by the way, if there are difficulties in the text you don't have answers for, confess your ignorance. In a sermon on Mark 7, I acknowledged I had no idea what "couches" were doing alongside the "cups and pitchers and copper pots" that the Pharisees were ostensibly washing ritually (v. 4). Also, if you don't have time to get into an ancillary but important issue—like the divine command to annihilate the Amalekites in 1 Sam. 15, which doesn't have direct implications for the thrust and force of the text but is nonetheless concerning for modern listeners/readers—you might want to acknowledge that the story raises significant questions that you will address on another nonsermon occasion (in a Sunday school, a Bible study class, etc.). Reserve preaching for discerning the theology of the text and deriving application for listeners—that is, demonstrating the text + theology so that listeners experience it fully and faithfully, resulting in changed lives.

7. I'll address the similarity between the headings of the theology moves (I. and II.) and those of their respective revelation submoves (I.A. and II.A.) below.

II. Theology: God's blessing of his people, redeeming (thus incorporating) them for his grand plan (1:1–8, 11–14)

    A. Revelation: God's blessing of his people, redeeming them for his grand plan

    B. Relevance

III. Application: *Bless God!*

As you create and flesh these revelation submoves, it is easy to be lulled into thinking that what you are doing is simply using the text to substantiate the fragmentary labels of your moves, those split portions of the Theological Focus. But when you preach the I.A. Revelation submove, you are not simply explaining and validating "God's grand plan to consummate all things in Christ." That's simply a label for the submove—a landmark on a map directing your travel, no more. What you want to do is go to the text and direct listeners to the clues therein that will help them discern the portion of its theology regarding the grand plan of God (Eph. 1:9–10). The text's intrinsic power and pathos are utterly lacking in the bald label of the I.A. Revelation submove ("God's grand plan to consummate all things in Christ"). All that to say, you are not preaching those labels; you are preaching the *text*. The labels are not the destination; the irreducible theology (which cannot be expressed in any form other than the text) is the destination. The labels are merely placeholders and memory joggers for you, the preacher.

As was noted in chapter 4, in standard outlining protocols, whether for sermons or essays, every main point encompasses the notions of all the subpoints within it. So if the sermon map above were a traditional outline, the label of I. Theology would subsume the labels of both I.A. Revelation and I.B. Relevance. Likewise, the label of II. Theology would encompass the labels of both II.A. Revelation and II.B. Relevance. But you may have noticed that, in the way we created the map for this sermon, the labels of I. Theology and I.A. Revelation are identical, as are the labels of II. Theology and II.A. Revelation. Remember, the map is *not* a standard outline that is constrained to follow certain structural rules. A sermon map is a different entity, shaped for a different purpose, with labels (not points) for each move and submove. Therefore, we are doing away with academic fussiness and tweaking standard procedures to adapt them for our cartographic undertaking.[8]

---

8. Warning: If you are a student, you may have to present your sermon conception formally as an outline that abides by limitations set by your professor. I had to do this myself in my student days but have since rejected such mandates as unnecessary, with few benefits to show for much cost.

What do we do with the similarity of the labels of I. and I.A. and of II. and II.A. in the map? We simply remove the labels for the main moves (I. and II.) and replace them with simpler keywords or phrases. Here is the result.

I. God's Grand Plan

    A. Revelation: God's grand plan to consummate all things in Christ (1:9–10)

    B. Relevance

II. Humanity's Glorious Place

    A. Revelation: God's blessing of his people, redeeming them for his grand plan (1:1–8, 11–14)

    B. Relevance

III. Application: *Bless God!*

These keywords/phrases will be significant in two places in sermon preparation: in the introduction (see chap. 7) and in sermon transitions (see below). For the moment, simply convert the longer phrase labels (portions of the split Theological Focus) into shorter keyword/phrase labels. You will catch the utility of this modification as we proceed.

Relevance: In the World

Essentially, the relevance submove brings home to the particular audience what is introduced in the revelation submove. The question being answered in the relevance submove is this: Where do the notions in the revelation submove show up in the world (and in our lives)? For some relevance submoves, the question might well be, Where (and why) do the notions *not* show up in the world (and in our lives)?[9] Necessarily, relevance submoves will involve the use of illustrations (see chap. 6, "Illustrating Ideas") that help concretely depict how the matters discussed in the respective revelation submoves show up in real life.

The relevance submove might also be the occasion to push back against objections you think your listeners are raising in their minds about what they heard in the revelation submove—the "Yes, but . . ." protests. Such demurrals

---

9. For instance, in the map for the Eph. 1:1–14 sermon, for I.B. Relevance, we might ask where the divine plan of consummation shows up in our lives and what it might look like. But we could also point out what the world looks like before that divine plan is consummated in Christ—the chaos and disharmony of a world *not* in Christ.

usually come from the listeners' contrary experiences or competing values. Contrary experience: "Yes, preacher, I hear you say God has co-opted us into his grand plan to consummate all things in Christ, but my life is such a mess. Nothing is going right. I don't see it in my life." You, the preacher, might need to address such dissent if you think a significant number of your listeners are thinking the same thing. Competing value: "Yes, preacher, I see the text calls us to align ourselves with God's grand plan to consummate all things in Christ, but isn't being rich and being able to afford a big house and a few cars and to send my children to elite schools more important?" Again, you might consider responding to this sort of resistance as necessary.[10]

There is much flexibility and fluidity here. Fundamentally, to show relevance we must be concerned for our listeners and know them well. Therefore, it is impossible to have relevance in our sermons if we are not shepherding in some capacity. I'd go so far as to say that preaching and pastoring/shepherding ought never to be divorced; they belong together.[11] We cannot know our listeners well enough to be relevant if we are not shepherding them. By being relevant we are considering their circumstances and their lives, their maturity and their growth, and their hesitations and their doubts as we execute relevance submoves. This is where we pastorally address their issues and answer their questions to the best of our ability, with the wisdom, discretion, and love of a shepherd for the flock.

Here we are, then, with the sermon map for Ephesians 1:1–14. I have added labels for I.B. Relevance and II.B. Relevance.[12]

I. God's Grand Plan

A. Revelation: God's grand plan to consummate all things in Christ (1:9–10)

B. Relevance: God's grand plan entails all things being set right in the world we live in [how things are *not* set right now; illustration]

II. Humanity's Glorious Place

A. Revelation: God's blessing of his people, redeeming them for his grand plan (1:1–8, 11–14)

10. Modified from T. Warren, "Developmental Questions," 84–85.
11. See Kuruvilla, "Preaching Is Pastoral," in *Vision for Preaching*, 31–49.
12. As was noted, for my own work I don't create move labels as full sentences. After all, they are only labels. An annotated manuscript of a sermon on this text is provided in app. C. You might want to go to the manuscript and glance at the revelation and relevance sections of each move. A version of the sermon may also be seen/heard as a live recording online. See Abraham Kuruvilla, "God's Grand Plan," Homiletix, April 10, 2018, http://homiletix.com/preaching-resources/abes-videos/gods-grand-plan/.

B. Relevance: God's co-optation of us is how we find purpose and
    fulfillment in life [purposeless and unfulfilled life without under-
    standing God's incorporation of us into his grand plan;
    illustration]

III. Application: *Bless God!*

Here are some other examples.

Proverbs 13:20[13]

> The one walking with the wise will become wise,
>   but the one dealing with the foolish will suffer detriment.

Theological Focus: "Those keeping company with the wise become wise, but
those keeping company with the foolish suffer."

Let's work with the Problem–Solution–Application map that we created
earlier.

I. Problem

A. Revelation: Keeping the company of fools leads to suffering
    (13:20b)

B. Relevance: Suffering that comes from keeping the company of
    fools is common[14] [where does this happen in life? why/how?;
    illustration]

II. Solution

A. Revelation: Keeping the company of the wise precludes suffering
    (13:20a)

B. Relevance: We too may be saved from suffering as we keep the

13. Preaching on a single proverb in this fashion is probably not going to be part of real
life for most of us. A single proverb may not always have enough in it to justify the thirty to
forty minutes of a standard sermon in evangelical assemblies. Instead, in a single sermon we
might handle a few proverbs collected together, all dealing with a single topic and thus yielding
a topical sermon. So there is a sense of artificiality in what we are doing with proverbs in this
work. However, the advantage of using proverbs for homiletical pedagogy is considerable:
we can discuss important issues of discerning theology, deriving application, creating maps,
and fleshing moves all without having to worry about a complex text and its complicated
context.

14. Or "Suffering that comes from keeping the company of fools happens to all of us."
But such phrases—". . . is common," ". . . happens to all of us," etc.—can become repetitive
in relevance submoves. Another option, and my personal preference, is to dive right into the
illustration that shows how this is common or how it happens to all of us without necessarily
stating the label of the relevance submove (see below).

company of the wise [where does this happen in life? why/how?; illustration]

III. Application: *Keep company with the wise!*

I kept the labels of moves I. and II. quite straightforward: Problem and Solution, respectively. You could get creative, of course: I. How to Suffer and II. How *Not* to Suffer.

Abe's Cutaneous Theology
"Theological" Focus: "Sun exposure is a cause of skin cancer."

   I. Sun as a cause of skin cancer

      A. Revelation: UV rays can lead to cancer-causing mutations in skin cells

      B. Relevance: Sun-related skin cancers occur frequently [statistics of skin cancer incidence;[15] what it can do to us; illustration]

  II. Sun exposure

      A. Revelation: How much sun exposure causes skin cancer

      B. Relevance: Who is affected by sun exposure and where and when [what skin types are affected at latitudes we live in and when during the day;[16] illustration]

 III. Application: *Wear sunscreen!*

Aesop's "The Fox and the Crow"
"Theological" Focus: "Avoiding prideful gullibility to flattery prevents loss."

   I. Attitude

      A. Revelation: Prideful gullibility to flattery [the story of the crow succumbing to flattery]

      B. Relevance: Pride is a common affliction, making us gullible to flattery [illustration]

  II. Loss

      A. Revelation: Prideful gullibility leads to loss [the story of the crow's response to flattery and the result—loss]

      B. Relevance: The consequences of prideful gullibility for us [illustration]

 III. Application: *Don't be proud(fully gullible and fall for flattery)!*

15. This deals with a potential objection that skin cancers are rare (contrary experience).
16. You may also want to address the competing value: "But then how do I get a nice tan?"

Proverbs 15:8
> The sacrifice of the wicked is abominable to Yahweh,
>> but the prayer of the upright his delight.

Theological Focus: "God is disgusted with the worship of the wicked but delighted with the worship of the upright."

  I. God's Disgust
   A. Revelation: God's disgust at the worship of the wicked (15:8a) [explain "abominable"; what else is abominable to God?][17]
   B. Relevance: Why God may be disgusted with our worship
  II. God's Delight
   A. Revelation: God's delight at the worship of the upright (15:8b) [other things that delight God][18]
   B. Relevance: What upright prayer looks like and why God is delighted[19]
  III. Application: *Delight God!*

Proverbs 21:16
> A man who wanders from the way of understanding
>> will rest in the congregation of the dead.

Theological Focus: "Straying from the way of understanding (i.e., God's way of living) has dire consequences."

  I. Straying
   A. Revelation: Straying from the way of understanding is to abandon God's way of living (21:16a) [explanation of the text]
   B. Relevance: How and why we tend to wander from God's way
    1. Illustration: Pastor A who was on prescription drugs (or was an Ashley Madison subscriber)
  II. Slaying
   A. Revelation: Abandoning God's way of living has dire consequences (21:16b) [explanation of the somewhat obscure phrasing]

---

17. See Prov. 3:32; 6:16–19; 11:1; 12:22; 15:9, 26; 16:5; 17:15; 20:10, 23; 28:9.
18. See Prov. 8:35; 11:1, 20; 12:2, 22.
19. Notice that II.B. Relevance, "What upright prayer looks like," might well merge into the application (in its "tell" and "show"; see chap. 4), which would also deal with how to delight God by prayer. In that case, II.B. Relevance could be omitted: the tell and show of the application serves to actualize (make relevant) what was discussed in II.A. Revelation.

    B. Relevance: What the consequences might be for us who wander

       1. Illustration: consequences for Pastor A

III. Staying: *Stay in God's way!*

You may have figured out by now that relevance submoves often need to include an illustration as an example. This is perhaps the best way to make things relevant to listeners: show them! This is not to say that illustrations shouldn't be used with revelation, but they invariably fit well with relevance (more on illustrations in chap. 6, "Illustrating Ideas"). The impact is powerful when such examples are employed. When you do use an illustration, include a brief note in your sermon map of what that illustration is about (as in I.B.1. and II.B.1. in the map above).[20]

The following sermon map is essentially Problem–Solution–Application, but I have chosen to remove those vanilla labels and create my own: I. Foes' Power; II. God's Power; III. Our Power.

Ephesians 1:15–23
Theological Focus: "Hostile powers at work to oppose God's plan and God's people are overwhelmed by God's incredible power in and through Christ— power that is extended toward believers, the body of Christ, his fullness, as Christ reigns."

    I. Foes' Power

       A. Revelation: The powerful supernatural foes arrayed against us and our fear of them [the list of supernatural foes (1:21); reason for their opposition (reflecting 1:10)]

       B. Relevance: Fearful foes are operating today, in our culture, against us [illustration]

    II. God's Power

       A. Revelation: God's incredible power in Christ (1:15–21) on behalf of believers, the body of Christ (1:22–23)

       B. Relevance: This divine power in Christ shows up in our lives and is working for us [illustration]

    III. Our Power: *Live powerfully!*

20. As was noted, in standard outlines, if there is no second point you don't need to number the first point (e.g., no need for "1." if there is no "2."). However, we are not dealing with standard outlines but with sermon maps, and so we will cavalierly break that rule and include numbered subsidiary moves even if they stand alone, all in service of making things clear to ourselves, the sermon preparers, the direction of our homiletical journeys.

Multiple Texts in a Single Sermon?

Topical sermons usually employ a number of superficially related but otherwise unconnected portions of Scripture.[21] While not denying the occasional
benefit of such sermons, I maintain that the need of the hour is preaching
pericope by pericope, respecting the trajectory of the book and the thrust
of the particular passage. All else, I maintain, is fast food, useful in certain
exigencies; by no means should it become a dietary staple. On the other hand,
preaching pericope by pericope (*lectio continua*), the preacher focuses on a
single text in a given sermon.

But what about referring to multiple texts in a sermon on a single pericope
as part of fleshing out individual moves (usually in the revelation submove)?
You may have noticed that in the sermon map for Proverbs 15:8 (above), in
I.A. Revelation, I suggested that one could explain "abominable" by showing
what else elicits God's disgust in Proverbs (and in II.A. Revelation, one could
explain "delight" in corresponding fashion). This might be one of those few
instances in a sermon when commandeering another verse or two to clarify
"abominable" may be helpful—perhaps picking a couple from the list provided in note 17. But referring to another verse should not take more than
a minute and certainly should not divert the focus of the sermon from the
chosen pericope.[22] Resort to such extra-pericopal operations as necessary, but
restrict the impulse to go fishing all over Scripture. Another occasion to point
to a text outside the chosen pericope is when you are preaching a series (*lectio
continua*) and you want to remind your listeners of what has been covered in
previous weeks. This is often helpful but should also take very little time and
can usually be done in the introduction of the sermon.

Another widely prevalent transaction is one that employs multiple texts
while the preacher ostensibly preaches a single Old Testament pericope; this
operation invariably ends up with the Old Testament text functioning as a
springboard for a dive into the New Testament. Often this is an attempt to
bring redemptive analogies into an older text, usually a mark of Christocentric
preaching. But here is a sound warning: "If the Old Testament no longer says
something to the Christian in its own right, to which the Christian still needs
to attend and on which Christian faith necessarily builds, its actual role within

---

21. My bias against topical preaching was already noted in chap. 1, "Getting Ready."

22. Again, the extra-pericopal references should subserve the thrust/force of the pericope
you are preaching; if they don't, then avoid such citations. By the way, if you do choose to
mention other verses, you can save time by projecting them on a screen, keeping listeners from
turning away from both the text of the sermon (in the pages of their Bibles) and the impact of
that text (in their minds).

Christian faith will tend to become marginal and optional, no matter what rhetoric is used to urge its importance."[23] I recommend you preach the New Testament text of interest when you get to it, but when you are preaching an Old Testament text, privilege that Old Testament text and discern its thrust and theology for listeners.[24]

You might ask whether the divine Author could be *doing* something across vast swaths of the biblical corpus that the human author was unaware of, conceivably justifying the use of discrete passages in a single sermon. Here are a few commonly cited examples of such canonical connections between parts of Scripture, no doubt the design of its divine Author alone.

> "Ambition," *philotimeomai*, showing up in three places in the New Testament (Rom. 15:20; 2 Cor. 5:9; 1 Thess. 4:11)
>
> Restoration of sinning believers (Matt. 18:15–17; Gal. 6:1; James 5:19–20)
>
> Occurrences of "take courage," *tharseō*, in the Gospels dealing with various facets of human fear (Matt. 9:2, fear of unforgiven sin; Matt. 9:22, fear of being found out; Matt. 14:27 = Mark 6:50, fear of demonic beings; Mark 10:49, fear of being left behind; and John 16:33, fear of tribulation)
>
> Caleb's "fully following" God in each phase of his life (Num. 14:24; 32:12; Deut. 1:36; Josh. 14:8–9, 14—as testified by Moses, Joshua, the narrator, and God himself)[25]

But notice that these examples, and others, are not *doings* in the sense that we have been talking about in this work. They are, for the most part, Authorial sayings.[26] Therefore, while there may be a place for preaching such coordinated sayings by the divine Author, these sayings should never vitiate

---

23. Moberly, *Bible, Theology, and Faith*, 140. I have addressed this issue of Christocentric preaching in Kuruvilla, *Privilege the Text!*, 211–69. Also see my essay "Christiconic View" and my responses to others' contributions in *Homiletics and Hermeneutics*.

24. This is not to deny that you can make mention of, say, a New Testament fulfillment of an Old Testament prophetic text, but the theological thrust/force of the latter is usually never its fulfillment in the former. Most New Testament citations of, or allusions to, the Old Testament are not expositions of the pericopal theology of the older text but often imaginative applications and creative redeployments thereof, albeit inspired in what they say. They can and should be addressed as such—when those *New Testament* texts are preached. See Kuruvilla, *Privilege the Text!*, 220–21.

25. Some of these were modified from T. Warren, "Topical Expository Preaching," 3, 11–12.

26. And they deal with entailments of the text. For example, an entailment of Matt. 28:19–20 is that the Godhead is a Trinity. But that clearly was not the thrust/force (pericopal theology) of the Great Commission passage. Entailments, derived from authorial sayings, have value in the creation of a body of systematic/biblical theology. However, for preaching, it is the *doing* of the author that must be attended to.

A/authorial *doings* pericope by pericope, following the trajectory of a particular book. The former approach, respecting the Author's sayings, yields topical sermons that colligate disparate texts. The latter approach, respecting the A/author's *doings*, yields sermons that focus on a specific pericope. There is a place—an occasional place—for topical (and canonically driven) sermons, but in this age when pericope-by-pericope preaching is hardly ever done, I find it unconscionable to impose any other method of preaching God's word upon God's people.[27]

So as a rule, you will rarely need to bring other portions of Scripture into your sermon. There is really no call to defend one text with another, for all of Scripture is equally inspired and authoritative. Besides, such support for one text by another is a figment of the imagination, for pericopal theology is exquisitely specific for a given pericope. I am convinced that no two biblical passages can ever have the same pericopal theology, and thus one text cannot render substantial support of another. The specificity of wording and structure and context of any given passage renders it impossible for one pericope to have the same theological thrust/force as another.[28] Thus the greatest danger of employing multiple texts in a single sermon is that the specificity of the main pericope will be blurred, dimmed, and clouded. This results in the neglect of that pericope's particular theology, which may otherwise never be encountered elsewhere in Scripture.[29]

Our call as preachers is to address faithfully the single text that we are allotted for a given sermon. There is no reason to think we need to give our listeners everything in the Bible, fearing this may be the last sermon they'll ever hear (or the last we'll ever preach).[30] You've heard it said, "One Lord, one faith, one baptism," but I say unto you, "*One text*, one sermon, one application."

27. Anatomists describe how things are (the saying). Physiologists describe how things work (the *doing*). Be a physiologist! I would therefore strongly urge the relegation of topical-style addresses to nonsermon occasions, such as a Sunday school class or an adult Bible fellowship. Preaching by a pastor, in the context of a worship service, respecting the theological thrust/force of a given pericope, focused on the conformation of the people of God into the image of the Son of God by the power of the Spirit of God for the glory of God, is a special species of Christian communication, the unique qualities, values, and efficacy of which must *never* be undermined.

28. This is true even when a passage is repeated verbatim in another location in Scripture, for instance, 2 Kings 18:13–20:11 and Isa. 36:1–38:8; Pss. 14 and 53; etc. The shift in context means that there will be a change in theological thrust. "Love all!" means one thing when proclaimed from the pulpit on Sunday morning. It means something entirely different when announced on Center Court in Wimbledon.

29. I take this indictment very seriously. Employing multiple texts in a single sermon does God a disservice, his word a disservice, his people a disservice, and even his world a disservice (for it is by seeing God's word come to life in his people that a dark world is enlightened).

30. You do not want your sermon assessed this way: "[It] began with the fall of man, touched on the principal doctrines of revelation, gave a Christian's experience, conducted him safely to

Audience Adaptation

One of my favorite commencement pictures was taken a few years ago showing four Dallas Theological Seminary faculty members—all University of Aberdeen alumni, splendidly arrayed in their *togae rubrae* ("red robes," the academic regalia of the alma mater) and John Knox caps (another idiosyncratic piece of gear donned by those with graduate degrees from bonnie Scotland). But on one of these solemn exercises of commencement, a student graduating chose to wear shorts to the event. No, he wasn't allowed to walk but had to collect his diploma in private after the event. All this to say, we need to know our audience and the event in order to dress appropriately.

Even more importantly, we need to know our audience to make our sermons relevant to our listeners. Socrates said, "Since it is the function of speech to lead souls by persuasion, he who is to be a rhetorician [speaker] must know the various forms of soul" (*Phaedrus* 271D).[31] For a modern version of this sentiment, we go to the nineteenth-century Presbyterian minister John Hall, who exhorted, "Come near your hearers. Letters dropped into the post office without addresses go to the dead-letter box, and are of no use to anybody."[32] Sermons insensitive to the audience, imperceptive to its composition, and inattentive to its needs are as good as letters without addresses—good for nothing and going nowhere.

The dual approach of revelation + relevance that we have taken in each sermonic move reflects the necessity for every sermon to be both text based (attending to revelation) and audience focused (attending to relevance). If a sermon is text based but only text focused, it is a lecture that has no relevance (though it may have plenty of revelation). On the other hand, if the sermon is audience based and audience focused, it is merely chatter that has no revelation (though loaded with relevance). To become preaching, a sermon needs to have both revelation (it should be faithful to the text) and relevance (it should be faithful to the audience).[33]

	Lecture	Preaching	Chatter
Based on	Text	Text	Audience
Focused on	Text	Audience	Audience

heaven, and wound up with the resurrection of the dead, the general judgement, the retribution of eternity, and an application of the subject" (Jeter, *Recollections of a Long Life*, 19–20).

31. In Plato, *Euthyphro. Apology. Crito. Phaedo. Phaedrus*, 553.

32. Cited in Gilbert, *Dictionary of Burning Words*, 479.

33. Modified from T. Warren, "Definition, Purpose, and Process," 14–15. Johnny Cash's sentiment might well be applied to some preachers: "So heavenly minded, you're no earthly good" ("No Earthly Good"). Preachers need to be both mindful of heaven (revelation) and considerate of earth (relevance).

Preaching is a different species of communication; it is not information driven, nor is it merely an explanation of the text: its structure, language, background, or history. Instead, preaching is transformation driven—motivational, spiritually forming, and Christlikeness inculcating (by the power of the Spirit).

Adapting to your audience involves almost every aspect of the sermon, including the language you use to preach your sermon, the Bible translation you follow, the clothes you wear, the illustrations you employ, the applications you offer (as we saw earlier in chap. 3), and so on. You will need to know the size of the audience, the character of its geographic location, and its economic and cultural standing. Be aware of the jargon your listeners use, the balance of their genders and ages,[34] their ethnicities and nationalities, their life experiences, their marital statuses, their educational levels, their leisure activities, what they read, and, most importantly, where they are in their walk with God. There are a number of demographical, psychological, and spiritual factors characterizing your listeners that must be attended to.

Max Warren's notion of "quadruple think" is helpful for preachers' adaptation of sermons to audiences. Essentially it involves (1) thinking out what one is going to say, (2) thinking out how what one has thought out will be understood by listeners, (3) rethinking what one is going to say, and (4) rethinking how what one has rethought will be understood by the audience.[35] Harry Emerson Fosdick's observation is apropos: "A wise preacher can so build his sermon that it will be, not a dogmatic monologue but a co-operative dialogue in which all sorts of things in the minds of the congregation— objections, questions, doubts, and confirmations—will be brought to the front and fairly dealt with. This requires clairvoyance on the preacher's part as to what the people are thinking, but any man who lacks that has no business to preach anyway."[36] This transaction of quadruple think (or of clairvoyance!) is a crucial undertaking that can only improve the sermon, at least with regard to its relevance to listeners. "The preacher must always try to feel what it is like to live inside the skins of the people he is preaching to, to hear the truth as they hear it. That is not as hard as it sounds because, of course, he is himself a hearer of truth as well as a teller of truth, and he listens out of the

---

34. At least 60 percent of sermon listeners on a Sunday morning will be women. "In the U.S., Religious Commitment Is High and the Gender Gap Is Wide," Pew Research Center, March 22, 2016, http://www.pewforum.org/2016/03/22/in-the-u-s-religious-commitment-is-high-and-the -gender-gap-is-wide/. Mathews, *Preaching That Speaks to Women*, is worth reading in this regard.

35. M. Warren, *Crowded Canvas*, 143. And you can keep going for several rounds of thinking and rethinking!

36. Fosdick, "What Is the Matter with Preaching?" 137.

same emptiness as they do for a truth to fill him and make him true."[37] We preachers should be willing to do whatever it takes (short of sin) to facilitate for our listeners an experience of the text + theology and to influence life change toward Christlikeness, for the glory of God by the Spirit's power. As Paul declared, "To all persons I have become all things, in order that I may by all means save some" (1 Cor. 9:22).

Making ideas and notions and concepts of the revelation (the theology of the pericope) relevant to hearers has other potent ramifications for the preaching event than just bringing everything into proximity with the audience. First, it unites the audience with the preacher. "The rhetor's [speaker's] turn from prose explanation to mimetic imitation [showing how it works in real life] brings the audience alongside the rhetor in a shared experience of the emotion. No longer is the rhetor speaking 'to' the audience but, instead, they are together caught up in the turmoil of the drama. . . . The boundary between 'speaker' and 'audience' becomes permeable or disappears altogether."[38] Together as one, preacher and listeners walk with God, guided by Scripture.

Second, and perhaps even more importantly, when caught up in the emotion and imagination that relevance invariably evokes, the audience itself becomes a unified body. As the preacher, in the relevance submoves, describes a shared situation that happens in "our" world and provides examples of how things happen in "our" lives, a community is being created rhetorically. A sense of unity is nurtured: "We are in this together." Neuroscience and cognitive psychology have shown that the "sharing of strong emotions within a group plays a central role in the formation of group cohesion. . . . Humans are hardwired to share in the emotional experiences of those around them, and that shared emotional experience is, to a large extent, what constitutes us as a group."[39] It may well be that, in a sense, the preacher is facilitating the formation of an *ideal* audience that would inhabit God's *ideal* world as projected by each pericope of Scripture. Such an audience is constituted by the very event of the sermon, as the preacher calls members, on behalf of their God, to experience the text + theology: "'Come,' our God invites us, 'come and live with me in my ideal world.'" And as the audience resolves to do so, according to the specific, striking, and singular application tailor-made for it, there is an excitation of the consciousness of a shared identity: the people of God living with their God. Thus sermonic language creates an audience in the relevance submoves

---

37. Buechner, *Telling the Truth*, 8. Or as David L. Larsen put it, "Our objective is to preach subcutaneously—that is, to get under the skin of our hearers" (*Telling the Old, Old Story*, 191). To a dermatologist, this makes perfect sense!

38. Selby, *Not with Wisdom of Words*, 146–47.

39. Selby, *Not with Wisdom of Words*, 154.

by evoking shared emotional states through the collective terms, unifying phrases, and bonding illustrations employed (as well as through the application proffered). And thereby the people of God are becoming—progressively and increasingly, pericope by pericope and sermon by sermon—citizens of the divine kingdom: an *ideal* audience, indeed!

All that to say, know your audience. "And he [David] shepherded them according to the integrity of his heart, and with the skill of his hands he led them" (Ps. 78:72). If you want to be like David in his shepherding, you have to know your flock well. This means engaging in pastoral ministry with integrity of heart and with skillfulness of hands. Care for the sheep. Meet with the ones you are responsible for, at church, in their homes, at their workplaces. Work on your memory: get that church directory into your brain—remember faces, names, and details. Show concern, demonstrate compassion, be gentle. And develop an attitude of deference to the audience—not a patronizing demeanor or an obsequious one but a heart for them driven by genuine love. After all, they are God's people, and God's word was written to them. We preachers are interlopers, standing between God's word and God's people (to whom God's word was addressed), no doubt for a good purpose. But the fact remains that the saints of God are the important human entities in this equation. Love them, respect them, and bring God's word to them faithfully and to the best of your ability.

Above all, pray for your listeners. As a shepherd, that should be one of your primary responsibilities. Maintain their prayer requests on a list you pray through, monitor church prayer chains, keep track of online requests, and so on. But do not forget to pray particularly in connection with your preaching, praying for listeners before, during, and after each sermon, specifically that they may experience the particular pericope of the word of God in a potent way that transforms their lives. Paul wrote to his protégé Timothy that, even from a distance, "I unceasingly remember you in my prayers night and day" (2 Tim. 1:3).

Transitions

Transitioning from one move/submove to another move/submove requires some finessing so that the sermon as a whole flows fluently and coherently. I will assume that you have shaped sermon moves in such a way that there is a natural and logical flow between them, but a brief transition at the various seams can be helpful to smooth the flow even further and to give listeners an explicit link between the parts of the sermon.

Types of Transitions

There are a number of ways to accomplish these transitions. Here are a few of the more common ones.

Phrases and Statements

"In addition . . ."

"Moreover . . ."

"Besides . . ."

"However . . ."

"Despite this . . ."

"Let's build on that . . ."

"Let's go a step further . . ."

"Look again at . . ."

"Reconsider this . . ."

"The real question is . . ."

"What if . . ."

"You might be thinking/asking/questioning . . ."

"OK, now I want us to pay attention to this" (as you arrive at any important concept)

"Let's look at the text again" or "This is what God says" (to transition into a revelation submove)

"Here's what it looks like" or "Here's what the world thinks" (to transition into a relevance submove)

"This is what I'd like us to do in response" or "God calls for action on our part; let's commit to doing this" (to transition into the application move)[40]

Questions

"Why is this so?" (to proceed to explain something)

"What does the text say?" or "Do you know what God says about this?" (to transition into a revelation submove)

---

40. Numbering—"first . . . second . . . third . . ."—may also be considered among transitions. I rarely use numbers and would recommend you not use them either. We logocentric, science-based, enlightenment-fancying, nonartists have a deep and abiding love of numbering (and the slicing and dicing that goes with it). But avoid multiple levels of numbering. They are difficult for listeners to hear and understand. (Numbering is easier for readers to see and understand.) Numbers also make for more prominent seams between sections in sermons than one might desire.

"So how does this look in our lives?" or "Where do we see this in the world?" or "What does this matter to us?" (to transition into a relevance submove)

"What concretely do we do?" or "So how do we respond?" or "How can we put this into practice?" (to transition into the application move)

Rhetorical questions, as a rule, are helpful devices that can serve as transitions anywhere in the sermon. They gently push listeners to think and follow along with the preacher. Options other than those listed above include "Well, you might ask me . . . ?" or "Have you ever had the experience of . . . ?" and so on. Feel free to be creative.

When you want to answer questions that you feel (by quadruple think) your audience is asking, you could say, "But some of you will counter . . ." or "You might think . . ." or "Others will say this is contrary to . . ." and so on. If you are making a necessary detour from the main trajectory of the sermon, try this: "Stay with me now. I'll get us to our destination—just hang on with me for a bit." If you don't have much time to spare, say, "We're going to move rapidly—seat belts on, please."

Signposts

Transitioning involves both entering into a new move and exiting gracefully out of a completed move. Entry signposts indicate arrival; exit signposts indicate departure. For this, you do not have to create anything new: the labels of the moves themselves serve as signposts for effective transitions into and out of moves. Announce the label of the move up front (as an entry signpost) as you arrive at move I., and then state that same label again (as an exit signpost) as you depart move I. and before you state the label of move II. (as an entry signpost).

"We are going to see / look at . . . [state the move label: entry signpost]"

"We have just seen / looked at . . . [state the move label: exit signpost]"

You can create a number of variants based on this basic structure. (See below for more on these entry/exit signposts.)

Movements

Movements are obviously not spoken transitions, but if you have a wide enough stage, you might use your position to demarcate the moves of the sermon. For example, you might choose to preach the first move from stage right (the point of view of the preacher on stage), the second from stage left, and the third (application) from stage center (behind the lectern/pulpit).

In sum, use your sound pastoral (and common) sense as you employ transitions. Too many, too frequently, can make the sermon seem formulaic and pedantic and may actually draw (negative) attention to the transitions themselves, which ought to be transparent and unnoticeable. One important way of transitioning is silence—a brief pause before launching into the next move or submove.

Transitions are not—and ought not to be—complicated. There should be a sense of inevitableness to them, so much so that the listener is implicitly thinking, "Yes, of course, that's the best way to move from I. to II. [or A. to B.]." In any case, aim for naturalness and variety, without affectation or ornamentation. Simplicity always wins.

Oral Clarity and Signposting

Remember that you are speaking and being heard (oral-aural communication), not writing and being read (manual-ocular communication). The audience has only one chance to listen and understand (unless they are watching or listening to a recording that they can rewind). There are no visual cues in a sermon like underlining, italics, or bold fonts, as there are in scripted material. Neither are there paragraphs, indents, running heads, and the like to indicate to listeners where they are in a sermon.[41] Signposts, discussed above, are helpful for this purpose. They are explicit cues for hearers, signaling transitions into and out of moves. As was noted above, at the beginning and end of each move, state that move's label—it forms entry and exit signposts, respectively. For instance, based on the sermon map for Ephesians 1:15–23 (see below), at the beginning of move I. you might say, "Let's look at our foes' power" (entry signpost). At the end of move I. (i.e., after I.B. Relevance) you might want to say something like, "We've seen our foes' power" (exit signpost). Then as you enter move II. give the label for that move: "Now let's see God's power" (entry signpost). However, at the end of move II. (after II.B. Relevance) it is better to say the labels of *both* moves covered thus far: "We've seen our foes' power and also God's power" (exit signposts).[42] Now you are ready to enter

---

41. See Sunukjian, *Invitation to Biblical Preaching*, 266–99, for a helpful chapter on oral clarity. More about writing sermons for the ear can be found in chap. 8, "Producing Manuscripts."

42. Feel free, if you so desire, to expand on each of these signposts. If time permits and necessity demands, make the signposts a sentence or two long or a collection of phrases. That being said, also feel free to omit them, as I often do, to make transitions between moves more seamless and one-B-like (see chap. 4, "Creating Maps," and the sermon manuscripts in apps. C and D). Again, there is plenty of flexibility here.

the Application move. Do so smoothly, with something like, "So what can we do?" or "How do we respond?" or some other similar transition before stating the label of the Application move: "Let's now see our power: *Live powerfully!*" (another entry signpost). These signposts and their locations are shown below.

Ephesians 1:15–23

> [Entry signpost I. Foes' Power]
>
> I. Foes' Power
>> A. Revelation: The powerful supernatural foes arrayed against us and our fear of them [the list of supernatural foes (1:21); reason for their opposition (reflecting 1:10)]
>> B. Relevance: Fearful foes are operating today, in our culture, against us [illustration]
>
> [Exit signpost I. Foes' Power]
> [Entry signpost II. God's Power]
>
> II. God's Power
>> A. Revelation: God's incredible power in Christ (1:15–21) on behalf of believers, the body of Christ (1:22–23)
>> B. Relevance: This divine power in Christ shows up in our lives and is working for us [illustration]
>
> [Exit signposts I. Foes' Power and II. God's Power]
> [Entry signpost III. Our Power: *Live powerfully!*]
>
> III. Our Power: *Live powerfully!*

We have seen the importance of stating the labels of the moves as entry and exit signposts above. The ultimate goal of all these transitioning maneuvers is the streamlining of moves (and submoves) so that the progression from one to another is frictionless and almost seamless.[43] You want to avoid abrupt entries into and exits out of parts of the sermon. You can be as creative and flexible in your wording as you care to be, appropriate for your speaking style and for your audience. And there is plenty of freedom in how exactly these transitions are created. As was noted, after mastering these somewhat mechanical and recipe-driven operations as described above, feel free to omit them as you see

43. You might also want listeners to catch the submove labels as you enter or exit the appropriate revelation and relevance submoves (a form of entry/exit signposting, but of submoves). Using the labels of submoves as signposts can further enhance clarity, helping listeners (and you, the preacher) to be oriented to where the sermon is going. I confess I rarely use submove signposts, considering them obstacles to the kind of smoothness I am shooting for in my one-B sermons.

fit for some moves if they feel redundant or excessively repetitive, tending to produce overly bumpy seams.

Here is a sermon map for Genesis 26:1–33 (see chap. 2 for the derivation of its Theological Focus), a variation on the usual scheme; note the signposts in particular.[44]

Genesis 26:1–33
Theological Focus: "God's promised blessings are sure and obviate any attempt to secure them by deception in fear or retaliation against opposition—instead, reconciliation is called for."

[Entry signpost I. God Ensures] First we'll see that God ensures—the blessings he bestows are secure and cannot be lost.

I. God Ensures

    A. Revelation: Deception in fear manifests distrust in God's promised blessings (26:1–13)

    B. Relevance: We too, when fearful, distrust God's promises to us [illustration]

    C. Application: *Remember the promises!*

[Exit signpost I. God Ensures] We've seen that God ensures—his blessings to his people are safe and secure. In response, God's people remember his promises of blessing.

[Entry signpost II. World Envies] Now we'll see that the world envies—God's blessings on his people evoke the enmity of the world.

II. World Envies

    A. Revelation: Not retaliating against opponents manifests trust in God's promises (26:14–29)

    B. Relevance: We too, oppressed unjustly, will be tempted to retaliate [illustration]

    C. Application: *Refrain from retaliation!*

[Exit signposts I. God Ensures and II. World Envies] We've seen that God ensures his blessings for his people and that, as a result, the world envies those who are blessed by God. In response, God's people are to refrain from retaliation.

[Entry signpost III. Isaac Entrusts] Now let's take a look at the patriarch's attitude in the midst of opposition—Isaac entrusts himself to God.

44. The signposts, though they give much clarity to sermons, can also become mechanical, repetitive, and ponderous. Therefore, I chose to omit some of them when I preached this sermon. (See app. D for an outline of the manuscript I created to preach Gen. 26).

III. Isaac Entrusts

    A. Revelation: Reconciling with opponents manifests trust in God's promises (26:30–31)

    B. Relevance: We find it difficult to reconcile with our enemies [illustration]

    C. Application: *Reconcile with grace!*

[Exit signposts I. God Ensures, II. World Envies, and III. Isaac Entrusts] We've seen that God ensures blessings for his people, that the world envies those who are blessed by God, and that Isaac forms a model for believers, entrusting himself to God when facing opposition. Like him, God's people can respond to their opponents by reconciling with grace.

I employed the Focus Splitting maneuver to shape the sermon into three moves: God's promises to Isaac and his distrustful response (the negative story in the pericope); Isaac's nonretaliation against enemies and his trust in God (the positive story in the pericope); and Isaac's reconciliation with his opponents (the conclusion of the pericope). So there are three submoves of revelation, one in each move, and three corresponding submoves of relevance. Rather than give a single application at the end as move IV., I decided to provide a three-pronged application on responding to opposition, with a portion in each of the three moves: *Remember the promises! Refrain from retaliation!* and *Reconcile with grace!* The advantage of separating the trio of responses was that each one became part of the move most pertinent to that prong of application, giving the whole sermon a greater sense of cohesion.[45]

Verse-by-Verse Preaching?

In chapter 2, "Discerning Theology," we discussed the discrimination between significant and insignificant matters in the text—one way to determine the text's saying on the way to discerning the text's *doing* (pericopal theology). Let me address that issue of significance and insignificance a bit more here.

Remember that what we are trying to do in a sermon is discern the theology of the text and derive its application for listeners—that is, facilitate their experience of the text + theology. We are not necessarily going verse by verse, giving a line-by-line running commentary on the text, which, unfortunately, is

45. Now is a good time to check out the transitions in the sermon manuscripts for Eph. 1:1–14 and Gen. 26:1–33 (apps. C and D, respectively).

a fairly common practice in pulpits.[46] I heartily echo Henry Mitchell's sentiments on verse-by-verse expository preaching, which, he said, "gives a wide
variety of sermon ideas and deals with none of them."[47] Such messages veer
toward becoming lectures; they dissect out the text's saying but neglect what
the text as a whole is *doing*. And without discerning the latter, such lectures
have no valid basis for application; sermons they are not.

For instance, in a sermon that goes verse by verse, tackling the pericope we
are about to examine, Ephesians 3:14–21, the preacher might start off with
Paul bowing his knees (3:14) and draw attention to the apostle's posture of
humility, which reflects a humble heart. A brief digression may be provided
on appropriate attitudes (and postures?) God's people must adopt as they
pray. Then one would head off in the direction of Paul's mention of the Father and point out another appropriate attitude of the praying apostle: inti-
macy with God. Then the preacher may tackle Paul's petitions, the Father's
riches, our need for power, the Trinitarian emphasis, and so on, collecting
disjointed observations on the text's saying and making no attempt to link
them to the author's *doing* in this pericope.[48] Now you might counter, "But
these elements are in the text, so are they not important?" Yes, they are in
the text, but the question is, How do they contribute to the author's *doing*
(pericopal theology), and how important are they in that contribution (significance versus insignificance)? Answering these questions is ultimately an
exercise in synthesis.

Here is the Theological Focus of Ephesians 3:14–21: "Believers, increasingly
conformed to Christ in faith by the Spirit, and comprehending, in community,
the immensity of Christ's love, glorify God, who dwells in them." So in this
particular case, Paul's posture and his beseeching of the heavenly Father are
not little sideshows that indicate proper attitudes of prayer; rather, they show
the intensity of Paul's desire that his readers become "increasingly conformed
to Christ . . . comprehending . . . the immensity of Christ's love." The reason
the A/author chose to include those elements describing the apostle's prayer
in the pericope is to emphasize the importance of what Paul was praying
about—the content of his prayer. What about the wordplay of "Father," *patēr*,
and "family," *patria* (3:14, 15)? In light of 2:19 (remember that 2:19–22 is
what Paul is referring to in 3:14 with "for this reason"), which mentions God's
household, the paronomasia further strengthens that image of a family. Paul is
fervently, humbly, and intensely praying to the Father that we, the members of

46. As we have seen in sermon mapping (chap. 4, "Creating Maps"), there is no constraint
that we should follow the text order in our maps or in our sermons.
47. Mitchell, *Black Preaching*, 118.
48. This was actually part of a student sermon in one of my classes.

that divine household, headed by and named for the Father, may be "increasingly conformed to Christ . . . comprehending . . . the immensity of Christ's love." Notice that the wordplays and other textual curiosities are not being considered for their own idiosyncratic interest; rather, they are coordinated with authorial *doing* (pericopal theology). If your diagnosis (discernment of the theology) is accurate, then every symptom you detect in the patient (every element of the text) will corroborate and validate your diagnosis (contribute to the pericopal theology: intrapericopal consistency). If you cannot link all the textual observations with what you believe is the theology of the pericope, then your interpretation of the theology is suspect.

It goes without saying that some elements and clues we detect in the text, even though they aid and abet the theological thrust/force, are not significant enough to warrant a mention in the time-constrained event of the sermon. This is why, in my commentary on Ephesians 3:14–21 below, I did not mention Paul's posture or the fatherhood/family wordplay. As I have just shown, they certainly do contribute in their own way to the theology, but they do so relatively insignificantly for sermon purposes.[49] For a sermon, within the constraints of time allotted, the preacher has to make some judicious decisions as to what to include and what to exclude. Remember, simplicity *always* wins.

---

49. You will find a plethora of observations like those in my monograph commentaries, but only a small fraction thereof should ever show up in sermons.

Ephesians and the Jacob Story[50]

6. Ephesians 3:14–21

This pericope is the continuation of Ephesians 2:11–22 (after which came the "digression" of 3:1–13). Paul concludes Ephesians 2 by saying that believers have been re-created as a holy temple, the dwelling of God (2:20–22). Here we find out how they should function as this "temple" and "holy dwelling" of God.

Paul, the one who became part of God's grand purpose by the "working of his power" (3:7), now prays that God would grant his readers to be "strengthened with power" (3:16). In other words, God wants the Ephesians to join him in this divine plan for the cosmos as he empowers them for this purpose.

Power for believers.

But how are they to play their part? The structure of the pericope is focused on the love of Christ (C, D, C').[51]

A   *every* (*pas*) family (3:14–15)
  B   strengthened with *power* (*dynamis*) (3:16)
    C   that Christ may dwell; rooted and founded in love (3:17)
      D   breadth and length and height and depth (3:18)
    C'   love of Christ (3:19)
  B'   to him who is *able* (*dynamai*); according to the *power* (*dynamis*) (3:20)
A'   to *all* (*pas*) generations (3:21)

There are three purpose clauses here: "that he may grant . . ." (3:16), "that you might be able . . ." (3:18), and "that you may be filled . . ." (3:19), each building on the preceding one. Empowerment by the Spirit for Christ's indwelling (3:16–17; this is not the event that occurs at justification but the ongoing indwelling and manifestation of Christ that occurs with sanctification: Christ being formed in the believer) leads to a comprehension of Christ's love in the context of community, where the magnitude of Christ's love is experienced visibly and tangibly. Thus there is an imperatival element here, the exhortation of believers to be active in love for one another. This comprehension

50. As was noted earlier, I have skipped commentaries on some pericopes altogether (providing only their Theological Foci), both to give you a chance to do your own work on them and to keep the current volume to a manageable size. My remarks on all these texts are available at http://www.homiletix.com/preaching2019/commentaries. For expanded curations of these texts, see Kuruvilla, *Ephesians*, 99–112, 113–32; and Kuruvilla, *Genesis*, 355–67, 368–82.

51. Modified from Heil, *Ephesians*, 25–26. Similar elements are italicized.

(and expression) of love, in turn, leads to the church being filled to the fullness of God, thus glorifying God and becoming the temple / holy dwelling of God it was intended to be (3:21; 2:20–22). In the Old Testament the construction of the tabernacle and the temple was followed by their filling with divine glory (Exod. 25–31; 35–40; 40:34–35; 1 Kings 5–9; 8:10–11); so also here in the New Testament (Eph. 2:19–22; 3:16–19). There is clearly an implication in this pericope that the fullness and glory of God is manifest in this temple of his people only as they experience and express the multidimensional love of Christ.

> Power for believers through the Spirit so that Christ may indwell them and thus they may understand the love of Christ and manifest it.

The thrust of this pericope is that, through the power of the Spirit and in faith, believers are increasingly conformed to Christ (his indwelling them). Thus they are able, as they live in community, to comprehend the immeasurable extent of Christ's love. Their conformation to Christ's image enables this love—manifested in community—to grow and flourish. Through all this they become, more and more, the temple of God, his fullness in them. And thereby God is glorified by the body of Christ.

> God empowers believers through the Spirit so that Christ may indwell them and thus they may understand the love of Christ and manifest it, thus becoming the dwelling of the Spirit, the temple of God's fullness.

Here is a simpler version.

> **Believers, increasingly conformed to Christ in faith by the Spirit, and comprehending, in community, the immensity of Christ's love, glorify God, who dwells in them.**

Here is a map for this pericope with the submoves of revelation and relevance (deliberately brief, in the interest of space).

I. God's Goal: Conformity to Christ
   A. Revelation: Increasing conformity to Christ: the work of the Father (3:14–16a), the Spirit (3:16b), and the Son (3:17a)
   B. Relevance: What it means to *not* look like Christ [specific examples of how we live in an *un*-Christlike fashion: selfishness, everyone for himself/herself; illustration][52]

---

52. Notice that all of my relevance submoves in this map deal with the negative—how life looks when we are not aligned with the theology of the text: selfishness, lovelessness, and not bringing glory to God.

II. God's Means: Love of Christ
   A. Revelation: Experiencing and expressing the love of Christ happens only in community (3:17b–19a)
   B. Relevance: The consequence of *un*-Christlike selfishness is lovelessness [illustration]
III. God's Purpose: Glory in Community
   A. Revelation: Conformity to Christ and the expression of Christ's love lead to the glory of God, as the community becomes full of Christ (3:19b–21)
   B. Relevance: *Un*-Christlikeness and lovelessness do not bring glory to God, for outsiders do not see Christ's fullness in believers [illustration]
IV. *Look like Christ by loving like Christ!*[53]

7. Ephesians 4:1–16

Selfless and loving exercise of Christ's grace gifts by leaders and saints, which leads to peaceful unity, builds up the body to the mature stature of its head, Christ.

Here's a suggested map.

I. Christ: The Head of the Body[54]
   A. Revelation: God's goal of peaceful unity (4:1–6);[55] Christ, the gift giver, the head of the body (4:7–10), accomplishing that unity
   B. Relevance: Lack of unity in the body [specific examples]
II. Leaders: The Facilitators of the Body
   A. Revelation: Gifted leaders are the equippers, the facilitators of the saints (4:11–12a), moving the body to maturity (4:13–14)
   B. Relevance: Dangers of immaturity of the body [illustration]
III. Saints: The Builders of the Body
   A. Revelation: Gifted saints are the ministers, the builders of the body (4:12b, 16), growing the body into Christ, in love (4:15–16)
   B. Relevance: Spiritual gifts, a brief excursus (Rom. 13; 1 Cor. 13; 1 Pet. 4)[56]
IV. *Bodybuilders, let's get to work!*

53. I will let you figure out specific, striking, and singular applications for the sermon maps in this chapter.

54. I chose a map here with moves that demonstrate the roles of the gifting head (Christ), the gifted facilitators (leaders), and the gifted builders (saints).

55. Conceivably, "God's goal of peaceful unity" could be a separate move of its own, preceding this one; however, for the sake of simplicity I've combined it with Christ's role as part of I.A.

56. Since this pericope does not deal with specific gifts (other than those of the leaders/facilitators), a brief excursus of spiritual gifts may be in order.

6. Genesis 29:31–30:24

Jacob is now married—to two sisters, Leah and Rachel. Though Leah is unloved, her womb is open, and she proceeds to bear four sons in what is literarily rapid succession (Gen 29:30–35a). Rather than speaking to Jacob, Leah addresses God in the naming of each son, hoping against hope that her husband's attitude toward her will change. There is no response from Jacob; in fact, the man does not even seem to play a role in the four instances of Leah's conception, let alone in the naming of his children!

> The pathos of Leah's unloved state [narrative detail].[57]

Also significant is that Leah stops bearing thereafter (29:35b; also 30:9). Why, we are not told. It cannot be age, for she seems fertile enough to bear three more children later (30:17–21). It could be a divine, sovereign act of womb closing, of course, but the text gives no hint about that. (We'll discover the reason later.)

> The pathos of Leah's unloved state culminating in a cessation of conception [narrative detail].

This frenzy of baby production by the unloved woman with the open womb puts the loved woman with the closed womb in the green grip of jealousy (30:1) and on a course of threatening, manipulation, monopolizing, exchanging, and domineering: a high-handed attitude. She wants to be blessed, but her idea of how this can be accomplished is way off the mark: she appeals to Jacob (not God!) in a fit of pique, demanding that he provide her with children (30:1–2). Nothing changes with that, so she takes matters into her own hands, arranging for her maid, Bilhah, to be Jacob's concubine (30:3–4): she will do anything to get blessed, even if it means offering Jacob a surrogate womb. But Leah counters with her own maid, Zilpah (30:9–13). So that strategy doesn't make Rachel a winner either.

At that juncture, Leah's oldest, Reuben, brings home mandrakes, considered in those days to be an aphrodisiac, and another exchange is accomplished: Jacob for mandrakes (30:14–16). Rachel gets the mandrakes; Leah gets Jacob. And with that we discover why Leah had stopped bearing: Rachel, apparently, had prevented Jacob from having relations with Leah (30:15). If she, Rachel, could not conceive, then her sister, Leah, certainly was not going to be permitted that privilege anymore. But despite all of these manipulative maneuvers, Rachel remains barren.

> The pathos of Leah's unloved state culminating in a cessation of conception. Rachel's attempts to force the blessing of pregnancy: throwing tantrums, arranging concubinage,

---

57. The narrative detail, being specific for the story's circumstances, is not really "theological" in the sense of going beyond the textual situation.

employing aphrodisiacs, preventing Leah from having relations with Jacob—all without
result [narrative detail]. Improper, high-handed posture in an attempt to experience
divine blessing.

Surprisingly, following the exchange, Leah continues to conceive and deliver not
once but thrice (30:17, 19, 21), after what had been negotiated as a one-night stand
(30:15). What happened? Were there more mandrakes that bought Leah a few more
nocturnal trysts with Jacob? Unlikely, since mandrakes are not mentioned after 30:14–16
(they had no effect on Rachel the first time anyway). Did Leah manage to consort with
Jacob unbeknown to Rachel? Unlikely. Nothing seems to have gotten past that scheming
woman thus far. Did Rachel forget the one-night deal she had made? Unlikely. With the
score now Leah 5 and Rachel 0, how could she forget? The only explanation is that Rachel
had given up. Nothing had worked for her, not jealousy, not tantrums, not concubinage,
not obstruction, not aphrodisiacs—nothing! The narrator is hereby implying that Rachel
had surrendered, renouncing her manipulative and conniving and deceptive tendencies.

No wonder, then, that immediately after we are nudged toward such a conclusion,
we are told, "*Then* God remembered Rachel and listened to her" (30:22). God remembered Rachel *when Rachel had given up* and, perhaps, when she called on God for the
first time in the narrative (God is said to have "*listened* to her"). Thus we learn that
the proper posture to experience the blessings of God is not one of high-handedness,
grasping, exploitation, and overbearing. If one is to experience the blessings of God, one
must take on the posture of openhandedness, of letting go, of gracious generosity and
humility, and of dependence on God.

Rachel's attempts to force the blessing of pregnancy: throwing tantrums, arranging concubinage, employing aphrodisiacs, preventing Leah from having relations with Jacob—all
without result. And so Rachel gives up and prays, appealing to God. Then she conceives
[narrative detail]. Proper posture for experiencing divine blessing: submission.

And with that, quite suddenly, it seems that Jacob too has come to his senses. After
all the frenzied conceptions, gestations, and parturitions in his household, he too has
fallen at the same place of helplessness as Rachel. Jacob realizes that if he is to experience God's blessings, he has to resolve his unfinished business back home in Canaan
involving a sibling and a parent whom he has treated most shabbily. It appears that
Jacob has perceived—as has Rachel—that manipulation and conniving and deception
never succeed. Rather, dependence on God alone does. And so, he says, "I have to go
back home" (30:25).

Rachel's attempts to force the blessing of pregnancy: throwing tantrums, arranging concubinage, employing aphrodisiacs, preventing Leah from having relations with Jacob—all

without result. And so Rachel gives up and prays, appealing to God. Then she conceives. And at her delivery of Joseph, Jacob too realizes the true posture for experiencing divine blessings. He plans to return home to take care of some unfinished business [narrative detail confirming proper posture for receiving divine blessing].

Converting this long-winded statement that has quite a bit of narrative detail into a crisp Theological Focus that removes the particularities of the story, we get the following.

High-handedness precludes the experience of God's blessing, but faithful dependence on God brings it about.

Here is a suggested map.

   I. How *Not* to Experience God's Blessing
      A. Revelation: Faithless high-handedness: wrong attitude (jealousy, 29:31–30:1a); wrong appeal (threatening, 30:1b–2); wrong action (manipulation, 30:3–13); wrong alternative (mandrakes, 30:14–15); wrong artifice (trickery, 29:35; 30:9, 15)[58]
      B. Relevance: What some of our own wrong attitudes, appeals, actions, alternatives, and artifices are [illustration]
   II. How to Experience God's Blessing
      A. Revelation: Faithful dependence (30:16–24, Leah's three children implying Rachel's surrender, prayer to God, and the result: pregnancy)
      B. Relevance: How we often come to the end of our tether before we learn the error of our high-handed ways
   III. *Let go . . . and let God bless!*

7. Genesis 30:25–31:16

God sovereignly works to bless his children, as they work responsibly, even in adverse conditions.

Here is a map.

   I. God's Sovereignty
      A. Revelation: Jacob's departure in line with God's will (30:25–26, 29–33; 31:3); Laban's deception (30:28, 35–36); God's hand at work (30:30, 43; 31:5, 7, 9, 11–13)

58. Yes, I got carried away with alliteration.

  B. Relevance: In times of opposition and turmoil, we wonder if God is working at all [illustration], but he is, even when that work is imperceptible

 II. Humanity's Responsibility

  A. Revelation: Jacob's claim for wages (30:29–31, 32–33); his determination to work (30:31, 33); his industry (30:25–42);[59] his obedience (31:3–16)

  B. Relevance: In the days of difficulty, we too tend to neglect our responsibilities to stick to the task[60]

 III. *Labor for God, with God!*

---

59. In the sermon, the preacher must necessarily summarize this rather intricate account.

60. With this relevance submove, the application becomes clear: Stick to it and *labor for God, with God!*

6

Illustrating Ideas

Artistic import, unlike verbal meaning, can only be exhibited. . . .
So the questions arise in art criticism: what is the artist commenting
on, what does he say, and how does he say it? These are, I believe,
spurious questions. He is not saying anything, not even about the
nature of feeling; he is *showing*.[1]

L et's take stock of where we are. We first created a long-term plan for
  preaching, chose a biblical book, divided it into pericopes, and performed the preliminary explorations of the texts (chap. 1, "Getting
Ready"). Then we discerned the theologies of the pericopes, with a Theological Focus for each (chap. 2, "Discerning Theology"). Next we derived a
specific, striking, and singular application for each pericope and its theology
(chap. 3, "Deriving Application"). Then we created sermon maps (chap. 4,
"Creating Maps") and fleshed them out with revelation and relevance (chap. 5,
"Fleshing Moves"). Now we move on to illustrating ideas.

Functions of Illustrations

Illustrations have four essential functions: to clarify, convince, concretize,
and captivate.[2]

1. Langer, *Feeling and Form*, 379, 394 (emphasis in original).
2. For a somewhat parallel classification, see T. Warren, "Supporting Materials," 106.

Illustrations Clarify

The primary function of illustrations is to clarify for listeners anything introduced in the sermon that may need explication. Charles Spurgeon put it well:

> Often when didactic speech fails to enlighten our hearers we may make them see our meaning by opening a window and letting in the pleasant light of analogy. . . . To every preacher of righteousness as well as to Noah, wisdom gives the command, "A window shalt thou make in the ark." You may build up laborious definitions and explanations and yet leave your hearers in the dark as to your meaning; but a thoroughly suitable metaphor will wonderfully clear the sense.[3]

He was right about comparing illustrations with windows (itself an illustration, by the way). The verb *illustrate* comes from the Latin *lústrâre*, "to make bright." Light and luster are let into a sermon by illustrations. While preaching on Ephesians 1:1–14, I observed in the sermon that God's plans were deliberate, not capricious or whimsical. He knows what he's doing, unlike us humans. I then provided an illustration—in two parts: a factoid (numbers of decisions humans make each year) plus an anecdote (of a faulty decision that I made)—to clarify that while humans constantly err in their decision making, God determines and acts perfectly.[4] Illustrations clarify.

Illustrations Convince

In the example referred to, while I was clarifying I was also implicitly convincing my hearers, first with the statistic provided and then with the personal story of something foolish I actually did, that they—and in fact all humans—are not very different in error-prone decision making. Clarifying and convincing go hand in hand, one aiding the other. Especially with a real-life story about someone who is close to or part of the audience, the conviction begins to take hold: "Yes, we're all like that; it has happened to me too! This is true!" Illustrations convince.

Illustrations Concretize

Not entirely separate from the clarifying and convincing functions of illustrations is their concretizing function: making things real, visible, and near. An illustration, like a picture, is worth more than a thousand nonillustrative

3. Spurgeon, *Lectures to My Students*, 349.
4. See app. C for an annotated manuscript of that sermon.

words. While such concretizing by means of illustrations may—and should—occur throughout the sermon, it is of particular importance in application. There illustrations play a key role in helping listeners visualize a specific and actual response, in addition to clarifying what they are to do and convincing them that such a response is appropriate (all part of the "show" of application; see chap. 3). The application statement may be fairly specific already: "At least once a week, make sure you bless God for what he is doing in your life" (the application in my Eph. 1:1–14 sermon—the "tell" of application). But it is made even more concrete when I illustrate it—that is, when I show someone doing it or, as I did, detail my own plans for doing it. This shows the audience what performing the application actually looks like. Illustrations concretize.

Illustrations Captivate

The fourth function that illustrations serve is to captivate, or to keep one's attention.

Conversational rates of speech vary from 140 to 180 words per minute. Experiments have shown that listeners comprehend normal speech successfully even when it is speeded up by compression to 425 words per minute.[5] This means that there is a significant gap between the rate of speaking and the rate of comprehending what is spoken. Our audiences can understand our sermons about three times faster than we can deliver them. This time differential is enough to seduce minds to wander. Add to this the short attention spans of average listeners, the cares and concerns of life weighing on our congregations, plans for Sunday lunch, the availability of smartphones, and other potential distractions in a large room holding a large number of people, and we have the perfect recipe for people abandoning us mentally in the middle of our sermons.

According to one study, the heart rates of students listening to a lecture drop continuously from the time the lecture begins until the time it ends (at the seventy-five-minute mark). But a five-minute break, or a change of activity in the middle, can restore heart rates to starting levels.[6] Which brings us to this fourth, somewhat indirect role of illustrations: to captivate. Illustrations provide listeners a space to breathe and a spot to rest, signaling a subtle shift in what's happening up front, akin to a dash of spice in a dish. Illustrations make for easier listening and can help restore some of the naturally sagging attention levels and flagging heart rates. Despite biblical precedent, I would

5. Wingfield, "Cognitive Factors in Auditory Performance."
6. Bligh, What's the Use of Lectures?, 57–59.

not recommend going on until midnight as Paul did (Acts 20:7–8), with a disastrous consequence for one of his listeners (20:9). Even that catastrophe apparently didn't faze our preacher, who kept on going until daybreak (20:10–11). Boring your audience is, if not a sin, at least close to being one. Haddon W. Robinson once said, "I have come closer to being bored out of the Christian faith than being reasoned out of it. I think we underestimate the deadly gas of boredom. It is not only the death of communication, but the death of life and hope."[7] Don't enervate; instead captivate—with illustrations.

Illustrations and Emotions

Illustrations work more by evoking emotion than by engaging reason. The ancients called this "presence." Aristotle, in the fourth century BCE, recommended that orators "set things 'before the eyes' . . . by words that signify actuality."[8] The first-century-CE Roman rhetorician Quintilian affirmed this notion of presence "by which the images of absent things are presented to the mind in such a way that we seem actually to see them with our eyes and have them physically present to us."[9] Speeches, according to Quintilian, should go "further than the ears" and be "displayed to [the] mind's eye."[10] Invariably, such captivations of the audience with presence involve their emotions.

> No doubt, simply to say "the city was stormed" is to embrace everything implicit in such a disaster, but this brief communiqué, as it were, does not touch [penetrat, "penetrate"] the emotions. If you expand everything which was implicit in the one word ["stormed"], there will come into view flames racing through houses and temples, the crash of falling roofs, the single sound made up of many cries, the blind flight of some, others clinging to their dear ones in a last embrace, shrieks of children and women, the old men whom an unkind fate has allowed to live to see this day; then will come the pillage of property, secular and sacred, the frenzied activity of plunderers carrying off their booty and going back for more, the prisoners driven in chains before their captors, the mother who tries to keep her child with her, and the victors fighting one another wherever the spoils are richer. "Sack of a city" does, as I said, comprise all these things, but to state the whole is less than to state all the parts.[11]

7. Quoted in Henderson, *Culture Shift*, 19.
8. Aristotle, *Art of Rhetoric*, 399, 405 (3.10.1410b; 3.11.1411b).
9. Quintilian, *Orator's Education*, 59–61 (6.2.29–30).
10. Quintilian, *Orator's Education*, 375–77 (8.3.62).
11. Quintilian, *Orator's Education*, 379 (8.36.70).

Quintilian concluded, "Emotions will ensue just as if we were present at the event itself."[12]

As we have noted before, neuroscientists have established that the same areas of the brain seem to be active in three discrete states: when the *speaker* experiences something, when the *speaker* recalls and recounts that same experience, and when the *listener* hears the speaker's recounting.[13] And the emotions play a significant role in this resonance between speaker and listener. The power of illustrations lies in the fact that they enthrall listeners not just with reason but also with emotion, enhancing their potential to clarify, convince, concretize, and captivate.

Daniel Goleman was on to something when he declared in a best seller, "The old paradigm held an ideal of reason freed of the pull of emotion. The new paradigm urges us to harmonize head and heart."[14] Increasingly, cognitive psychology is showing that our decisions are affected by emotions far more than we realize.[15] Emotions are an integral part of who a human being is. This is important for preachers, who are in the application business, to recognize: "Unless we are reaching people on all levels—mind, heart, will—we are not even communicating, let alone motivating. . . . A major part of the totality of the preaching-event is the joining of the affective and cognitive."[16] One of the three main means of persuasion of an audience through a speech, Aristotle declared, was the use of *pathos*, the passion of the speaker and the emotions evoked in listeners.[17] "*Pathos* . . . is the means of persuasion that is most concerned with understanding how to *move* the audience into caring about and then acting on what is said," so much so that "listeners tend to *unconsciously* persuade themselves" as a result.[18]

12. Quintilian, *Orator's Education*, 61 (6.2.32).

13. Stephens, Silbert, and Hasson, "Speaker-Listener Neural Coupling"; and Zadbood et al., "How We Transit Memories to Other Brains." While the research is still in a nascent stage, the existence of mirror neurons in primates has excited a great deal of attention. Motor neurons discharge when a person performs an action, but apparently a subset of these neurons also discharge when the person views *someone else* performing a similar action (mirror motor neurons). And it seems there are mirror neuron subsets of sensory nerves as well: they fire, for instance, when a person is touched and *also* when that person sees *someone else* being touched. The ramifications for imitation (by mirror motor neurons) and empathy (by mirror sensory neurons) are considerable. Mirror sensory neurons may explain much of listeners' emotional response to speakers, particularly to their illustrations. See Rizzolatti, "The Mirror Neuron System."

14. Goleman, *Emotional Intelligence*, 29.

15. See, for instance, Bechara et al., "Deciding Advantageously before Knowing," 1294.

16. Sleeth, *God's Word and Our Words*, 69.

17. Aristotle, *Art of Rhetoric* (1.2.1356a).

18. Hogan and Reid, *Connecting with the Congregation*, 78–79 (emphasis in original). Of course, if you want your audience to care about something, you must care about it yourself, and that care, concern, and passion for what you are talking about must be manifest in the

We preachers, as guardians of our flocks, as their pastors and shepherds, must treat our listeners holistically, as integral humans. Humans are not disembodied brains or mere buckets of emotion tossed here and there. We should acknowledge and respect the integral association of reason and emotion in those who listen to us. We must involve both the cognition and emotion of listeners to stir volition—to effect life transformation through God's word by the Spirit. And illustrations play a significant role in this coalition of mind and heart.

At this point, one might wonder whether the preacher's engagement of the audience's emotions is a form of manipulation. Yes, one can manipulate audiences because words have power and because the pastoral office has authority. But don't forget that one can manipulate people with logic as well, even with seemingly rational numbers when they are presented in less than honest fashion. Mark Twain once said, quoting Benjamin Disraeli (who never said this), "There are three kinds of lies: lies, damned lies, and statistics."[19] This is all the more reason that the preacher be, first, a spiritual person after God's own heart. Otherwise one is nothing but a demagogue and not to be trusted. Preachers must handle the power of words and the authority of their office with great caution. No wonder James warns, "Not many should become teachers, brothers [and sisters], knowing that we will receive greater judgment" (3:1).

In sum, treating our listeners with respect as the people of God involves comprehending the importance of both their reason and their emotions. And unless the latter are also engaged, habits cannot be formed. Unless habits are formed, dispositions cannot be created. Unless dispositions are created, character cannot be cultivated. And unless character is cultivated, Christlikeness cannot be developed in the power of the Spirit.

All of this is true for every element of the sermon, not just for illustrations. Nonetheless, we preachers need to be careful in our choices of illustrations. Not just any illustration will do to clarify, convince, concretize, and captivate. We must make sure to engage not just listeners' reason but also their emotions.

Types of Illustrations

Here are the main categories of illustrations preachers commonly use.

---

preaching event. "The heart of the matter as regards arousing emotions, so far as I can see, lies in being moved by them oneself" (Quintilian, *Orator's Education*, 59 [6.2.26]).

19. Twain, "Chapters from My Autobiography," 471. Even something as simple as an average can be misleading. If ten of us make $100 a day, but two others make $1,000 a day, the average—$250 a day—is quite skewed.

Narration

When one hears the word *illustrations*, stories of different kinds, shapes, and colors come to mind—narration. Narratives that work well as illustrations are about people and success and are proximal to the audience (i.e., stories they can relate to without much difficulty). Narration can be fact or fiction. Here's one, and I'm not sure which it is, fact or fiction—hence the qualifier "A story is told . . ."

> A story is told of one of the czars of Russia who, when walking in his palace park one day, came upon a sentry standing before a small patch of weeds. The czar asked him what he was doing there. The sentry did not know; all he could say was that he had been ordered to his post by the captain of the guard. The czar then sent his aide to ask the captain. The captain replied that regulations had always called for a sentry at that particular spot.
>
> His curiosity by now aroused, the czar ordered an investigation. No living person at the court could remember a time when there had not been a sentry at the post, and none could say what he was guarding.
>
> Finally, the archives were opened, and after a long search, the mystery was solved. The records showed that over a hundred years ago, Catherine the Great had planted a rosebush in that plot of ground and a sentry had been assigned to see that no one trampled it.
>
> Catherine the Great was now long dead. The rosebush was now long dead. But orders were orders, and for over a century, the spot where the rosebush had once been was being guarded by men who knew not what they were guarding.

Fiction and parables and hypothetical situations can all be used as illustrations. These would usually begin with something like, "Suppose it is nighttime, and you come to the scene of an accident . . ."; or "Let's say you are the bride's father and . . ."; and so on.[20] If a story is not true, please don't tell it as if it is or as if it happened to you.[21]

You might want to consider occasionally taking on the role of characters in a narrative pericope to bring vividness to the account and to hit home the thrust of the text—also a form of narration. For instance, to emphasize how strongly Esau felt about his deception by Jacob (Gen. 26:34–28:9; see commentary in chap. 3), I read 27:41: "So Esau bore a grudge against Jacob . . . and said in his heart, 'The days of mourning for my father are approaching;

---

20. Modified from Delnay, *Fire in Your Pulpit*, 63.

21. I once had a student preacher use an illustration in which he and his wife were shown arguing about his marital infidelity. The student, we listeners knew, was married, and he lost us all for the rest of the sermon, worried as we were about his marriage vows. In the debriefing after the sermon, he confessed that it was a made-up story.

then I will kill my brother Jacob.'" And then I continued, in Esau's voice, "I'm gonna kill that kid brother. I'm gonna finish him off. Just wait." In a sermon on Genesis 32:1–32 (see chap. 7), I read 32:28, "And he [God] said, 'Your name will no longer be called "Jacob," but "Israel," for you have fought with God and with men, and you have endured.'" Then I threw in this:

> No more grabbing of heels, snatching of dreams, clutching at straws, chasing of wind. No more Yakov. No more chasing. Henceforth "Israel." "Israel," meaning "God fights." No more will you grab heels. No more will you *need* to grab heels. Because, you know what? God fights for you.
>
> *I'm gonna be your fighter. You don't have to fight any more. You don't have to chase anything anymore. You don't have to run after anything anymore. I'm gonna fight for you, Israel.*
>
> "Israel"—God fights . . . for you.

Not only was I attempting to adopt God's voice in the italicized portion, but I was also subtly identifying the community of God's people with Jacob by using the slippery "you" everywhere. Is God addressing Jacob or the listeners? Both! Sometimes the thrust of the text is clarified more by this sort of role-playing than by description.

Also, for narration, current issues are usually more interesting and catchier than things that happened in the days of the czars. But not always. As long as you don't go into unnecessary historical detail, the story will drive itself. Success stories in which everyone lives "happily ever after" are also preferred, but again, not always. Tragedies aren't taboo, as long as they make a point and go somewhere. Chris Anderson, the owner of TED and curator of the immensely popular TED Talks, opines that "tales of failure, awkwardness, misfortune, danger, or disaster, told authentically, are often the moment when listeners shift from plain vanilla interest to deep engagements. They have started to share some of your [the speaker's] emotions."[22] Variety, of course, is highly recommended in the choice of narrations for any given sermon.

Confession

Confession may take the form of a story, but it is personal—you lived it. You saw what happened, and now you describe it so vividly that your listeners see it too. The other advantage of confession is that you are more comfortable and confident as you recount the event—after all, it is a part of your life you

22. Anderson, *TED Talks*, 60.

know well. Here's one embarrassing incident, a confession from my sermon on Ephesians 1:1–14 that I already alluded to: "The other day I was headed to the Landry Fitness Center. As was my habit, I grabbed a stick of gum on my way out. Collecting my gym bag and my keys and phone, I unwrapped the gum, threw the gum into the trash can, and carefully put the wrapper in my mouth. For paper, it tasted pretty good! If you haven't done things like that, just wait till you get to be my age. It's coming. Our choices are rotten. We're clueless."

Confessions (they don't have to be confessional, of course; any personal anecdote falls into this category) are best when they show the confessor in a dim light, as did my story above. People love it when the preacher is the victim of the events being recounted. Throwing a confession / personal experience into a sermon shows vulnerability and helps to humanize the preacher. After all, preacher and listeners are on the same spiritual journey together, none of them having "arrived." We are all broken and equally in need of divine grace. So there is nothing wrong with tactful self-disclosure. On the other hand, too much airing of dirty laundry should be avoided, lest it cause you to lose credibility and stand in the way of God's message reaching God's people. And please do not constantly harp about your dog, your hobbies, your family, and so on. People tire of them quickly.[23]

With both of these categories, narration and confession, you are primarily telling stories. Storytelling is an art—the art of painting pictures with words. The better the painter you are, the more your audience will hang on your words.

> Auditors respond to direct evidence such as statistical data with much greater levels of counterargument than they do to exemplars such as stories, illustrations, and personal testimony. . . . Whereas direct argument tends to put the auditor in a position as a judge or critic of the evidence, which inherently undermines the argument's power to convince, certain other kinds of discourse have the power to draw the listener *into* an immersive experience, a stance that tends to lower their resistance to being persuaded.[24]

Listeners' imaginations are the best props to use in a sermon (for more on props, see below). Stoke their imaginations with pictures that you paint with words. Such an immersive experience draws people into the story and diminishes pushback against whatever notion you are illustrating.

---

23. By the way, don't disclose confidences. Get permission to tell stories about people in your life, especially if those in the audience know them personally.
24. Selby, *Not with Wisdom of Words*, 128–29 (emphasis in original).

There needs to be some tension in any story you tell—suspense, intrigue, danger, puzzlement, curiosity, and so on. Don't leave out details that are the fine brushstrokes of the picture you are painting, but then again, make sure you don't overburden listeners with unnecessary information that misdirects them and camouflages the purpose of the illustration. Some kind of neat ending, a resolution, is also always necessary. Generally speaking, leaving listeners hanging, especially if the story has raised some unintended questions in their minds, should be avoided.[25] I would strongly recommend watching professional storytellers, and even stand-up comedians (more about humor later), for what stories they choose to tell (as well as for how they tell them). Beginning preachers would do well to try out their storytelling skills on others in one-on-one conversations and other non-pulpit speaking situations.

Enumeration

Enumeration is the use of statistics as illustrations. Keep in mind that statistics can quickly overwhelm if employed carelessly and thoughtlessly. They have to be concise and compact—not too many decimals for any given number (instead, round them off and/or use percentages). If it is important for listeners to remember the numerical data, repeat the numbers. Here's an example of a cleverly created enumeration: "Consider a protein made up of twenty amino acids that are arranged in a precise sequence. The probability of this protein forming by pure chance, by random association of amino acids is 1 in 1,000,000,000,000,000,000. On a practical level, this is like saying that we can flood the entire state of New York with quarters, one hundred feet high, and pick out, blindfolded, the one quarter we had painted red and thrown in with the rest." The denominator of the fraction is a mind-boggling number with an abundance of zeroes. But those incredible odds were immediately pictorialized—a sort of illustration within an illustration. Startling numbers are attention grabbing, but relating them to something visible or tangible (like coins flooding New York State) is even more impactful.

This coin illustration has been with me for many decades, and I have forgotten where I found it.[26] Don't let that happen when you collect illustrations (more on that below); keep track of their sources. Don't just copy a good one you find somewhere; make sure you note where you found it or who said it.

---

25. There are times when one can break a story in midstream and finish it later in the sermon (see chap. 7, "Crafting Introductions and Conclusions"). But such maneuvers are best avoided until you know exactly what you are doing and why and how.
26. Neither have I done the calculations to verify its mathematical accuracy.

Later on, that notation will come in handy, especially if someone challenges your numbers. Also, don't simply accept numbers put forth by anyone with an internet connection. Be discriminating and avoid sources that are dodgy. Ensure accuracy of your data or at least the respectability of their sources. Here are a few more enumerations.

Every day 5 percent of all garbage collectors get hurt on the job.[27]

Is 99 percent good enough? That would mean medical errors killing four thousand people each year.[28] And power outages for fourteen plus minutes every day. No, 99 percent isn't good enough.

Every two minutes a child under eighteen is arrested for a crime.[29] Every twelve hours a child five years or younger is murdered.[30]

If the sun were the size of an orange, about 3.5 inches in diameter, the earth would be a grain of sand about 30 feet away from the fruit. The nearest star, Proxima Centauri, by that same measure would be 1,500 miles away! And the diameter of the Milky Way (580 quadrillion miles in actuality) would be, on this sun-as-an-orange scale, 37 million miles. Even on this miniaturized scale, the numbers are mind-boggling.[31]

Quotation

Quotations are often employed with good effect to illustrate a concept or to emphasize a point. You are better off using surprising sources (I have used Ann Landers, Yogi Berra, and Randy Travis)[32] than relying on the usual suspects, like William Shakespeare, Winston Churchill, Chuck Swindoll, and others. In any case, contemporary and real-life quotations work better than historical or literary ones, unless they are bitingly relevant and apropos. In other words, Chuck is better than Winston or the Bard.

27. I made that up. It sounds reasonable, but I'm not a good source of on-the-job injuries suffered by garbage collectors. (Please don't concoct statistics.)

28. Apparently, four hundred thousand people die each year from medical errors, as reported in Makary and Daniel, "Medical Error."

29. The US Department of Justice reported 856,130 arrests of juveniles in 2016; https://www.ojjdp.gov/ojstatbb/crime/qa05101.asp; accessed May 1, 2018.

30. For the tables from the US Centers for Disease Control relating to this statistic, see https://webappa.cdc.gov/sasweb/ncipc/mortrate.html, accessed May 1, 2018.

31. This illustration takes only a bit of math to create, from actual sizes and distances of astronomical bodies.

32. Country music song titles like "How Can I Miss You When You Won't Go Away" (Dan Licks) and "If the Phone Doesn't Ring, It's Me" (Jimmy Buffet) can be gainfully cited. Make one up yourself. "They May Put Me in Prison, but They Can't Stop My Face from Breaking Out" has poignant meaning for a dermatologist, though I doubt it is an actual song. It ought to be.

Chasing the source and accuracy of a quotation can be quite a chore. The amount of error that has crept into others' sayings—usually to render them spicier—is unimaginable. For instance, John Kenneth Galbraith's "If all else fails, immortality can always be assured by spectacular error" is frequently quoted by one and all. There is only one problem: he never said it that way. What he actually wrote was, "If all else fails, immortality can always be assured by adequate error," which is not as striking as the mutated and commonly used version.[33] Attributions of pithy statements to Mark Twain are legion, as are those to Abraham Lincoln. Use them at your own risk. You can safely say, "Apparently [name of person being quoted] once said . . ."[34] If you don't know who said it, "An old philosopher once said . . ." or "Somebody once told me about . . ." will work.[35]

Exemplification

Exemplification includes all other kinds of illustrations that serve as examples of a notion you are trying to convey. These might include *definitions*. Check the dictionary or even an etymological dictionary,[36] or make up your own: "expensive means 'you don't get one.'" Or get your kids to define something; their creations are usually funny or eye-opening or both.[37]

Then there are *analogies*: "preachers are like footballs" (or fire hydrants—useful in emergencies but, oh, the daily indignities); "[something] is like the Holy Grail," or whatever. The possibilities are endless and limited only by your creativity.

You can use *cartoons* but describe them in words. I personally think these verbalized cartoons work much better than the visualized ones, at least in public speaking: you can control the speed and sequence at which the cartoon

33. Galbraith, *Money*, 204.

34. A decent place to play detective is https://quoteinvestigator.com.

35. Please don't say "quote . . . unquote" with quotations. That goes for prefaces like "Let me illustrate . . ." and "Here is a story to show . . ." as well. Neither do you have to provide footnotes in your sermon for your illustrations—where you discovered them, who published them, when, and on what page. But you do need to know where you found anything you cite. If someone asks you afterward, you should be able to point them to the source. See chap. 8, "Producing Manuscripts," for my take on plagiarism.

36. A good one is https://www.etymonline.com/.

37. I heard of a child who, when asked to read the word *resuscitation*, tried long and hard until she finally landed on "rescutation." I used that marvelous "definition" in a sermon once. There are entire websites dedicated to the funny sayings of kids. Who knows if they are true? Who cares? Use them as appropriate—but no more than one definition per sermon and then only infrequently. Kenny, age seven, supposedly declared about love and marriage, "It gives me a headache to think about that stuff. I'm just a kid. I don't need that kind of trouble." Me neither.

is gradually revealed, and the punch line is entirely yours to deliver, with all your listeners hearing it at the same instant. Here's one: "Two shipwrecked survivors are on a tiny tropical island. One is holding a bottle that floated onto the shore. He looks at the note and says to his companion, 'It's from your alumni association.'"[38]

Lists are good exemplifications too. "Did you know that the biggest fear of all Americans is public speaking? Death is number 7, with fear of heights, insects and bugs, financial problems, deep water, and sickness falling in between."[39] Consider using a list of predictions that failed. For instance, in 1925, during the heyday of the silent movie, Harry Warner of Warner Bros., when told of the latest technological advances that would enable sound to be synchronized with video, exclaimed, "Who the h___ wants to hear actors talk?"[40]

You can use whatever strikes your fancy as exemplification. I've employed *letters* as exemplifications and once used a "Nigerian scam" email to illustrate gullibility (only a fraction of such letters originate in Nigeria, apparently).

Finally, I've *read the text wrongly* to illustrate a concept, adding words in brackets: "And all who wish to live godly lives in Christ Jesus will [sometimes, occasionally, infrequently, rarely] be persecuted" (2 Tim. 3:12). Or "Husbands love your [godly, rich, beautiful, obedient, submissive, loving] wives" (Eph. 5:25). Be creative!

Visualization

Visualization is the use of what are commonly called "props." Such modalities include handouts, projected slides, audio, video, physical objects, and other similar means of illustration. Yes, the Bible does affirm that "the hearing ear and the seeing eye, Yahweh made them both" (Prov. 20:12), but—and I'm giving away my bias right at the outset—you are better off not employing things for the ear to hear (besides your words) and for the eye to see (besides your person and the text). These are not called "props" without reason: they "prop" the speaker up. They help us, or so we think, to be clear when we are not. They help us stand, we suppose, when we are floundering. That's not altogether bad. But the problem is that with the use of visualizations of any kind, preachers will almost always sacrifice oral clarity—the art of being clear

38. In other words, "You can run, but you can't hide!" From Kushner, *Public Speaking for Dummies*, 330.

39. But alas, this is apparently not true anymore. See "America's Top Fears 2017," Chapman University, October 11, 2017, https://blogs.chapman.edu/wilkinson/2017/10/11/americas-top -fears-2017/. So now I find I've been lying to my preaching students all these years! But http:// listverse.com/ is a useful website for a whole universe of lists.

40. Warner and Jennings, *My First Hundred Years in Hollywood*, 168.

with just one's words, the perspicuous painting of verbal pictures—because they have props to lean on. Mastering the art of oral clarity is one thing all of us—novices, veterans, and everyone in between—need to be doing. And guess what? Once you have become competent in that business, you'll find yourself asking, "Why do I need these props and visualizations?" Visualizations are necessary only if the matter being discussed is so complex that without them listeners are unlikely to catch the thrust of the text. After more than two decades of preaching, I have yet to encounter a text that mandates the use of such aids.

An Arabian proverb declares that a good speech "turns the ears into the eyes." In fact, it has been shown that for preschool children, listening to stories is associated with activation of areas of the brain that support mental imagery.[41] The lead author of that study, commenting on the research, said, "It will help [preschoolers] later be better readers because they've developed that part of the brain that helps them see what is going on in the story. . . . When we show them a video of a story, do we short circuit that process a little? Are we taking that job away from them? They're not having to imagine the story; it's just being fed to them."[42] Thomas G. Long is right: "Preachers should remember that the spoken word can take hearers to places in their imaginations where the visual cannot so easily go."[43]

It is true that the bigger the extravaganza, with slides and movie clips and all, the smaller the preacher becomes. And needless to say, the more ambitious your electronics are, the greater the risk of things breaking down midsermon. You also need a cadre of tech wizards and design mavens spending hours (and money) to create and manage quality visualization material.[44] The errors of employing media (outside of the spoken voice of the preacher and the text of Scripture) are considerable and, unfortunately, commonplace: the lack of any discernible purpose for using particular visualizations; oversaturation with screens and monitors, lights and sounds; equipment and technical failures;

41. Hutton et al., "Home Reading Environment."
42. Hutton, cited in Klass, "Bedtime Stories for Young Brains."
43. Long, *Witness of Preaching*, 275–76. The idea that there are varieties of learning styles (that call for the use of varieties of media in pedagogy) has been shown to be a myth. "The contrast between the enormous popularity of the learning-styles approach within education and the lack of credible evidence for its utility is, in our opinion, striking and disturbing," concluded a respectable team of researchers (Pashler et al., "Learning Styles," 117). Pomerance, Greenberg, and Walsh describe the theory of learning styles as "debunked" (*Learning About Learning*, 13). Others "suggest that educators' time and energy are better spent on other theories that might aid instruction" (Willingham, Hughes, and Dobolyi, "Scientific Status of Learning Styles Theories," 266). Preachers' time and energy, likewise, ought to be better directed.
44. See Hoff, *"I Can See You Naked,"* 142.

operator incompetence; sloppy design; copyright infringements; and so on. If any of these weak links can break, they will, and usually when you are preaching, as the venerable Irishman declared in his eponymous law. The result will be a distracted audience, switching back and forth from speaker to screen (or whatever), succumbing to multiple, simultaneous, disjointed streams of cognitive input. I would affirm that you, the pastor / shepherd / spiritual director, are an essential part of the sermonic undertaking and that listeners' attention should not be allowed to wander from you and the text you are preaching from.[45] There is something special about the connection that is forged between God's people and God's preacher, a link strengthened by the Holy Spirit and undisturbed and undisrupted by visualizations or anything else going on at the same time.

My Personal Practice

I rarely use visualization; I hardly ever see a need for it. Handouts and slides, the most common forms of visualization, I employ only when the churches I'm preaching at are used to them and expect them.

On those rare occasions when I use slides, I employ as few of them as I can get away with. My home church has a graphic designer on staff who saves me much anguish in their creation. Slide backgrounds are conformed to the house style for that sermon series and delivered to me; I do the rest. Usually my slides are restricted to one with a title for the series/sermon, some with the one-word labels of my sermon moves (that fill the corresponding blanks in my handout; see below), a few with verses that are located outside the pericope I'm preaching from (rarely), and occasionally a slide with important details of the text's structure or language (I have shown chiasms and Hebrew/Greek terms).[46] I also print out a hardcopy of the slides for

45. With videos, particularly, tight control of what the audience is seeing is impossible unless you create your own material. A clip from a particular movie may cause listeners to go off on a tangent in their minds about other scenes in the movie or wonder about other movies this actor was featured in, and so on. Before you know it, they are far away from you and your sermon. But editing borrowed video is painstaking and time consuming and usually truncates the clip inelegantly and incoherently. Even if appropriate clips are commercially available, vetting them is time consuming. In any case, without careful management of what is shown, rarely will viewers think what you want them to think or go in the direction you want them to go. C. S. Lewis was talking about writing, but his sentiment holds true for speaking too: "I sometimes think that writing is like driving sheep down a road. If there is any gate open to the left or right the readers will most certainly go into it" (*God in the Dock*, 291). Keep those gates padlocked!

46. Here are a few more tips: use PowerPoint (preferred) or Keynote; use a 16:9 slide layout; have no more than a dozen slides per sermon; create your own background texture (or get

the operator (six to a page), with written cues to aid transitions. During the sermon, I call for the next slide (I prefer not to run my own slides while I'm preaching—that's one less thing to worry about). The technical experts at my home church are used to my idiosyncrasies; we make a good team.

The time needed to create sober, well-conceived, artistically designed slides is considerable, especially for a beginner. You definitely don't want any of that poor-resolution clip art, that rainbow of colors, that torrent of fonts and stampede of texts, all in upper case, accompanied by a plethora of bizarre transitions, on a canned OEM template. If you really need slides, *get professional help.* Of course, that takes even more time, coordination, effort, and back-and-forth, not to mention money. Don't discount the time needed to rehearse your sermon with all those fancy maneuvers. My opinion? The benefits are minimal compared to the costs. I'd rather spend time working on my sermon and its application and praying and meditating.

Of the two, slides and handouts, the one I use more frequently is the latter. If listeners are in the habit of writing things down, it is a good idea to give them something to write on. But my main reason for providing a handout is not primarily to aid their writing but to give them the text I'm preaching on, usually in my own English translation, which highlights wordplays and other textual elements that I want to draw attention to (see the italicized and underlined words in the sample handout, fig. 6.1). I often include blanks in the sermon move labels for them to fill in. These are usually alliterated words (the word also shows up on a slide at the right moment, if I'm using PowerPoint). The alliteration is innocent fun for me. I like the challenge of confinement, of trying to find three or four words that begin with the same letter. And listeners try to keep one step ahead of me, attempting to guess what the next *P* word is going to be (see the numbered list to the right of the text in fig. 6.1). At least that keeps them focused and listening.[47]

---

someone to do it for you); use a dark background/texture with light-colored text (off-white; avoid multiple colors); employ a thirty- to forty-point font with decent weight; use a sober and matched mix of serif (e.g., Constantia, Minion Pro) and sans serif fonts (e.g., Calibri, Candara, Gotham); avoid underlining; be sparing with italics and bold; use drop shadows only to help legibility of the text; avoid text animations; leave bullets alone—"bullets belong in *The Godfather.* Avoid them at all costs" (Anderson, *TED Talks,* 122); keep audio and video out of your slides; have a copy of your presentation file handy (in the cloud and/or on a flash drive); and practice, practice, practice your sermon with the slides. Above all, never forget that simplicity always wins.

47. Please see app. C for an annotated manuscript of the sermon on Eph. 1:1–14. Here are some other tips: use the largest font size you can, given the size of the page/bulletin used by the congregation; add your contact information to your handout; and get help with the design, copying, and distribution.

Figure 6.1
GOD'S GRAND DESIGN

EPHESIANS 1:1–14
Translation © Abe Kuruvilla 2015

1 Paul, an apostle of Christ Jesus, by the will of God, to the saints who are in Ephesus and believers in Christ Jesus.

2 Grace to you and peace from God our Father and the Lord Jesus Christ

3 Blessed [be] the God and Father of *our* Lord Jesus Christ, who has blessed *us* with every spiritual blessing, in the heavenlies, in Christ,

> **1. God's P**

4 because He <u>chose</u> *us* in Him before the foundation of the world, that *we* may be holy and blameless before Him; in love

5 He <u>predestined</u> *us* for adoption as children, through Jesus Christ, unto himself, according to the <u>good pleasure</u> of His will,

6 for the praise of the glory of His grace [with] which He engraced *us* in the Beloved.

7 in whom [Christ] *we have* redemption through His blood, the forgiveness of trespasses, according to the riches of His grace

8a which He lavished on *us*;

8b with all wisdom and insight

> **1. Man's P**

9 He made known to *us* the mystery of His <u>will</u>, according to His <u>good pleasure</u> that He <u>purposed</u> in Him

10 for the administration of the fullness of times, the consummation of all things in Christ—the things in the heavens and the things on the earth in Him;

11 in whom also *we have been claimed* [by God] as an inheritance, having been <u>predestined</u> according to the <u>counsel</u> of His <u>will</u>,

12 that *we*, who hoped beforehand in Christ, may be for the praise of His glory;

13 in whom also *you*, hearing the word of truth, the gospel of *your* salvation—in whom also believing, *you were sealed* with the Holy Spirit of promise

> **1. Our P**

14 (who is the pledge of *our* inheritance) until the redemption of [God's own] possession, for the praise of His glory.

Handouts are one of the more trouble-free modes of visualization, though there is many a slip 'twixt the cup and the lip: poor design (always seek help from someone with a good sense of graphics),[48] improperly made copies (malfunctioning copier, manipulation of handout size to fit a standard bulletin, miscounting so there are not enough copies for all in attendance,

---

48. The graphic designer at my church beautifies my work, formats it to church bulletin constraints, adds a logo appropriate for the series (that matches the schema on my slides), puts in a QR code (providing a link to the sermon video on the church's website), and prints it out on colored paper, and so on. But what I have done myself, approximated in figure 6.1, is quite sufficient, and I've frequently used this format in other churches, simply printed on letter-sized sheets and copied in black and white.

miscommunication—when you get "What handout?" from the church administrator on Sunday morning), and so on. That being said, handouts are quite a safe form of visualization.[49]

Using Illustrations

Perhaps the first essential to bear in mind when using illustrations is this: know your audience.[50] Tailor your illustrations to have maximum impact for most of your audience. And use a variety of illustrations, those that appeal to older people, younger folks, those from different ethnicities, and so on. Sports are not necessarily interesting to everybody; neither is cricket avidly followed in most parts of the United States by the average churchgoer (alas!). Battles and wars are gory to many. Not everyone is a movie fan. Be aware of the marital statuses of your listeners as well. How many are parents? Be sensitive to the gender composition of your audience: at least 60 percent of sermon listeners, if not more, are women. Many of these issues of audience were touched on in chapter 5, "Fleshing Moves."

Generally, one illustration per move is sufficient. In fact, if you use too many illustrations, you run the risk of confusing listeners and consuming precious time allotted for the sermon. You should be very clear about why you are using *this* illustration and why it is being deployed *here* in the sermon. Plan illustrations carefully; place them strategically.

The illustration itself should be crisp so that the point is smartly made with an economy of words and a precision of structure. Don't add unnecessary detail that might sidetrack hearers and obfuscate the issue being addressed. Don't talk about things that might raise irrelevant questions you have no intention of answering. Unlike with video and audio clips, you do have total control over the verbal illustrations you use. Keep things tight; let listeners hear only what you want them to hear. No more, no less. All that to say, make sure your illustrations are appropriate, relevant, and helpful. While the Olympic motto calls for "Faster, Higher, Stronger" execution in athletics, I'd recommend "Fewer, Sharper, Briefer" illustrations in homiletics. And prepare those illustrations well. David G. Buttrick's comment is wise:

49. At one church where I served as interim preacher, I created a separate handout for kids in attendance called "Catch the Word" with a verse or two and some key words that they had to circle when I uttered them.

50. This is true for every aspect of the sermon but especially for illustrations, which are usually part of relevance submoves and the application move. You might remember that my application dealing with Evernote, which I mentioned in chap. 3, was totally lost on an elderly couple who weren't as tech savvy as some of my other listeners.

Many ministers today do not write out illustrations ahead of time; while they may be listed in a manuscript, they are often ad-libbed in delivery. As a result, ministers are apt to get carried away as raconteurs, overelaborating stories or slipping in tangential comments. Extraneous fat on illustrations can fog understanding, and tangential remarks destroy the coherence of illustrations. . . . Advance preparation will reduce the tendency to destroy illustrations' effectiveness through careless improvisation.[51]

Melodrama, sensationalism, and gimmickry have their own dangers. Several years ago, Melvyn Nurse, thirty-five, youth minister at Livingway Christian Fellowship Church International in Jacksonville, Florida, wanted to prove his point that sin is like playing Russian roulette. In front of 250 of his young adults, their parents, and his own wife and children, Nurse took out a pistol, put in a blank, spun the cylinder, put the weapon to his head, and pulled the trigger. He died![52]

In that same vein, I recommend avoiding gags and tricks and games and other such inanities, unless you are sure why you are doing it and are equally sure you can get away with it. Few of us can. In a church I attended some years ago, I was struck one Sunday by how emotionally powerful the first part of the worship service was, with a moving testimony, carefully chosen songs, and a passionate prayer. Then the pastor came up to preach. He started off with a goofy game in which we had to stand up, touch the person on our right, and complete a few other jejune maneuvers I've since forgotten. But I remember this: it ruined the entire atmosphere, and there was a general sense of deflation, a puncturing of the high that had been achieved in the service thus far. That is not to say there is no place for humor (more on that below). But we need to calibrate our illustrations for our audiences appropriately, respecting their personalities and culture as well as considering the event and the ambience thereof. Some illustrations can be insipid. Others can be too powerful and so shocking that you lose your listeners as they remain caught up in the power of what you just described. Nobel Laureate Elie Wiesel, a Holocaust survivor, recounted a story of how two adults and a child were hanged for hoarding arms in a Nazi concentration camp, with all the inmates forced to line up and watch the gruesome spectacle. I've used this as an illustration in the past, but I always forego the last line. Wiesel

51. Buttrick, *Homiletic*, 147.
52. Yes, blanks can kill at close range. This illustration (mine) about using an illustration (Nurse's) demonstrates how visualizations can sour on you. See "Minister Fatally Shoots Himself during Sermon," *Los Angeles Times*, October 4, 1998, http://articles.latimes.com/19 98/oct/04/local/me-29125.

ended his account with, "That night the soup tasted of corpses."[53] That's just too strong in my opinion.

Needless to say, don't use illustrations—especially personal stories or confessions—to drop names, to boast, to show off, and the like. Doing so will only lose you points, favor, and credibility with your listeners, and these the preacher can ill afford to lose.[54]

It is also best to avoid using biblical stories from one part of Scripture as illustrations for a sermon on another part. I will grant that the New Testament authors used the Old Testament in this way often, as did Jesus, employing, for instance, David as an illustration when discussing the newness of kingdom life in Mark 2:23–28. But remember, this was at a time when the only stories audiences were familiar with were those from their own biblical traditions and the narratives of their forefathers. In those days, a much less literate and media-saturated age than ours, they had no newspapers, internet, TV, movies, or other modern forms of entertainment and information. Without any other common fund of knowledge or storehouse of memes to draw from, biblical writers had to pull from the Old Testament primarily.[55] So employing biblical illustrations was a reasonable and appropriate operation. But Scripture-writing *methods* are not inspired; only the *text* itself, the product of those scripting enterprises, is. Therefore, there is no call for preachers to imitate the illustrative methods, hermeneutical modalities, rhetorical structures, or lingua franca of the writers of Scripture.[56]

I would therefore warn against employing the Bible as an illustration book. In the first place, biblical narratives are not the best illustrations. In a day when biblical literacy is at a low, throwing in the David and Bathsheba story to illustrate (negatively) a command elsewhere in Scripture that calls for purity means you are going to spend valuable minutes telling that story, explaining who David was, who Bathsheba was, and so on.[57] If you want an illustration

53. Wiesel, *Night*, 65. For the illustration as I told it in a sermon introduction, see chap. 7.
54. Also avoid hobby horses and pet peeves. These can, if you are not careful, hijack your sermon. Issues that you have strong opinions about—and I don't mean doctrinal matters—should be avoided or handled with restraint. Likewise, if you are going through life crises, vigilance is necessary so that those issues, whatever they may be, do not creep into your sermons and render you incapable of meeting the needs of your flock.
55. The New Testament writers infrequently drew on other noncanonical works as well: the Book of Jasher (perhaps in 2 Tim. 3:8), the Book of Enoch (perhaps in 2 Pet. 2:4; 3:13; Jude 4, 6, 13–15); the Epistle to the Laodiceans (Col. 4:16); the Assumption of Moses (2 Tim. 3:8; Jude 9); the Martyrdom of Isaiah (Heb. 11:37); a work of Epimenides of Crete (Titus 1:12); etc. Surely no modern preacher would seek illustrative quotes for their sermons from these ancient tomes.
56. See Kuruvilla, *Privilege the Text!*, 246–48.
57. By that same token, if you employ abstruse allusions to movies and to other current trends, you might have to spend your scarce time explaining what you mean: not everyone has seen the recent movies, read the latest books, or stayed up to date on esoteric terms or jargon.

on adultery, Ashley Madison or Tinder would serve you better. Second, those biblical stories pulled out as illustrations have a theological thrust/force of their own that usually has nothing to do with the theology of the pericope you are preaching. In fact, the theology of the David and Bathsheba story of 2 Samuel 11–12 does not directly relate to adultery (or murder).[58]

Here's a dictum we have encountered before: one text, one sermon, one application. Preach one *text*, without supplementing it with portions of other Scripture, whether as illustrations or otherwise.[59] Preach one *sermon* (i.e., with one textual thrust/force) each time, not going in multiple directions or trying to pour into that one sermon every bit and byte of systematic and biblical theology that you know. And deliver one *application* (we talked about singular application in chap. 3).

Finding and Organizing Illustrations

I've already warned you off canned sermon maps. What about canned illustrations, the kind you pick up in compilations of anecdotes? The problem here is that most such books have a lot of items that are worthless; weeding out the good from the bad is laborious. That being said, I've trawled most of the standard collections, with some benefit.[60]

But if you keep your eyes, ears, and mind open, you will discover illustrations as you observe life. We generally tend to forget interesting things that happen to us. Don't! Take note of them, figuratively and literally (on the literal part, see below). This observation of life also involves reading widely; within reasonable limits, read anything and everything, alert for illustrative material.[61] Please do not restrict yourself to theological reading or just catching up on the news. Read for pleasure: fiction, blogs, dermatology, cricket, or whatever else strikes your fancy. Expand your horizons. Broaden your interests. Develop

58. See Kuruvilla, *Privilege the Text!*, 118–27, 146–48.

59. See the discussion in chap. 5, "Fleshing Moves."

60. Some of the better ones are Larson and *Leadership Journal, 750 Engaging Illustrations*; Evans, *Tony Evans' Book of Illustrations*; and Swindoll, *Swindoll's Ultimate Book of Illustrations*. Useful websites include the following: for quotes, http://www.quotationspage.com /search.php3; for jokes, http://www.rd.com/jokes/; for statistics (which you can also often find by simply googling), https://www.usa.gov/statistics. If you are looking for just the right word that begins or ends with a particular letter or letters, this online dictionary is your best friend: https://www.onelook.com/. For rhyming words, check this one out: https://www.rhymezone .com/. You can even try specific searches: "illustration for [greed/pride/ . . .]."

61. I would strongly recommend subscribing to a number of newsletters put out by *Christianity Today* (https://www.christianitytoday.org/myaccount/?page=newsletters) and to a more literary compilation from Micah Mattix (http://www.prufrocknews.com/) or the *Chronicle of Higher Education* (https://www.aldaily.com/).

hobbies. And take interest in the horizons, interests, and hobbies of those in your congregation; ask to be taught, learn well, and remember.

There are usually reams of articles on the internet that I want to read but don't have the time for. Some time ago I decided I needed to keep from succumbing to the busyness of life and the brevity of my attention span that left many potentially interesting essays languishing as TL;DR. Here's what I did (and what I recommend you do too). I set up an account on https://www .instapaper.com and installed the Instapaper app on my iPad and an Instapaper extension on my Chrome browser (these are available for many different platforms). Anytime I find something on the internet that I want to read but don't have time for right away, a click on the Instapaper browser extension puts that article into my Instapaper account, which syncs with my iPad—all ads removed and only text showing. Later I can access all my saved, to-read articles on my tablet, which I tote with me to the gym. There, while slaving away on an exercise bike, I peruse and whittle down my Instapaper collection.[62] I can even copy quotations and paragraphs and email them to myself (for later retrieval and storage) or archive articles that I want to investigate further, all the while cycling away my calories.

Here are three words to remember: collect, collect, collect! Collect illustrations from wherever you can, from whomever you can, however you can, whenever you can.[63] To repeat myself, always be on the lookout for illustrations, whether you are surfing the internet, browsing an airline magazine, or listening to another preacher. But finding them is not enough; you also have to assemble them in some meaningful fashion.

One of the first steps in collecting is to create a database of illustrations. Start now, before it is too late. If you are a preaching student about to embark on an exciting career in homiletics, this is the best time to begin—while you are yet in school. I have the Microsoft Office Suite that includes the database Access, which I've been using for several decades now. But the suite (and even the standalone database) will put you back a nice chunk of change. You might consider it a worthwhile expense, but let me suggest some alternatives that may work even better. And they are free! If you aren't familiar with Evernote, it is time you were (https://evernote.com/). The best way to describe this cross-platform app (iOS, Android, Windows, and MacOS) is to call it a

---

62. Once Instapaper is synced to your tablet, you do not need to be online to access those articles, making it a great tool for long flights, train rides, and road trips. (A similar app is Pocket: https://getpocket.com/.)

63. One speaker exhorts us to beg, borrow, and steal illustrations, rationalizing that last nefarious act this way: "We're all thieves stealing from other thieves" (Mark L. Bailey, personal communication, 2008). I am not disagreeable to that sentiment.

set of notebooks. You can create a notebook for whatever you want.[64] Let's talk about one for illustrations. Into this notebook you copy your various illustrations, one to a page, tagging them as you desire. Every element and tag (in every notebook) is searchable. You can even input photographs from your smartphone, and Evernote does a good job with its optical-character recognition engine, rendering even words in those pictures searchable. I recommend downloading this app to your smartphone and your computer (it is free, as I noted, but if you want to put it on more than two devices, you have to pay).[65] The advantage of this multidevice enterprise is that any new note you enter in Evernote on one of your assigned devices syncs via the cloud to the app on all the others. You can walk around with your phone and all your illustrations in your pocket.[66]

Now how do you categorize them all? Here's the ideal situation: whatever database you employ, tag each illustration with multiple tags—for topic(s), for date and place it has been used, and for what sermon on what text. I confess, though, that my practices are far less than ideal. Tagging by topic has never worked for me, simply because by tagging, aka pigeonholing, I find I have confined an illustration to just that topic (or topics if it has multiple tags). I always find unusual uses for illustrations when I'm scrolling through my collection with a particular sermon in mind, uses that I would never have thought of when tagging those illustrations as I added them to my database. In other words, if I searched for illustrations with only a particular tag, I would never find a new use for an old illustration. And trust me, that happens often—far too often. So I have given up tagging illustrations for the most part.

But this creates an intractable problem: finding the right illustration when I am looking for one. I confess that I take the labor-intensive route, going through *all* my illustrations for *each* sermon I plan to preach. That sounds backbreaking, but in actuality it doesn't take as much time as one might expect; having repeated this process often, I know the six thousand illustrations currently in my database reasonably well and can click through them at a rapid pace. Still, the process does take me several hours, and I admit it is not the

64. I have an odd assortment of notebooks, including one for the different cheeses that I like. When I find one, I simply take a picture of the label and insert it into my "cheese" notebook.

65. You will also have to pay if you want to upload more than 60MB per month or if you have more than 100,000 items ("notes") or more than 250 notebooks. There are a number of tiers you can upgrade to, with varying prices payable monthly or yearly.

66. Another database, more stripped down compared to Evernote (which has its share of diversionary bells and whistles), is Bear (http://www.bear-writer.com/). It too has multiplatform support and can sync across devices. Yet another option is Microsoft's OneNote (https://www.onenote.com).

ideal way to utilize my collection. But I don't have a better option. If some sort of topical tagging works for you, by all means create those categories and apply those tags (and let me in on your secret). Of course, if I know I have a particular illustration that talks about, say, dermatology, and I remember that it has the word *skin* in it, I can search for that particular word and quickly locate what I want. That is probably the best function of a database: it can search through not only tag headings but also the body of the illustrations for any keyword you might be interested in. In any case, here is the bottom line: collect, collect, collect!

Using Humor

While the preacher ought not to be the resident church comic, the judicious use of humor in preaching is highly recommended for a number of reasons: reducing potential tension, dismantling listeners' defenses, enabling an entrée into topics that otherwise may be taboo, showing yourself as human, not taking yourself too seriously, inculcating a sense of joy and celebration in the sermonic event, fostering a sense of community in listeners as they laugh together, and even increasing your own credibility. Frivolity is not what is being advocated here; after all, we deal with matters of great substance and seriousness—the relationship of God to his creation. But cheerfulness is always to be aimed for. Proverbs puts it well: "A joyful heart promotes wholesomeness, good medicine, but a broken spirit dries the bones" (Prov. 17:22). All that to say, you are not called to be funny, but you can show yourself as one with a good sense of humor and a willingness to laugh—especially at yourself. And much of this sense of humor ought to show up in your illustrations.

Learn to deliver humor well: how to tell a story, how to time your lines, what facial expressions to adopt, what gestures to employ, how to deliver the punch line, how to be conversational, and so on. As already noted, watching stand-up comedy is a great way to adopt some of these things. Beware of the language and risqué jokes, though. Keep in mind that all sermonic humor must be appropriate—no off-color remarks; no offensive language; no sarcasm; no belittling of another's religion, ethnicity, gender, race, nation, political viewpoint, or hair color. "Make 'em laugh—but not squirm!"[67] A Christian leader should never be deprecatory or derogatory. Offending your listeners could turn them off from the rest of the sermon and, frequently, from the rest of your ministry. Don't even take a chance on remarks that might sound

---

67. Anderson, *TED Talks*, 63.

humorous to you but are pejorative to others. As the old public speaking adage goes, "When in doubt, drop it out!"[68]

There is, however, one exception to humor that slights a person: it is appropriate if you are the subject of the slight. Self-deprecation is the best and safest kind of humor. I don't think I've gotten as much of a laugh from my listeners as I did when I recounted my chewing gum and wrapper experience.[69] Your mistakes and crazy experiences will go far to endear you to your listeners.

One-liners are useful too, since they don't take much time to tell and are winsome because of their punning, wordplay, and cleverness. Some of them also turn out to be eye rollers that people listen to not with a grin but with a grimace and a groan. But even these aren't bad and have their use, for people will then laugh at you and your clumsy attempts at humor—self-deprecation in operation again![70]

At the same time, don't just hop from one joke to another, or even one illustration to another. We've all heard sermons that were nothing but strings of jokes and stories. They were boisterously mirthful, but as for what was being conveyed from the text, they were utterly forgettable. Also, any joke can fall flat on occasion. Not to worry. Keep going without trying to retell it or expound it. And learn from your mistakes.[71] In every case, whether you go boom or bust, clearly and explicitly make the point you were trying to make with your humor—at least listeners will appreciate that—and move on.

68. Ask yourself, "What would my mother say if she heard me deliver these lines?" Or "What if my joke turned up on the front page of the local newspaper?" There are enough fires in pastoral ministry to put out without the preacher adding to the conflagration. Run your humor (and illustrations as necessary), especially those you aren't sure about, by a trusted individual or two.

69. See app. C for an annotated manuscript of the sermon with that confession. I've also poked fun of my other job as a dermatologist in a sermon on 1 Sam. 17; 17:42 notes that David "was a youth, with a ruddy complexion." I added as an aside, "In other words, he was a dermatologist's dream." Dig into your life. Has a toilet overflowed? Have you fallen off a roof? Blessed are you if you have!

70. Check out the more than two thousand items, including numerous one-liners, in Bramer, *The Bible Reader's Joke Book*, ably arranged by book, chapter, and verse; it also comes with a topical index. Kushner, *Public Speaking for Dummies*, 315–48, has helpful tips on the use of humor in public speaking.

71. This has happened to me more than once, especially in cross-cultural ministry in foreign lands and even in ethnic churches in the United States.

Ephesians and the Jacob Story

8. Ephesians 4:17–32[72]

> **Believers, no longer living licentiously, are being divinely renewed into the likeness of God that is manifest as they maintain unity and engage in activities that build up one another.**

Here's a suggested map with some illustrations added.

I. Past: The Lifestyle of Unbelievers
    A. Revelation: Licentious living rooted in hard-heartedness (4:17–19)
    B. Relevance: How and why believers regress into such a degenerate lifestyle [example(s)][73]
        1. Illustration (narration) of Lou Dinarde, an example of a person not living as he could be

> For years, there have been rumors among the homeless downtown that a drifter in North Beach in San Francisco was sleeping in the gutter while he had all the money he needed in the bank. It's true. That drifter is sixty-eight-year-old Lou Dinarde.
>
> Dinarde is homeless, he often sleeps in the gutter or on the sidewalk, and he has plenty of cash—a trust fund that at one point was worth nearly $700,000. He draws $2,500 a month from the fund plus $500 a month in Social Security. Dinarde has had this money rolling in since 1992, when his mother died and her assets were sold to create the trust.
>
> Trouble is he can't resist the bottle. He abandoned his career as a carpenter three decades ago for life on the streets. "I'm rich, but I like it out here. I ain't sleeping inside," Dinarde mumbled through sips of vodka last summer as he sat in front of St. Francis of Assisi Church. "You can't make me."[74]

II. Present: The New Status of Believers
    A. Revelation: Learning, hearing, being taught in Christ, the exemplary Man (4:20–21), and the ongoing renewal of believers into Christlikeness (4:22–24)

---

72. For a brief commentary on this pericope, see http://www.homiletix.com/preaching2019/commentaries. For an expanded curation of this text, see Kuruvilla, *Ephesians*, 133–49.

73. Not implying loss of salvation, of course. But Paul's exhortation to the Ephesians implies that backsliding is possible for believers.

74. Modified from Kevin Fagan, "S.F. Man Is Homeless—by Choice," SFGate, January 2, 2004, https://www.sfgate.com/bayarea/article/S-F-man-is-homeless-by-choice-He-has-a-2833486.php. Be sure such a narration is concluded appropriately: "Many believers are like Mr. Dinarde . . ." (and tell listeners how).

B. Relevance: Applying what we are learning, hearing, and being taught is therefore important

    1. Illustration (exemplification) of growth in Christlikeness, a slow and steady process, like multiple doctor visits

> This is like multiple, weekly visits to a doctor. Say you are visiting me, a dermatologist, this week. I might tell you how to take care of your dry skin. Next week, if you return, I might advise you on how to take precautions in the sun. The week after that, you might be given recommendations regarding your moles. After that, I'd offer tips on how to care for your hair. Then your nails. (Skin, hair, and nails, by the way, are the domain of a dermatologist.) As you follow my recommendations, your dermatological status is being improved, week by week, and you are well on your way to developing perfect skin.

> After several weeks of seeing me, you might decide to visit your cardiologist. The first week she might advise you on controlling your blood pressure. The week after that, how to maintain an exercise regimen. Then how to control your cholesterol with diet and a prescribed statin. And so on, week by week, till you attain a perfect cardiovascular state.

> You might then move on to an endocrinologist, and after a few weeks of that, a gastroenterologist, and then a nephrologist. In short, slowly and steadily, you are being perfected in health.

> So also our new status as believers—learning, hearing, and being taught in Christ. Slowly and steadily, as we align ourselves with what we are learning, hearing, and being taught, we are being gradually molded into the image of Christ.

III. Future: The Lifestyle of Believers

    A. Revelation: Abandoning evil words (4:25–27, 29, 31–32), evil deeds (4:28), and evil thoughts (4:31–32) that grieve the Holy Spirit (4:30)

    B. Relevance[75]

IV. *Delight the Spirit!*

8. Genesis 31:17–55[76]

> **Remaining in the will of God ensures protection from harm (even from the most unexpected source), a blessing to be gratefully acknowledged.**[77]

---

75. This submove of relevance could be omitted since the next move of application will likely deal with the practicalities of delighting the Spirit.

76. For a brief commentary on this pericope, see http://www.homiletix.com/preaching2019/commentaries. For an expanded curation, see Kuruvilla, *Genesis*, 383–93.

77. I'll let you think about potential sermon illustrations for the moves created here by Focus Splitting.

7

Crafting Introductions and Conclusions

> Passengers want a smooth takeoff. They want to eat peanuts, drink sodas, read magazines, and get where they're going. They don't want to sit on the runway forever, gain altitude too fast, have the plane career wildly through the sky, or use the barf bag. . . . The same considerations apply to your introduction. . . . The conclusion is the landing. The passengers—your audience—don't want the landing to be sudden or bumpy. They don't want to land in the wrong place. And most important, they *do* want you to land.[1]

We have so far looked at the text and discerned the theology of the pericope, derived application, mapped out the sermon, fleshed out its moves, and mulled over illustrations. The final elements to be added to the sermon are an introduction and a conclusion (which also need illustrations, as we shall see). Crafting the introduction and the conclusion *after* you've created the body of the sermon makes sense, because if you don't have the body ready, you won't know what to introduce and what to conclude.

The metaphor of airplane travel for a speech, as used in the epigraph, is helpful: if the body of the sermon is the flight, then the introduction is the takeoff and the conclusion is the landing. Together the introduction (takeoff) and the conclusion (touchdown) make up about 25 percent of the sermon.

1. Kushner, *Public Speaking for Dummies*, 119, 140.

Sermon	
Introduction	15%
Body	75%
Conclusion	10%

These two sermonic elements, the introduction and the conclusion, are critical. They are, respectively, the first and last impressions the preacher makes on the audience.

Elements of the Introduction

Passengers want an uneventful flight, and for that, a hassle-free takeoff is essential. A sloppy ascent and the pilot loses credibility with passengers, making them worry for the rest of the flight, "What else can go wrong?" Likewise with preaching. The introduction sets the tone for the rest of the sermon; it prepares the audience to listen. The first three minutes after you get up in front of everyone are when listeners' attention is at a natural high. That's when they size you up. That's when you set up their expectations. That's when they are going to decide if they are going to hang with you for the rest of the sermon. And that's your best chance to make a terrific first impression—and a lasting one at that.

Here are the elements of an effective introduction, the first letters of which spell out INTRO.[2]

1. Image
2. Need
3. Topic
4. Reference
5. Organization

Let's look at each one.

Image

The image is what has commonly been called the *hook*. With an opening image, you bait the listeners. Each person comes to listen to you burdened with

2. Using Arabic numerals is a standard way of numbering the elements of an introduction (unlike the moves of the sermon body, which take Roman numerals).

his or her own cares, concerns, and worries. You need to grab all your hearers by the ears (using your voice and words) and give them no choice but to listen to you because what you've begun to say is so powerful, relevant, interesting, and attractive. This calls for an opening image that creates emotion, raises tension, and grabs attention.[3] Essentially, it is the entrée into your sermon, specifically connecting a somewhat disinterested audience with the need (which immediately follows the image). Images can be divided into the following categories: novelty, activity, proximity, disparity, anxiety, and jollity.[4]

Novelty

A startling statement or statistic, an unusual discovery, a striking prediction—in other words, something that is novel, even an old idea in new garb—makes for a good image. Here's one I heard on the radio some time ago from a well-known Christian preacher (who shall remain unnamed): "Did you know that the majority of the world—six to seven billion people—living today do not know Jesus Christ and are damned? [Pause] And I bet most of you are worrying more about my language than about the billions who are going to be lost eternally!" Needless to say, that six-letter word was not bleeped out. I don't recommend swearing in your sermons, but this preacher certainly got my attention.

On one of those rare occasions when I've employed a visualization (a prop), I wore a particular watch on my wrist and asked someone sitting in front to come up to the podium, examine my watch, and announce the make of the timepiece into a microphone. "Rolex," the volunteer duly noted. I sent the person back and continued, "Rolex! Did you hear that? *Rolex!* Not bad, huh? *Geneve.* Good for a yuppie, a fat cat, a big shot. That makes me a favorite of the gods, right? The cost? Well . . . let's just say it's worth it for a successful preacher like me." I continued in that egotistic vein for a minute. Then pausing, I confessed, "Before you chase me off the pulpit and start sending emails and texts to the elders, let me add a few more observations about my 'Rolex.' I bought it for $7.99. This thing doesn't work. It never has. But it keeps perfect time twice a day! Oh, and if you look carefully underneath, it says 'Made in Taiwan.' Rolex? Hardly! Looks good on the outside, but it's dead inside."

---

3. And draws some blood! As Chris Anderson advises, in the introduction, one ought to "deliver a dose of drama" and "ignite curiosity" (*TED Talks*, 157, 160).

4. These categories are not watertight compartments. Some images may fit more than one category, and some categories will no doubt overlap with others. Neither is this an exhaustive list of categories; you might be able to create more.

This was the image in the introduction to a sermon on Revelation 3:1–6, Christ's letter (through John) to the church at Sardis, which says in 3:1, "I know your deeds, that you have a name that you live, but you are dead."

All kinds of possibilities exist for novel images. The other day a student in my class began her sermon with "Failed! We failed! Miserably." That certainly perked up our ears. She went on to describe a church-planting experience she and her husband were involved in that had ended unsuccessfully. Also, anything that begins with "Did you know that . . . ?" has the potential to be interesting. Lists are usually fascinating too: "Five ways to . . ."; "The top ten . . ."; and so on. Unusual stories (illustrations of narration) also work well.

Activity

Anything that is active and dynamic, with movement conjured up in vivid wording, will catch listeners' attention. Stories are prime candidates for images in this category, since they are active—things happen in stories. That's why the four most powerful words employed in the English language to grab someone's attention probably are "Once upon a time . . ." The contemporary version of that fairy tale introduction is "About a [week/month/year] ago . . ." There is nothing like stories, or events recounted, to captivate listeners. We humans live in stories ourselves, and the stories of others seduce us, especially if they are personal ones. You might even check history websites for anything that might have happened "this day in history," including births and deaths. If a "date factoid" will fit your introduction, use it.[5]

Proximity

Items of interest usually are things that are proximal to listeners, relevant to them, familiar to many: things that happened in their community, something you spotted in the local newspaper, an interesting tidbit about the locality, a conversation you had with a person familiar to them, and so forth. Proximity and life relatedness always help make things relevant to listeners and may be gainfully employed as attention-getting images.

Chaplain Bill was a beloved fixture at Dallas Theological Seminary for many years—he and his trumpet led music and worship at most of our functions. Before his retirement, I took an opportunity to put him into an introduction image (a version of a Texas-is-the-best canned joke) for my sermon on Genesis 22, the story of a "test."

5. Check out http://www.history.com/this-day-in-history or http://www.historynet.com /today-in-history or https://www.timeanddate.com/on-this-day/.

A man went to a church here in Dallas and asked to join. The preacher said, "OK, but you have to pass a short Bible test first. Where was Jesus born?"

The guy tried tentatively, "Longview?"

"What! Sorry, you can't join our church," was the reply.

So the man went to another church in town and requested membership. The pastor there said, "We would love to have you, but you have to pass a Bible test. Where was Jesus born?"

This time the fellow answered, "Tyler."

The pastor exclaimed, "Tyler? Find another church, buddy; you can't come here."

Finally, the man ended up at Grace Bible Church, where he ran into Chaplain Bill, who was pastoring there . . . oh, about two hundred years ago! "You want to join Grace?" Chaplain inquired. "We welcome you with open arms and loud trumpets."

The man asked, "I don't have to pass a Bible test first?"

"Of course not," said the good reverend.

"Oh! Well, then, can I ask *you* a question? Where was Jesus born?"

"That's easy," Chaplain replied. "You know, in Palestine."

"Palestine!" the guy said, groaning. "I knew it was in East Texas somewhere."

Of course, to understand this joke, you need to be familiar with the names of some of the towns in Texas and their locations within the state (and also with Chaplain Bill and his horn). All three locations named in the story are in East Texas (yes, we have a Palestine: population 18,712). So this piece wouldn't work in Watertown, Massachusetts; it would not be proximal to people there. You need to know your audience.[6]

Disparity

By "disparity" I mean some conflict, some inconsistency, some puzzlement, something that doesn't add up. Here is an example.

He was the most brilliant man ever born in the US. At eighteen months of age, he was reading the *New York Times*. When he turned three, his father taught him the Greek alphabet, and he promptly began reading the poet Homer—in Greek, of course. At the same time, he also taught himself to read Latin. By age five, he had written a treatise on anatomy, and by six, he spoke seven languages fluently. At seven years, he passed Harvard Medical School's anatomy exam. At eight, he passed MIT's entrance exam, and at nine, Harvard's entrance exam, but they judged him too young to enter. They made him wait till he was eleven!

---

6. That was not a true story, of course. I did not have to offer that caveat, since its apocryphal nature was quite obvious to my listeners.

He graduated from Harvard at sixteen while already teaching part-time. His IQ was between 250 and 300. Bear in mind that Einstein's IQ was only a paltry 200. William Sidis was his name.

I usually pause here in my delivery to relish the utterly blank looks on my listeners' faces.

Amazing, isn't it, that with that kind of intelligence you never heard of him. So brilliant he could conquer any language in one day—one twenty-four-hour day!

He died in 1944 at age forty-six. What was he doing? He was working as a minor clerk with menial duties in a New York business office. Sidis had wasted his life pursuing trivia, refusing to accept responsibilities, and turning down great opportunities and large salaries, finally to die unknown, unheard of.

Started well but did not finish strong![7]

The disparity is spelled out in the last line. This image was for a sermon on the Israelite leader Caleb, who both started well and finished strong.

Anxiety

Images of anxiety involve some suspense, dread, or challenge and create unease. They are emotionally powerful and should be carefully calibrated for one's listeners. Here's an anxiety-inducing image that I referred to in chapter 6, "Illustrating Ideas."

Elie Wiesel, a Nobel Peace Prize winner whose writings have focused on the Jewish Holocaust and its atrocities, was himself imprisoned by the Nazis at the age of sixteen. He endured unspeakable horrors at Buchenwald and Auschwitz concentration camps. One incident lives forever in his memory. Two adults and a child—maybe twelve years old—had been caught hoarding arms inside the camp. They were sentenced to death.

The boy had a refined and beautiful face, so different from the gaunt, disfigured faces of most prisoners—the face, said Wiesel, of a sad angel. They erected three gallows, the three victims mounted chairs, and the SS placed their necks in nooses. All the other prisoners were forced to line up and watch the gruesome spectacle. "Long live liberty!" cried the two adults. The child said nothing. But from the rows of anguished spectators, a cry came up. "Where *is* God? Where *is* he?"

The chairs were tipped over and the bodies jerked, then dangled limply from the ropes. It was a terrible sight. The two adults died in seconds, but the third

7. In case you were wondering, this one *is* a true story. Google him!

rope was still twitching lightly. The child, being so light, was still alive. In all it took the boy perhaps half an hour to die.

"Behind me," said Wiesel, "I heard the same man asking, 'Where is God *now?*'"[8]

This is a provocative image that creates anxiety. (I used it in the introduction of a sermon on Mark 4:35–41, Jesus's stilling of the storm; see below for the rest of the introduction.)

Jollity

Images involving jollity,[9] or humor, can be powerful. However, you shouldn't let such images hijack the sermon or the introduction. Keep the jollity in control, tightly reined. My Chaplain Bill joke served as a bit of comedy, at least for us Texans. Remember the guidelines for humor discussed in chapter 6. All those apply here as well (the image in an introduction is, after all, an illustration employed for a particular purpose).[10] You do not have to be funny in a comical way; demonstrating a good sense of humor is enough. And you can do that with a Yogi Berra quotation, an Ann Landers epistle, a Mark Twain-ism, a humorous anecdote or personal story, or something similar.

Need

The second element of the introduction is the need. Commonly neglected in sermons, the need is important to establish at the very beginning. It responds to an apathetic listener's hypothetical question, "Why should I spend the next thirty minutes listening to this sermon from this text?" by answering, "Because you are [or are going to be] in a situation in which you will find help from this text." The preacher is, in a sense, overcoming the inertia of indifference that one can safely assume is etched into the minds of most listeners. As Harry Emerson Fosdick complained, "Only the preacher proceeds still upon the idea that folk come to church desperately anxious to discover what happened to

---

8. Modified from Wiesel, *Night*, 63–65.

9. Yes, *jollity* is a word. And it means what you think it does: merriment or humor. I am, in my obsession with alliteration and assonance, employing words here that need explanation. If you have to explain your alliterated or assonant labels and titles and such, that's a reliable sign that you've gone too far. But I do it anyway, since I enjoy the mental exercise of finding the right word within certain linguistic constraints.

10. Every type of illustration discussed in chap. 6 will work for introductions too: narration, confession, enumeration, quotation, exemplification, and, rarely, visualization.

Jebusites."[11] They do not. The preacher has to draw listeners into the sermon, and the need in the introduction accomplishes that.

You might think answering this implicit question from listeners—a version of "What will I get out of this, if anything?"—is pandering to a mentality of consumerism. It is not. Scripture is profitable for life, a sine qua non for becoming conformed to the image of our Lord and Savior, Jesus Christ (Col. 1:28–29; 2 Tim. 3:16–17). Therefore, every pericope of the Bible—and by extension every sermon that discerns pericopal theology—is *needed* by every child of God. Here, at this point in the introduction, the preacher is simply spelling out the need for the given pericope in specific fashion. For instance, after the Chaplain Bill image (jollity), I provided this need: "Life is full of tests. We want to do well in them, especially in those tests given by God."

Notice that I used the verb "want." Perhaps that is a better descriptor than "need."[12] The preacher has to make listeners *want* to hear the sermon. Often the want/need may not be one that is felt. In that case, it is up to the preacher to elicit that feeling; this will likely happen with the image. After the harrowing incident recounted by Elie Wiesel (in the sermon on Mark 4:35–41), I went on to say:

> I hope you are never in the situation of witnessing such abominable evil and abysmal cruelty. But I bet there have been times in your life when you have asked that same question: "God, where are you?" When life is crumbling around you and there seems to be no help in sight—no, not even God. Bills are due, but the bank account is empty. A loved one receives an ominous call from the doctor's office—that X-ray, that mammogram . . . cancer! You are called to your boss's office: there is to be a layoff and your name is on the list. It is just a matter of time. We will all be stricken, in one way or another.

People may not have thought about disaster striking, so I draw their attention to it, creating a felt need—that is, transforming the need that they were not aware of into a *want* that they now keenly feel: "Yes, we too will have times when we think we are all alone in our tragedy. We *want* to know what to do then."

After the William Sidis image (disparity: started strong but finished poorly), I continued, "In Christian life too it is not only how you start the race that matters but also how you finish. How will we be doing as Christians in the future, in ten, twenty, thirty years?" Though I did not explicitly express it, I raised the specter of listeners *not* finishing strong, even though they may have

---

11. Fosdick, "What Is the Matter with Preaching?" 135.
12. But then how would I have my acronym INTRO?

started strong. Implicit here was the need: "We all *want* to finish strong." No, you don't have to spell everything out. In this case, for a sermon delivered in Dallas Theological Seminary's chapel, I anticipated that most of my listeners, having sacrificed much to be in seminary, would have such a need (want) to finish strong. And with the story of one who failed to finish well, I caused a need to be felt: "Yes, of course, unlike Sidis, *I* want to finish well!"

While being specific on the one hand, you should be careful not to give away too much in the need on the other. You don't want to lose the sense of suspense by revealing, in the introduction, everything the sermon is going to address later. Play your cards close to your chest. Do not disclose the thrust of the pericope or where you are going in the sermon, except in very general terms. This is a delicate balancing act that only experience will train you to perform well. Like most things in life, the more you do this—thoughtfully and reflectively—the more adept you will become.

So the need is the first place where relevance enters the sermon. We could add to figure 5.1 from chapter 5, "Fleshing Moves," to look like figure 7.1.

Figure 7.1

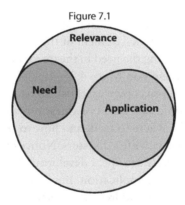

Need, like application, is an integral part of relevance. Here you are con-necting to your listeners with emotion and pathos, in the place where they live, in the nitty-gritty of their lives, in the rough-and-tumble of daily wear and tear. And that's the only way to draw them into the sermon. Harry Emerson Fosdick is right: raising a need "is the only way I know to achieve excitement without sensationalism."[13]

In the English language, we tend to conflate "need" and "should." I am reminded of a *Garfield* comic strip (created by Jim Davis) that shows the eponymous fat and lazy cat being admonished by its owner, Jon Arbuckle:

13. Fosdick, "What Is the Matter with Preaching?" 138.

"You need to lose weight." To which the wisecracking feline, holding up a "finger," replies, "Correction: I *should* lose weight. I *need* cookies."[14] In English "need" is a polite substitution for "should"; it takes the edge off what might sound like a dictatorial demand. For instance, I might tell my students on the first day of class, "You need to turn in your assignments on time." That really is not a need/want my students have. What I really mean is "You *should* turn in your assignments on time." The need/want for my class, however, is to get good grades on their work. My requirement could more accurately be phrased this way: "You *should* turn in your assignments on time if you *need* [want] a good grade." All this to say, the *need* is not the same as a *should*. The latter is objective—something imposed on listeners from another. The former is subjective—something listeners feel, want, and desire (or are *made* to feel, want, and desire) for themselves.

Topic

The third element of the introduction is the topic—what you are going to be talking about. In essence, the topic answers—in very general terms—the need you just raised. Therefore, need and topic are closely related, and the two may even be considered a unified element of the introduction: need + topic.

Here's the topic following the need in the introduction that employed Elie Wiesel's story (for a sermon on Mark 4:35–41): "What will you do? Where will you turn? How will you cope with those disasters, those distresses? Can you?" I phrased the topic as a series of questions implying, "This sermon will tell you what to do, where to turn, and how to cope." That is the topic: what/where/how to cope with life's disasters. Notice that I didn't give listeners the full answer: how *exactly* to cope. I developed the answer throughout the sermon and especially in the application. But in the introduction, I promised them that this topic would be addressed in response to the need elicited. My listeners were (or were going to be) in situations of distress and wanted to know what to do, where to turn, and how to cope (the need), and this sermon on this text was intended to give them an important way (or some ways) to handle such crises (the topic). As I illustrated above, I generally tend to lay out the topic as one or more questions.

For the sermon introduced by the William Sidis story, this was the need + topic (the topic is the five-word question in italics that follows the [implied] need): "In Christian life, too, it is not only how you start the race that matters but also how you finish. How will we finish? How will we be doing as Christians

14. Jim Davis, "You Need to Lose Weight," Garfield, accessed May 1, 2018, https://garfield.dale.ro/garfield-2008-january-21.html.

in the future, in ten, twenty, thirty years? *How can we finish strong?*" The topic of the sermon was how listeners might finish strong. I told them what they could expect from the sermon but without providing any specifics.

Let's try a few more examples of need + topic, from texts inspired and otherwise, some of which we have encountered already.

Proverbs 12:25

> Anxiety in the heart of a man weighs it down,
> but a good word cheers it up.

Theological Focus: "Anxiety depresses/downs, but encouragement uplifts."[15]

Let's assume you decide to go with a Problem–Solution–Application map for the sermon body.

    I. Problem: Anxiety is downing (12:25a)

    II. Solution: Encouragement is uplifting (12:25b)

    III. Application: *Be an encourager!*[16]

Now ask yourself, Why do my listeners need to hear this? An obvious reason is there are anxious people all around us to whom we want to minister (the need). How will we do that (the topic)? In other words, this sermon is geared toward people who have a need to minister and want to alleviate the cares and concerns of others. The answer, of course, is developed later in the sermon as you discern pericopal theology and derive specific application.

What image might work here that would lead naturally, smoothly, and seamlessly into the need? Perhaps a situation of anxiety within the community, a story of someone who experienced distress and how he or she spiraled into depression. That would move straight into the need.

Proverbs 10:25

> When the storm passes, the wicked one is no more,
> but the righteous one [has] a foundation forever.

Theological Focus: "Unbelievers will be judged by God, but believers, escaping judgment, will be established eternally in relationship to God."

---

15. The use of "depresses/downs" and "uplifts" here is an attempt to make the wordplay in the Hebrew obvious in the English: 12:25a has *yashkhennah* ("weighs it down"), and 12:25b has *yesammekhennah* ("makes it glad" or, as I have it, "cheers it up").

16. Do make applications more specific than how I have them.

And here's a suggested set of moves for the body, also using the Problem–Solution–Application style.

I. Problem: Unbelievers will not escape God's judgment (10:25a)

II. Solution: Believers will escape God's judgment (being established forever in relationship to God) (10:25b)

III. Application (for believers): *Tell your unbelieving friends/neighbors . . . !*

Why do listeners need to hear this sermon on this text? Because their caring nature and concern for their unbelieving neighbors make them want to help their neighbors escape God's eternal judgment (the need). This sermon will tell them how they can do that (the topic). Notice that the need is going to have to deal with I. Problem, that unbelievers will not escape God's judgment. So we will have to say pretty much the same thing in the introduction (the need) *and* in the first move of the body (I. Problem). Some careful negotiation may therefore be necessary so as not to repeat matters in this fashion.[17] One way out of this complication is to tweak the need: "As children of God, we want to be helpful and kind, gracious and compassionate toward those around us" (our need to be benefactors of others as agents of God's grace). "Today we'll find out the *best* way to benefit our neighbors" (the topic). This way we have revealed nothing about I. Problem, neither the issue of God's judgment nor the consequence thereof for unbelievers. This modification thereby moved the need + topic to a more generic level, away from the specificities of the text, to preclude tedious repetition and maintain the suspense.

Let's think for a moment about what image might fit this need + topic. We could use one that shows a Christian being helpful to others but probably not one that shows a believer witnessing—that would give the application away. Or we might try something like this:

[Image: novelty] Ancient Hindu traditions have a version of the Golden Rule; Isocrates said it in ancient Greece in the fifth century BCE; Zorastrianism propounded this; so did Seneca the Younger, a Roman philosopher of the first century CE. But the biblical version is the best known, as Jesus put it: "Love your neighbor as yourself."

[Need] And, of course, we as Christians want to obey this, one of the two great commandments. We want to be helpful and kind, gracious and compassionate toward those around us.

17. This might also be an indication that the Problem–Solution–Application canned map is not ideal for a sermon on this proverb.

[Topic] How do we do that? There are probably many ways of obeying this command, but today we're going to find out one of the *best* ways to benefit our neighbors.

As you probably realize by now, there are many ways to skin this cat. Be creative. Be concerned for your flock. Think. Think again. Think once more. And yet again.[18] And pray throughout for wisdom, for ideas, for "accidents."[19]

Aesop's "The Fox and the Crow"
Remember the "Theological" Focus of this story? "Avoiding prideful gullibility to flattery prevents loss." Here is the sermon map we created in chapter 4.

I. Attitude: Prideful gullibility to flattery [the crow's succumbing to flattery; pride as a common affliction that makes one gullible to flattery]

II. Aftermath:[20] Causes loss [the crow's loss; consequences of prideful gullibility]

III. Application: *Don't be proud(fully gullible and fall for flattery)!*

Here is the need: "We are all justly proud of all that we have done. But often there are dangerous consequences of pride, and we want to avoid such nasty ramifications." And here is the topic: "Today we'll find out one way to avoid them." But the application—how to avoid these "nasty ramifications"—turns out to be quite obvious after hearing the need: *Don't be proud!* A listener might therefore not be compelled to listen to the rest of the sermon, since the need + topic has given most of it away. So a tweak that raises the need to a more generic level is necessary: "Life is full of complications and dangers, trip-ups and losses, all of which we'd prefer to avoid [the need]. How do we do that [the topic]?" As an image for this sermon introduction, one might give an example not of pride causing a fall (which would give away the sermon) but of a complication or a danger, a trip-up or a loss (that does not dwell on the cause thereof). Of course, if you can tell your listeners about a complication or danger caused by pride *but without revealing the cause*, you might be able to revert to that image later in the body (perhaps in II. Causes loss)

18. I.e., quadruple think (see chap. 5, "Fleshing Moves").
19. By "accidents" I mean things that pop into your head while in the shower, perusing a magazine, or on the treadmill. I can't tell you how many times such "accidents" have saved me and my sermon (not to mention my listeners). This, of course, goes not just for introductions but for every part of the sermon. Indeed, an utter dependence on God's providence is worth cultivating for *all* of life.
20. I know, I know—I'm stretching it. What I really want to say is "Loss" (or "Consequence"), as I did in an earlier iteration of this map, but I badly wanted to alliterate and couldn't think of a better *A* word.

and *then* give the cause (pride), thus finishing off the story that you started in the introduction's image.

Proverbs 15:8
> The sacrifice of the wicked is abominable to Yahweh,
>> but the prayer of the upright his delight.

Theological Focus: "God is disgusted with the worship of the wicked but delighted with the worship of the upright."

Here is the sermon map.

I. God's disgust at the worship of the wicked (15:8a)
II. God's delight at the worship of the upright (15:8b)
III. Application: *Delight God!*

The need jumps out at us: "We children of God want to delight our heavenly Father." And you could/should go on in this vein for a bit, not restricting it to a single sentence as I have just done. Here's the topic: "So how do we delight God? Today we'll discover one way to delight our Father."

The image might well be the story of a man trying to delight his wife (or vice versa) or of a parent delighting a child (or vice versa).[21] The possibilities are limited only by your creativity. The more extreme the effort the "delighter" makes to delight the "delightee," the more effective that image will be. "If that's what we're willing to do for our earthly loved one, how much more for our heavenly loved One, who first loved us?" That's the need, implicitly declaring that we want to greatly delight our Father.

Reference

This element is straightforward. The reference announces the biblical text of the sermon, which people can locate in their Bibles. You might want to say the reference at least three times, in different ways, of course, so people catch it. Here's what I did for a sermon on Ephesians 1:1–14: "I think we'll find some answers in our text for today, Ephesians 1:1–14. Lots of stuff going on here in Ephesians 1:1–14. But we're going to focus on what God is doing, God's grand design, his purpose. Ephesians 1:1–14." As you repeat the reference, you are giving listeners time to locate the text in their Bibles. If listeners are using pew Bibles, let them know the page number where the text is located; doing

---

21. An image of a child wanting to delight a parent is particularly apt; it lends itself to an easy transition into the need: "We want to delight our parent too—our heavenly Father."

so might minimize embarrassment (if listeners have no clue where Ephesians is) and also save time. If you need to make a brief statement about the context of the text, or "where we are in this series on Ephesians," or some other pertinent remark, this is the time to make it, as listeners are getting ready.

I would not recommend you read the entire pericope here. Of course, if it is a verse or two, like our Proverbs examples, by all means go ahead. For a longer pericope, as in Ephesians and the Jacob Story, such a reading takes far too much time. You are going to be dealing with most of the verses of the pericope anyway within the sermon body. In any case, it is always best to lead your listeners through the text the way *you* want them to experience it rather than giving them an unglossed straight reading that lets them make up their minds about what it means before the sermon. No, you, the preacher, want to be their curator, their docent, and you want to guide your listeners through the text and its experience as you preach.

I have nothing against the public reading of Scripture (1 Tim. 4:13). Just listening to the words of the Holy Writ is appropriate—the word of God for the people of God—and such an event ought to be part of every worship service. However, I would separate such a reading from the sermon and keep it as a discrete activity in the worship service, for the reasons mentioned above. Indeed, the preacher does not even have to be the one who reads the text. I've had a Markan narrative pericope performed vocally by a group of people taking on the roles of the characters. Separating such readings from the sermon with a song, the offertory, or something else is always wise.[22] Let the sermon be the sermon.

Organization

The organization element of the introduction simply sets forth the number of moves you will have in the body. Again, be careful not to give away too much here. All you need to do is announce the keyword/phrase label of each move (see chap. 4, "Creating Maps"). For Proverbs 10:25 and 12:25 you already have the labels Problem, Solution, and Application, so here's what you would say for the organization element in the introductions to sermons on these texts: "First we'll see a Problem, then a Solution, and then an Application." That's all you need to do.[23] For a sermon on Proverbs 21:16 you

22. Or one could choose to have a psalm read publicly, a chapter or portion thereof that is somewhat tangentially related to the thrust of the preaching pericope, instead of reading the text itself.

23. You could get creative for a sermon on Prov. 12:25 and announce, "First we'll see a downer, then an upper, and finally an application." This doesn't give anything away but instead serves to intrigue the audience: "Where's the preacher going with downers and uppers?"

could say, "First we'll see a straying, then a slaying, and finally a staying."
Listeners understand that there will be three major moves and that the labels
of those moves are Problem, Solution, and Application (Prov. 10:25; 12:25) or
"straying," "slaying," and "staying" in this case (Prov. 21:16). They are also
being primed to catch these labels later as entry signposts for the respective
moves. For a "sermon" on the Aesop's fable we considered, you could say,
"First we'll see an attitude, then we'll look at its aftermath, and finally we'll
discover an application." For a sermon on Proverbs 15:8, the phrases "God's
disgust," "God's delight," and "application" will work for the organization
element of the introduction, forecasting that there are three moves to the
sermon's body.[24]

As noted, these organization keywords/phrases serve as cues that audiences
can watch for later in the sermon. And when you get to a particular move in
the body, using the keyword/phrase label of that move—as an entry signpost
(see chap. 5, "Fleshing Moves")—will clue listeners in to where you are in the
sermon. Listeners will link those signposts with what they heard earlier in the
introduction (in its organization element) and will derive a sense of pleasure
and security in knowing where they are in the sermon. Thus your oral clarity
is significantly improved.

Here are the reference and organization elements of the introduction that
commenced with Elie Wiesel's story (the image) for my sermon on Mark
4:35–41.

I would like to draw your attention to a well-known incident recorded in
Mark 4:35–41—the stilling of the storm. The disciples were in a catastrophic
situation. Calamity loomed ahead. Death stared them in the face. Mark
4:35–41.

We are going to find answers to three questions: First, Where *was* God? That
is, What had the disciples already seen of Christ before this incident? Second,
Where *is* God? That is, What were the disciples not seeing while being tossed
in the storm? And three, Where *will* God be? That is, What will *we* see when
we are assaulted by tumults, torments, terrors? Mark 4:35–41.[25]

24. I often skip the organization element, as I attempt to mold my sermons into a one-B
shape (see chap. 4). For such single-move sermons, organization is unnecessary (see the annotated manuscript for my sermon on Eph. 1:1–14 in app. C for an example). After all, there
is only one move in the body, apart from the application that constitutes the final move in
most of my sermons. But feel free to tweak things according to your own style, for your own
voice—and you should.

25. I gave the location of the text three times: twice in the reference element and once after
the organization element. I did not explicitly label the third move "application," though that
is what it was.

Putting the INTRO Together

I assume that by the time you get to crafting the introduction, the body of the sermon is in good shape, including the application, of course. Once you decide to work on the introduction, the first thing to think about is the need + topic. Then consider what image you might use that would flow smoothly into the need. Reference and organization are ready to go, of course, since your sermon body is already done.

Let me summarize the elements of the introduction.

The *I*mage says: Get ready to hear this sermon.

The *N*eed says: This is why you should hear this sermon.

The *T*opic says: This is what you are going to hear.

The *R*eference says: This is from where you are going to hear it.

The *O*rganization says: This is how you are going to hear it.

Basically, the introduction should be viewed as a contract for communication, a mutual agreement between preacher and listeners that catches listeners' attention, explains why the sermon is important, and delineates what will be communicated, from which passage of Scripture, and how it will be heard.[26] Or as Thomas G. Long put it, an introduction "should make, implicitly or explicitly, a promise to the hearers." It should be a covenant listeners desire to see kept, a pledge that they want the preacher to honor. And based on that promissory deal, "listeners are using the opening statements of the sermon to form a guess about what the rest of the sermon holds in store. The hearers, then, are not only listening *to* the sermon; they are also listening *for* the sermon they have been led to expect."[27] But as was mentioned, play your cards close to your chest. "Full disclosure is not essential, nor is it desirable. What listeners need at the beginning of a sermon is not necessarily a thumbnail prospectus of the whole sermon but rather an orientation, a reliable direction for listening. . . . To make a promise is to point toward a certain kind of future without necessarily specifying precisely how that promise will be fulfilled."[28]

Here's the introduction to my sermon on Ephesians 3:1–13. See if you can distinguish the individual elements of the introduction.

The other day a French tourist had an unusual experience in New York City. Karine Gombeau, a Paris native, was visiting New York's famous Little Italy

26. Nichols, *Building the Word*, 101.
27. Long, *Witness of Preaching*, 201–2 (emphasis in original).
28. Long, *Witness of Preaching*, 202–3.

neighborhood. She'd just eaten lunch and was carrying her leftover pizza back to her hotel when she saw a man sifting through garbage bins.

"He looked like a man having a rough time," Ms. Gombeau explained. "Here he was, going through a garbage bin, and I had food with me. And so I thought, 'You know, he should have my pizza instead of digging through that bin.' And so I gave my doggy bag to the homeless guy."

Well, he wasn't exactly a homeless guy. You see, Karine Gombeau had unwittingly stumbled onto the set of a film shoot. The movie was *Time Out of Mind* (2014), in which sixty-five-year-old Richard Gere plays a homeless man. Yes, Ms. Gombeau had unwittingly given her half-eaten pizza to Hollywood megastar Richard Gere, who is worth over $100 million dollars.

What can *we* ever do for God as we participate in his grand design to consummate all things in Christ—a glorious plan that we saw introduced in Ephesians 1? Doing something for God is kind of like giving the Creator of the universe a half-eaten pizza. I mean, what do *we* have to give him? What can *we* do for him, insignificant and immaterial and irrelevant as we are?[29] We saw in Ephesians 1 that God has involved us in his grand plan. But he uses *us*? Strange.

Well, we're going to solve this strangeness in Ephesians 3:1–13—why and how God plans to use us and, importantly, how we should therefore respond. So here we are in Ephesians 3:1–13.[30] First we'll see a paradox, then a paradigm, and finally an application. So off we go. Ephesians 3:1–13.

The Pre-introduction

There might be a number of things you want to say from the pulpit before launching into the sermon proper (which begins with the first sentence of the introduction's image). Routine pleasantries may be necessary: "Good morning, folks. I'm glad to be here." Or "Let me acknowledge my gratitude to the organizers for their invitation." Or "I can't believe the Cowboys lost again!" Or "Wasn't that a great song by the praise team?" There is a distinct need for making such public and social connections with your listeners every time.[31] You are being friendly and amiable, wishing your listeners well and complimenting them, not only with these preliminary remarks but also

29. I'm implying here that my listeners *want* to do something for God but are feeling insignificant, immaterial, and irrelevant.

30. For the sake of smoothness, I interwove topic and text, and I announced the reference three times, while at the same time providing organization. Such bleeding/blending of one element of the introduction into/with another is perfectly acceptable.

31. Of course, the preacher who is also pastoring is making *private* connections with individual members of the flock frequently, outside the pulpit and throughout the week.

with your facial expressions, open posture, and inviting words and gestures. This is a bonding moment. If you are a guest preacher, this is a good place to name someone everyone knows, the pastor who invited you, the friends you see in the audience, or the person you talked to by the coffee machine. If you are a regular in the pulpit, this may be the time to make a general comment about the sermon series or to encourage people to take out their handouts (if you have distributed one). Don't forget, in all this, to respect the tone of what has gone on before and the mood of the audience as you go up to speak.[32] Also, don't ask how much time you have (that should have been decided on a long time ago); don't apologize for anything (most of the time no one will notice a problem until you bring it to their attention); don't admit you were too busy to prepare (even if that is true, and if it is, they'll find out anyway); and don't admit you've preached the sermon before (every audience likes to feel unique).

Any such preliminary remark falls into the pre-introduction. By all means, engage in these socializing utterances, but keep them brief. And as with Scripture reading, separate them from the actual sermon. Making that distinction is easy: after completing your opening remarks in the pre-introduction, call the audience to prayer.[33] The first word after "Amen!" belongs to your sermon (which begins with the image of the introduction).

There is one more element to the pre-introduction. If you are not known to your listeners and are not preaching to them on a regular basis (or are meandering from pulpit to pulpit like me), you need to make yourself known to them. Credibility is a big factor in creating a receptive audience for your sermon. The best time to create credibility is *not* just before you preach. And the best person to do it is *not* you, the preacher. Ideally, some sort of write-up about you distributed the week before is best, with a briefer introduction just before you preach being made by the local pastor or worship leader or whoever is in charge of the day's events.[34] Needless to say, do not toot your own horn. "Let a stranger praise you, and not your mouth; an alien, and

32. I mentioned in an earlier chapter the puncturing of the audience's somber mood that had been created in the worship service until the preacher employed an inane game in his sermon introduction. This was both insensitive and inappropriate, trivializing strong emotions. By the same token, if something major has happened that week on the local, national, or global stage, you should probably acknowledge it, even if you don't plan to discuss it further in the sermon. Depending on the seriousness of the incident, you might even pray about it, right before the sermon or in a separate pastoral prayer elsewhere in the worship service.

33. Or you could deliver the pre-introduction in front of the lectern and the sermon behind it. Or you could insert a pregnant pause between the pre-introduction and the sermon.

34. Churches that invite me to preach usually solicit an autobiographical summary; I have a prepared version always ready.

certainly not your lips" (Prov. 27:2). In the unfortunate situation in which you don't get the leg up you deserve, never try to redeem the situation with braggadocio. A few words about who you are and why you are preaching that day will be sufficient. Let the Holy Spirit, his text, and your sermon do the talking.

Things to Avoid in the Introduction

There are a few things you must *not* do in the introduction. Don't do the following:

Introduce and promise something you won't deliver (aka "bait and switch"). This happens when the need + topic goes in one direction and the rest of the sermon goes in another, and you end up never providing what was promised.

Say, "Before I begin . . ." Anything you want to say before you begin falls into the pre-introduction. And if you have to do a pre-introduction, separate it from the sermon (as noted, prayer works well for this purpose).

Use offensive humor, inappropriate anecdotes, or sarcasm that pokes fun at someone. His or her sister-in-law might be in the audience. And no dissing of local people, places, or establishments. Indeed, no dissing of anyone, period. And watch out for gender, age, race, and ethnicity discrimination. Needless to say, no politics either.

Use long-drawn-out and slow-moving images. Start energetically. People know you are going to preach (fly); don't keep on introducing the sermon (taxiing for takeoff). Get on with it and move to your sermon (flying altitude). Remember, the introduction should be only about 15 percent of the entire sermon.

Start with equipment failure, if you can help it. Do a dry run, testing the microphones, lighting, or whatever else you plan to use.

Fumble. Have the introduction down pat—word for word. If you want to memorize any part of your sermon, the introduction is a good choice (as also is the conclusion). The introduction may be the most anxiety-producing time for you, so it helps to know that element of the sermon really well. Knowing it by heart also enables you to maintain unflagging eye contact with listeners. An introduction done well inspires listeners' confidence in you. They will then pay attention to what you are saying rather than worrying about whether you are going to self-destruct.

The Conclusion

You have taken off, you have flown your aircraft well, you are arriving at your destination. Now you have to get the plane on the ground. That's the role of the conclusion. It prepares people to go out into the world and respond appropriately to what they've heard from their God and experienced in his text. The conclusion forms the last 10 percent of the sermon.

Sermon	
Introduction	15%
Body	75%
Conclusion	10%

The way we've considered sermon mapping (see chap. 4, "Creating Maps"), application is the last move of the body. In other words, listeners discern the thrust of the text (pericopal theology) in the moves of the body preceding the application move; then appropriate application is derived that gets them one step closer to being conformed to the image of Christ. That closes out the body. Given that you have—hopefully—provided a specific, striking, and singular application and developed it well, telling and showing how it's done (see chap. 3, "Deriving Application"), you don't want to add much more after that in the conclusion. Keep the passion intense, keep the demand high, keep the momentum strong, and end on a vigorous note. That being said, the conclusion is a simpler part of the sermon than the introduction. Because of the simplicity of the conclusion and its (usual) location right after the application, it is somewhat fungible and malleable, particularly in how it follows and fits with the application move.

If the introduction was your first chance to make an impression, the conclusion is your last chance to make one. In other words, land the sermonic aircraft well. Your passengers will forever remember a violent touchdown, forgetting all the perfect flying you performed until then. Land, by all means (no flying around forever and ever), but take care to land well.[35]

The standard elements of the conclusion to a talk of any kind are generally a summary of what was heard, a stirring depiction of the action the talk calls for (image), and a final challenge to apply what was heard to change one's life.

For a sermon, the summary is the précis of what was heard in the body (usually the keyword/phrase labels of the sermonic moves, which may be expanded into one or more sentences in the conclusion's summary);[36] the

35. Modified from Kushner, *Public Speaking for Dummies*, 141.
36. Basically, this is the same as the organization element in the introduction, perhaps with more detail. If the organization was a preview of the sermon, the summary in the conclusion is a "postview."

image is a strong emotional illustration powerful enough to launch the next element, the challenge that closes the sermon (corresponding to the image that launched the need in the introduction); and the challenge is a restatement of the application as a spur to action, a call to commit, an exhortation to go forth and do.

Conclusion	
Summary	Précis of moves (including application)
Image	Powerful illustration
Challenge	Brief restatement of the application as a closing call to action

Here's a reminder of the elements of the application move (see chap. 3, "Deriving Application").

Application	
Tell	Say what to do
Show	Detail how it is done by someone

The difference between show in the application move and image in the conclusion is that the application's show is simply a detailing of someone (yourself or another) doing the application—mostly descriptive of how things are done, in order to picture for listeners the actual steps of the application. The conclusion's image is ideally a more powerful and emotionally resonating illustration, designed for a compelling impact on listeners and intended to lead naturally into the challenge, an equally influential and rousing exhortation to application (see examples below).[37]

The normal placement of the conclusion after the application move calls for a nuanced negotiation of how the two may be designed together. My practice has been to combine application and conclusion into a unified entity, application + conclusion, for maximal efficiency and efficacy. The major tweak I make when I combine application and conclusion in this way is the elimination of the summary in the conclusion. I find the rehearsal of prior sermonic moves to be somewhat mechanical and jerky, coming right after the application move; linking the application move directly to the image of the conclusion makes for

37. Again, the image in the conclusion resembles the image in the introduction in that each is an impactful illustration that moves smoothly into the following element—the challenge in the conclusion and the need in the introduction, respectively. If you have an appropriate narration conducive to being split in half, telling the first part in the introduction's image and the closing part in the conclusion's image might work. Of course, don't do that in every sermon. Never be that predictable; unpredictability always adds spice, both to life and to sermons.

a greater emotional impact.[38] Thus the application + conclusion unit hangs together better when the telling and the showing of application link seamlessly with the image and the challenge of the conclusion. Here's what I do.

Application + Conclusion

Tell	Say what to do
Show	Detail how it is done by someone
Image	Powerful illustration
Challenge	Brief restatement of the application as a closing call to action

There is considerable freedom in sculpting this application + conclusion combination. Use your discretion and good homiletical and pastoral sense. For example, if the telling of the application is quite precise and detailed, it may not need much showing. At times, I skip the image due to either a lack of time or the inability to find a suitable illustration. The image is one element in the application + conclusion that needs as perfect an illustration as you can find, one that is vivid, potent, and laden with pathos. On other occasions, if the sermon is to be followed by the Lord's Supper or even by the offertory—if by design these are placed at that point after the sermon—I omit the emotionally powerful image, since I want what follows the sermon to take on that role, particularly when those post-sermon elements of a worship service are linked in theme and tone to the sermon's application + conclusion.[39]

Now for some examples of application + conclusion.[40]

Proverbs 5:15

Tell

Now in the privacy of our homes, we can lust to our hearts' desires. And no one need know! No one else can monitor my sexual purity unless I let them—and

38. Also, for the one-B sermons I try to create, a summary doesn't make sense in the conclusion, since there are no clearly demarcated moves in the sermon body. If you choose to do a summary in the conclusion, I suggest restating the organization element of the introduction (the preview of the sermonic moves), perhaps with a bit more expansion. As was noted, that should make for a sufficient "postview" of the moves of the sermon in the conclusion.

39. In other sermons, I have omitted the conclusion's challenge and incorporated that into the benediction (if I am allowed to do that as a guest preacher and if it follows immediately after the sermon or right after a song that follows the sermon). All that to say, feel free to experiment, but always aim for smoothness and seamlessness, power and potency. Also see the annotated sermon manuscripts in apps. C and D for their conclusions.

40. I'll let you work out the Theological Focus on your own, but I took the sermon in a direction that called for personal purity in sexual matters, particularly the avoidance of lust.

that I need to do. So here's what I'd like us to do: be accountable. Find one or two persons of the same sex whom you can trust and who will be willing to ask you tough questions.

Show

There is a person in my life, a trusted friend, to whom I have given authority to check my browser history on my computer any time he wants to. Besides, my laptop is owned by Dallas Seminary, and I'm certain all my moves on the web are being logged somewhere in cyberspace (by parties other than my ISP). Big Brother isn't watching my every step, but I'm sure he could check if he wanted to. That alone is enough to keep me accountable. Let us be accountable and eliminate lust from our lives.

Image

"This bull has killed me" were the last words of José "Yiyo" Cubero, one of Spain's most brilliant matadors, before he lost consciousness and died. Only twenty-one years old, he had been enjoying a spectacular career. However, in this 1985 bullfight José made a tragic mistake. He thrust his sword a final time into a bleeding, delirious bull, which then collapsed. Considering the struggle finished, José turned to the crowd to acknowledge the applause. The bull, how-ever, was not dead. It rose and lunged at the unsuspecting matador, its horn piercing his back and puncturing his heart.

Just when we think them dead, sinful desires rise and pierce us from behind. We should never consider the sinful flesh dead before we are.[41]

Challenge

Never neglect the frequent decontamination of lust from your life—be account-able. Let's decide right here, right now that we will constantly be accountable. And may the grace of God strengthen and establish us all.

Ephesians 3:1–13 (Application + Conclusion)

Tell

41. This bullfighting illustration showed the catastrophic consequences of carelessness and neglect (a negative picture). I chose this story for its drama and emotional punch and the power it lent to the closing challenge.

Here's what I want us to do. No doubt each of us knows one or more believers going through times of distress and despair. I want us to be the agents of encouragement to them, like Paul was to us in Ephesians 3:1–13.[42]

Show

This week I want us to call or write or email or text one or two people going through tumultuous times with a word of encouragement: *Your life is valuable to God and his design. Hang in there.* Just a simple note to enable them to persist in ministry.

And if you are going through a dark period yourself, well, hear it from Paul: *Your life is valuable to God and his design. Hang in there.* If you, like me, were wondering how *we* could do something for God, let me say it again: *Your life is valuable to God and his design. Hang in there.*

Image

Let me close with the story of a shoemaker's apprentice in England, William Carey, who was so consumed with a passion for spreading the gospel that he organized the first missionary society in the world, the Baptist Missionary Society. At its first meeting, he preached on the Great Commission. On entreating members to develop a heart for the pagan societies abroad, he was told, "Young man, sit down, when God pleases to convert the heathen, he will do it without your help or mine." Thankfully, he didn't listen. He hung in there despite opposition.

In 1793, William Carey left for India with his wife and four small children. "He is mad," his father declared. Two months later, he was in debt. His five-year-old boy, Peter, died. His wife became mentally disabled. He labored for seven years without a single convert. Hanging in there!

While he was engaged in the translation of the Bible into several languages, his entire press, his notes, the types, years of hard work, everything burned— reduced to ashes. He started all over again. Hanging in there!

To make a long story short, let me tell you some of the tangible results of this man's persistence. He printed the first Bible ever in an oriental language. He translated the Scriptures into twenty-nine languages entirely by himself. He printed the first Chinese Bible. He started a seminary in India that exists to this day. All this over two centuries ago and in a land foreign to him.

Lest you get the impression that this was some high-achieving hero with a cartload of spiritual gifts and natural talents unlike any of us, here's what Carey told a relative of his about his strengths: "If after my death anyone

42. See chap. 4 for a commentary on this pericope.

should think it worth his while to write my life, I will give you a criterion by which you may judge its correctness. If he gives me credit for being a plodder, he will describe me justly. Anything beyond this will be too much. I can plod."[43]

Challenge

Fellow believers, we need to plod. Never give up. Persist in ministry! Because *your life is valuable to God and his design*, no matter what your circumstance or situation, *hang in there!*

In the early phases of sermon preparation, think of the application move and the conclusion of the sermon as distinct. Later, seek to unite them as the application + conclusion. Only if you initially conceive of application as an integral move in the sermon body will you give it adequate time to be developed—telling and showing—without reducing it to a mere postscript or tag to the rest of the sermon. Over time, such an approach that devalues application will cause both you and your listeners to regard it as less important than the other parts of the sermon, simply a nod to a meaningless traditionalism, a legalistic and moralistic add-on to an otherwise brilliant lecture. That warning being given, let me encourage you, when you are preparing the conclusion, to consider how you can make the application + conclusion a seamless unity. Above all, remember to exercise your common sense, your creative sense, and your pastoral sense as you structure and shape this single unit with discretion and freedom.

In sum, the conclusion, perhaps more than any other part of the sermon, affords the greatest leeway for flexibility and personalization to one's own idiosyncratic approach to preaching. I would not worry too much about the precise titration of the ingredients of the conclusion.

Things to Avoid in the Conclusion

As with the introduction, there are a few things you must *not* do in the conclusion. Don't do the following.

Consider the application merely an add-on to the sermon (as already noted). While the application is placed next to the conclusion and both can be seen as a single entity—the application + conclusion—when you prepare the sermon, treat the application separately, developing

43. Carey, *Memoir*, 623. (Of course, sermons ought not to be footnoted thus.)

its elements to the full. When you get to crafting the conclusion, that's when you can consider an amalgamation of the two.

Add new elements in the conclusion. The conclusion is not the place to put in that great story you forgot to tell in the body or to smuggle in that move you inadvertently omitted. Do not say you forgot to mention something and lob it at the audience in the last minute. Let those things go. Bygones are bygones.

Be impersonal. Instead, connect and be relevant. As we saw earlier, the introduction (its need element in particular) is a facet of relevance, connecting specifically and particularly with your audience (see fig. 7.1). But so also is the conclusion, especially its challenge (see fig. 7.2). Let it be a direct address to your flock.

Figure 7.2

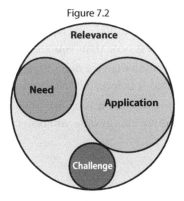

Lose eye contact. Because the conclusion is the last thing listeners hear in your sermon, with the final exhortation to "go forth and do," engaging them with your eyes is crucial in this part of the sermon. So, as with the introduction, the conclusion may also be memorized for maximal effect.

Lose energy. Rather, sustain the intensity. This is definitely not the place to ramble, go astray, chat idly, and lose your bearings.

Be overly dramatic by using an image that is far too gripping. In such cases, the image is all that listeners will remember about your sermon.

Just stop. Instead, finish smoothly and well. Just stopping is like a plane disappearing into the Bermuda Triangle.[44] We don't know what happened to those aircraft, but we do know what happens to preachers

44. As Kushner observed, in *Public Speaking for Dummies*, 146.

and their sermons when they just stop—they crash and burn! Learn to say, "Good-bye."

Skip the conclusion. For a proper sense of closure, the conclusion (or the application + conclusion) is essential. And there should not be more than *one* conclusion. If you have to say, "In conclusion" (or "Finally") more than once, you are asking for trouble.

Say, "Thank you" (unless you are asking for donations or votes). Doing so only weakens a powerful ending. However, a fervent prayer is a terrific way to close out the sermon, perhaps even asking for the Holy Spirit's help to perform the application.

Go on forever. Land the plane! Make listeners sorry you have arrived! George Burns supposedly said, "The secret of a good sermon is to have a good beginning and a good ending and having the two as close together as possible."[45] For the same reasons that the introduction should not start late, the conclusion should not end late. Stick to your allotted time. In fact, take slightly less time than you are given.

Conclude a different sermon than the one you promised in the introduction. That is, as we labeled it before, a "bait and switch" operation.

Apologize for anything. Unless it is a very obvious mistake or faux pas, don't draw attention to things only you observe or are aware of.

---

45. I stole that one from somewhere but couldn't trace the primary source. Burns may never have said it.

Ephesians and the Jacob Story[46]

9. Ephesians 5:1–20

> The imitation of God and Christ's selfless love call for abandonment of sexual immorality and the adoption of a wise and worshipful lifestyle.

9. Genesis 32:1–32

> Remembering that God fights for him or her, the child of God lives life with confidence and fearlessness.

Here's a suggested map for a sermon on this pericope, with an introduction and an application + conclusion.

Introduction

People will go to amazing lengths to find satisfaction and happiness or "blessedness." Several years ago, undercover agents for the Arizona Department of Fish and Game arrested several people for—get this!—toad licking! That's right, toad licking! They had in their possession the Colorado River toad (*Bufo alvarius*). This toad, which is found in the Arizona desert, deters predators by secreting a milky white substance on its skin that includes a powerful drug classified as psychoactive under Arizona law. It is poisonous. It is dangerous. Drug aficionados get high by licking the toads directly.[47]

Toad licking! There it is—the secret of happiness. Go lick a toad! People will do anything to find happiness and blessedness.

But really, does licking toads and frogs produce happiness? What does? How *do* we find happiness and blessedness?

Isn't that what all of us are really searching for? Isn't that our hearts' deepest longing? The pursuit of happiness. Enshrined in the US Constitution. How can we achieve it? Will accumulating titles, and power, and money, or a better car, or a bigger home make us happy? Or athletic prowess, or beauty, or a good education, or perfect health, or the perfect mate? That great job, high status, glorious reputation?

Today from the story of Jacob in Genesis 32:1–32, we are going to see how we can find that blessedness we are searching for. This part of the patriarch's life, the narrative of Genesis 32:1–32, comes toward the end of the Jacob Story in Genesis. He is arriving

---

46. For brief commentaries on these pericopes, see http://www.homiletix.com/preaching 2019/commentaries. For expanded curations, see Kuruvilla, *Ephesians*, 150–66; and Kuruvilla, *Genesis*, 394–406.

47. Modified from Larson and *Leadership Journal*, *750 Engaging Illustrations*, 404.

back in Canaan, and his brother, Esau, is on his way to meet Jacob's caravan. That's where we are in Genesis 32, but to get a sense of the momentum of this story, we'll see a recap of Jacob's life thus far—Jacob, the self-made man. Then we'll see what God does to this headstrong individual—Israel, the remade man. Finally, we'll talk about an application for ourselves, how we can be blessed by God.

Body

I. Jacob, the Self-Made Man[48]

    A. Revelation: Recap of Jacob's life thus far (cheating his brother, 26:34–28:9; getting cheated himself, 29:1–30; his current attempt to appease Esau, 32:1–8, 13–21; his prayer, 32:9–12)

    B. Relevance: Our inclination to trust ourselves and our own initiative to find blessing for ourselves [example/illustration]

II. Israel, the Remade Man

    A. Revelation: Jacob's grappling with God, the true source of blessing (32:24–26); God's renaming of Jacob (32:27–32)

    B. Relevance: Only God's blessings will satisfy, fulfill, and delight—nothing else will

III. Cling to God alone because God fights for me!

Application + Conclusion

What can we do? Cling to God alone!

Let's give up our chases, our fights, our struggles. Ultimately all of that is unfulfilling, unsatisfying. Only God—God is enough, more than enough. Be dependent on God.

So in response, I'd like to get us to do something strange. Yes, strange! I'm going to hijack an ancient church custom. I'd like to rehabilitate that custom back to its original focus.

The custom is the sign of the cross, a practice that arose in the early church. That custom was to serve as a reminder that God [holding out the three fingers of my right hand] came down from heaven [making the vertical motion: mid-forehead to mid-chest] to move me from the kingdom of darkness [pointing to left shoulder] to the kingdom of light [making the horizontal motion: left shoulder to right]. I want us to make the sign of the cross a daily habit. But I want us to do it this way, saying aloud, *God fights for me!*

Do it every morning as you lie in your bed. *God fights for me!* It simply serves as a tangible jog to our memories to *Cling to God alone because God fights for me!* He loves

---

48. I put in a recap of the Jacob Story as the first move because it helped to make the contrast between Jacob as he has been thus far and the change wrought in his character (and body) as a result of his recognition of God as the true, and only, source of blessing.

me, he gave himself for me [making the sign of the cross]. *God fights for me!* His love sustains me, his grace suffices for me, his presence surrounds me [making the sign of the cross]. *God fights for me!*

Just as the Israelites had a custom to remember that God fought for them, we make the sign of the cross to remember [making the sign of the cross] *God fights for me!*

The Barcelona Olympics of 1992 provided one of track and field's most moving moments. Britain's Derek Redmond had dreamed all his life of winning a gold medal in the four-hundred-meter race, and his dream was in sight as the gun sounded in the semifinals at Barcelona. He was running the race of his life and could see the finish line as he rounded the turn into the backstretch. Suddenly, he felt a sharp pain go up the back of his leg. He fell face first onto the track with a torn right hamstring. As the medical attendants approached, Derek fought to his feet. "It was animal instinct," he would say later. He set out hopping, in a crazed attempt to finish the race. When he reached the stretch, a burly man in a T-shirt came out of the stands, thrust aside a security guard, and ran to Derek, embracing him.

It was Jim Redmond, Derek's dad. "You don't have to do this," he told his weeping son.

"Yes, I do," insisted Derek.

"Well, then," said Jim, "we're going to finish this together."

And they did. Fighting off security men, the son's head buried in his father's shoulder, they stayed in Derek's lane as they hobbled together all the way to the end. The crowd gaped, then rose and applauded. And then wept.

Derek didn't walk away with the gold, but he left with an incredible memory of a father who, when he saw his son in pain, left his comfortable seat in the stands to help him finish the race.[49]

That's our God. The One who came to earth and died for us. You cling to him. He'll fight for you. He'll see you through. He'll bless you. And only God, God alone, can do that. You can't find it anywhere else. Nowhere else.

Be like Jacob: Cling to God alone because [making the sign of the cross] God fights for me!

---

49. Modified from Rice, *Hot Illustrations for Youth Talks*, 93–94.

8

Producing Manuscripts

A good speaker usually finds when he finishes that there have been four versions of the speech: the one that he prepared, the one that he delivered, the one that the newspapers said that he delivered, and the one that he wishes, on the way home, that he had delivered.[1]

We have covered a lot of ground thus far. This might be a good time to put together a chronological sequence of how to craft a sermon—that is, the ordering of the steps one takes in the process.[2] Here is the sequence I follow in my own sermon preparation, and it follows the order of the chapters of this book.

1. Get ready
2. Discern theology
3. Derive application
4. Create maps
5. Flesh moves

1. Carnegie, *How to Develop Self-Confidence*, 48.
2. I will assume your life is in order and your spirituality is growing as you walk in discipleship with our Lord Jesus Christ. I will also take for granted that every step of sermon preparation— and every facet of every ministry you undertake—is bathed in prayer. These, therefore, will not show up in the listed sequence.

6. Illustrate ideas

7. Craft Introductions[3] and Conclusions[4]

8. Produce Manuscript

9. Deliver Sermon

All through the sermon preparation process, I encouraged you to keep writing as you got ready, discerned theology, derived application, created a map, fleshed out moves, illustrated ideas, and crafted an introduction and a conclusion. At this point your sermon has, no doubt, come together quite well in some written state. In this chapter we'll address the issue of getting this product fashioned into the final form of a manuscript.

Why Produce a Manuscript?

There are a number of reasons why I strongly recommend creating a manuscript. It is an immensely profitable exercise, a critical step in sermon preparation.[5]

Precision

You might already know *what* to say, but writing helps you figure out *how* to do so, in the most efficient and verbally economic way possible. You don't want to waffle, digress, chase red herrings, or pursue rabbit trails in your sermon. You want to be on track, and writing things down is invaluable for the accuracy and precision it affords. Francis Bacon's words are apropos: "Reading maketh a full man, conference [speaking] a ready man, and writing an exact man."[6] Write for exactitude and simplicity, so that your sermon is sharp and definite, polished and styled, beautiful and concise.[7]

---

3. You might create the introduction in this order, though this not the sequence of presentation, of course:
    A. Need + Topic
    B. Image
    C. Reference and Organization
4. You might create the unified entity application + conclusion in this sequence:
    A. Tell
    B. Show
    C. Image
    D. Challenge
5. I will address the issue of using manuscripts in sermon *delivery* later in this chapter. Here I focus on creating manuscripts as a tool in sermon *preparation*.
6. Bacon, *Selected Writings*, 128–29.
7. That's an ideal, of course. No one is perfect, and God's power is "perfected in [our] weakness" (2 Cor. 12:9). In fact, imperfections themselves can be beautiful according to the

Timing

With increasing experience you will be able to tell, with just a word count of your document, how long the sermon will take to deliver. I can usually figure out the length of a sermon—within two minutes—simply by knowing how many words I've employed. The words-per-minute rate of delivery, of course, differs with each preacher.[8] Knowing your own delivery speed comes with experience (as you prepare manuscripts and check word counts sermon after sermon). In any case, stick to the allotted time for your sermon.[9] Particularly when it is part of a bigger corporate event, like a worship service, that has many moving parts, lots of people are depending on you to stick to the clock. Otherwise you disrupt a number of planned activities and disturb a host of participants in the Sunday morning endeavor: the worship band may have to adjust their songs on the fly; those involved with childcare will have to be responsible for restless kids longer; parking lot attendants are going to have a mess on their hands with one service finishing too close to when the second service is set to begin; and so on. Of course, if you are live on radio or TV, no one will cut you any slack as far as time is concerned. So, by all means, surprise your listeners and finish a few minutes early—everyone will thank you. The late-eighteenth- and early nineteenth-century minister and theologian Nathaniel Emmons once quipped, "Better leave the people longing than loathing."[10] Yes, it is better to be short and sweet than long and sour! And producing a manuscript helps you accomplish that goal.

Hearability

There is a difference between the readability and the hearability of a sermon. One must write sermons for the ear and not the eye, to be heard and not to be read (more on this below). Perhaps this sounds paradoxical initially, but writing a manuscript does help improve hearability. There are tools built into many word-processing programs that assess writing style. If you shoot for a style meant to be *read* by a sixth-, seventh-, or eighth-grader, that piece of writing, when orally delivered, will be suitable to be *heard* by everyone, youngsters and adults.[11]

---

traditional Japanese aesthetic concept of wabi-sabi: "a beauty of things imperfect, impermanent, and incomplete" (Koren, *Wabi-Sabi*, 7).

8. Mine is about 125 wpm. Adjust for nervousness, audience response to your humor, etc.

9. In the circles that I preach in, thirty-five to forty minutes is the average time given for a sermon.

10. Gilbert, ed., *Dictionary of Burning Words*, 484. And an "old philosopher" once observed that a speech need not be eternal to be immortal.

11. If you use Microsoft Word, you should enable readability statistics and then do a spelling and grammar check on the sermon manuscript. At the end of this process, you will get a numerical readout of the Flesch Reading Ease scale or the Flesh-Kinkaid Grade Level test. These

Preparation

One of the most important advantages of producing a manuscript is that it significantly improves the process and flow of your sermon preparation. The manuscript is a snapshot of what you were thinking as you were producing it. When you come back to that work in progress a day or two later, you can easily continue where you left off. A cooling-off time may also give you a better perspective on things and help you see your manuscript with an uncluttered mind. What you thought was quite clear two days ago might not appear so today. You might decide to delete a paragraph, move an illustration to another location, change the application altogether, or undertake any number of other manipulations of substance and style. But the final product of each preparation session is available in the form of your manuscript, and you get to improve on it the next time you engage it.

The manuscript will also be of great help for rehearsing your sermon. You have a product you can internalize, and as you rehearse, you have something to go back to and check and rework. The manuscript exposes moves that need more illustrations or better transitions and also reveals redundancies and irrelevancies in content. Wrestling with the words and the content in your manuscript can itself clarify your thought process.

Reuse

With a saved manuscript, you can revisit the sermon a few years later, change what needs to be changed for the new day and the new audience, and preach it again. But the core of the sermon (the revelation submoves especially) will remain the same, of course. You've already done the hard work, so why not reuse the fruit of your labor on another occasion?

So all things considered, *do* produce a manuscript! After a quarter century of being in the preaching business, I still write a manuscript for every one of my sermons.

Writing for the Ear

It is critical to remember, as you write your sermon, that the final product is not being read by the eye but being heard by the ear. In fact, that written

---

are *readability* assessments, so if you want to gauge *hearability*, you need to aim for a maximum of 6.0 or 7.0 on the scale. For instructions for Mac users, see https://support.office .com/en-us/article/determine-the-reading-level-of-a-document-in-word-for-mac-acec642a-f4 e5-44ee-bb08-d47fb381bb94; for PC users, see https://support.office.com/en-us/article/Test -your-document-s-readability-85b4969e-e80a-4777-8dd3-f7fc3c8b3fd2. These links (and those in the rest of this work) are reproduced at http://www.homiletix.com/preaching2019/links.

product should be called not a *manu*script (from the Latin *manus*, "hand") but an *ora*script (from the Latin *os*, *or-*, "mouth"), indicating its essentially oral nature, even though it happens to be scripted.[12] Unfortunately, preaching students, enduring the seminary rigors of producing academic papers all footnoted and Turabianed, find it exceeding difficult to exchange their verbose and long-winded writing styles (meant to be read) for something more appropriate for sermons (meant to be heard).[13] One has to alter those deeply ingrained habits of composition, the rules of which include the following:

> No sentence fragments. None. Run-on sentences are an abomination and you should never use them because you'll get marked down when the teacher grades your paper. Don't use contractions. It's not a good idea to ever split infinitives. A preposition is something you should never end a sentence with. And don't begin sentences with "and." Never, never, never repeat yourself.[14]

But we never follow those rules when talking. Ever. We simply open our mouths and let the motor keep going any which way we want until we run out of things to say and every detour and rabbit trail have been taken. All without any punctuation or indentation or fonts or caps or boldface or italics. That's speech. We should get used to writing sermons that way. All the time. As if we were speaking. Because that's the form in which sermons are delivered. Speech. We *speak* sermons; we don't read them.

So write the sermon to be *heard*, not read. As Henry Grady Davis said, "The serious writer, the poet, and the preacher must write for the ear, not simply for the eye. . . . He must lay on himself the discipline of listening to his language as he writes until it has become second nature. Like deaf Beethoven, he must write a music of language heard by his inner ear."[15] One option to ease yourself into writing for the ear, though a bit laborious, is to record your sermon by talking into a recorder or a smartphone and then transcribe the vocalized product into a manuscript. Thus you have created an *ora*script that can be subsequently modified and improved in writing. Though he is discussing how to write better (i.e., for the eye), Jacques Barzun's advice is invaluable for the preacher wishing to write better for the ear.

> Reading abundantly, in good books, is indispensable. It is only in good writing that you will find how words are best used, what shades of meaning they

---

12. As suggested by Larsen, *Telling the Old, Old Story*, 135.

13. I refer, of course, to the venerable Kate L. Turabian and her *Manual for Writers of Research Papers, Theses, and Dissertations*.

14. Jacks, *Just Say the Word!*, 2.

15. Davis, *Design for Preaching*, 268.

can be made to carry, and by what devices (or the lack of them) the reader is kept going smoothly or bogged down in confusion. You may think the sense of motion and pleasure depends on the subject matter. That is not so. It depends on tone, rhythm, sentence structure, selection, and organization. The *composition* of all the elements of writing is what occasions the reader's pleasure while ensuring his comprehension.[16]

Here are a few guidelines for writing for the ear and not the eye:

Be direct. Freely use first- and second-person pronouns as well as direct discourse that is vivid and climactic.

Be repetitive. Repetition (saying the same thing in the same words) is a close cousin of restatement (saying the same thing in different words). Have both relatives visit your sermons often. Some things have to be repeated; others restated. Repetition and restatement of important statements, key notions, sermon signposts, application slogans, and the reference and organization elements in the introduction are critical.

Use contractions. "Don't," "can't," "that's," and so on may be used freely, as may ellipses (when, in the passion of your delivery, you stop in the middle of one sentence and launch into a new one) and run-on sentences (when the aforementioned passion leads you to link multiple sentences with "and"—they do have a powerful rhetorical effect). Of course, don't overuse or overdo anything: just as too much sugar—a good thing in and of itself—is bad for you, so too is an excess of anything in your sermon.

Permit irregular grammar. Not as a rule but only for effect, and only if it crops up naturally. Such vocal irregularities include sentence fragments; split infinitives; prepositional endings; sentences beginning with "and," "but," or "because"; and the use of "ain't" and "nothin'."[17]

Use words appropriate to your vocabulary. No need to impress anyone with big words. In Lincoln's Gettysburg Address (its Alexander Bliss version, 1863), 222 words out of its total of 278 are five or fewer letters in length.[18] The Great Emancipator notwithstanding, I would remind you

16. Barzun, *Simple & Direct*, 9–10 (emphasis in original).

17. Normally such language only makes you sound both "uneducated and ordinary" (*agrammatos kai idiōtēs* [Acts 4:13]), not to mention unclear and obscure. There is nothing wrong, of course, with being like the good apostles, but you want to avoid anything that creates an obstacle between you and your listeners. That said, go ahead and break those grammatical rules you were taught in grade school, but only with deliberateness—in the interests of effectiveness—and only on occasion.

18. See http://www.abrahamlincolnonline.org/lincoln/speeches/gettysburg.htm, accessed May 1, 2018.

that though the sermon is a conversational monologue, it is an *elevated* conversational monologue, manifesting a level of refinement, artistry, and decorum higher than what you might demonstrate in a one-on-one with your best friend. The sermon should have polish, so go back over your first draft and choose your words with more care the second (and third and fourth) time around. As in all things, seek balance—here, the balance between the informality of a conversational monologue and the aesthetic of an elevated conversational monologue.

Use the active voice. It is far more effective than using the passive. I'd suggest you go through the manuscript and eliminate passive usages.

Use verbs. Employing verbs is generally better than overusing nouns, but try to remove all forms of the verb "to be" if you can.

Omit unnecessary "junk" words and phrases, such as "I remember when . . ."; "This reminds me of . . ."; "Let me illustrate . . ."; "Quote . . . unquote"; euphemisms; vague adverbs such as very, highly, quite, rather, really, truly; all jargon; any kind of -ism; "a lot," "okay," "all right"; and all the ums and uhs and the rest.

Reduce reliance on modifiers. Eugene L. Lowry puts it well:

> When in English composition class, I thought "being descriptive" meant using a lot of adjectives and adverbs. But typically, the use of a modifier does what the term suggests—it *modifies*. That is, it alters or shapes. Most of us are not greatly impacted by an alteration. We are impacted by a radically new and different image. To do that, one needs the power of nouns and verbs. Moreover, modifiers clutter, complicate the sentence structure, which again tends to dilute the power. They also call attention to the sentence and hence to the speaker.[19]

Use rhetorical questions. These stimulate thinking in the audience and make your sermon more conversational.

Root out clichés. They are as old as the hills and, unlike clouds, do not have silver linings. The writing is on the wall for these figures of speech. Rare ones may be as good as gold, but the frequently heard specimens are as useful as a lead balloon.[20]

Vary sentence lengths. Short sentences are good, but sentences of varying lengths are better.[21]

19. Lowry, *How to Preach a Parable*, 163 (emphasis in original).
20. Check out http://www.clichelist.net/.
21. Here's one of the longest sentences I've ever employed in a sermon—and it was deliberately done for effect. "Do we want to just spend the rest of our lives selling sugared water,

Don't overenumerate. Do not use "First, . . . Second, . . . Third, . . ." in one move and a new sequence of "First, . . . Second, . . . Third, . . ." in another. All these successive numbers (in parallel? serial?) are extremely difficult for listeners to keep straight. It may be easy for readers to do so, because they can see the indentations and Roman and Arabic numerals and such in written text, but it is impossible for listeners to accurately track these concatenated numberings in speech.

Create dialogues and take on roles. "What! You want me to play a role and act? Me? In a sermon? Whatever for?" An occasional sprinkling of such asides to an imaginary interlocutor can add life to a sermon.

Tell stories in the historical present tense. "So Jacob wrestles with God at night. Finally, at dawn, God miraculously dislocates the patriarch's hip bone, and the battle is over. After this, Jacob limps through life, never again fighting for himself, because he knows that 'God fights' (Isra-el) for him." This makes the action vivid. Do the same for illustrations that are narration.

Employ vocabulary tools. The liberal use of a good dictionary, a thesaurus, and perhaps even a rhyming dictionary is highly recommended.

Employ the tricks of rhetoric. These include hyperbole ("Coming to this North Dallas church from downtown Dallas, where I live, is like driving to Oklahoma."); allusion ("David, go take care of your lambs with their fleece all white as snow."); personification ("The bear fell to its knees and prayed."); alliteration ("from black holes to badgers, from nebulas to nightingales"); metaphor ("The conclusion is the landing."); simile ("Man's destiny in the universe is like a colony of ants on a burning log."); rhetorical questions ("Do we want to change the entire cosmos as we join God's grand design?"); rule of three ("Move and dig. Move and dig. Move and dig."); repetition ("disservice to God, disservice to his word, disservice to his people, and disservice to his world"); antithesis ("Man proposes, God disposes."); and so on.[22]

Minimize alliterations and puns. I love both, but don't overdo them. If you do, let your listeners know that you know that they know it is overkill

---

building bigger homes, buying better clothes, clawing up social ladders, building big churches, big ministries, writing big books, finding fame and fortune—living like flies in the Sistine Chapel—or . . . do we want to change the world—no, not the world—do we want to change the *entire cosmos*—as we join God's grand design, his glorious venture, his great plan?" It worked well—all seventy-five words of it. Break the rules if you must. (For the annotated manuscript of the sermon containing this sentence, see app. C.)

22. Check out Kushner, *Public Speaking for Dummies*, 164–70, or any decent textbook on English composition for rhetorical devices.

and that you are doing it just for the fun of it, as a challenge. Listeners—especially if you preach regularly to the same ones—may appreciate a bit of droll humor and may even take you on, trying to come up with, say, a *P* word to match the other *P* words you've already employed.

Relegate Hebrew and Greek to your study and do not invite them into the pulpit unless doing so is essential and without which listeners will not catch the theology of the text.

Watch your language. Don't be chauvinistic or discriminatory. Avoid the excessive use of second-person pronouns. First-person plural pronouns are appropriate and necessary, seeing that we preachers have not yet "arrived." We too, like our flocks, are following Jesus as broken humans saved by grace, and are being sanctified by grace.

Start writing a blog that is conversational and informal, even if it is for a nonexistent audience. This will help you move away from the seminarian's default style of pedantic, academic composition.[23]

Read your manuscript out loud or listen to a recording of yourself doing so to get a sense of how the sermon sounds to the ear.

Find your own voice and develop a style of your own. Whatever you read, especially good literature, read with eyes open; whatever you hear, especially good talks, hear with ears open. Attend and absorb. Take notes. Build your vocabulary. Expand your pool of metaphors. Think in pictures. Gauge emotional impact. Employ pauses and silences effectively. And be yourself.

All of this brings us to the next question: How should I plan to deliver my sermon?

Types of Sermons

There are at least four ways to deliver a sermon.

The Impromptu Sermon

An impromptu sermon is entirely unplanned, delivered on the spur of the moment. It is totally spontaneous and akin to what you would deliver if you were picked, without any notice, to lead a group in a devotional. Lest you

23. Most of my own writing is in the service of the academy, and all of it is pedantic. But having to post a six-hundred-word, conversationally written blog every Sunday on http://www.homiletix.com for well over a decade now has helped me break away from that formal style of writing to a more informal one, at least when blogging and scripting sermons.

think this rarely happens in pastoral ministry, let me warn you that it will! If you are in seminary or have gone to one, you are a leader among God's people, no matter what your vocational track or ministry leaning. And if you are a leader, everyone will look to you for words of wisdom, consolation, and advice in times of crisis and trouble, celebration and joy—or when the scheduled preacher cancels at the last minute. You are "it" at those critical moments. What will you do? Well, if you have several already-preached sermons in your barrel, grab an appropriate one and go with it, making changes on the fly. If you aren't that adequately stocked, ask for thirty minutes to think (and pray!), pick a proverb, choose a canned map, and take off. Even if you have the gift of gab, you might fumble for words and ideas, and the product might be clumsy in structure and disjointed in order. You just haven't had enough time to collect your thoughts, gather your illustrations, straighten out the kinks, and so on, but then you didn't have any choice. It was do or die!

That being said, let me say unequivocally, do not deliver impromptu sermons on a regular basis. Save them for times when you are stuck. The people of God deserve better. And the word of God deserves more careful handling, with extended time for thought, study, and prayer.

The Memorized Sermon

The memorized sermon is exactly that—a sermon learned by heart, word for word. There may be several reasons for doing so: lack of confidence, fear of looking amateurish by using a manuscript (or because your professors prohibit you from using one in class), unfamiliarity with the language in which you are preaching,[24] and so on. The advantage of a memorized sermon is that you will likely not grope for words, and you will not have to think too much about what to say (though you might become preoccupied with trying to remember what comes next). You can also maintain continuous, unbroken eye contact, which aids engagement with your listeners (see chap. 9, "Delivering Sermons"). The danger is that you might hit a mind-block, forget everything, and be stranded without any means of recovery. Memorized sermons also tend to be delivered in a stilted and inflexible style, almost as if one is reading what is being seen in the mind's eye (this is also a problem with manuscripted sermons; see below). All things considered, I feel that the cost-benefit ratio is high—too much time spent memorizing (and the more your gray hairs, the longer it takes) with too few gains. My recommendation again is don't do it.

---

24. I see this with international students in my preaching classes. They are thinking in their mother tongues and delivering in English, and I've no idea how they do it. Kudos to all of them!

I would, however, encourage you to memorize the sermon *map*, because you can then deliver an extemporaneous sermon (see below). I also think memorizing the introduction and the conclusion is a good idea: the opening and the close of a sermon are when you want maximal engagement with the audience, and memorized introductions and conclusions are conducive for sustaining such rapport. You may also consider memorizing any statistic or quotation that you plan to use and even illustrations that need to be told exactly as you planned them.

The Extemporaneous Sermon

While *extempore* means "spoken or performed with little or no preparation or forethought," that is not what an extemporaneous sermon entails. You have prepared well, produced a thorough manuscript, and practiced often. You have worked long and hard, but you have not memorized the sermon. And now you are carrying only a sermon map (ideally, on a single page) into the pulpit.[25] You work off that map and deliver the sermon in words that are fresh and mostly spontaneous, since you are not using the exact words found in your manuscript or the wording you employed in your practice sessions (which also were conducted with only your map). Thus for each iteration of your rehearsals *and* for the final iteration—the actual sermon—the words are necessarily different as you work off the map each time, though the structure is the same and the ideas are in the same sequence in each instance. Extemporaneous delivery gives the sermon a degree of freshness and attractiveness. It sounds conversational, looks spontaneous, and seems effortless, facilitating audience engagement and involvement. In addition, it takes less work than memorizing a sermon, but you also have an escape hatch: the sermon map available for reference—a boost to confidence. This is the kind of sermon most recommended by teachers of preaching, and I join my colleagues in its endorsement.

However, this is not my personal practice. I love the English language and the breadth and depth of its vocabulary. Therefore, I am picky about the words I use in public speech—remember, a sermon is an *elevated* conversation. The extemporaneous sermon, by necessity, has a less-finished style that I personally don't care for. Far too often the chatty tone of such sermons is

25. The amount of detail in the map you carry with you is your call. Do not add too much or the map will approximate a manuscript; hence, the one-page restriction. Of course, you might wonder why you even need the one-page map. You might as well memorize this skeleton and put flesh on those bones as you preach. But the sermon is extemporaneous, whether the map is in front of you or in your mind's eye.

distracting, tending to trivialize important matters. I prefer to say things in my sermons exactly the way that I planned to say them (in my manuscripts). I have found the extemporaneous route unwieldy and error-prone, reducing me to an awkward mess as I strain and struggle for words. Not everyone retrieves words from the mind's lexicon the same way or with equal fluency.[26] If you can do it with ease and aplomb, more power to you. For me, generating words, phrases, sentences, and paragraphs from just a map has always been a struggle. So I gave that up a long time ago; instead, I rely almost exclusively on the manuscripted sermon.

The Manuscripted Sermon

Preaching without any notes is impressive—like walking a tightrope far above terra firma without a safety net! Doing so is worth the risk if one is creating a masterpiece de novo and wants to awe the audience. But preachers serve Scripture and its Author and are not out to dazzle anybody. Their job is not to produce works of art but to curate one, the Holy Writ, so that listeners may experience the text fully. Curators and handmaids of the Bible do not need to be impressive; they are called only to be faithful. I, therefore, consider preaching without notes overkill, a vestige of ancient rhetoric and of the not-so-ancient Great Awakening, when George Whitefield waxed mighty in his itinerant orations sans notes. Here is Ernest G. Bormann on eighteenth-century American homiletical practice:

> Extemporaneous speech [i.e., without notes] was glorified because it opened the way for the inspiration of God and because it was more natural and less learned and impractical than the written discourse. The unlearned minister preaching because of a call from God could speak extemporaneously with much greater ease than he could write a sermon. In an important sense, the stress on narrative material and extemporaneous speaking elevated inspiration and downgraded scholarship as virtues for the speaker.[27]

Such delivery was so dramatic, especially Whitefield's declamation of set sermons that became more polished with each iteration to a high gloss of

26. Psycholinguistics has demonstrated that there are different ways in which words are stored in the mind: by sound, by first letter, by last phoneme, by semantic field, by association, and so on. And mental recall works differently in different people, with potential for error and a host of pathologies threatening to unravel this cryptic process. See Altmann, *Ascent of Babel*; and Levelt, "Accessing Words in Speech Production." For me, a classic introvert, always nervous before a crowd, who preaches in his second language (even though I think—and dream—in my adopted tongue), such spontaneous and extemporaneous recall of the mot juste never comes easily.

27. Bormann, *The Force of Fantasy*, 166.

brilliance, that even Jonathan Edwards began to emulate Whitefield's extemporaneity, as did Charles Finney, later in the nineteenth century.[28] The latter even went so far as to declare that "we can never have the *full meaning* of the gospel, till we throw away our notes."[29]

The advantages of going without notes are touted as follows (with my counterarguments alongside).

Spontaneous leading of the Holy Spirit. But can a manuscript obstruct the sovereign work of the Spirit? Can't the Spirit spontaneously lead while one prepares?

An act of faith. If this argument is extrapolated, one might have to avoid preparation altogether. There is always a fine line between faith and presumption. Preaching from a manuscript also requires dependence in faith on the Holy Spirit; it is as creditable an act of faith as any other form of sermon delivery—a means of trusting God to use one's feeble efforts, with or without notes.

Ability to focus on the audience and speak out of a burden for the flock. The real focus on listeners should be during the preparation and writing of the sermon—careful, thoughtful, and prayerful focus. Permit me to quote in full the nineteenth-century American clergyman and author Phillips Brooks:

> The real question about a sermon is, not whether it is extemporaneous when you deliver it to your people, but whether it ever was extemporaneous,—whether there was ever a time when the discourse sprang freshly from your heart and mind. . . . The main question about sermons is whether they feel their hearers. If they do, they are enthusiastic, personal, and warm. If they do not, they are calm, abstract and cold. But that consciousness of an audience is something that may come into the preacher's study; and if it does, his sermon springs with the same personalness and fervor there which it would get if he made it in the pulpit with the multitude before him. I think that every earnest preacher is often more excited as he writes, kindles more then with the glow of sending truth to men than he ever does in speaking; and the wonderful thing is that that fire, if it is really present in the sermon when it is written, stays there, and breaks out into flame again when the delivery of the sermon comes.[30]

28. Bormann, *The Force of Fantasy*, 84.
29. Finney, *Revivals of Religion*, 202 (emphasis in original).
30. Brooks, *Lectures on Preaching*, 172–73.

Adaptability to the exigencies of the situation. One should know one's audience and the situation even as one prepares and writes the sermon weeks before it is delivered. I wonder what exactly one is able to learn about the circumstances of the audience during pulpit time? Of course, if one spots boredom or incomprehension in listeners, one should veer away from the script momentarily. That being said, preachers should know and love their audiences so well that such midstream adjustments are rendered unnecessary. This is yet another reason not to divorce preaching and pastoring.

Authenticity in preaching. I am unsure why preaching from a manuscript is inauthentic. Wasn't the sermon prepared from the heart, without artifice, fraud, or farce? In any case, what exactly does one mean by "authenticity"? I wonder if being who we are, broken and bruised sinners, ought to be the major goal of our lives and ministry. Perhaps *real* authenticity—and I realize that sounds redundant—is being what *God* wants us to be. We are all inauthentic as we are, and we become *really* authentic only insofar as we become more Christlike. Here is what Michael Gerson, once a speechwriter for President George W. Bush, had to say about authenticity in governance and speaking—quite valid for pastoring and preaching:

> Governing is a craft, not merely a talent. It involves the careful sorting of ideas and priorities. And the discipline of writing—expressing ideas clearly and putting them in proper order—is essential to governing. . . . When it comes to rhetoric, winging it is often shoddy and self-indulgent— practiced by politicians who hear Mozart in their own voices while others perceive random cymbals and kazoos. Leaders who prefer to speak from the top of their heads are not more authentic, they are often more shallow—not more "real," but more undisciplined.[31]

More engagement with the audience. There is some truth to this, but it all depends on how one utilizes the manuscript come sermon time (see below). Eye contact is clearly oversold. How much of it does one need? It is impossible, in any case, to keep eye contact with every individual in the audience for every second of the sermon. The legendary storyteller Garrison Keillor once described preachers in this way: "Ministers. Men in their forties mostly, a little thick around the middle, thin on top, puffy hair around the ears, some fish medallions, turtleneck pullovers, earth tones, Hush Puppies. But more than dress, what set them apart

31. Gerson, "Obama Speeches Gain from Teleprompter."

was the ministerial eagerness, more eye contact than you were really looking for."[32] Let's not forget that there is more to engaging an audience than eye contact, including passion in delivery, power in content, proximity in relevance, and aptness of illustration, all in the context of the church at worship. Besides, the value of eye contact varies from culture to culture.[33]

On the other hand, the advantages of preaching from a manuscript are considerable.

A product of substantial, careful, prayerful preparation. What one has worked hard at, shaping, phrasing, and word painting, is retained in sermon delivery. Therefore, a manuscripted sermon achieves a greater economy and precision of expression, carefully calibrated to reflect the text's power and pathos and the needs of the particular audience.

A degree of control. One can pour out one's personality and passion into the sermon with deliberateness and thoughtfulness, with a degree of control not achievable with other modes of preaching.

Respect for the exalted text being preached. Preaching the word of God for the people of God calls for utmost humility from the preacher (the handmaid/midwife to the text). As was noted, one is not creating masterworks; one is curating the Master's work. The more one plans, prepares, and programs the curation, the greater the chance listeners will experience the text + theology with all its power and pathos as its A/author intended.

Adequate audience engagement. Engaging the audience is still possible when preaching from a manuscript. However, the work done before pulpit time is hopefully so thorough that eleventh-hour adjustments are obviated. In other words, manuscript preaching calls for prior audience analysis rather than reliance on a last-minute, on-the-fly, in-the-pulpit assessment.

32. Keillor, "Pontoon Boat," 17–18 (emphasis removed).
33. I haven't tried a teleprompter for my sermons. I've used the iPad version for a video podcast or two. But you can't mark up the teleprompter copy or make last-minute changes to the document easily. And unless you are experienced in using the device, it can appear artificial. Also, who's going to drive the scrolling of the text? Automatically setting the rate will not sync with the variations in your vocal speed during delivery. Controlling it yourself, say with a smartphone, adds more complexity than is desirable. And if someone else is controlling it, that is yet another layer of potential disaster. Far too much rides on technology, and the risk of complications is high. I'd recommend avoiding this modality altogether.

Prayer. One can pray for what is going to be said when one knows ahead of time exactly what one is going to say.

No mental blocks or forgetting crucial moves.

Greater confidence. While a manuscripted sermon will not necessarily preclude the fear of failure, it will considerably diminish its intensity. Confidence is a terrific boost to sermon delivery in all its facets. If one is more relaxed, one smiles more, and such a sense of assurance and safety furthers engagement with listeners.[34] This confidence is also infectious. Listeners will catch it and will see the preacher as more credible. They can relax and absorb the sermon without worrying whether the preacher will bomb.

No going off on tangents. I have experimented with ad-libbing portions of a sermon, even with a manuscript in front of me, but I realized how much clearer and tighter everything was when I followed the manuscript. I've also found myself on occasion adding something on the spot that I thought was not in the manuscript. I'd say to myself, "Hmm. . . . I don't think I wrote this insight down; I'd better say it here." A few minutes later, on another page of my manuscript, there it was, exactly what I wanted to say (and what I had already said in my haste), but better phrased and fitting better in the preplanned context than where I threw it in while improvising on the fly.

Better control over time. As noted earlier, with experience one can tell from the word count of the manuscript how long the sermon will take. Keeping to a set time in the pulpit also respects listeners and everyone else involved in the event, on stage and behind it, on the sidelines and in the sound booth.

All that being said, let me confess that there are two disadvantages to manuscript preaching, *if done poorly*. First, one has to exercise extra care in writing the manuscript for the ear, because unlike other methods of sermon delivery, what is written by the preacher is exactly what will be heard by the listeners. One expert points out, "People who sound like they aren't reading from a script are probably really good writers. They know how people talk, little nuances, and how to structure sentences so they sound natural. . . . This

---

34. It's like the confidence one has driving while being aided by a GPS device. I recently undertook a driving tour of the North and South Islands of New Zealand with my nephew. It was just the two of us and the disembodied GPS lady. We had a whale of a time, even though we were driving on the left side of the road, which, of course, is not the right side but the wrong one! Thanks to the aforementioned device, we were entirely confident and fully able to appreciate the incredible scenic beauty of that country with freedom and joyful abandon, even while negotiating a vehicle along its sinuous and unfamiliar roads.

is not a gift. It takes practice and doing it over and over again."[35] In addition to writing to be heard, one must also *read* (the manuscript in the pulpit) to be heard. Frequently, readers adopt a stilted, singsong tone, a mechanically modulated and robotic reading style commonly employed when one is learning to read. The voice goes up and then down, and then up and then down again, ad nauseam. No pauses, no breaks, no thoughtful display of the sermon's emotions. This is distracting and artificial and drains listeners' interest rapidly. Therefore, preaching from a manuscript requires one to do it well, and that takes practice and experience.

Second, whenever one carries a manuscript into the pulpit, said document exudes a magical magnetism that unwittingly draws one's eyes to it. And it holds those eyes there unremittingly, so much so all the audience sees is the top of the preacher's head. If that describes you, avoid the manuscripted sermon at all costs, for it completely squelches any connection with the audience and puts emotional distance between you and your listeners. But this is not a problem without remedy. Here is the cure: never open your mouth when you are looking at your notes but only when you are looking at your listeners. In other words, look down, take a mental snapshot of a small portion of your notes, look up, connect with a member of the audience, and conversationally deliver what you see in that snapshot. Then look down, take a snapshot of the next chunk, look up, connect with someone else, deliver, and so on.[36]

Winston Churchill, the British prime minister whose oratory rallied a nation roiled by the Nazi onslaught during World War II, won the 1953 Nobel Prize in Literature. The citation reads, in part, "for his brilliant oratory in defending exalted human values."[37] He, by the way, was a manuscript speaker![38] No doubt, such delivery takes considerable skill. Here are three words to help you get to that level of success: practice, practice, practice! Reading the manuscript out loud in rehearsal is a good idea so that you become familiar with how it sounds; then you will not need to look down at the manuscript as often when you actually preach. All that to say, I recommend manuscripted sermons, but only if you can deliver the sermon conversationally without sounding pedantic and maintain adequate engagement with your audience.

---

35. Manoush Zomorodi, host of WNYC Studio's *Note to Self*, cited in Bellis, "Let Your Favorite Podcast Hosts Fix."

36. You might find that when you are tethered to notes or a manuscript, you are not as free to move around the stage or podium. That depends on how large a chunk of the manuscript you can retain in your mind as a single snapshot. But I have never been convinced that one must move around just for the sake of moving around (see chap. 9, "Delivering Sermons").

37. See https://www.nobelprize.org/nobel_prizes/literature/laureates/1953/, accessed May 1, 2018.

38. Manchester, *Last Lion*, 34.

Accomplishing this takes work, but I would emphatically affirm from personal experience that it is worth the effort.

Here are some practical hints for using manuscripts, some that we've already encountered.

> Don't allow thoughts/ideas to continue from the bottom of one page to the top of the next. Even though you can turn pages unobtrusively with a swipe (on a tablet; see below) or a flip (of the hard copy), discontinuities can throw you off.
>
> Read as if talking. But for that, you first need to *write* as if talking.
>
> Mark up the manuscript. At least in the early days of learning to preach, give yourself cues for gestures, for pauses, and so on. It is said of Churchill, "Because his delivery gives an illusion of spontaneity and the notes include stage directions ('pause; grope for word' and 'stammer; correct self'), each of his speeches is a dramatic, vibrant occasion."[39]
>
> Become familiar—*very* familiar—with the manuscript; doing so keeps you from being buried inextricably in it.
>
> Steal glances subtly at the manuscript. Do this not so listeners won't know you have help before you but because you do not want dependence on your notes to interfere with audience engagement. There is no need to pretend you don't have notes; there is no need to announce it either. People always see me carry an iPad into the pulpit. I don't make a big deal of it, and while it's in use, I don't draw attention to it.
>
> Make eye contact. Get your nose out of your notes.
>
> Actively engage with listeners throughout the sermon with passion, relevance, illustrations, gestures, and so on.
>
> Make sure you look at the audience at the end of sentences. I frequently find myself, at the end of a sentence, looking down to get ready for the next one before I have finished uttering the first. Don't. Maintaining eye contact with listeners at the end of a sentence or a thought emphasizes the importance of what you are saying.
>
> Use a podium, lectern, or music stand to hold the manuscript.
>
> Put everything you want to say into the manuscript, including, in the appropriate locations, Bible verses you want to read. Then you won't have to carry anything else other than the manuscript (ideally on a tablet; see below) into the pulpit.

39. Manchester, *Last Lion*, 34.

Find a system that works for you. Practice it often. Use it frequently. Fine-tune it to your comfort. Commit to it totally.

Materials and Methods for Producing a Sermon Manuscript

Here are the details of how I go about producing manuscripted sermons, what I use and how I use them.[40]

Materials

Microsoft Word on a Mac

iPad or equivalent tablet that is the right size for your hands (and your eyes), plus a stylus[41]

iBooks, a standard app that comes with the iOS system

iAnnotate, an iOS app, well worth the $9.99 it costs (I'm sure you can find comparable apps for Android and Windows.)[42]

A Dropbox account[43]

Methods

Once the manuscript is finalized on your computer (whether you intend to deliver a manuscripted sermon or not, let me affirm again that preparing a manuscript is essential), convert the document into a page size suitable for your tablet. Some trial and error may be necessary to enable a good fit that utilizes all the space on your device.[44] Remember that you are going from an

40. I am, of course, dealing with the resources available to me and the routines with which I am familiar. You should make the necessary changes to fit your equipment and your style. Also be aware that what I recommend in terms of technology is current only as of this writing.

41. I use a 9.7-inch iPad Pro (Apple) and an Apple pencil (though there are other considerably cheaper options for the latter that work well: https://www.amazon.com/Friendly-Swede-Micro-Knit-Universal-Capacitive/dp/B071H7BFGN?ref=ast_p_ep). The iPad Pro also comes in 10.5-inch and 12.9-inch models; I find them too large for convenient handling. There are other versions of the iPad that also have 9.7-inch screens and will suffice. I wouldn't recommend anything smaller. In any case, don't use notecards or sheets of paper for the manuscript; in this day and age, you should invest in a tablet. Convenience beats cost!

42. See https://www.iannotate.com.

43. See https://www.dropbox.com. The paid level of Dropbox Plus ($99 per year with 1 TB cloud storage) is a good deal. Assign a folder for Dropbox on your laptop/desktop. And make sure you download the free app to your tablet as well. Other options include Apple's iCloud, Amazon Cloud Drive, and Google Drive.

44. I've found that 8.5 x 11 is good enough. I adjust the top and bottom margins to 0.2 inches and the left and right margins to 0.3 inches to utilize the entire screen of my iPad.

8.5 × 11 letter-sized page to the smaller dimensions of your tablet. You will need to increase the font size of the document to compensate for this reduction and to make reading it easy on your eyes.[45] Once you are satisfied with the formatted document, convert it into a pdf and save it in a Dropbox folder.

Now to the iPad. Fire it up and open iAnnotate. Give the app permission to access your Dropbox folder, then open the sermon manuscript pdf in the app. iAnnotate contains a number of annotating tools that you can utilize to mark up the manuscript with a stylus. I generally use a variety of pen colors to underline and annotate and a few highlighter colors to emphasize words, phrases, and sentences. I don't have a particular code for these colors. My intention is simply to make parts of the sermon stick out so that my eyes are easily drawn to certain words, sections, and sentences as I preach; I don't want to lose my place in the manuscript in the middle of the sermon. Once you are satisfied with your markings, save the document, flattening the annotations.[46] The document, still a pdf, is automatically saved to the same Dropbox folder as the original, with a new name indicating its flattened status.

Next, open up Dropbox on your iPad and navigate to the folder that has the annotated (and flattened) sermon manuscript pdf. Open it within Dropbox and choose the option to export it to iBooks. iBooks will open, and with it your manuscript pdf, all marked up and shiny.[47] You are now ready to preach.

But before you preach, there are a few important things to attend to on your tablet.

Check the charge on your device, making sure it is at 80 percent or higher.

Adjust the brightness of the screen to a suitable level, perhaps a tad brighter than normal.

Lock the screen orientation in portrait mode.

Put auto lock to "Never" (otherwise the screen can go black on you, requiring a password, fingerprint, or face ID to unlock the device).

Put the tablet in airplane mode (you don't want to receive annoying notifications in the middle of the sermon).

Switch off all sounds (for the same reason).

45. My main font size in the manuscript as I prepare is 11 points (in a serif font); when I convert the document for my iPad, I increase the size to 16 points. I put all my illustrations in a different font (sans serif), placed in outlined text boxes on the page, to make them stand out.
46. This sounds complicated, but flattening is actually easy to do, since iAnnotate has a macro that performs it for you with the touch of a button.
47. I have found that turning pages by swiping from right to left works better in iBooks than in iAnnotate. In any case, left-to-right swiping to turn pages is the way to go when you are preaching; top-to-bottom scrolling is far too imprecise, and you can get lost easily.

Turn on "Do Not Disturb" (just in case).

Exit all apps except iBooks. You want total, absolute silence and complete, unswerving submission to your will from your tablet. No unruliness should be tolerated.

Feel free to experiment and modify any or all of this, or come up with an entirely different mode of operation to suit you and your way of preaching. Hopefully, the specifics I have provided will spark ideas of your own.

Simplicity Always Wins

Here's one more thing to remember as you work on every portion of your sermon, especially your manuscript—and I've said it before: simplicity *always* wins. You and I, preachers who have spent years studying the Bible, theology, history, Greek, and Hebrew, have a serious affliction: the "curse of knowledge." We know too much, at least when compared to our listeners. And this malady has a very unhelpful manifestation: we are inclined to regurgitate all we know in every sermon.

A well-known study in the 1990s that earned the researcher a doctorate involved tappers and listeners. Tappers had to beat out the rhythm of common songs ("Happy Birthday," "The Star-Spangled Banner," etc.) on a table. Listeners had to guess what the song was just from hearing the tapped rhythm. Tappers performed their tasks expecting that listeners had a 50 percent chance of guessing the name of the tapped tune correctly. They were wrong. Listeners got it right 2.5 percent of the time.[48] The reason for this discrepancy between expectation and result? Tappers knew too much. They, hearing the song in their heads, assumed everyone (or at least one out of every two people) would recognize the tune. It was impossible for them to imagine someone *not* knowing what they, the tappers, knew. But listeners were completely oblivious to the tappers' intentions. They were hearing only a series of rhythmic taps that, for thirty-nine out of forty individuals, meant absolutely nothing. "Our knowledge has 'cursed' us. And it becomes difficult for us to share our knowledge with others, because we can't really re-create our listener's state of mind."[49] The curse of knowledge is a dangerous thing for the preacher. Cure yourself of that affliction by swallowing the pill called "simplicity."

48. Newton, "Rocky Road from Actions to Intentions."
49. Heath and Heath, *Made to Stick*, 20.

R: SIMPLICITY. One pill every hour when preparing a sermon. Refills for a lifetime of ministry. No substitutes.

Stephen Pinker is right: "The main cause of incomprehensible prose is the difficulty of imagining what it is like for someone else not to know what you know."[50] A key task when attending to simplicity in the preparation of sermons is deciding what *not* to use, from commentaries and one's own research.[51] This alone will remove most of the foul effects of the curse of knowledge that has befallen us.

As for sermon titles, here is my advice in three words: forget about it! That's all you need to know. I've rarely found it necessary to create a perfect title for any of my sermons. If the goal is to be catchy, go ahead and craft one. Once, at the behest of conference organizers who insisted on a title for my scheduled sermon, I concocted this one as I prepared to preach on Mark 7: "Dogs and Demons." Other than the fact that Mark 7 mentions both dogs and demons, it really had nothing to do with the text (or with the sermon). Did it draw a huge crowd? I doubt it. And no one asked me after the sermon why I had misled them either. Most importantly, I hope you will be preaching *lectio continua*, and in that case, titles assume even less importance.

Plagiarism

There is, these days, "a crime wave of homiletical petty larceny," lamented Thomas G. Long.[52] He was referring to the borrowing of another's sermonic material and incorporating it into, or using it as, one's own. The widespread access to the internet, the plethora of sermon podcasts available, and the proliferation of sermon-hawking sites have tempted many a preacher to buy, borrow, or burgle material for the coming Sunday (or whenever a sermon is required). One can appropriate an entire sermon verbatim, a sermon map or portions thereof, specific sentences or phrases, one or more illustrations, or even just the application—the possibilities in scope and scale of the adoption are almost endless. A student of mine once preached a sermon in class that contained several hundred of *my own words*—not to mention my entire sermon map—taken verbatim from a sermon on the same text I had preached

---

50. Pinker, *Sense of Style*, 57.
51. As far as my own commentaries are concerned, no more than 15–20 percent of what is in their pages—clues to the theology of the pericope—should show up in the revelation submoves of the sermons.
52. Long, "Stolen Goods," 18.

just a year earlier. Now that's guts! Listening to it was like an out-of-body experience for me.[53]

A quick word on definition: if attribution is made, borrowing material is not plagiarism[54]—assuming, of course, that copyright is not violated in the process.[55]

> Plagiarism occurs . . . whenever a writer appropriates material that falls outside the sphere of common knowledge, and is from any source not [one's] own *without indicating [one's] indebtedness* to that source. The theft may have to do with substance (i.e., ideas or information taken from a source *without acknowledgment* in the form of proper documentation), or it may have to do with verbal expression (i.e., wording or phraseology taken from a source *without acknowledgment* . . .).[56]

Putting aside this definition of plagiarism as a criterion, here are my two gauges for assessing whether the borrowing constitutes a "felony" for preachers: desertion and deception. If the borrowing falls into one (or both) of these categories, then the act is, indeed, "homiletical petty larceny" or at least a deed worthy of condemnation, regardless of whether it is technically plagiarism.[57]

Desertion

If the need for borrowing from another's sermon arises because I have deserted my post as the shepherd of my flock, as the pastor of God's people, and as their spiritual formation director, then that borrowing is cause for concern whether acknowledged or not. I am declaring that because of my slothful and cowardly desertion—I didn't work hard enough, I didn't allocate

---

53. I, the prof, got an A+ for that sermon, and he, the student, got an F.

54. From the Latin *plagiárius*, "kidnapper" or "plagiarist"; from *plagium*, "kidnapping"; from *plaga*, "net."

55. As long as there is no commercial use being made of these elements, it is the rare borrower who violates copyright. Check out the helpful information sheet from the General Council on Finance and Administration of the Methodist Church: "Copyright Compliance for Local Churches," http://s3.amazonaws.com/Website_GCFA/reports/legal/documents/Copyright _Compliance_for_Local_Chuches_2015.pdf, accessed May 1, 2018.

56. *Student Handbook 2016–18* (emphasis added).

57. Both of these categories, desertion and deception, as we shall see, deal with intentional borrowing. There is also a form of unintentional borrowing, the unwitting use of another's material, in whole or in part, due to sloppy research and note taking without marking sources or due to a long-term interaction with that source material and a tacit absorption of its ideas and words into one's psyche. This too falls under the category of plagiarism, because the borrowing of material remains unacknowledged. But I will not deal with this inadvertent variety of borrowing here. Due diligence and care in one's handling of others' material should preclude such unpremeditated and unconscious incorporation into one's own work.

my time well enough, I was too lazy, I went AWOL (or some other excuse for dereliction of duty)—I will make use of someone else's work. Martin Luther noted:

> [There are] some lazy pastors and preachers, who are no good themselves, those who count on getting their sermons from these [commentaries] and other good books. They do not pray, do not study, do not read, do not meditate on anything in Scripture, just as if on account of [these books] one did not have to read the Bible. . . . And they are nothing but parrots or jackdaws that learn to repeat without understanding.[58]

Desertion-driven borrowing is inexcusable whether or not I give attribution to the source from which I borrowed. That is, my slacking is not exonerated even if my borrowing does not fall into the category of plagiarism. Desertion is culpable, regardless of my integrity in crediting the source(s) of my copying.

Deception

I will be the first to grant that there may be occasions—no, there *will be* occasions—when you just do not have enough time to get ready for the next sermon. And not because you have deserted your post. All manner of pastoral exigencies can tyrannize your days even if you have been dutiful and responsible to the best of your ability. All kinds of shepherding responsibilities can hijack your schedule, leaving you bereft of the energy, resources, space, and time needed to prepare an upcoming sermon.[59] Or perhaps you are burning out, at the end of your tether. Maybe you just aren't as good as you thought you were at this whole sermon-production business. You don't have a staff to do the research, or you don't have the books, or access to them, in the small town where your church is located.[60] Or maybe you have encountered some other difficulty not easily and immediately correctable. What do you do then? Your heart is well-intentioned. You want to meet the needs of your flock to the best of your ability, and in this situation, you find

---

58. Luther, "Preface to Johann Spangenberg," 285.

59. I would, of course, strongly recommend planning ahead, as was discussed in chap. 1, "Getting Ready." Such planning does not make preparation waterproof, but the chances of taking on an unexpected leak (an emergency of some sort) that causes scuttling of preparation time will be considerably less.

60. A preacher delivering thirty-minute sermons once a week for at least forty weeks a year, at the rate of 125 words per minute, has to compose 150,000 words every year. Most PhD dissertations do not contain that many words, and they take several years of blood, sweat, and tears to produce, and that only once in a lifetime. The preacher's mandate to keep on producing for a perpetuity of ministry is almost unimaginable.

that another's words, phrases, illustrations, structure, or entire sermon would work far better than your own material would. After all, "there is nothing at all new under the sun" (Eccles. 1:9).[61] When David Yonggi Cho, pastor of the world's largest church of almost eight hundred thousand members—Yoido Full Gospel Church in Seoul, South Korea—was asked how he put his sermons together, he replied, "Honestly, I have never given an original message in all my years of ministry here at Yoido Church. Each week, I preach word-for-word messages from either Billy Graham or W. A. Criswell from Dallas First Baptist Church. I can't afford to not have a home run each weekend when we gather. I don't trust my own ability to give completely original messages."[62] The same Luther who decried borrowing because of laziness (desertion) seemed to excuse it when done for this reason: "If Dr. Martin [Luther] cannot write such good epistles as St. Paul did to the Romans, or cannot preach as well as St. Augustine did, then it is honorable for him to open the book, to beg a morsel, from St. Paul or from St. Augustine, and to follow the pattern of their preaching."[63]

I am of the opinion that in such a situation, do whatever you want with another's sermon material, but *do not practice deception*.[64] Augustine would agree: "There are indeed some people who can give a good speech but not compose one. If they borrow from others something composed with eloquence and wisdom and commit it to memory and then bring that to their audience, they are not doing anything wrong."[65] In other words, feel free to borrow in the dire circumstances noted above, but give credit to the fountain(s) whence you drank. If you don't, your borrowing constitutes deception—and it is plagiarism. Yes, Luke observed in Acts 2:44 that "all who were believing

61. However, it is quite unlikely that sermons available elsewhere on specific pericopes will meet the standards propounded in this work, with its unique approach to the hermeneutic and rhetoric of preaching, at least in the near future. However, topical sermons are more conducive to being borrowed, seeing that they employ multiple texts in a more general fashion (*lectio selecta*), without the focused theological exegesis called for in pericope-by-pericope preaching of the kind promoted here (*lectio continua*). You will rarely find exemplars of the latter in sermon anthologies.

62. Cited in Sjogren, "Don't Be Original, Be Effective!"

63. Luther, "Psalm 101," 162.

64. I, for one, don't buy the argument that borrowed sermons are not suitable for congregations. That is true only if the sermon is adopted in its entirety and that too, verbatim without regard for the hearers. Hopefully, that kind of appropriation rarely happens. A borrowed sermon can be tweaked, adjusted, and fine-tuned for the benefit of the current audience. Likely, even the application can be changed, not to mention the illustrations. Modifications can also be made to phrasing and structure for impacting the audience (not for disguising the borrowing). All these redesigns are means of tailoring another's work to the particular audience of the borrower.

65. Augustine, *On Christian Teaching* 144 (4.29.62).

were together and had all things in common," but I doubt that "all things" included words of sermons.

Clearly, the remedy for deceptive borrowing is straightforward: acknowledge one's sources. But the issue of how exactly to make this acknowledgment is not as obvious. Of course, one does not want to include footnotes in sermons, creating awkward insertions in what ought to be a smooth delivery. Besides, there is also the question of whether every kind of borrowing requires the same level of source citation. Admittedly, gray areas abound, but the bottom line is *do not deceive*. If you are wondering whether a seemingly minor borrowing requires citation, ask yourself, What would happen if I told the truth about that duplication? If you think the congregation would mind, then that is a good indication that a tacit sermonic agreement existing between preacher and congregation has been broken and that trust has been breached.[66] Or imagine that the author of the sermon you borrowed from without attribution is in attendance on the day you preach. Would you be embarrassed? If you would be, then citation is in order. In any case, be sure to involve the leadership of the church in your decisions if you are borrowing—your elders, your board, those in authority over you. Make such sermon adoptions a joint venture with shared responsibility. Accountability is critical, and there are benefits to the wisdom that comes with collective input on these matters.

Here are a few ways of acknowledging sermonic debt, many of which may be combined.[67]

Formal vocal announcement at the start of the sermon

Less obtrusive vocal acknowledgments within a sermon

   "I am indebted to . . . for this helpful insight."

   "Thanks goes to . . . for clarifying . . ."

   "I recently read / once heard . . ."

   "As one Bible scholar said . . ."

   "A colleague told this story . . ."

   "I learned something from . . ."

   "I wish all of you would read . . . where I found . . ."

   "One writer clarified it all for me, saying . . ."

66. Long, "Stolen Goods," 20–21.

67. The more that is borrowed from the sermon of another, the more detailed the acknowledgment should be. If you haven't given listeners a sense of the extent of your borrowing, that too is deception, though, of course, it also depends on the quantity borrowed.

Acknowledgments of forgotten/unknown sources
  "An old philosopher once observed . . ."
  "I've heard it said that . . ."
  "As I read somewhere . . ."
Note in the worship bulletin or sermon handout indicating the extent of
  the borrowing
List of the sources in bulk in the bulletin or handout
  "The following resources were helpful in the preparation of this
    sermon . . ."
Footnotes in the bulletin or handout for individual sources
Announcement in a blog maintained by the pastor-preacher[68]

Agreements with the elders or the board as to the kind and extent of bor-
rowings that are acceptable to all parties involved is wise. Such blanket statements may even be included in the preacher's contract. So in sum, discharge,
don't desert! Disclose, don't deceive!

That being said, even if you are discharging (your duty) and disclosing (your
sources), my recommendation is that you not borrow sermons (in part or in
whole) for yet another reason. Your confidence may be low at the beginning
of your career. If you get into the habit of borrowing, it will destroy whatever
confidence you have in your ability to create sermons and to preach. It may
affect your ability to learn and grow in your preaching capabilities. The danger
of borrowing is that it can become a habit, each instance gnawing away at
your self-assurance until one day you lapse into desertion and deception. It's
just a matter of time. So nip it in the bud.[69]

68. Hopefully, the blog is linked to the church's website so that it gets the attention it deserves.
One might even divide sources into "extensively used" and "moderately used" and publish these
at the beginning of the sermon series. I'll let you (and your conscience) make the call as to what
you want to do with "minimally used" sources.

69. Borrowing from commentaries and nonsermonic resources is a different matter. You are
unlikely to be borrowing en masse from them; besides, they are helping you catch the meaning of the text—its saying and *doings* (they are not necessarily giving you sermonic material).
Therefore, the criteria for borrowing ideas from these resources is less stringent. As far as my
own commentaries are concerned, here's my standard advice to readers: digest all the material
thoroughly and carefully assess my validation of pericopal theology. If you accept my conclusions, feel free to use them in your sermons—after transforming my academic writing for the
purposes of your spoken sermons (designing your manuscript to be heard). And adopt one of
my suggested sermon maps if you wish, but you will need to come up with the fleshing and the
application on your own, since my skimpy maps don't offer much of either. In other words,
borrow the blueprint and the tools and the "engineering" ideas freely, but build your own
house—no desertion, please! Of course, you have to decide how you want to acknowledge your
borrowing—no deception, please! As far as illustrations (and perhaps even creative applications)

Ephesians and the Jacob Story

Here are the Theological Foci of the remaining pericopes in Ephesians and the Jacob Story.[70]

10. Ephesians 5:21–33

> The filling by the Spirit manifests in the mutual submission of believers and in the modeling of the husband-wife relationship after the Christ-church relationship.

11. Ephesians 6:1–9

> Children obey their parents and parents gently instruct their children, and slaves obey their masters with sincerity and masters treat their slaves likewise as they both serve God—all furthering unity and promising reward.

12. Ephesians 6:10–24

> Victory against supernatural foes is achieved by divine empowerment in the form of God's armor (commitment and dependence on God) and by Spirit-driven prayer.

10. Genesis 33:1–20

> Faith in God is marked by seeking and extending forgiveness, thus restoring relationships with others and also with God.

11. Genesis 34:1–31

> Enjoying God's blessings calls for responsible maintenance of moral standards in the face of worldly evil.

12. Genesis 35:1–36:43

> The blessings of God fulfilled in the past promote worship of God that, in turn, continues the cycle of divine blessings for the future.

---

are concerned, I abide by the words of the wise one I noted earlier: "We are all thieves, stealing from other thieves." Go right ahead!

70. For brief commentaries on these pericopes, see http://www.homiletix.com/preaching 2019/commentaries. For expanded curations, see Kuruvilla, *Ephesians*, 167–68, 184–200, 201–19; and Kuruvilla, *Genesis*, 407–15, 416–30, 431–44. Do your best to discern the theology yourself before you glance at any resource.

9

Delivering Sermons

> The poet is not a man who asks me to look at him; he is a man who says "look at that" and points; the more I follow the pointing of his finger, the less I can possibly see of him. . . . I must make of him not a spectacle but a pair of spectacles.[1]

On July 8, 1741, Jonathan Edwards, thirty-seven, America's foremost theologian, strode into his pulpit in Enfield, Connecticut, and began to read in calm measured tones: "My text this evening is found in Deuteronomy, chapter 32, verse 35: 'Their foot shall slide in due time.'" Then he began profiling the wrath of the Almighty Lord of heaven and earth in a sermon that shook not only the little town of Enfield but all of New England. The Great Awakening had begun!

> There is nothing that keeps wicked men at any one moment out of hell, but the mere pleasure of God. . . . The God that holds you over the pit of hell, much as one holds a spider, or some loathsome insect over the fire, abhors you, and is dreadfully provoked: his wrath towards you burns like fire; he looks upon you as worthy of nothing else, but to be cast into the fire; he is of purer eyes than to bear to have you in his sight; you are ten thousand times more abominable in his eyes, than the most hateful venomous serpent is in ours. . . . And yet it is nothing but his hand that holds you from falling into the fire every moment.

1. Lewis and Tillyard, *Personal Heresy in Criticism*, 11–12 (emphasis removed).

As Edwards continued, his listeners, crowding the narrow pews before him, began to shake with moans, tears, and shrieks. Several times he had to pause and ask the people to quiet down so he could continue. "The wrath of God burns against them, their damnation does not slumber; the pit is prepared, the fire is made ready, the furnace is now hot, ready to receive them; the flames do now rage and glow. The glittering sword is whet, and held over them, and the pit hath opened its mouth under them." Men and women were out of their pews now, collapsing on the floor. "O sinner! Consider the fearful danger you are in: it is a great furnace of wrath, a wide and bottomless pit, full of the fire of wrath, that you are held over in the hand of that God, whose wrath is provoked and incensed as much against you, as against many of the damned in hell. You hang by a slender thread, with the flames of divine wrath flashing about it, and ready every moment to singe it, and burn it asunder." People were clinging to the pillars of the room as if to keep their feet from sliding out from underneath them, as Edwards's text warned, and their cries continued even after the preacher had concluded.

Edwards's sermon "Sinners in the Hands of an Angry God" is often thought of as typical "fire-and-brimstone" preaching. It is easy to imagine the theologian as a passionate orator, playing on the emotions of rustics, gesticulating wildly, spitting words of condemnation at a quaking congregation. That picture, however, could not be further from the truth. Standing solemnly, six feet tall, at his high pulpit, hunched over the tiny writing of his seven-thousand-word manuscript, Edwards actually *read* his whole sermon! He delivered those incendiary statements in a monotone for an hour, only occasionally looking up to stare without expression at the back wall of the meeting hall.[2]

There is hope for us, folks! We who are gauged in our sermonic enterprises by the fiery pulpiteering of renowned preachers—we have hope! That hope lies in the fact that in preaching God's word and God's agenda in each pericope, we are blessed by the presence of the Author himself, the Holy Spirit. Preachers are not alone. As John Calvin said, "In the preaching of the Word . . . there are two ministers, who have distinct offices. The external [human] minister administers the vocal word, . . . external, earthly and fallible. But the internal [divine] minister, who is the Holy Spirit, freely works internally, while by his secret virtue he effects in the hearts of whomsoever he will their union with Christ through one faith."[3]

2. I have borrowed liberally—in places verbatim with only minor changes—from the imaginative description of Edwards's sermon in Colson and Vaughn, *Being the Body*, 95–97, and have also incorporated the Puritan's words from his "Sinners in the Hands of an Angry God."
3. Calvin, *Summary of Doctrine*, 173 (article 5).

Who can assay the work of the Spirit in the lives of our listeners? When God's word is proclaimed, it will not go back to him void (Isa. 55:11). "I planted, Apollos watered, but God caused growth," declares Paul (1 Cor. 3:6). That, of course, does not mean we shouldn't work hard at preaching, with diligence and responsibility and to the best of our ability: Paul *did* plant, and Apollos *did* water. That too is part of the conscientious and faithful stewardship of what God has entrusted us with. So along with laboring at discerning theology, deriving application, creating maps, fleshing moves, crafting introductions and conclusions, illustrating ideas, and producing manuscripts, we must also strive to deliver well the final product, the sermon. In this chapter we will deal with the facets of sermon delivery—all the aspects of sermonic communication besides actual words and content.[4]

"[W]hen Demosthenes [the legendary fourth-century-BCE Greek orator] was asked what was the most important thing in the whole business of oratory, he gave the prize to Delivery, and he gave it the second and third place too, until they stopped asking; we must therefore suppose that he thought of it not just as the first faculty needed, but as the only one."[5] So committed was Demosthenes to the importance of delivery that he is said to have practiced enunciation with pebbles in his mouth to get rid of a lisp.[6] How much more should we be burdened by the preaching of the word of God to the people of God! Delivery is critical and has been known to be so from the time of the ancient rhetoricians onward. Pliny the Younger (61–113 CE), the Roman writer and magistrate, said, "We are always being told that the spoken word is much more effective; however well a piece of writing makes its point, anything which is driven into the mind by the delivery and expressions, the appearance and gestures of a speaker, remains deeply implanted there."[7]

A study in the late 1960s by Albert Mehrabian achieved canonical status among those who write of delivery, giving rise to the 7%-38%-55% rule, demarcating listeners' positive feelings toward the speaker/speech: total liking = 7% verbal liking + 38% vocal liking + 55% facial liking.[8] In other words, 93 percent of listeners' liking of a speech depends on nonverbal, non-content-related communication. Therefore, we preachers, who are in the motivation business, *must* take delivery seriously. And dealing as we do with God's truth

---

4. "Delivery" comes from the Latin *de* + *liberāre*, "to free from." A speech delivered is a speech liberated, released, unloosed by the speaker for listeners. Delivery, then, deals with how this liberation occurs.

5. Quintilian, *Orator's Education* 87, 89 (11.3.6).

6. Plutarch, *Lives* 27 (11.1).

7. Pliny the Younger, "To Maecilius Nepos," 87, 89 (2.3.9–10).

8. Mehrabian, "Inference of Attitudes"; Mehrabian, *Silent Messages*, 43–44.

from God's word for God's people to conform them to the image of God's Son in the power of God's Spirit, we must be ready to do whatever it takes—short of sin—to deliver our sermons well.[9] "To all I have become all things, so that by all means I might save some" (1 Cor. 9:22). We should therefore endeavor to remove every obstacle that stands in the way of effective communication.

Preachers must remember, however, that the closer the message is to the needs of the listeners—or the better they have created felt needs that match the thrust and force of the text—the less the importance of nonverbal communication. For instance, if you, a medical researcher, have just won the Nobel Prize in Medicine for discovering the cure for breast cancer, and you are speaking to a group of breast cancer patients, you might be the most boring speaker on the planet with an utterly unimpressive delivery, but your listeners will hang on to your every word, simply because they have a pressing need and perceive that you have an answer to that need. No doubt, your communication will be improved by your being smart and persuasive in delivery, but the intensity of your listeners' need/want for a life-saving cure and their expectation that you can provide that cure will obviate, to a great extent, the necessity of any pyrotechnics in delivery.

That being said, there is no doubt that nonverbal communication (delivery) has a significant effect on the speaker's credibility and the audience's persuadability. Listeners tend to trust those nonverbal facets of communication because they are usually unplanned and unprogrammed by the speaker; such spontaneous cues are considered difficult to fake or manufacture.

The fundamental principle behind delivery is that you be natural and yourself—the best version of yourself that you can be with God's help. Don't try to be someone else or what you'd like to be. With naturalness comes confidence, and listeners will sense your assuredness and that you seem to be comfortable preaching. As a result, they will forget you and focus on what you are saying and thus experience the text with its fullness of force. Thus delivery must become almost transparent and not draw attention to itself. That is to say, when accomplished well, it will not stand out. However, *poor* delivery will draw attention to itself and be a hindrance to the audience catching the thrust of the text. Let nothing prevent God's people from experiencing God's word and, indeed, from experiencing God himself. Remember, the message isn't yours—it's God's; the messenger isn't you—it's God's Spirit; and the people aren't yours—they're God's. Preaching is not about us preachers—not at all!

9. This is vital not just in sermon delivery, of course; we will strive to do well, God willing, in every aspect of preaching and, indeed, of our lives!

Elements of Delivery

So again, sermon delivery deals with all the aspects of homiletical communication besides the actual words and content. The standard elements of delivery include proxemics (utilization of space), kinesics (appropriateness of movement), ophthalmics (expressions of eyes [and face]), vocalics (control of voice), and extrinsics (management of appearance).[10]

Proxemics

Proxemics deals with how speakers use surrounding space for their communicative acts. You want to be as close as possible to your audience for maximum impact. Bring listeners forward if there are empty rows in the front. If it is within your control, use whatever means available—rope, ribbon, tape—to block off the last few rows and force everyone to be seated in front.[11] Here is a rule of thumb: if the number of listeners is fewer than thirty, use a semicircular seating arrangement; if the count is between thirty and sixty, use a double semicircle; if it is over sixty, set up classroom rows.

Empty chairs are also best avoided if you can help it. Pack everyone together; doing so brings everyone closer and increases the energy of the audience as a unified body. They laugh louder, they react more emphatically, they respond more freely. This is because in a packed room individuals tend to act not so much as discrete persons, one separate from another, but as a single organism, each member feeding off the others.

As does distance, elevation also separates you and your audience. If you are on a raised platform, listeners may perceive that they are being talked down to. Amphitheaters, on the other hand, avoid that problem, since most seats are at a higher level than the stage.

Big, ornate pulpits also tend to stand in the way, blocking the space between preacher and congregation. Depending on the building and its facilities, there may not be much you can do to minimize obstruction, but, generally speaking, the fewer the pieces of furniture between you and your listeners, the better. All you need is a place for your notes/tablet/Bible.[12] A simple music stand should

10. I have modified and expanded on some of the categories mentioned in Litfin, *Public Speaking*, 314–30.
11. Here's an easy ploy to get people to move: ask the audience if anyone needs more exercise. Most will raise their hands. Then make them move up to the front. From Berkun, *Confessions of a Public Speaker*, 49. You could even ask them to stand up, shake hands with someone they don't know, *and* move one row forward.
12. I carry only my iPad. My manuscript includes all the Bible verses I intend to read. I don't take water, cough drops, stopwatch, or anything else into the pulpit. A digital clock or timer located somewhere, visible to the preacher, is useful, though I hope that after carefully

suffice, its unobtrusiveness being a big plus. Even a more substantial lectern, if made of acrylic and transparent, works well. But I wouldn't eliminate some sort of placeholder for your tablet. I prefer to keep my arms free to gesture, so I need a place to put my notes.

Kinesics

Kinesics deals with body language in communication. In actuality, your body language as a preacher is important even before you set foot in the pulpit and utter the first word of your sermon. By your actions, demeanor, and posture, before, during, and after your sermon, you are communicating, and people are watching.[13] Needless to say, these basics are worth remembering: sit dignified and straight without slouching, demonstrate your active participation in the worship (or in the scheduled events before you preach), move to the lectern purposefully and quickly (you *are* excited to be there, aren't you?), hold your head high, stand tall with your feet slightly apart and your arms ready to gesture, lean forward (but do not prop yourself on the lectern or hold on to it for dear life), catch a few eyes, pause a few seconds, and smile. You're essentially communicating that you are ready, eager, and privileged to preach God's word to God's people and that you want them to settle down, get ready, and give you—their pastor, preacher, elder, parent figure, spiritual director, or mentor—their full attention. Then, and only then, should you launch into your sermon. Cultivate a sense of drama as you preach—it is powerful, particularly when it occurs in the context of corporate worship.

You should utilize the stage around you comfortably, economically, and naturally. All your movements, usually side to side,[14] must be purposeful and answer the question, Why am I moving in this fashion? Moving out from behind the lectern periodically (or moving the lectern to the side and not having it directly between you and your listeners) is a good idea. If the congregation is seated in a wide arc in front of you, movement to better connect with those

producing your manuscript you are confident about the length of your sermon even without a time-keeping device.

13. This projection of pastoral presence actually begins when you leave home, arrive at the church, walk in, and interact with others. It continues as you participate in the worship, preach, pray, distribute the elements of the Lord's Supper, deliver the benediction, interact with more people, leave the church, and arrive home. The whole package—indeed, the entire life of the preacher—is critically important, including what's happening inside the head and the heart. Take care to walk with God *all the time*, in public and in private.

14. For most audiences, depth perception is minimal, so back-to-front movements on the stage do not accomplish much.

at the ends of the arc is advisable.[15] But never pace the floor pointlessly, like a lion going back and forth in its cage in a predictable pattern. Avoid swaying on your heels, rocking to and fro, and every other kind of rhythmic weaving, bobbing, and shuffling. All these inutile agitations only weary both you and your watchers. If you have excess energy, don't let it drop down to your feet, impelling you to prance around restlessly. Instead, channel that energy into your upper body, your arms, and your voice. Show variety in your movements.[16]

As far as mannerisms go, these are best recognized and avoided early in your preaching career. Not that any particular action is taboo, but repetitive, habitual maneuvers—such as playing with a button, a lock of hair, keys, coins, or glasses—are distracting. In the initial phases of your ministry, watching yourself on video and performing a self-critique (perhaps with the sound turned off) can be useful.

If you are unsure what to do with your hands, let them hang at your sides (at least at the start of the sermon). Gently touching the tip of the thumb to the tip of the forefinger on each hand will give you a feeling of contact and a sense of stability.[17] A Merkel rhombus is appropriate, as is a hand steeple on top of the lectern.[18] Such neutral hand positions serve as launching pads for other gestures, which will take off, automatically and naturally, once you get into your sermon. But if you put a hand in your pocket, clasp your hands together (creating a "fig leaf" in front of you or hiding them behind your back), or cling to the lectern, these nonneutral positions have a tendency to become permanent for the rest of your sermon. You thus lose an arm or two with which you could have gestured.

So what about gestures? Generally speaking, these will (and should) come naturally. But there are a few things worth attending to.

Let your gestures be natural—flowing from your personality, expressing what you feel—not stiff, sparse, or repetitive.

Use broad gestures that become more expansive the larger your audience. Employ hand, arm, and shoulder; try to avoid small, self-conscious movements isolated in a tiny one-cubic-foot (imaginary) box in front of your navel.

15. However, even that may not be entirely necessary. You can comfortably pivot around a central location to take in those seated on the sides without necessarily having to ambulate toward them.
16. I have already suggested that you might, on occasion, deliver the various moves of the sermon from specific points on the stage. In that case, movements also help structure the sermon in physical and explicit fashion.
17. Hoff, "I Can See You Naked," 64.
18. Look up Merkel-Raute at https://en.wikipedia.org/wiki/Merkel-Raute.

Be bold, confident, and authoritative in your gesturing, not tentative, half-hearted, or ambiguous. And engage the whole body as a single unit, reinforcing the message spoken.

Vary your gestures. Keeping still is also a valid "gesture." When you move around the stage, listeners focus on your whole body; when you gesture, they zoom in on your upper body; when you stand still, they focus on your face; and when your face is relatively motionless, they focus on your eyes and mouth. In other words, you can, to some extent, control the attention of your listeners and the zoom lens they are using to watch you simply by employing techniques to focus listeners on your body, chest, face, or eyes and mouth.

Thoughtfully perform your gestures. On occasion you may want to make notations in your manuscript in advance as to the gestures you intend to execute (remember Winston Churchill). Indeed, early on you may even want to write in certain things to say just so that you can gesture in a particular fashion. Consider practicing your gestures before a mirror. As you become more comfortable in your role, all of this will become natural.

Avoid any cultural no-nos (pointing at individuals, clenched fists, etc.).

Demonstrate numbers with fingers, size with arms (spread or together), importance with your right hand on your heart, unity or similarity by joining your hands, goodness with thumbs up, and so on.

Place groups of people or things that show up in your sermon to the left or the right of the stage to help listeners track distinct groups in discrete physical locations. This is especially important with biblical stories or an illustration that is narration. For example, you might place Jesus stage left and the disciples stage right as you deal with them in a sermon. This helps the audience locate and "see" those characters and clarifies the movement of the narrative (and the moves of the sermon).

Involve the congregation with inclusive and embracing gestures that signify "us/we," "you and I."

Indicate time appropriately. In most cultures (that write from left to right), past is on the left and the future is on the right. When you face an audience, this is, of course, reversed: the past is on your right (the audience's left) as you preach, and the future (including heaven) is on your left (the audience's right). In other words, "preach in Hebrew."

Ophthalmics

Ophthalmics refers to the expressions of eyes and face in delivery.

Eye contact, in many cultures, is a valuable facet of audience engagement. It also improves the credibility of the speaker, making him or her more believable. "Make regular eye contact with members of the audience. Be warm. Be real. Be you. It opens the door to them trusting you, liking you, and beginning to share your passion."[19] While I believe the overemphasis given to eye contact in most seminary homiletical curricula must be tempered (see chap. 8, "Producing Manuscripts"), there is no gainsaying the importance of connecting with your listeners with your eyes. Here are some tips.

When you arrive at your preaching position, don't just launch right in with your first sentence. Take a couple seconds, pick out an individual or two, make eye contact, nod, and smile.

Be aware of cultural differences regarding eye contact; in Western cultures, it usually improves credibility. Accepted frequency and duration of eye contact may also vary by culture and the preacher's personality.

Divide the audience into sections and move your eyes from section to section; each time you gaze at a particular section, pick one individual in that section (a different person each time) to make eye contact with.

Don't forget to look at people in the back rows, the balcony, the choir loft, and so on.

Look at each of the chosen individuals in the eye for a second and move on instead of rapidly and randomly moving your head and eyes all around. Practice is essential, and one of the best ways to do so is to make deliberate eye contact—briefly, and not creepily—in one-on-one interactions with the grocery check-out clerk, the person at the front desk at the gym, the office administrative assistant, your neighbor over the fence, your kids, and so on.

Don't break eye contact at the end of a sentence or thought, particularly if you are using a manuscript. Having notes makes you prone to do so, as you run on ahead, seeking the next sentence.

Know your sermon well enough to maintain eye contact for as long as possible. Read ahead in your notes, and work hard at not speaking when you are looking down but only when your head is up and you have made eye contact with somebody (see chap. 8, "Producing Manuscripts").

Be aware that the closer you are to your listeners, the more eye contact (and facial expression) matters.

19. Anderson, *TED Talks*, 50.

Your face is an important tool in your sermonic toolbox, so be familiar with it and practice using it, as musicians do their instruments. Here are a few tips.

Maintain a normal and relaxed facial expression. A pleasant expression makes you human, amiable, and engaging and improves your credibility and persuasiveness.

Take care to match your facial expression with what you are saying at the moment.

Smile. At least think the word *smile*. That alone will relax your features and put a twinkle in your eye. "Humans have evolved a sophisticated ability to read other people by looking at their eyes. We can subconsciously detect the tiniest movement of eye muscles in someone's face and use it to judge not just how they are feeling, but whether we can trust them. . . . The best tool to engender that trust? Yup, a smile. A natural human smile."[20] Watch your eyes in a mirror as you smile, and you'll see how this works. Scientists have shown strong linkage between the observation of others' expressive faces and the reflection of those expressions on observers' own faces—mostly unconsciously. Mirror motor neurons seem to play a role in this. These nerve cells discharge both when a specific action is performed and when that action is observed being performed by another individual (see chap. 6, "Illustrating Ideas"). In fact, there is significant overlap between areas of the brain that respond to the observation of smiles and those responsible for the execution of smiles.[21] When you watch someone smile, you are being programmed to smile yourself. That means, preacher, your smile will make others reciprocate, keeping everyone in an agreeable state of mind, open, trusting, and amenable to your ideas.

Avoid facial expressions that may not be conducive to persuasion (watching videos of yourself will reveal these): lifted brows, squinted eyes, tight jaw, flared nostrils, pointed stares, constant frowns, random smiles, and so on.

Consider practicing facial expressions, especially your smile, in front of a mirror.

Vocalics

Vocalics deals with the voice, but beyond the actual words uttered. This is also called paralanguage, communication occurring alongside language. In

20. Anderson, *TED Talks*, 49.
21. Hennenlotter et al., "Common Neural Basis," 589.

effect, paralanguage is an extra layer of communication added to the words and content of the sermon. Think of it as doubling your communication time without having to add a single word. *How* you utter the words you have already prepared is the essence of vocalics.

The human voice has a number of elements and parameters: volume, pitch, pace, timbre, tone, and prosody (the lilt of the voice that, e.g., helps one distinguish between a statement and a question). We'll address some of them here, but variety is the key for all these vocal components.

> Often when listeners react to a reader or speaker with distaste, they mislabel the speaker as a "monotone." In fact, there are far fewer true monotones than there are mono-rates. Reading at a too-steady rate is a nearly ubiquitous problem. It may well be that a slow and steady rate is the most common oral interpretative problem of all. Natural speech is downright erratic compared to the way many people read. Full of explosive starts, sudden stops, side trips, spurts, jogs, and even foot dragging, natural speech moves forward unevenly. Its rhythms are endlessly interesting, and they do the crucial job of packaging content into hearable bits. Pauses of varying length, sometimes in surprising places, keep listeners' attention and give them time to digest what is being communicated.[22]

"Variety," truly, "is the very spice of life, That gives it all its flavor."[23] This variety and vibrancy of voice reflects the emotions of the preacher. It is essential that you let your passion for the text and its thrust/force manifest naturally, even in your voice. Of course, this means the passion has to captivate you before you get to the pulpit—the ink of the text has to be turned into the blood of the preacher.[24] To be as natural as you can be, you must yourself have experienced the thrust and the power and pathos of the text you are preaching.

Some might suspect that all this talk about passion makes the entire sermonic undertaking very artificial. Scott Berkun asserts, "I'm not suggesting you should be phony. Don't act like a game-show host or a cheerleader. Instead, be a passionate, interested, fully present version of you."[25] Exactly! To be passionate simply means to demonstrate the passion that the experience of the text has already evoked in you so that you might, by the power of the Spirit, evoke that same passion in your listeners as you help them experience

---

22. Childers, *Performing the Word*, 93–94.
23. Cowper, "The Timepiece," 2:606–7. That spice must also be incorporated into the words of the sermon as you write to be *heard*.
24. "Turning Ink into Blood" is the title of a chapter in Bartow, *God's Human Speech*, 53–94.
25. Berkun, *Confessions of a Public Speaker*, 89.

the text. Enthusiasm and dynamism go a long way toward inducing credibility and sustaining audience attention. And in return, listeners respond
better in every way, listening, laughing, weeping.[26] Because the gains are high,
let your passion show, boldly and unashamedly. "That means to risk losing
control—ever so slightly—in the desire to generate a storm of excitement."[27]
Being passionate makes you vulnerable, because you are revealing the *real*
you, baring your feelings, your emotions, and your very soul. Now you are
not just a messenger; your message contains a piece of you—your passion
for the experience of the text and for the God it depicts and for the people
of God it is intended for.

So again, your voice is an important means of manifesting that passion.
Here are a few tips for utilizing this critical tool.

Variety is always appropriate for every element of vocalics. It is also always
   helpful to repeat and restate important content in a different tone, rate,
   or volume.

Slow down for emphasis and feel free to accelerate if the emotion of what
   you are saying calls for doing so. But be careful. Often, vocal speed
   increases with emotion, and with increasing speed, articulation wors-
   ens. There is no absolute rate that should be your goal: it depends on
   your normal speed, your content, your personality, and your listeners.
   If you are usually a rapid-fire speaker, make sure your ideas-per-minute
   speed does not match your words-per-minute rate. You can still retain
   your fast vocalizing, but repeat and restate your content so you are not
   bouncing from idea to idea at an equally breakneck speed. Even if you
   are hurtling along in words per minute on the sermonic autobahn, you
   need to give time and space for what you have said to sink in. Slow down
   your ideas-per-minute rate, not necessarily your words-per-minute rate
   (though that might help too).

Use amplification so you can vary your volume considerably and be heard
   even in a whisper. Don't be afraid to modulate from loudness to soft-
   ness and vice versa; it can be incredibly effective. But don't trail off in
   volume at the end of sentences (a habit I'm still working to change).

Get used to using microphones. Avoid handhelds; they will paralyze one
   of your very expressive tools—your extremities. Free-standing (fixed)
   microphones are fine, but when you turn to face different parts of the

26. As the first-century-BCE Roman poet Horace said, "If you would have me weep, you
must first [weep] yourself" (*Ars Poetica* 102–3 [my translation]).
   27. Hoff, *"I Can See You Naked,"* 90.

audience, make sure you are still speaking into the microphone. Of course, you will be limited to standing within a couple feet of that immobile device. Wireless mics that clip on to your clothing or hug the side of your face are best. With these, hide the wire that runs to the battery pack inside your outerwear if you can.

Warm up your voice before the sermon. Sing the songs in the worship set before you preach reasonably loudly, though not so loudly that you strain your vocal cords. Sipping a warm liquid (decaffeinated preferably) is helpful.

Articulate. Deliberately exaggerate consonants a bit; this is appropriate for public speech and especially important if you have an accent that might be unfamiliar to most of your listeners.

Be aware of the importance of stressing certain words. Try saying, "I never said she stole my purse" seven times, each time with the emphasis on a different word. You have just said seven different things.[28]

Identify and minimize verbal habits, such as your favorite go-to words and phrases ("This is about . . . ," "So now . . . ," "Here we see . . . ," "OK," "All right," "So then," "Yeah," etc.).

Don't neglect to pause as appropriate, all the while maintaining eye contact. A pause emphasizes what you just said, permitting it to be absorbed. And don't be afraid of brief silences; you'll have the undistracted attention of your listeners as they await your next word. Pauses are also effective in transitioning between moves.

Avoid vocalized punctuations or verbalized pauses—those ums and ahs and ers. Just as physical tics are distracting, so are vocal tics when overdone. Silence is better than attempting to fill pauses with trivial sounds.

Work on rhythm. This involves tempo and rate *and* the actual sounds, all of which move prose into the domain of poetry, and poetry into the realm of song. The choice of words, taking into account how they sound, is important, as are repetitions of catchwords, phrases, slogans ("I have a dream!" is a striking example). Alliteration, assonance, syllabification, and parallelism all fall into this category.

Vary your pitch. As with most of the other elements of vocalics, variety is essential. See that you don't remain in a high register throughout (or in a *basso profundo*). Be natural and stay with your normal conversational pitch, but pick up the pitch a notch for clarity of sound, projection of voice, and ease of listening.

28. Childers, *Performing the Word*, 85.

Ensure that the timbre of your voice is fairly neutral, not too resonant, not too airy, not too nasal, not too harsh. Crispness of voice is critical for maximum comprehensibility by listeners.[29]

Minor issues of vocalics can be corrected by yourself (perhaps with help and feedback from a trusted few). Ron Hoff suggests "spend[ing] a day or two with your own voice." He recommends recording yourself throughout the day—while driving, taking the elevator, eating lunch, sitting in your office, working out—talking about any topic: the weather, how you feel, what you see, or whatever else takes your fancy. At the end of the day, listen to yourself. How do you sound?

> You're getting better acquainted with your voice. You'll hear things you never heard before. You may notice that you laugh when you're surprised or self-conscious. You may find that your voice deepens when you become relaxed. You may detect that you pause before certain words. You may realize that the words are beginning to come more easily as you let your thoughts flow. . . . You may discover that you *like* to talk and that your voice doesn't sound so bad after all.[30]

Based on the tips on vocalics offered above, pick one thing from the recording you would like to change and work on it the next day while repeating the exercise. Keep going for as many days as you want.

If you have a major vocal problem—a lisp, a stutter, or other anatomical and pathological issues affecting voice production—a speech pathologist and/or a vocal coach can be of considerable help.[31]

Extrinsics

Extrinsics deals with the externals and appearances, how you look. God once informed his prophet that he "does not see as man sees, for man sees by eyes [the outward], but Yahweh sees the heart [the inward]" (1 Sam. 16:7). I cite this verse only to make the point that while inside-gazing is all well and good for God, man still looks at the outside. Your listeners, while they may try to gauge your heart, can see with their eyes only what's external. And you do not want your outward appearance to be a hindrance to their experience

---

29. Here is a helpful booklet from Toastmasters International on vocal quality: https://www.toastmasters.org/~/media/B7D5C3F93FC3439589BCBF5DBF521132.ashx.

30. Hoff, *"I Can See You Naked,"* 122 (emphasis modified).

31. I have found the following handout from the Texas Voice Center (run by an otolaryngologist in Houston, TX) useful for voice maintenance: http://www.texasvoicecenter.com/advice.html.

of the word of God. *Nothing* should stand in the way of the text of Scripture and the voice of God therein. The sum of extrinsics is this: look appropriate on the outside—don't draw attention to anything on your person. I'll cite it again: "To all I have become all things, so that by all means I might save some" (1 Cor. 9:22). It is not that clothes make the (wo)man or the effectiveness of his/her sermon but that you will do anything—short of sin, that is—to facilitate the experience of God's word by your listeners without permitting any obstacle to stand in their way.

Here are some tips regarding extrinsics.

Look put together. Unless you are an Einstein or a Hawking, uncombed hair and disheveled clothing or anything else that suggests shoddiness and neglect will destroy your credibility. Your listeners will perceive that you didn't care enough to clean up for them. Remember, your clothes and your grooming reflect not only your person but also your perception of your audience. Make sure you respect your listeners and show it: dress up and look decent. Everything—*everything*—communicates.

Dress conservatively—shoes shined, clothes pressed, jacket buttoned (if you are wearing one).

Whenever possible, dress like your audience—maintain the "I-am-one-of-you" tone. A rule of thumb is to dress like 30 percent of those who will be attending. If you aren't sure how they will be attired, dress up a little. Somewhat naively, I once wore a jacket and bow tie to a speaking function when everybody else was in jeans. But that was an easy problem to remedy: I simply took off the out-of-place articles of clothing. The situation would have been more complicated had I worn jeans when the rest of the people were in formal wear. If you can determine the dress code beforehand, do so; it will preclude a lot of pain.

Wear appropriate footwear. I've worn it all: shoes, sneakers, loafers, with and without socks. I've preached in flip flops on a beach and barefoot at a camp. Be appropriate.

Wear clothing that gives you a sense of confidence; that confidence will project and be discerned by your listeners. It will keep you at ease speaking to them, and it will put them at ease listening to you.

Avoid extremes of fashion—both new and old. Alexander Pope was right: "Be not the first by whom the new are tried, Nor yet the last to lay the old aside."[32]

32. Pope, *Essay on Criticism*, 2.133.

If the worship service is streaming live or being recorded, you may want to avoid wearing bright white or jet black. Small patterns on garments can also create odd optical effects when seen through a lens. If you know the background against which you will be standing, choose clothes that will keep you from becoming a chameleon.

Avoid anything that may be a distraction. This includes pockets bulging with pens, markers, keys, phones, and other miscellaneous stuff; distracting jewelry; noisemakers such as coins, bangles, and necklaces; and a purse or wallet (no need to carry these to the pulpit; secure them elsewhere).

Don't keep your phone with you. If you do, most assuredly it will ring while you are preaching or praying. Put it on vibrate and leave it with your other paraphernalia—somewhere else.

As noted earlier, hide microphone wires as best as you can.

Carry yourself with "presence." This involves the whole package: walking up briskly and purposefully, gesturing confidently, speaking energetically, demonstrating care for your listeners, being sensitive to their situation and circumstances, projecting positivity and preparedness. All of these will infect listeners with a sense of confidence in you and a keen anticipation for what is going to happen, even before the sermon begins.

Rehearsing

We have, throughout this book, discussed the process of preparing a sermon. You are almost ready now. What about rehearsing the finished product? Besides the confidence such practice builds, rehearsal also improves the sermon.

> The primary purpose of practicing a sermon aloud . . . is to place ourselves in the role of the listener. Indeed, as we speak our sermon out loud, we become its first hearer. . . . Listening to our own sermon being spoken [before the fact, in rehearsal] makes us aware of the rhythms, movements, and intrinsic timing of the sermon in ways that studying notes or a manuscript can never do. We realize, perhaps, that a sentence that looks good on paper sounds convoluted in speech. . . . In speaking our sermon aloud, we discover places where pauses will be necessary to allow the hearers time to reflect, where our speech will need to be more rapid, or slower, if the power of that part of the sermon is to be felt.[33]

33. Long, *Witness of Preaching*, 268–69.

These days I don't do much rehearsing out loud. Occasionally I try out loud an illustration or some other section of the sermon where timing and pacing may be critical. For the most part, "hearing" myself say things in my mind as I silently read my manuscript is sufficient, much like musicians "hear" the music as they scrutinize scores. If you are a beginning preacher, however, vocal rehearsal can be profitable. It may also be helpful to practice before a live audience of a few trusted friends. Perhaps you could even do a dry run in the actual location, simulating live conditions. Then listen to what your invited audience has to tell you; take it to heart, resolve to change.

It is also not a bad idea to record yourself rehearsing your sermon and then listen to or watch the recording. It may reveal problems with your rate of speaking, volume, mannerisms, enthusiasm or lack thereof, flow of ideas, and so on. Warning: this can be depressing. After all this time preaching, I still can't bear to see and hear myself on video.

But nothing can compare with preaching often—whenever you get the chance, wherever you are invited.[34] Doing so will only improve your preaching, increase your confidence, and strengthen your faith in the God who deigns to use you for the sake of his people. And remember that it is perfectly fine to repeat a sermon one has preached before; it only improves with time.

Despite your best efforts and careful rehearsals, there will be breakdowns in almost every aspect of the human side of the homiletical undertaking, especially in its final iteration, the actual sermon. Have a backup plan and prepare and practice some responses to those breakdowns.

Nervous flubs. "Oops, let me do that again"; "Sorry, let me try it in English now"; and so on.

Tech failures. "OK, while that's being sorted out, let me tell you why we're doing this sermon/series"; "Let's review what we looked at last week"; "Great, we've got a couple minutes to kill. I know what, we'll take offertory again." Or invite the music team up for an extra song (they'll love you for it); or interview someone on the spot (might make for good comedy); or ask for prayer requests and pray for them.

Interruptions. When someone's phone goes off, jolting everyone, preacher and listeners, off their rhythm, try what I did once: "If that was Mom, tell her I'll call her back in a few minutes." Once I was heckled in church;

34. This includes (from my own experience) preaching at nursing homes, homeschool events, outdoor evangelistic meetings, wakes and funerals, home gatherings for international students, devotionals for medical students, lunchtime Bible studies for elderly women, etc. You can't be picky! These experiences are sure to help you find your own feet and discover your own voice.

I graciously thanked the person for his comments—which I couldn't hear—and moved on. If that happens to you, be sympathetic, never show your ire, never get into an argument, and never attempt a put-down; if you feel it necessary, ask the person to speak with you afterward.

Other catastrophes. Make sure you have cell phone numbers of those you might need to notify should you run into trouble the day you are scheduled to preach. I have had a flat tire on Sunday morning, major leaks in the house—twice, and both times just hours before I preached—and other assorted disasters. Each time I managed to notify the appropriate people about my predicament and warn them I might be late, and each time I was able to call upon trusted friends to render aid in some fashion. If things can go wrong, they will, so be prepared.[35]

By the way, don't let your iPad, notes, Bible, or any appurtenances you absolutely depend on out of your sight even for a moment. Things tend to disappear. Once, a few minutes before I was scheduled to speak, I couldn't find my Bible with my printed notes in it. I panicked. The Bible, thankfully, had only fallen behind my theater-style seat. Another time I left my iPad on the lectern between services, and one of the members of the setup team swung the lectern off the stage without realizing my tablet was on it. I watched my tablet fly high into the air, and both it and my heart fell with resounding thuds (it still worked—and so did my heart).

Nervousness

Rehearsing sermons might diminish, but will not completely abate, nervousness. It is part and parcel of public speaking of any kind, "the only sure cure" for which is "embalming fluid."[36] Mark Twain once said (maybe he really did), "There are two types of speakers; those who are nervous and those who are liars."[37] The question is, Can we convert that inevitable anxiety into something of utility?

35. Things going wrong include the next-door neighbor having a party on Saturday and playing the drums all night, your protests notwithstanding, finally necessitating a call to the cops at 3:30 a.m. I preached that Sunday morning after less than an hour of sleep. I have since moved.

36. Kemper, *Effective Preaching*, 124.

37. Why is there such apprehension over public speaking? We who put ourselves frequently under a public microscope will often find it impossible to extirpate every vestige of the fleshly desire for the respect, support, and plaudits of others. Fear of failure therefore drives some, if not much, of our nervousness. But preachers of Scripture ought not to take on the responsibility of enhancing their own standing and social currency, certainly not in and through the preaching of

Edward R. Murrow, the journalist (or was it Walter Cronkite? or Zig Ziglar?), reportedly affirmed, "The best speakers know enough to be scared. . . . The only difference between the pros and the novices is that the pros have trained the butterflies to fly in formation."[38] Lepidoptera are going to do their thing in the alimentary tract, so it is best to anticipate the adrenaline, to welcome and embrace it. I have gotten to expect and even enjoy the rush. It improves the performance, gives you a nice edge, gets you raring to go, and makes you active, dynamic, and passionate.[39] But too much of said chemical can give you the jitters, especially if you are already fortified with caffeine. Experts suggest draining off some of that excess adrenaline if you have an outpouring of the stuff. Physical activity helps: take a walk beforehand or do some sit-ups or other calisthenics in the restroom or someplace private (without wrinkling or sweating on the fine items of your carefully chosen wardrobe). Massage your neck. Breathe deeply, in and out. I confess I have never engaged in any of this. Instead, before the worship service, I put myself at ease by wandering around with a cup of coffee[40] and chatting with people about all kinds of things. During the service I throw myself with abandon into enjoying the music in worship, making a point to engage my body—feet and hands—as I sing.[41] And I pray, pray, pray!

In any case, fear is a good motivation—the fear of looking foolish but, even more, the fear of doing God a disservice, his word a disservice, his people a disservice, and his world a disservice with shoddy preaching. Fear can focus your attention, motivate you to work hard to prepare sermons, and, more importantly, push you to an utter dependence on God for the entirety of the preaching endeavor.

So expect nervousness as the norm. The key, however, is not to show it. A visibly nervous preacher creates nervous listeners who are unsure about whether the preacher will deliver the goods. If your listeners detect your timorousness and trepidation, they will be concerned that you may collapse in a nervous wreck. Please relieve them of their trepidation by hiding any extreme

God's word. Let God handle reputations. That being said, we are human, and given that we are social animals and sinful beings, any focus on the self in so public a transaction as preaching will create insecurity and cause nervousness. Let's be constantly working on the right spiritual attitudes.

38. This is another of those quotations for which finding the source was well-nigh impossible. I tried.

39. In fact, a recent study showed that the presence of an audience enhanced the performance of a skill-based task: the potential of being judged by others increased the motivation of performers to excel (Chib, Adachi, and O'Doherty, "Neural Substrates of Social Facilitation").

40. But I am careful not to drain the whole cup; I use it simply as a warm liquid to sip on.

41. Sing lustily enough to express your emotions. Doing so also stretches your diaphragm and improves your breathing.

displays of fear, such as fidgeting (don't!), dry mouth (sip water), sweating (antiperspirant and/or an undershirt is helpful; handkerchiefs aren't), tremors (don't hold up a Bible or tablet or notes), and so on. Just smiling will quiet your (and their) nerves more often than not. But however much you try, when all is said and done, your lack of confidence and apprehension will manifest themselves in some way during the sermon; listeners are perceptive and can pick up on diffidence. But that, in its own way, can also be endearing to the audience. Nervousness announces to everyone that you believe preaching is a big deal and that you consider your listeners a discriminating crowd.

Preaching is my greatest fear. Granted, I don't do roller coasters, bungee jumping, or even Ferris wheels—I am risk averse, yes. But preaching remains my greatest fear—and my greatest joy. What a privilege to be used by God!

Pre- and Post-sermon Routines

What follows is a summary of my routines before preaching (on the day before and on the day of) and after the delivery of a sermon (assuming it is delivered on a Sunday in the corporate worship of a local body of Christians). These routines are, of course, based on my own practices. I share them here simply to encourage you to develop your own rituals based on your own circumstances, constraints, and capabilities.

Pre-sermon Routines

I'm a late riser, especially on Saturdays. My Saturday morning routine resembles that of any other day: coffee (I'm not a breakfast person), Bible reading, and prayer to start me off. Saturday is my laundry day. I don't go out all day (except to the gym). I try not to engage with others.[42] If I have any social activity scheduled, I am content to let others be the life of the party. I rest my voice. I may work on other writing projects. I read, but not sermon-related material. I watch cricket if there's a game on (and there always is, somewhere in the world, praise God!). I listen to music. I eat leftovers.[43] I pick my clothes for Sunday.

Saturdays before I preach are, therefore, deliberately slow, marked by the disciplines of abstinence, particularly silence and solitude. I reflect about random things. Throughout the day, I pray for those who will be listening to me the next day, for the worship team, for all that goes on in the service.

---

42. Not a particularly hard restriction for a confirmed bachelor who thrives on solitude.
43. What's new? Another idiosyncrasy of the single life.

I do everything but sermon preparation. Unless I'm pushed to polish the manuscript at this eleventh hour, I prefer to leave it alone.[44] The day before I preach is always leisurely and unhurried. I am "gliding," as Ron Hoff puts it:

> You're sitting there, by yourself, at just a little after 7:00 PM—the night before. You've got about six waking hours until your presentation. *What are you going to do?*
>
> You put your nervous system on "fluid drive." From now on, you're just going to *glide.* Any crashing calamities or "crises"—unless life-risking—will be quietly put aside. . . . Your mind is reserved for your presentation and your private thoughts about it.
>
> Have a quiet dinner, with a quiet person. Nice, but quiet. Don't talk business if you can possibly avoid it. If you're alone, *glide.* . . .
>
> Practice positive self-imagery. . . . You are minimizing the possibility of surprise. You hear what you sound like. You visualize what you look like. And you're already familiar with the environment. . . .
>
> The night before is the time for settling into your presentation. It is not the time for massive, unsettling changes. . . .
>
> Go to bed at a reasonable hour. . . . It's 11:00 PM. The night before. Lights out. Sleep well. You're going to be terrific.[45]

Though, as I noted, I am not into formal breakfasts, my routine the morning I preach includes some flavored yogurt (a single guy's staple). I also make sure I am well hydrated, but not so overhydrated to need frequent bathroom breaks.

I always arrive early at the church or the location where I will be preaching; I am more relaxed that way. If I get the chance, I hop onto the stage and take a look at everything from the preaching position, familiarizing myself with the view. I ensure that all the requisite technology works and that there is a lectern in place (at a height suitable for me—usually elbow level works for most preachers). I fit on the microphone and do a sound check; getting used to hearing myself on the location speakers is helpful.

To reduce last-minute stress, I meander through the halls and aisles of the facility before the service, meeting people I know, befriending those I don't, cracking jokes and laughing a lot. This also helps my breathing and the dissemination of some of my nerves, not to mention making me more human and credible to one and all, even before I get up to the pulpit. I also arrange

---

44. However, there is one aspect of preparation that I save till Saturday evening, and that is marking up my manuscript (on my iPad with iAnnotate; see chap. 8, "Producing Manuscripts") while supine on my couch.

45. Hoff, *"I Can See You Naked,"* 66–67 (emphasis in original).

to pray for a few minutes with one or more of the elders and/or with the worship team. Having people pray for me is another remarkable stress reliever.

Post-sermon Routines

After the sermon, don't get high on compliments or low with brickbats—and both are sure to come your way. While the reactions of your listeners are not unimportant, our call as preachers is to be faithful to the one who called us into his service. "One should consider us this way—as servants of Christ and stewards of the mysteries of God. Now what is sought in stewards is that they be found faithful" (1 Cor. 4:1–2). Paul explicitly observed that his goal as one "approved by God to be entrusted with the good news" was that he might "speak, not as pleasing men, but God, who examines our hearts" (1 Thess. 2:4).

Preaching takes its toll on me, physically, mentally, and emotionally, as I'm sure it does on most preachers. Lunch after church is usually with friends with whom I can be whatever I care to be: loquacious or silent, vocal or pensive. There is rarely any discussion of the sermon unless my friends have questions for me; it's usually the same crowd, and they know me well. This is my time to come down from the high-energy level of delivering a sermon.

Soon, I'm back on my own again, recovering. A trip to the gym and a dip in a hot tub (a standard Sunday regimen), followed by a forty-minute nap, bring me back to life. Because I juggle other jobs, I don't have the luxury to be off on Monday, so Sunday evenings are spent getting ready for the next day's activities (clinics and classes for me), though I do make sure to get to bed earlier than my usual midnight hour.

At some point during the week, I try to listen to or watch the sermon I delivered from the viewpoint of the audience. How did they hear and see me? I gauge myself for animation, the comfort and chemistry I projected, and my amiability, trustworthiness, and degree of confidence. Sometimes I even turn the sound down on the video—just watching myself can be revealing. Getting feedback from those you trust—spouse, children, parents, elders, professors—is invaluable. If I decide there is something I want to do differently the next time I preach that text, I jot it down somewhere, often in the manuscript of that sermon.

And now for the bottom line: Prepare, prepare, prepare! Practice, practice, practice! Pray, pray, pray! And may God bless our efforts to glorify him and to edify his people through the preaching of his word. Thy kingdom come!

Conclusion

Cujus vita fulgor, ejus verba tonitrua.
The one whose life is lightning, his words are thunderbolts.[1]

In the fourth century BCE, Aristotle made a profound observation about public speech: "Now the proofs [persuasion] furnished by the speech are of three kinds. The first depends on the moral character [*ēthos*; of the speaker], the second depends upon putting the hearer into a certain frame of mind [i.e, *pathos*], the third upon the speech itself [*logos*]."[2] Several centuries later, Paul seemed to echo those same ideas: "Our gospel did not come to you in word only [i.e., *logos*], but also in power and in the Holy Spirit and with great and complete confidence [i.e., *pathos*], just as you know the kind of men we were among you for your sake [i.e., *ēthos*]" (1 Thess. 1:5).

In this work, we have considered primarily the *logos* of the sermon (its content) and to a lesser extent its *pathos* (the passion of the speaker and that evoked in listeners). But Aristotle had this to say about the third element, *ēthos*: "for it is not the case . . . that the worth [goodness/virtuousness] of the orator in no way contributes to his powers of persuasion; on the contrary, moral character [*ēthos*], so to say, constitutes the most effective means of proof [persuasion]."[3] In other words, with regard to influencing the flock, the character of the pastor-preacher is at least as important as, if not more than, all that was discussed in the last nine chapters. For a Christian, of course, character is equivalent to one's spirituality and walk with God. Augustine

1. Medieval proverb.
2. Aristotle, *Art of Rhetoric* 17 (1.2.1356a).
3. Aristotle, *Art of Rhetoric* 17 (1.2.1356a).

declared, "More important than any amount of grandeur of style to those of us who seek to be listened to with obedience is *the life of the speaker*."[4] And so, Timothy, the pastor-preacher at Ephesus, was exhorted, "Become an example for believers in speech, in conduct, in love, in faith, in purity" (1 Tim. 4:12).

But along with becoming an exemplar of spirituality in one's daily walk with God, how is the pastor-preacher to *preach* "spiritually"? What does it mean to engage in preaching—or any ministry for that matter—"in the Spirit"? What does that involve?

One of the classes I had to take in seminary—decades ago—was on leading worship. For that class, all the students were divided into groups of five or six, and on each day of class one group was assigned to lead a ten-minute worship session before class commenced. A few days before my group had its turn, we got together to plan what we would do. "Jake will lead us with this song, and we'll sing a verse for one minute, thirty-six seconds. Then we'll have the class stand, and Matt will lead a responsive reading for one minute, forty-two seconds. Then we'll all sit and Joe will pray. That will bring us to three minutes, eighteen seconds, and then we'll have the second verse of the song for one minute, thirty-six seconds." Right in the middle of our meticulous planning, John, one of my classmates, exclaimed, "Hold it, hold it, hold it, guys. We're planning too much. We've got to leave room for the Holy Spirit to work."

That has made me wonder ever since. Does letting the Holy Spirit work mean we work less? Does inviting the Holy Spirit to use my sermons mean I work less on getting ready, discerning theology, deriving application, creating maps, fleshing moves, illustrating ideas, crafting introductions and conclusions, producing manuscripts, and delivering sermons? What does that say about the sovereignty of God and his ability to show himself and act whenever he wants and however he wants, all our planning and preparing notwithstanding? I am sure you will agree that we have to work as hard as we can, plan as best as we can, *and* trust the Holy Spirit to work in and through all our readying, discerning, deriving, mapping, fleshing, illustrating, crafting, producing, and delivering: human responsibility *plus* divine sovereignty. Well, how different would that be from working in the flesh? How does one discharge one's responsibility to God "in the Spirit"? Another way to examine this issue is to ask, What would the discernible difference be between a spiritual preacher and an unspiritual preacher (assuming a level of omniscience on the part of the judge)?

4. Augustine, *On Christian Teaching* 142 (4.27.59) (emphasis added).

I've had a few years to think about this, and I've come up with at least seven elements of distinction between a spiritual preacher and an unspiritual one.

Purpose. The purpose of the spiritual preacher is clear: to glorify God by conforming his people into the image of Christ through the preaching of Scripture. The unspiritual preacher may have other goals for the sermonic undertaking, likely egoistic.[5]

Purity. Without a doubt, the life of a spiritual person manifests godliness even before stepping foot in the pulpit. The unspiritual preacher, on the other hand, shows little sign of godliness.

Prayer. The spiritual preacher bathes sermon preparation and delivery in prayer. (And if one has failed in purity, there will also be a prayerful confession of all outstanding sin.) The unspiritual preacher couldn't care less about praying.

Presence. The spiritual preacher, preaching in the context of a gathering of the people of God for worship, is conscious of the presence of Christ in the singing, in the praying, in the testimonies, in the offertory, in the ordinances, as well as in the preaching, where the image of Christ is proffered pericope by pericope for the edification of God's people. There is a conscious and deliberately cultivated awareness by the preacher of the presence of Christ in corporate worship—especially during the preaching of God's word. The unspiritual preacher will be quite oblivious to divine presence.

Power. The one who walks with God, the spiritual preacher, is fully aware of human frailty, feebleness, and incapacity and so is utterly dependent on divine power, succor, and sustenance. After all, this is *God's* word being exposited to *God's* people so that they may become conformed to the image of *God's* Son by the power of *God's* Spirit. The spiritual preacher is acutely conscious of the necessity of divine power in preaching.[6] The

---

5. An integral part of "purpose" is the burden of the preacher for the flock, driven by love. You have heard it said one way, but I say unto you, "Love covers a multitude of homiletical sins." Your relationship with your auditors as their caring shepherd will enable your words to go further, even if you are not the best pulpiteer in the business. See Kuruvilla, *Vision for Preaching*, 31–49.

6. There is no question that the divine power of the Spirit in and through the text of Scripture must be experienced first by the preacher. Gordon D. Fee warns ministers of the "great danger" of becoming a "professional": the tendency "to analyze texts and to talk *about* God, but slowly to let the fire of passion *for* God run low. . . . If the biblical text does not grip or possess one's own soul, it will likely do very little for those who hear" (*Listening to the Spirit*, 7 [emphasis in original]).

unspiritual preacher is not, seeing such power as unnecessary for the sermonic endeavor, undertaken solely in the flesh.

Product. If the power is God's, then the product is God's too: the outcome of the sermon belongs to God. The unspiritual preacher, on the other hand, lays personal claim to most of the credit—that can never be!

Praise. If the power is God's and the product is God's, then the praise must belong to God as well. The spiritual preacher thanks God—from preparation through delivery—for what God is going to do (and has done) in and with the sermon. No such thanksgiving is forthcoming from the unspiritual preacher.

Ultimately, an inward attitude of trust of and commitment to God—that manifests in determined purpose, uncompromising purity, incessant prayer, consciousness of divine presence, reliance on divine power, recognition of divine product, and continual praise—ought to be the touchstone of spirituality.[7] Growth in spirituality should be a lifelong ambition and an unceasing endeavor for the preacher. May God help us, through his Spirit—not just to preach but also to live lives pleasing to him, lives worthy of the name of his Son!

So as far as ministry activity is concerned—and our concern here is, of course, with preaching—it is a partnering with God in his mission. That is why Hebrews 13:20–21 says (as we have seen before), "Now may the God of peace . . . equip you with every good thing to *do* his will [*poieō* = our doing], [he] *doing* in us [*poieō* = God's doing] what is pleasing before him, through Jesus Christ, to whom be glory forever. Amen." Our doing *and* God's doing. We work *and* God works! What a marvelous mystery!

Feeding the flock is a remarkable privilege afforded to us preachers. The charge is solemn, the responsibility great. As the seventeenth-century French theologian François Fénelon urged, "O pastors . . . , be fathers—no, that's not enough, be mothers: give birth in pain; suffer again the pains of childbirth, with every effort that must be made to complete the formation of Jesus Christ in the heart [of the listener]!"[8]

In that vein, here's what an aficionado of Aaron Franklin, the barbecue virtuoso, has to say about that pitmaster.

What I most admire about the man and what I think is his greatest asset and the greatest secret of his success—is the absolute, utter commitment he has to

---

7. Feel free to add other elements to this list—just make sure they all begin with *P*! Also see Kuruvilla, *Vision for Preaching*, 167–85.
8. Fénelon, "Éloquence et Critique," 115 (my translation).

the customers who truly humble him every day by waiting for hours in line for his food. His obsessive dedication to the happiness and satisfaction of every person who eats at Franklin Barbecue is awe inspiring, especially given how easy it would be for him to kick back, drink some beers, and rest on his smoky laurels. I've never met anyone who, while running an overwhelmingly popular restaurant, welding, working on books, and filming television shows, also tries so hard to make sure people get what they want.[9]

Preacher, the lover of God's flock and the curator of God's word, may the Triune God bless you, your preaching, *and* your people—the ones God has entrusted to your care.

9. Mackay, "Coauthor's Note," viii–ix.

Big Idea versus Theological Focus

Haddon W. Robinson, a stalwart of evangelical preaching theory and praxis, is the one who tagged and named the Big Idea in his magisterial *Biblical Preaching* (1980). The multiple editions of this work have made it one of the most widely used homiletics textbooks in evangelical seminaries worldwide. Expository preaching, according to him, is "the explanation, interpretation, or application of a *single dominant idea* supported by other ideas."[1] Essentially, this Big Idea is a proposition, comprising a subject and a complement.[2] Though a variety of terms have been employed, the label "Big Idea" has stuck, and the notion has influenced evangelical preaching for almost four decades.

Concerns with the Big Idea

My concerns with the Big Idea stem from the assumption of its adherents that behind every text is an essential truth that can be distilled and expressed in propositional fashion as a Big Idea (distilling the text) and that this Big Idea is what is to be preached to listeners (preaching the distillate).

This appendix is a modified version of Kuruvilla, "Time to Kill the Big Idea?" (available at http://homiletix.com/kill-the-big-idea/).

1. Robinson, *Biblical Preaching* (1980), 33 (emphasis added). Subsequent references to this work indicate its third edition (2014).

2. Robinson, *Biblical Preaching*, 22.

Distilling the Text

The Big Idea is extracted from the biblical pericope in question by means of a reduction, involving "an ability to abstract and synthesize," Robinson confesses. "An idea, therefore, may be considered a distillation of life. It abstracts out of the particulars of life what they have in common and relates them to one another."[3] By deriving such Big Ideas from texts, declares Timothy S. Warren, "specific contextualizations are eliminated and specific behaviors [in the text] generalized." Such a distilled extract and core of the text is the "timeless, transcultural theological proposition" (aka the Big Idea).[4] And according to Grant R. Osborne, a key step in the move from text to sermon is the determination of "the underlying theological principle behind the text."[5] For such interpreters, then, cultural issues "intrude" on the text, seemingly a distraction from the principle behind the text. "Principles . . . must be given priority over accompanying cultural elements."[6] Thus the dross of a text is smelted off to leave behind the gold of a Big Idea, which is then preached. As Fred B. Craddock puts it, "The minister boils off all the water and then preaches the stain in the bottom of the cup."[7]

One would then have to wonder at God's wisdom in giving the bulk of his Scripture in nonpropositional form. Perhaps deity would have served himself and his people better had he just stuck to a bulleted list of timeless Big Ideas rather than messy stories and arcane prophecies and sentimental poetry, all of which turn out to be merely illustrations or applications of "underlying . . . principle[s] behind the text." This Big Idea approach of traditional evangelical homiletics may even suggest that once one has gotten the distillate of the text—that is, the coffee stain (or the gold in the nugget), the reduction of the text into a Big Idea—one can abandon the text itself. That is naive at best, perilous at worst. The text is what it is, theology and all, and will suffer no transmutation into anything else. Any distillation incurs significant loss of textual meaning, power, and pathos. Such a "lossy"[8] formatting is equivalent to a photo (of a person), or the theme (of a musical work), or the summary score (of a ball game), or any number of other reductions that can never substitute for the real thing. What we must

3. Robinson, *Biblical Preaching*, 20.
4. T. Warren, "Theological Process," 342, 346.
5. Osborne, *Hermeneutical Spiral*, 343.
6. Kaiser, "Principlizing Model," 21.
7. Craddock, *Preaching*, 123.
8. "Lossy" primarily describes the mp3 digital audio coding format, which, in comparison to CD-quality ("lossless") versions of music, utilizes compression that discards much of the original data to create a file of considerably smaller size.

preach, then, is the *text*, not a reduction, not a proposition, not a doctrine, not anything else but the text.[9]

All this to say that the text is not merely a *plain glass* window that the reader can look *through* (to discern some core Big Idea lurking behind it). Rather, the text, with all its nuances of language, structure, and form, is a *stained-glass* window that the reader must look *at*.[10] Such a window is carefully designed by the craftsperson: the glass, the stains, the lead, the copper, and everything else that goes into its production are meticulously crafted to generate a particular experience. So too with texts. The interpreter must therefore pay close attention to the text, privileging it not to discover some kernel hidden in it but to experience the thrust and force (theology) of the text as text, in toto and as a whole, that is inexpressible in and irreducible into any other form.

Preaching the Distillate

For those of the Big Idea persuasion, the Big Idea is not only the distillate of the text; it is also the main message that sermon listeners should be hearing, catching, taking home, and assimilating. In other words, the distillate is what must be preached. Robinson asserts that "it's what a congregation is to remember"—not the text, not the sermon, not the application, but the Big Idea. "The rest of the sermon is often like the scaffolding: it's important, but the major thing is for people to get hold of an idea or have an idea get hold of them."[11]

Almost every proponent of the Big Idea subscribes to the thesis that the sermon simply expands on the distilled Big Idea core of the text. Robinson again: "So one purpose of the big idea is that you organize the sermon around it. . . . Everything leads up to it or everything develops out of it. . . . You want to drive it home."[12] The Big Idea governs everything in the sermon, from its structure/shape to its application. After recommending a hunt for the Big Idea, John R. W. Stott calls on preachers to "arrange your material to serve the dominant thought. . . . Now we have to knock the material into shape, and particularly into such shape as will best serve the dominant thought."[13] The Big Idea is king; everything else serves this monarch who keeps his recalcitrant

9. I made the point in chap. 2, "Discerning Theology," that the text and its theology (i.e., what its author is *doing*) are inseparable, the latter supervening on the former. I, therefore, designate the unified entity as text + theology.

10. This metaphor was borrowed from Greidanus, *Modern Preacher*, 196.

11. Robinson, "Better Big Ideas," 353.

12. Robinson, "Better Big Ideas," 353, 357.

13. Stott, *Between Two Worlds*, 224, 228.

subjects (text, preacher, sermon, and listeners) in line! Likewise, Warren says, "The biblical preacher must recognize and represent the timeless truth of God's Word and then relate that truth to his audience."[14] So also Osborne: "The details of the text or main points of the sermon will actually develop aspects of this thesis statement [Big Idea]. Each main point will be one part of the larger whole, much like pieces of a pie."[15] The Big Idea is *it*! The rest of the sermon is merely a series of riffs on this main theme, ornament and embellishment, whipped cream on the pie. But as Thomas G. Long warns, "Sermons should be faithful to the full range of a text's power, and those preachers who carry away only main ideas . . . are traveling too light."[16] Indeed!

Traditional evangelical homiletics seeks to reduce the pericope to a Big Idea (distilling the text) and then preach that reduction (preaching the distillate), supported by textual proofs, real-life illustrations, and practical application. This is founded on a misunderstanding of how language functions, how texts work, and what a sermon does. Flannery O'Connor perceptively observed, "The whole story is the meaning, because it is an experience, not an abstraction."[17] Or each pericope as a whole (text + theology), regardless of genre, "is the meaning" intended to be experienced. Distilling the text and preaching the distillate will not do.

Theological Focus

That said, I am not against reductions per se; there is a specific, narrow, and circumscribed use for them in homiletics. In this work, such a reduction of the pericopal theology is called the Theological Focus. Though this Theological Focus, like the Big Idea, is a reduction, it is not the same as the latter—it is a different species in derivation, structure, function, and context.

Derivation. The Theological Focus is a reduction of what the author is *doing*—pericopal theology, the pragmatics of the text. The Big Idea, on the other hand, is a distillation of what the author is *saying*—the semantics of the text. There is usually no attempt to discern pericopal theology in these Big Idea transactions, for the underlying hermeneutic does not see texts as nondiscursive objets d'art but only as discursive objects for scientific examination (see app. B).

14. T. Warren, "Paradigm for Preaching," 463.
15. Osborne, *Hermeneutical Spiral*, 358.
16. Long, *Witness of Preaching*, 116.
17. O'Connor, *Mystery and Manners*, 73.

Structure. No particular format is assigned for the Theological Focus. One can make it a phrase or a collection thereof, a single long sentence or a paragraph, or whatever helps the preacher. After all, it serves only as a label (or shorthand, title, or handle) for the pericopal theology. The Big Idea, on the other hand, is generally mandated to be structured as a proposition, with a subject and a complement.

Function. Did the sermon preparer need the Theological Focus to understand the text in the first place? Of course not. The reduction was created after the fact, after the preacher caught what the text was *doing*. Following that discernment of the text's theology, a subsequent reduction of that inexpressible theology into the lossy format of the Theological Focus serves as a label for that pericopal theology, a quick reminder of the direction the preacher is to move in, like a compass pointing north. In chapter 3 ("Deriving Application"), we also observed that the Theological Focus serves as a launching pad for thinking about possible applications.[18] And as we saw in chapter 4 ("Creating Maps"), the Theological Focus also helps with sermon mapping, its various parts forming convenient labels for sermonic moves. It is never, and can never be, a stand-in for the text to ferry the experience of the text + theology to listeners. The Big Idea, on the other hand, is considered the all-important kernel of the text and a seemingly adequate and lossless substitute for it, obtained by distilling the text. Implicitly, the text itself (the shell) becomes dispensable, its Big Idea (the kernel) having been conveniently extracted from it. And so what listeners are now expected to catch in the sermon is this Big Idea core. The rest of the sermon is simply an expansion of that proposition, explaining, proving, and applying it—that is, preaching the distillate.

Context. The context of the Theological Focus is the conception of the sermon as a *demonstration* of pericopal theology inextricably interwoven with the text: text + theology. The preacher is only a handmaid/ midwife to the text, and the sermon only a curation thereof, so that listeners may experience the text + theology as its A/author intended. The context of the Big Idea, on the other hand, is based on the sermon as a novel and stand-alone entity (based, no doubt, on the text but as a new creation of the preacher and as distinct from it). And such a

---

18. Application is also a reduction of sorts—the same application can fit a number of different pericopal theologies. This explains the utility of the Theological Focus, itself a reduction, in the derivation of application. Indeed, the Theological Focus, obtained from the pragmatics of the text (pericopal theology), is better placed than the Big Idea, obtained from the semantics of the text, to play this role.

sermon is constructed as an *argument* to explain, prove, and apply the Big Idea of the text.

In sum, I would strongly recommend that preachers work with a Theological Focus rather than a Big Idea for the constrained functions noted above, recognizing the significant differences between these two entities.

Preaching—Argumentation versus Demonstration

Following the lead of classical rhetoricians, preaching came to be seen as an argument made by the preacher to influence and persuade listeners. During the Reformation, preaching as an argument became de rigueur, perfectly suiting doctrinal debates. While those controversies have died down, argumentation has been the norm in Protestant sermons ever since. The influential homiletician John A. Broadus was of this stock: "Preaching and all public speaking ought to be largely composed of argument."[1] Generations of preachers have followed after this sage, endorsing the precept that an argument maketh a sermon.

Besides the polemics of the Reformation, the scientific advances of the Enlightenment in the late seventeenth and eighteenth centuries also fostered this momentum of homiletics toward arguments that sustained Big Ideas, or propositions. David G. Buttrick called such an operation a "parody" of scientific procedure.[2] The text of Scripture, like an object for scientific study, is sliced, diced, parsed, and atomized to generate an underlying Big Idea that is then preached with persuasive arguments (distilling the text and preaching the distillate; see app. A). William H. Willimon acknowledged the perils of

---

This appendix is a modified version of Kuruvilla, "Time to Kill the Big Idea?" (available at http://homiletix.com/kill-the-big-idea/).

1. Broadus, *Treatise on the Preparation and Delivery of Sermons*, iv–v.

2. Buttrick, "Interpretation and Preaching," 47.

using the Big Idea to control a sermon. "The danger of this device is that it may encourage me to treat my text as an abstract, generalized idea that has been distilled from the text—such as 'the real meaning behind the story of the prodigal son.' I then preach an idea about the message rather than the story which *is* the message. My congregation listens to ideas about a story rather than experiencing *the* story."[3] What, then, is the alternative?

One of the first things to note is that preaching is a new form of rhetoric, unknown to ancient rhetoricians. Though the exposition of sacred text does occur in the Old Testament, this act achieved prominence and developed into a new genre of communication in the practices of the synagogue and the early church. In the description of Paul's speech in Acts 13:15–41, labeled *logos parakleseos* ("word of exhortation," 13:15), one detects a pattern: Scripture citations/references coupled with a concluding exhortation to action.[4] The utilization of a text in this fashion—an *inspired* text—to generate application is an unusual form of communication.

> The weekly confrontation with a revered text set the stage for a new rhetorical occasion, defined by the necessity of actualizing the significance of that sacred but often strange piece of literature for a community in, but not entirely of, the social world of the Hellenistic polis. Paraclesis, I suggest, is the newly minted rhetorical form that actualizes traditional scripture for a community in a non-traditional environment. It certainly has affinities with the classical forms of oratory, and those who regularly practised it probably had some training in rhetorical art, but paraclesis is in fact a mutant on the evolutionary trail of ancient rhetoric.[5]

Classical rhetoric never conceived of a speech that was not topical; such topical discourses dealt with particular subjects of importance and relevance and were always delivered without recourse to texts and with an emphasis on propositions (Big Ideas). Preaching, however, is unique. The use of a normative text on which to base a sermon sets this form of oral communication apart from all other genres of public address. And new forms of rhetoric call for new approaches to homiletics.

Along with the textual basis of a sermon, there is another important reason to consider preaching a different form of communication. It is founded on a hermeneutic that sees authors *doing* things (the pragmatics) with what they

3. Willimon, *Preaching and Leading Worship*, 68 (emphasis in original).
4. This pattern is also reflected in the Letter to the Hebrews—Heb. 13:22 labels the writing as *logos tēs parakleseōs* ("word of exhortation")—as well as in other early Christian documents. See Stewart-Sykes, *From Prophecy to Preaching*, 31–33.
5. Attridge, "Paraenesis in a Homily," 217.

say (the semantics), projecting the *world in front of the text*, the ideal world of God, and inviting God's people to dwell in that world, abiding by the call of that text (pericopal theology; see chap. 2). Semantic (scientific) analysis of a text generates only the author's saying. One must go beyond that to pragmatic (artistic) analysis, which alone can yield the author's *doing*.[6] In other words, text analysis for preaching should involve semantics *and* pragmatics, science *and* art. Consider a picture, photograph, painting, or poem. One does not need Big Ideas or even words to experience these and to catch what they do.[7] Likewise for texts: texts are not only discursive (lending themselves to scientific analyses of their sayings) but also simultaneously nondiscursive (bearing an artistic element—their *doings*). That's why distillation of texts that ignores authorial *doings* is problematic: such operations result in significant loss of textual meaning, emotion, power, and pathos. Again, I affirm that a canonical text such as Scripture is *both* scientific (with authorial sayings to be deciphered) *and* artistic (with authorial *doings* that must be inferred). And this calls for a major shift in how preaching is conceived, for "artistic import, unlike verbal meaning, can only be exhibited. . . . [The artist] is not saying anything . . . ; he is *showing*."[8] In other words, the experience of a text can be fully and faithfully shared by a preacher with the congregation only by *demonstration*, not by argumentation.[9]

Henry H. Mitchell once said that "the dullness of most mainline preaching is due to its being conceived of as argument rather than art—as syllogism rather than symbol."[10] Instead, Scripture calls for its experience to be demonstrated, not for a Big Idea to be argued. By this demonstration of what the text is *doing*, preachers facilitate listeners' experience of the text as they encounter God's ideal *world in front of the text*—the theology of the pericope. And, thereby, lives are transformed by the power of the divine Author. It is this hermeneutic (and the resulting conception of preaching) that is the foundation

6. For more on semantics versus pragmatics and the scientific code-model versus the artistic inferential process of interpretation, see Kuruvilla, "'What Is the Author *Doing* with What He Is *Saying*?'" For this article, a response to it, and my rejoinder to that response, go to http://www.homiletix.com/KuruvillaJETS2017.

7. This applies to other forms of art too—dance, drama, music, and movies. In fact, most of life is lived without Big Ideas. How do we experience John 3:16? As a proposition? Quick, can you reduce all the verses of "Amazing Grace" into one Big Idea? How about a visit to the Holocaust Museum in Washington, DC—what's the subject and the complement of what you saw/heard/experienced? How about your spouse—can you distill your loved one into a Big Idea?

8. Langer, *Feeling and Form*, 379, 394 (emphasis in original).

9. This is not to rule out the use of ideas or arguments in sermons. It simply denies that Big Idea distillation and its argumentation (distilling the text and preaching the distillate) are sufficient to facilitate the experience of Scripture for listeners.

10. Mitchell, "Preaching on the Patriarchs," 37.

for this work. The primary task of preachers is to help their listeners experience the text + theology—the agenda of the A/author—in all its fullness.[11] That is to say, preachers let their listeners encounter and experience the text as they themselves did (sans Big Idea) when they were studying the text. What is needed in the pulpit, then, is a creative exegesis of the text undertaken with a view to portraying for listeners what the author is *doing*—pericopal theology—enabling their experience of the text + theology.

I propose the analogy of a curator guiding visitors in an art museum through a series of paintings. Each pericope is a picture, the preacher is the curator, and the sermon is the curating of the text-picture and its thrust for the congregants, gallery visitors. The preacher is not producing new ideas, or even old ones in new guises, or anything of the sort. Instead, the preacher, standing between God's word and God's people to whom it was written, has the primary role of facilitating listeners' experience of the theology of the biblical text preached. Eugene L. Lowry quotes a comment made by a friend during a conversation on preaching: "'I see myself as a stagehand who holds back the curtain so that some might be able to catch a glimpse of the divine play—sometimes—perhaps—if I can get it open enough.' . . . If we could just get a better handle on how to pull back the curtains."[12] Precisely! That's the role of the preacher/stagehand—to pull back the curtains from the text. Or as Thomas G. Long describes, the preacher is a "witness" of the text: "The move from text to sermon is a move from beholding to attesting, from seeing to saying, from listening to telling, from perceiving to testifying, from *being* a witness to *bearing* witness."[13] The verb "to witness" has a dual sense that corresponds to this twofold responsibility of the preacher. First, "to witness" means to see/experience—to take something in. Second, "to witness" means to speak about what one has seen/experienced—to give something out. The preacher is thus a personal witness *of* the text and its *doings* and then a public witness *to* the text and its *doings*, "one who sees and experiences and tells the truth about what has been seen and experienced."[14] We preachers, as handmaids to the sacred writ, as midwives to Scripture, as curators and witnesses of the text, want the audience to experience it as the A/author intended. Otherwise, with our Big Ideas and arguments, they are getting only

11. The theology is integral to the text and inseparable from it, just as the mind is integrated with and inseparable from the brain: hence, text + theology designates an indivisible and irreducible entity.

12. Lowry, *The Sermon*, 52.

13. Long, *Witness of Preaching*, 100 (emphasis in original).

14. Long, "Distance We Have Traveled," 16. The US Department of Homeland Security knows a thing or two about this: "If you see something, say something" (https://www.dhs.gov/see-something-say-something, accessed May 1, 2018).

an already-chewed and predigested meal, a condensation and distillation of the text's saying, devoid of the power and pathos of the text's *doing*.

The seventeenth-century scientist and theologian Blaise Pascal was right: "People are generally better persuaded by the reasons which they have themselves discovered than by those which have come into the mind of others."[15] To facilitate this goal, the preacher is primarily a clue pointer who curates the picture (text) and the clues therein that point to its thrust/force (theology) so that the gallery visitors (congregants) might experience it as intended by the painter (A/author).[16] Then the text becomes the people's, its claim theirs, its call on their lives their own experience: the word of God for the people of God!

---

15. Pascal, *Pascal's Pensées*, 4 (1.10).

16. Or as Long puts it, we preachers pass out the eggs, and the hearers make the omelets themselves (*Witness of Preaching*, 193).

Annotated Sermon Manuscript— Ephesians 1:1–14

[IMAGE]

A few years ago, a circus parade was moving gaily through the streets of Milan, Italy. Suddenly, one of the elephants veered from the line and marched right into a church. (In Italy, church doors are large, and in the summer, they are often left wide open.)

Well, our friend Jumbo wandered up the center aisle, trumpeted a bit, looked at the surprised congregants, swung her trunk around, and headed back to the parade.

ILLUSTRATION: Narration
INTRODUCTION IMAGE: Disparity

[NEED]

I wonder if many of us are like this pious pachyderm.
Every week, we lurch into church, make a few noises,
    look around at everybody else,

A version of this sermon was delivered in Dallas Theological Seminary's chapel. See it here: http://homiletix.com/preaching-resources/abes-videos/gods-grand-plan/. The indentations and line breaks in the manuscript reflect the original I used in my sermons (with some accommodation to the page size of this book); the manuscript was structured thus for the purposes of phrasing, prosody, and rhythm, as well as to catch my eyes easily. Of course, my manuscripts are also extensively marked up in color using iAnnotate (see chap. 8).

then step out to resume our place in the
parade of life.
    Elephants in church! Elephants in ministry!
      Elephants in seminary!
Attend classes. Take in a few chapels. Get a nice
grade. Preach a few sermons. Counsel a bit.
Sing a few songs.

I wonder if many of us are like that.
    Not knowing what we are doing or
      what all this is about.

[TOPIC]

What are we Christians here for? What is God up to?
    Why did he create us and redeem us,
      and where is all this going?

[REFERENCE]

I think we'll find some answers in our text for today,
    Ephesians 1:3–14.
    Lots of stuff going on in Ephesians 1:3–14.
But we're going to focus on what God is doing—
    what all this is about: God's grand design—
      his purpose. Ephesians 1:3–14.

[ORGANIZATION]

First, we'll see God's grand plan,
    then humanity's glorious place,
and then an application.
    So God's grand plan, humanity's glorious place,
    and application.

When preaching this sermon, I omitted the organization element in an attempt to create a one-B sermon (see chap. 4).

I. God's Grand Plan
    A. [REVELATION] God's grand plan to consummate all things in Christ

[ENTRY SIGNPOST I.]
I omitted the entry signposts in this sermon. In a one-B shape, such transitions are best avoided or understated.

Paul begins Ephesians with
    a fairly standard salutation in 1:1–2
and then comes the rest of our section, 1:3–14.
It's one long sentence from 1:3–14,
    the longest sentence in the New Testament:

202 words in Greek. 202 words! Clause upon clause
upon clause upon clause.
It's as long as . . . as . . . a tapeworm!

The first word of this extended sentence is "Blessed."
So in effect, all of 1:3–14 is a blessing, in standard
Jewish fashion:
"Blessed be God who . . ." This is all about God
and why he is blessed.

If you look at this section, there is clearly an emphasis
on God's sovereign action.

> TRANSITION: Statement

Eph. 1:5 He *predestined* us for adoption as sons . . . according
to the good *pleasure* of his *will*.
Eph. 1:9 He made known to us the mystery of his *will*, according
to his good *pleasure* that he *purposed*.
Eph. 1:11 *predestined* according to the *purpose* of him who
works all things according to the *counsel* of his *will*.

> The italicized words in these verses were emphasized when read.

Will, purpose, counsel, pleasure, predestination.
Whatever God is doing, it is deliberate.
God is not capricious or whimsical.
He knows what he's doing.

Columbia researcher Sheena Iyengar has calculated that
the average person makes about seventy decisions each
day. That's over twenty-five thousand decisions a year. Over
seventy years of your lifetime, you've made over half a million
decisions. You put all of those half million choices together,
and that's who you are and what you've become. And, I hate
to remind you of this, but most of our choices and decisions
are terribly faulty and error prone.

> ILLUSTRATION: Exemplification

The other day I was headed to Landry. As was my habit, I
grabbed a stick of gum on my way out. Collecting my gym
bag and my keys and phone, I unwrapped the gum, threw the
gum into the trash can, and carefully put the wrapper in my
mouth. For paper, it tasted pretty good.
If you haven't done things like that, just wait till you get
to be my age. It's coming. Our choices are rotten. We're
clueless.

> ILLUSTRATION: Confession
> Landry = Baylor Tom Landry Fitness Center, Dallas, TX. The Dallas Theological Seminary community gets special privileges at this institution named after one of our erstwhile board members, a successful former coach of the Cowboys.

Not so God. In fact, his plans were made
way back when.

Eph. 1:4 ... He chose us in him *before the foundation of the world.*

This is no fanciful, impulsive, harebrained scheme
   that God cooked up at the last minute.
A grand design is under way—
   governed by his *will*, his *purpose*,
      his *counsel*, his *pleasure*.
      And intentionally designed "before the
         foundation of the world."

What was this purpose, this grand design of God?   `TRANSITION: Question`
   Jump to 1:9–10.

Eph. 1:9–10 ... with all wisdom and insight he made known to us the mystery of his will ... for the administration of the fullness of times.

What is being managed and administered
   and arranged and ordered
   is the "fullness of times"—the end times,
      the last days,
      the final end of all things:
   where everything is headed,
      where everything is going,
      where everything is ending up.

And how is God managing and ordering   `TRANSITION: Question`
   and arranging the end of things?

Eph. 1:10 ... the consummation ["summing up"] of all things in Christ—the things in the heavens and the things on the earth in him.

"The consummation of all things in Christ"—
   the redoing, repairing, reworking of all things
      into alignment with Christ.

   B. [RELEVANCE] God's grand plan entails setting all things right in the world

Right now, everything is broken, undone, chaotic.
An untuned orchestra, producing only cacophony:
   violence, materialism,
      gender identity crises, race identity crises,
         power struggles, nuclear threats,

breakdown of marriage,
    breakdown of the family,
    breakdown of society . . .
    Chaos everywhere.

But one day . . . in God's grand design . . . everything
    is going to be
    integrated, harmonized, and aligned with Christ.

Everything is coming together—*everything* is being
    consummated—in him.

The entire universe, "the things in the heavens
    and the things on the earth"—
    from black holes to badgers,
        from nebulas to nightingales,
    from transgalactic forces to intermolecular forces,
        from planets to potatoes—
    everything—*everything!*—is being administered,
        arranged, harmonized—
    consummated in Christ,
        the unifying Agent of all things.

> The consummation of all things in Christ, introduced in I.A. Revelation, is made relevant here with references to specifics in the world (black holes and badgers, nebulas and nightingales, etc., and, below, diseases and dangers, injustices and inequalities, etc.).

This is the grand design of God; this is the omega,
    the endpoint, the zenith of creation.
    Everything, everywhere is headed for
        this glorious end:
        the consummation of all things in Christ!

Outside of Christ are diseases and dangers,
    injustices and inequalities,
    despair and discrimination, pain and persecution,
        disorder and disaster, tumult and tribulation.

But *in Christ*, all things are being resolved, remedied,
    reformed, restored, renewed.
In Christ, all things are being set right,
    harmonized under the rulership of one Lord,
        Jesus Christ.
In Christ, all things are being made whole,
    transformed by one Lord, Jesus Christ.
And *in Christ*, all things are achieving
    their divinely intended end,

consummated under the preeminence of one Lord,
Jesus Christ.

This is the direction, the trajectory of all creation.
This is the purpose of God.
God's grand and glorious purpose.   EXIT SIGNPOST I.
The consummation of all things in Christ.
God's grand design has been revealed.
The end has begun. The clock has begun ticking.
And to that, all we can say is, "Wow!"

But . . . what's all this got to do with us?
Good question. Let's go back
to the beginning of our section.   TRANSITION: Question

II. Humanity's Glorious Place

A. [REVELATION] God blesses his people, redeeming them
into his grand plan
While this passage is focused on God   [ENTRY SIGNPOST II.]
and his grand design   I omitted this signpost.
to consummate all things in Christ
the many first- and second-person plural
pronouns and verbs
demonstrate something crucial.
Look at those, will you?

Eph. 1:3 Blessed [be] the God and Father of *our* Lord Jesus
Christ, who has blessed *us* . . .   TRANSITION: Statement
Eph. 1:4 because he chose *us* in him before the foundation of
the world, that *we* may be holy and blameless . . .   The italicized words in
Eph. 1:5 He predestined *us* for adoption as children . . .   these verses were empha-
Eph. 1:6 for the praise of the glory of his grace [with] which he   sized when read.
engraced *us* in the Beloved.
Eph. 1:7–8a in whom *we have* redemption through his blood,
the forgiveness of trespasses, according to the riches of his
grace which he lavished on *us*.
Eph. 1:9 He made known to *us* the mystery of his will . . .
Eph. 1:11 *we have been claimed* [by God] as an inheritance . . .
Eph. 1:12 that *we*, who hoped beforehand in Christ, may be for
the praise of his glory;

Eph. 1:13 in whom also *you,* hearing the word of truth, the gospel of *your* salvation—in whom also believing, *you were sealed* with the Holy Spirit of promise.

Eph. 1:14 the pledge of *our* inheritance . . .

Our, us, we, y'all. The grand design of God
involves us.
God's plan for the cosmos involves the church.

This passage is hardly an abstraction
far removed from us.
God is actually co-opting us, his people,
into his grand design
to consummate all things in Christ.
We are part of his great plan! He's chosen us
to be part of his grand plan.
What a glorious privilege!

> B. [RELEVANCE] God's co-optation of us, a blessing, is how
> we find fulfillment in life

And get this, folks: our place in God's purpose   *TRANSITION:* **Phrase**
is a *blessing!*
It is a blessing to be involved in God's grand design.
Look at 1:3.

Eph. 1:3 Blessed [be] the God and Father of our Lord Jesus
Christ, *who has blessed us.*

He blessed us into his grand and glorious plan
to consummate all things in Christ.
No one else has that privilege. No one else
and nothing else.
Not planets, not plants; not earth,
water, wind, or fire.
Not animals or even angels—at least
not to the extent that believers are involved.

Our place in God's purpose is a blessing—
a privilege and an honor.
And you know what? The only way—
the only way—we can ever be fulfilled
is by taking our place in God's grand design.

Nothing else will delight. Nothing else will satisfy.
  Nothing else will fulfill.
Without consciously being involved
    in the glorious purpose of God,
  we will never have purpose,
      we will never find our rightful place.

At a Florida track some years ago, a big greyhound race was about to begin. The sleek, beautiful dogs crouched in their cages, ready to go, while betting spectators finished placing their wagers. The gun went off, the mechanical rabbit with artificial fur began zipping down the track, and the dogs took off chasing it. As the rabbit made the first turn, however, there was an electrical short in the system, and the rabbit stopped, exploded, and went up in flames—poof! All that was left was smoldering black stuff at the end of a wire.

> *ILLUSTRATION:* Narration

Their prey having disappeared, the bewildered, perplexed dogs didn't know what to do. According to news reports, several dogs simply stopped running and lay down on the track, tongues hanging out, panting. Two dogs, still frenzied with the chase, ran into a wall, breaking several ribs. Another dog began chasing its tail, while the rest howled at the spectators in the stands. Not one dog finished the course.

Hopeless, fruitless, and worthless we are
  when we don't have a goal.
      Like Jumbo in church.

But we—we *have* a goal—to align ourselves
  with God's purpose—
          his grand design to consummate all things
            in the cosmos in Christ.

And look at this, the last part of verse 4:

> *TRANSITION:* Statement

Eph. 1:4–5 *In love,* he predestined us for adoption as children . . .

This blessing of us into God's grand and glorious
    plan is a choice of love,
  because it's the greatest thing we can ever be
      part of.
    So he loved us and blessed us into his plan,
        by saving us through Christ.

> Here and below, I am obviously dealing with revelation in a relevance submove. Yes, for smoothness of flow, particularly in a one-B sermon, you *can* break rules. But make sure that in such sermons you don't go too long with revelation without relevance, which is the underlying principle behind the focus splitting maneuver (see chap. 4).

Eph. 1:7–8 in whom we have redemption through his blood, the forgiveness of trespasses, according to the riches of his grace which he lavished on us.

Saved to be part of his grand design,
    his glorious purpose to consummate
        all things in Christ.
    Truly amazing!

Ernest Hemingway is supposed to have said, "Life is a dirty trick, a short journey from nothingness to nothingness. There is no remedy for anything in life. Man's destiny in the universe is like a colony of ants on a burning log."

ILLUSTRATION: Quotation
This is one of those quotations that are impossible to trace to accurate primary sources; hence, "supposed to have said."

If that's the way you feel, I want you to take another
        look at this text.
Life is *not* a remediless nothingness.
God's got a grand design for the cosmos,
    and he chose us as his children, way back when,
        in love, and with delight,
            to be a part of his glorious purpose
                to consummate all things in Christ.

And nothing else will ever give the kind of joy
    that having a place in God's purpose will.
Nothing will be as exhilarating,
    enjoyable, or exciting.
No thrill on earth can compare
    with this cosmic joyride God has involved us in.

You may have been a believer for many years,
    but if you haven't done so yet,
    get ready to consciously align yourself
        with God's grand design.

If we don't, we're like flies crawling on Michelangelo's masterpiece in the Sistine Chapel. Yeah, we flies have some sense of light and dark colors, and smooth and rough spots, but we remain clueless about the glory of the artist's creation as we crawl around the frescoes, oblivious to the grand design, totally missing out on the real fulfillment, the real satisfaction, and the real delight of partnering with God in his glorious plan.

ILLUSTRATION:
Exemplification
The last sentence of this illustration is sixty words long!

The rest of Ephesians spells out our responsibility
   as we participate in God's grand design—
      but here it is briefly in 1:4:

> **Eph. 1:4** He chose us in him before the foundation of the world,
> *that we may be holy and blameless before him.*

<aside>In order to explain how God's choice of us was a blessing, I returned to revelation in this relevance sub-move (here and below).</aside>

Our responsibility, as ones chosen to be part of
   God's grand design,
      is to be "holy and blameless."

God is serious about this.
Look at how God sees us,
   this "holy and blameless" people:

<aside>*TRANSITION:* Statement
Most of my transitions are statements pointing to the text.</aside>

> **Eph. 1:11** We have been claimed [by God] as an inheritance.

No one else and nothing else is ever described
   as being God's inheritance in this fashion.
      Only of believers is it said that they are
         the very inheritance and possession of
            God himself.
What an exalted status! What a place for humanity
   to be in! Mind-boggling!

And if that weren't enough,
   this glorious privilege of believers
   is guaranteed with a warranty—no ifs, ands,
      or buts—we *will* be God's possession.
      It *will* happen, and it's a done deal,
         as we find in 1:13–14.

> **Eph. 1:13–14** You were sealed with the Holy Spirit of promise
> (who is the pledge of our inheritance).

Sealed with the Holy Spirit as a guarantee
   of God's ownership.
   His ID stamped on us: we're his own. Spectacular!

There aren't words to describe the sublimity
   of all this:
   I think I've already used "amazing," "breathtaking,"
      "mind-boggling," and "spectacular."

Nothing can describe the magnificence
   of our incorporation into God's grand design
      of cosmic consummation in Christ.

We don't have words for this.
   And Paul didn't either.
After 202 nonstop words, he runs out of breath
   and calls for a period as he lands at verse 14.
And thus the longest sentence
   in the New Testament—
         majestically appropriate for God's glorious
            design—comes to an end.

This is just incredible: God's grand design and—
   wonder of wonders!—
   his joyful, delighted incorporation of us
      into his purpose.

Will you join him?

> Many years ago, when the then-fledgling company Apple fell
> on difficult days, Apple's young chairman, Steve Jobs, trav-
> eled from Silicon Valley to New York City. His purpose was
> to convince Pepsico's CEO John Sculley to move west and
> run this struggling company.
>
> As the two men chatted in Sculley's penthouse office
> overlooking the Manhattan skyline, the Pepsi executive began
> declining Jobs's offer.
>
> At that, Steve Jobs issued a challenge to John Sculley: "Do
> you want to spend the rest of your life selling sugared water,
> or do you want to change the world?"

ILLUSTRATION: Narration

God issues us a challenge:
Do we want to just spend the rest of our lives selling
sugared water,
   building bigger homes, buying better clothes,
      clawing up social ladders,
   building big churches, big ministries,
         writing big books, finding fame
            and fortune—
            living like flies in the Sistine
               Chapel—or . . .
   do we want to change the world—no,
      not the world—
   do we want to change the *entire cosmos*—
      as we join God's grand design,
         his glorious venture, his great plan?

This is another long
sentence—seventy-six
words (not as long as
Paul's)—but it worked
well for the emotion I was
feeling and wanted to
convey.

That's what we were created for.

That's God's purpose,
    and now it's *our* purpose as well.
    Will you join?

| | You can tell I am priming the pump for the application move that is to follow. |

It starts right here in Ephesians 1
    by recognizing the magnificence
    of what God is doing—
    consummating all things in Christ,
    co-opting us into his grand design as his partners.

EXIT SIGNPOSTS I. AND II.

No wonder this God is a blessed God!

> **Eph. 1:3** Blessed [be] the God and Father of our Lord Jesus Christ, who has blessed us.

III. Application + Conclusion

[ENTRY SIGNPOST III.]
I omitted the entry signpost at the application move, again trying for a seamless transition in the one-B shape of this sermon.

You know, we should do more of this:
    calling God blessed—
    the only one worthy to be called blessed.
        Especially in light of Ephesians 1:3–14
            and God's grand plan to consummate
            all things in Christ.
We should make a *habit* of calling God blessed.
    At least once a week.

APPLICATION + CONCLUSION: Tell

Here's what I plan to do: every Sunday,
    if I am dining with other believers or family,
    I'm going to take the lead to invite everyone
        at the table
        to share a blessing for God that begins,
            "Blessed be God who . . . !"
Bless him for his grand design and
    one way that his glorious plan
    has directly touched our lives this week.

APPLICATION + CONCLUSION: Show

And as you do so, focus on
    the grand things God's doing,
    not just on helping us get over
        computer problems and car problems,
        acne and gall stones,
            bad weather and bad grades,
            and stuff like that.

No, think of the big things God is doing
  in which you are involved.
Take all week to think about it;
  keep your eyes and ears open for
  what God is doing with his grand design
    in your life—
    and share it at Sunday lunch:
      "Blessed be God who . . . !"

In fact, let's practice for that this afternoon.
  As you sit down for lunch today after chapel,
    join someone else and share a blessing:
      "Blessed be God who . . . !"

> As I got ready this morning to come here and preach, I really didn't feel like it. It's been a tough couple of months that involved major crises at my medical practice (still unresolved). All the while I was the primary caretaker of a ninety-year-old parent who is getting more frail each day. I really didn't feel up to preaching. That seems to be a recurring theme: most days, I don't feel up to ministry.
>
> But then I thought to myself, "I may not be up to it or ready for it, but God is working, and he won't fail his people, even if his preacher fails."
>
> So here's my lunch blessing for this afternoon: "Blessed be God who will never fail his people. *Never.*" To think that he uses me—*me*, who cannot even tell the difference between gum and wrapper! Just amazing! Blessed be God!

APPLICATION + CONCLUSION: Image

ILLUSTRATION: Confession

Find something big God is doing in your week.
And bless God for his grand design:
  the consummation of all things in the cosmos
    in Christ. Soon . . . and very soon.
      Blessed . . . be . . . God!

APPLICATION + CONCLUSION: Challenge

I managed to repeat "Blessed be God" at least six times in this application + conclusion move.

Annotated Sermon Manuscript— Genesis 26:1–33

[IMAGE]

Once upon a time there was a man who went hunting. He was hunting bears. As he trudged through the forest looking for bears, he came upon a large and steep hill. He climbed the hill and just as he was pulling himself up over the last outcropping of rocks, a huge bear met him nose to nose. The bear roared fiercely. The man was so scared that he lost his balance and fell down the hill with the bear not far behind. On the trip down the hill, the man lost his gun. When he finally stopped tumbling, he found he had a broken leg. Life is messy!

ILLUSTRATION: Narration

INTRODUCTION IMAGE: Jollity

Escape was impossible, and so the man, who had never been particularly religious (in fact, he was hunting on Sunday morning), prayed, "God, if you will make this bear a Christian, I will be happy with whatever lot you give me for the rest of my life. I'll enroll at Dallas Seminary. Please, just make this bear a Christian!"

The bear was no more than three feet away from the man when it stopped dead in its tracks, looked up to the heavens quizzically, and then fell to its knees and prayed in a loud voice, "Lord, bless this food which I am about to eat. Amen."

A version of this sermon was delivered at a Dallas Theological Seminary chapel. See it at http:// homiletix.com/preaching-resources/abes-videos/isaac-confident-in-god/. The indentations and line breaks in the manuscript reflect the original I used in my sermons; the manuscript was structured thus for the purposes of phrasing, prosody, and rhythm, as well as to catch my eyes easily (also helped by my colorful annotations with iAnnotate [see chap. 8]).

[NEED]

I tell you, life is messy.
  Even Christians give us a hard time.
Have you ever been in a situation like that—
  everyone against you, antagonism all around?

> Several years ago, I was an elder in a church that had a dragon. Boy, did Milton spew fire from his mouth. His grandfather and uncles had started the church; they literally had built the structure some sixty years prior. So you know Milton's type. They think they "own" the church.
>
> This guy, for some reason, was full of anger and spite, and he almost split the church singlehandedly. A dragon. Nothing was ever satisfactory. He didn't like the worship style, our outreach to the homeless, the children's pastor (who later resigned), the senior pastor, and, after I came on the elder board, he didn't like me either. Milton was one *baaad* dragon!

ILLUSTRATION: Narration

Yes, I added another illustration to the introduction so that I could carry parts of this true story (with details changed) through the sermon.

Dragons like Milton are everywhere;
  you *will* encounter them, if you haven't already.
  Maybe you are experiencing antagonism
    of that kind in your life right now.

[TOPIC]

How will you deal with such
  opposition and hostility?

[REFERENCE]

I would like to draw your attention to
  two rather obscure incidents in the life of Isaac
    in Genesis 26.
  From these we will learn how we can handle
    such hostility and enmity.
Genesis 26 has two Isaac stories in it,
  a two-sided coin.
  One side, negative; the other positive.

[ORGANIZATION]

But this double-sided coin in Genesis 26 teaches us
  a single message in three steps:
    How to cope with dragons—three steps!

I left the organization element sparse. I didn't see any reason to expand it.

I. God Ensures

A. [REVELATION] Deception in fear manifests distrust in God's promised blessings

[ENTRY SIGNPOST I.]
I omitted the entry sign-post, here and before the other moves, for a smoother flow.

The story is actually a flashback and happens
before Isaac has any kids.

> **Gen. 26:1** And there was a famine in the land, besides the previous famine that had occurred in the days of Abraham.

Things look bleak, so God urges Isaac
to remain in the land of the Philistines.
God says:

> **Gen. 26:3–4** Dwell in this land and I will be with you and bless you, for to you and to your descendants I will give all these lands, and I will confirm the promise which I promised Abraham your father. I will multiply your descendants as the stars of heaven, and will give your descendants all these lands; and all the nations of the earth shall be blessed by your descendants.

This is an unambiguous promise
confirmed by an oath.
In the midst of a famine, God declares that
Isaac will be safe.
Isaac can be absolutely, positively sure that
God is going to keep his promise.

Now look again at Genesis 26:3–4.
What word keeps repeating itself?

> **Gen. 26:3–4** To you and to your *descendants* I will give all these lands. . . . I will multiply your *descendants* as the stars of heaven, and will give your *descendants* all these lands; all the nations of the earth shall be blessed by your *descendants*.

The italicized words in these verses were emphasized when read.

Which word is repeated?
Four times: "descendants," "descendants,"
"descendants," "descendants."
Hold that thought for a minute, will you?
We'll come back to that later.

OK, now here's where the story gets a bit hairy.
Isaac's now in Philistine land.

> **Gen. 26:7** When the men of the place asked about his wife, he
> said, "She is my sister," for he was afraid to say, "[She is]
> my wife," [thinking] "lest the men of the place kill me for
> Rebekah, because she is attractive in appearance."

His life threatened, Isaac falls apart
  and resorts to subterfuge,
  even risking his wife's safety.

> **Gen. 26:8–9** And it happened, when he had been there a long
> time, that Abimelech king of the Philistines looked down
> through a window and saw—and behold!—Isaac caressing
> Rebekah, his wife. Then Abimelech called Isaac and said, "Be-
> hold, surely she is your wife! So how did you say, 'She is my
> sister'?" And Isaac said to him, "Because I said [to myself],
> 'Lest I die because of her.'"

Isaac was terrified. Afraid. Afraid he'd be killed.
  Afraid for his life.

So now here's my question: TRANSITION: Question
  Was Isaac's fear legitimate? Was it?
Remember the repeated word in Genesis 26:3–4?
  "Descendants"—four times.
  Remember that?
Now if God promised Isaac kids—
  four times "descendants" is mentioned—
  how on earth would Isaac be allowed to die
    without having at least one descendant?
    (Remember, all this happened
      before they had any kids.)

The fundamental issue here is that Isaac,
  afraid for his own life,
  is actually mistrusting God and his promises.
    Afraid. Scared. Faithless.
And stricken with fear, Isaac lies,
  risking the safety of his wife.
  Afraid his blessings, indeed, his very life,
    would get stolen,
      he forgets God's promises.

What are *you* afraid of, Christian?   TRANSITION: Question
  So afraid that you've forgotten
  God's promises?

B. **[RELEVANCE]** We too when fearful distrust God's promises to us

I admit there are lots of things around to fear.
The uncertainty of finances, the failing of health,
the bleakness of the future,
the difficulties of ministry,
the struggles of relationships . . .
Has the noise of the world gotten so loud
we don't hear the voice of the Lord?

The voice that promises us
the constancy of his presence?

Heb. 13:5 I will never abandon you, nor will I ever forsake you.

The voice that promises us
the sufficiency of his grace?

2 Cor. 12:9 My grace is sufficient for you.

The voice of his love, from which
nothing can separate us?

Rom. 8:38–39 neither death, nor life, nor angels, nor authorities, nor things present, nor things to come, nor powers, nor height, nor depth, nor any other creation . . .

> While I usually prefer not to introduce verses from other parts of the Bible into my sermons, in this case, in order to point to God's promises for believers in the current dispensation, I made an exception.

C. **[APPLICATION]** *Remember the promises!*

So here's step 1 for coping with dragons.
1. *Remember the promises!*
Drown out the dragons' scary noises
with the sure voice of God.

Fear not, child of God, ours is a God
who keeps his word.
1. *Remember the promises!*

Etch them in your mind. Memorize them.
Meditate on them.
1. *Remember the promises!*
The three that I mentioned are great for starters,
but there are many like them.
1. *Remember the promises!*

Back to our story.
Thankfully, it ends well for Isaac and Rebekah.

> This is also somewhat unusual for me: I have three nonapplication moves, but I derived a three-pronged application and put one in each of the three moves (i.e., I have an application submove in each move). And for each of these application submoves, here and below, I did the *tell* but did not *show* the applications; they were sufficiently clear, I thought.

> *TRANSITION:* Statement

Gen. 26:11–14a So Abimelech ordered all the people, saying, "The one who touches this man or his wife will surely be put to death." Now Isaac sowed in that land and reaped the same year a hundredfold. And Yahweh blessed him, and the man became rich, and continued to grow richer until he became very rich. And he had possessions of sheep and possessions of cattle and a great many servants.

The man became rich, grew richer,
  and became the richest.
    God is faithful to his promises and blesses Isaac,
      despite Isaac's failure to trust.

That's side one of the Isaac coin—a negative side.
But there is side two—
  a positive side to the Isaac story.

II. World Envies
A. [REVELATION] Not retaliating against opponents manifests trust in God's promises

[EXIT SIGNPOST I.]
Since each of my three moves ends with an application submove, I chose to omit exit signposts here and elsewhere.

TRANSITION: Statement

[ENTRY SIGNPOST II.]
I omitted this signpost

Gen. 26:14 And he had possessions of sheep and possessions of cattle and a great many servants, so the Philistines envied him.

And look at what the envious world does to Isaac.

TRANSITION: Statement

Gen. 26:15 Now all the wells which his father's servants had dug in the days of his father Abraham, the Philistines stopped up and filled them with earth.

The Philistines stop these wells.
  So what does Isaac do? He digs elsewhere.

Gen. 26:19–20 And when Isaac's servants dug in the valley and found a well of running water there, the herdsmen of Gerar quarreled with the herdsmen of Isaac, saying, "The water is ours!"

The Philistines quarrel for these wells too.
  So . . . Isaac goes someplace else.

Gen. 26:21 Then they dug another well, and they quarreled over it too.

Philistines oppose the third round of well digging.
  So . . . Isaac moves away.

Gen. 26:22 He moved on from there and dug another well.

Every time Isaac hits water, the envious Philistines
     attack his wells. Constantly.
This was a sustained, ongoing, ceaseless antagonism,
     a blatant attempt to drive him away.
          Out there in the Middle East,
               no water meant no survival.
          The Philistines were going to take him out.

He did nothing wrong. He was simply obeying God,
     minding his own business.
And wham, wham, and again, wham,
     these Philistines were out to get him.
For no fault of his own.
     Innocent, doing his thing, troubling nobody.
     And then this.

> B. [RELEVANCE] We too oppressed unjustly will be tempted
>   to retaliate

Isaac was like Chippie the parakeet, who never saw it coming.
As Max Lucado tells one of my favorite stories, one second
the bird was peacefully perched in his cage singing, the next
moment its life changed forever.

> *ILLUSTRATION:* Narration
> Modified from Max Lucado,
> *In the Eye of the Storm:*
> *Jesus Knows How You Feel*
> (Nashville: Thomas Nelson,
> 2012), xi–xii.

     Its problems began when its owner decided to clean its
cage with a vacuum. She stuck the nozzle in to suck up the
seeds and feathers from the bottom of the cage. Then the
phone rang. Instinctively, she turned to pick it up. She had
barely said hello when—ssswwwwwwwapppp!! Chippie got
sucked in.

     The woman gasped, let the phone drop, and snapped off
the vacuum. With her heart in her mouth, she unzipped the
bag. There was Chippie—alive, but stunned—covered with
heavy black dust.

     She grabbed the bird and rushed to the bathtub, turned
on the faucet full blast, and held Chippie under a torrent of
ice-cold water, power washing him clean.

     Then the good lady did what any compassionate pet
owner would do: she snatched up the hair dryer and blasted
the wet, miserable, shivering little bird with hot air.

     Chippie doesn't sing much anymore.

Are you in a situation like that?

Have you lost your song, suffering through no fault
 of your own?

Get ready: Satan's world will throw everything at you.
 Dragons and all.
 Be assured that the enemy's lethal arrows
  will be targeted at you, and in full force.
  Perhaps especially at those in ministry—
   all of us here.

How will we respond? How did Isaac respond?   `TRANSITION: Question`

Philistines stop up the wells. He moves on.
 Philistines quarrel for the second dig. He moves on.
  Philistines oppose him the third round.
   He moves on.
   Move and dig. Move and dig. Move and dig.

This is really amazing!
 Because of what Isaac does *not* do.
 He doesn't fight. He doesn't so much as
  lift a pinky in resistance.
  Could he have?   `TRANSITION: Question`

Go back to . . .

> **Gen. 26:12–14** And Yahweh blessed him, and the man became
> rich, and continued to grow richer until he became very rich.
> And he had possessions of sheep and possessions of cattle
> and a great many servants.

And also . . .

> **Gen. 26:16** Then Abimelech said to Isaac, "Go away from us, for
> you are too powerful for us."

See, Isaac was not your average landowner.
 This guy was a huge enterprise, an institution.
Abraham, his father, had a homegrown army
 of 318 men
  that fought wars successfully.

Isaac wasn't too shabby himself—
 notice "great household" and "too powerful."

Isaac could probably have gone after Abimelech's men
   who were sabotaging his wells.
   He could've put their noses out of joint,
      cooked their geese,
      knocked their socks off, and wiped the floor
         with them with ease.

But, instead, what does Isaac do? Move and dig,
   move and dig, move and dig.
   No threats. No reloading weapons.
      No flash of steel.
      Just . . . move and dig, move and dig,
         move and dig.

In the earlier story, side one of Genesis 26,
   we had a guy quaking in his sandals.
   What happened here? In side two,
      he's quiet, calm, and peaceful.
   Move and dig. Move and dig. Move and dig.

You see, after side one, Isaac had learned his lesson.
He had seen God work. He was now trusting
   in God's promises.
   No contention, no conflict, no clashing.

C. [APPLICATION] *Refrain from retaliation!*

So here's step 2 for coping with dragons
      2. *Refrain from retaliation!*

In the face of unremitting virulent antagonism,
   how will our inner trust in God show outside?
      2. *Refrain from retaliation!*
Will our attitude and approach to our opponents
   be marked by a peacefulness?
   Or will we claw and clamor, chafe and complain,
      clash and confront?

When I got onto the elder board at that church, and Milton
turned his fire on me, I was all for ejecting him from the
church.

   In the Third Psalm, David begged God, "Strike all my enemies on the jaw and shatter their teeth!" After a few months
of Milton, I must confess that that verse came to mind often.
"Do him in, Lord!"

ILLUSTRATION: Narration

Hey, he was attacking poor innocent ol' me for no good reason, blaming me for events that happened before I had even moved to that city. Ego and self-righteous anger took over. Invariably, retaliation is related to our own egos.

How dare he? How dare anyone touch my wells?

| I engaged in a bit of role playing here (italicized). |

What should our attitudes be
   in circumstances of antagonism?
      2. *Refrain from retaliation!*

| [EXIT SIGNPOST II.] |
| Omitted in the sermon. |
| TRANSITION: Question |

And the result in Isaac's life?

| [ENTRY SIGNPOST III.] |
| Omitted in the sermon. |

III. Isaac Entrusts
   A. [REVELATION] Reconciling with opponents manifests trust in God's promises

Gen. 26:28–29 They [Abimelech and his officers] said, "We clearly see that Yahweh has been with you; so we said, 'Let there now be a pact between us—between you and us—and let us make a covenant with you, so that you will do us no harm. . . . You are now blessed of Yahweh.'"

Isn't that amazing? Even the unbelieving world
   recognizes that the Christian is blessed.
And trusting God, Isaac even responds
   with an overture of gracious friendship.

Gen. 26:30–31 Then he made for them a feast, and they ate and they drank. In the morning they arose . . . and they departed from him in peace.

His trust in God is so complete
   that Isaac can feed his enemies.

   B. [APPLICATION] *Reconcile with grace!*
So here's step 3 for coping with dragons:
   3. *Reconcile with grace!*

| Because of the trajectory of the sermon, I did not include a separate revelation submove here; the application submove took its place effectively. |

This, folks, is a hard lesson to learn and apply.
   What? Treat kindly those who oppress me?
      But what about my rights?
         Who's gonna take care of me?

| Role playing again (italicized). |

It all boils down to this:

Will you trust God to take care of you?
   Will we place ourselves in God's hands?
   Only then can we let go of our egos
      and let God handle the situation.
      Only if we trust God. Like Isaac did:
   *Remembering the promises! Refraining from
   retaliation! Reconciling with grace!*

If the name of an adversary or opponent
   who has been a dragon in your life comes to mind
      even as I speak,
      I want you to decide right now that you will:
   Remember the promises! Refrain from retaliation!
   and *Reconcile with grace!*

Has that person been giving you a hard time?
   Has pressure been mounting?
   Are you even dreading seeing them
      or being in their presence?
   Entrust yourself to God and *remember,
      refrain, reconcile.*

Today, tonight, tomorrow, or this week,
   give them a call,
   or write an email, or set up a meeting.

> Because I had an application submove in each move, in lieu of an APPLICATION + CONCLUSION, I went with a straightforward conclusion comprising summary, image, and challenge (below).

They may not accept it;
   they may reject your overtures.
      But God asks us to entrust ourselves to him
         (as Isaac did):
   *Remembering the promises! Refraining from
   retaliation! Reconciling with grace!*

I struggled with this in my church situation with Milton. This was not easy for me. *Show grace to those who are attacking you? How odd. How unnatural.*

> *CONCLUSION:* Summary

But the board of the church did exactly that. The leadership approached Milton (and his wife, Vicky) very peacefully and charitably and outlined their concerns. In the interests of keeping the peace, I was asked to stay away from that meeting so that I wouldn't be tempted to accidentally unleash a left hook or something. The leaders were not going to act

> *CONCLUSION:* Image
> *ILLUSTRATION:* Narration

with brute force. They were going to trust God to work. They kept me away.

Milton didn't take it well. He and Vicky left the church in a huff, uttering vague threats about lawsuits. I told the others, "That's it. We won't see him again . . . and good riddance too." I was wrong.

Recently, several years after I'd left the city, I got an email from one of the elders. "Abe," it said, "Abe, you will be interested to know that Milton and Vicky have returned to the church. I know you will rejoice with us [!] that Milt is now a changed person; last Sunday he publicly and formally apologized to the church."

I was amazed!
Milton seemed to have learned his lesson,
but I think it was I who learned a greater lesson—
that I needed to . . .
Remember the promises!
Refrain from retaliation!
Reconcile with grace!

CONCLUSION: Challenge

Our God is trustworthy:
Remember! Refrain! Reconcile!

Bibliography

Altmann, Gerry T. M. *The Ascent of Babel: An Exploration of Language, Mind, and Understanding*. New York: Oxford University Press, 1997.

Anderson, Chris. *TED Talks: The Official TED Guide to Public Speaking*. New York: Houghton Mifflin Harcourt, 2016.

Anelli, Melissa, and Emerson Spartz. "*The Leaky Cauldron* and *Mugglenet* Interview Joanne Kathleen Rowling: Part Three." *The Leaky Cauldron*, July 16, 2005. http://www.accio-quote.org/articles/2005/0705-tlc_mugglenet-anelli-3.htm.

The Ante-Nicene Fathers. 10 vols. Edited by Alexander Roberts and James Donaldson. Edinburgh: T&T Clark, 1869.

Aristotle. *Art of Rhetoric*. Translated by J. H. Freese. Loeb Classical Library 193. Cambridge, MA: Harvard University Press, 1926.

Attridge, Harold W. "Paraenesis in a Homily (λόγος παρακλήσεως): The Possible Location of, and Socialization in, the 'Epistle to the Hebrews.'" In *Paraenesis: Act and Form*, edited by Leo G. Perdue and John G. Gammie, 211–26. Semeia 50. Atlanta: Scholars Press, 1990.

Augustine. *On Christian Teaching*. Translated by R. P. H. Green. Oxford: Oxford University Press, 1997.

Bacon, Francis. *Selected Writings*. Edited by Hugh G. Dick. New York: Random House, 1955.

Barth, Karl. *Dogmatics in Outline*. London: SCM, 1966.

———. "Preface to the Second Edition." In *The Epistle to the Romans*, 2–15. 6th ed. Translated by Edwyn C. Hoskyns. London: Oxford University Press, 1933.

Bartow, Charles L. *God's Human Speech: A Practical Theology of Proclamation*. Grand Rapids: Eerdmans, 1997.

Barzun, Jacques. *Simple & Direct*. 4th ed. New York: Quill, 2001.

Bechara, Antoine, Hanna Damasio, Daniel Tranel, and Antonio R. Damasio. "Deciding Advantageously before Knowing the Advantageous Strategy." *Science* 275 (1997): 1293–95.

Bellis, Rich. "Let Your Favorite Podcast Hosts Fix Your Public Speaking Problems." *Fast Company*, July/August 2017. https://www.fastcompany.com/40452672/let-your-favorite-podcast-hosts-fix-your-public-speaking-problems.

Berkun, Scott. *Confessions of a Public Speaker*. Sebastopol, ON: O'Reilly, 2009.

Bligh, Donald. *What's the Use of Lectures?* 5th ed. Exeter, UK: Intellect, 1998.

Boice, James Montgomery. *Romans*. 4 vols. Grand Rapids: Baker, 1992–95.

Bonhoeffer, Dietrich. *The Cost of Discipleship*. Rev. ed. Translated by R. H. Fuller. New York: Macmillan, 1963.

Bormann, Ernest G. *The Force of Fantasy: Restoring the American Dream*. Carbondale: Southern Illinois University Press, 1985.

Bramer, Stephen J. *The Bible Reader's Joke Book*. N.p.: CreateSpace, 2014.

Broadus, John A. *A Treatise on the Preparation and Delivery of Sermons*. 2nd ed. Philadelphia: Smith, English,1871.

Brooks, Phillips. *Lectures on Preaching: Delivered before the Divinity School of Yale College in January and February 1877*. New York: E. P. Dutton, 1877.

Buechner, Frederick. *Telling the Truth: The Gospel as Tragedy, Comedy, and Fairy Tale*. New York: Harper & Row, 1977.

Buttrick, David G. *A Captive Voice: The Liberation of Preaching*. Louisville: Westminster John Knox, 1994.

———. *Homiletic: Moves and Structures*. Philadelphia: Fortress, 1987.

———. "Interpretation and Preaching." *Interpretation* 35 (1981): 46–58.

Calvin, John. *Summary of Doctrine concerning the Ministry of the Word and the Sacraments*. In *Theological Treatises*, edited by J. K. S. Reid, 170–77. Library of Christian Classics 22. Philadelphia: Westminster, 1954.

Carey, Eustace. *Memoir of William Carey, D.D*. London: Jackson and Walford, 1836.

Carnegie, Dale. *How to Develop Self-Confidence and Influence People by Public Speaking*. New York: Pocket Books, 1991.

Carter, Terry G., J. Scott Duvall, and J. Daniel Hays. *Preaching God's Word: A Hands-On Approach to Preparing, Developing, and Delivering the Sermon*. Grand Rapids: Zondervan, 2005.

Cash, Johnny. *Man in White*. New York: Harper & Row, 1986.

———. "No Earthly Good." In the album *The Rambler*. Produced by Charlie Bragg, Jack Routh, and Johnny Cash. New York: Columbia, 1977.

Chapell, Bryan. *Christ-Centered Preaching: Redeeming the Expository Sermon*. 2nd ed. Grand Rapids: Baker Books, 2005.

Chib, Vikram S., Ryo Adachi, and John P. O'Doherty. "Neural Substrates of Social Facilitation Effects on Incentive-Based Performance." *Social Cognitive and Affective Neuroscience* 13 (2018): 391–403.

Childers, Jana. *Performing the Word: Preaching as Theatre.* Nashville: Abingdon, 1998.

Colson, Charles, and Ellen Vaughn. *Being the Body.* Nashville: Thomas Nelson, 2003.

Cowper, William. "The Timepiece." In "The Task," book 2. https://ebooks.adelaide .edu.au/c/cowper/william/task/book2.html.

Craddock, Fred B. *As One without Authority.* Nashville: Abingdon, 1979.

———. *Preaching.* Nashville: Abingdon, 1985.

Davis, Henry Grady. *Design for Preaching.* Philadelphia: Fortress, 1958.

Delnay, Robert G. *Fire in Your Pulpit.* Schaumburg, IL: Regular Baptist Press, 1990.

Edwards, Jonathan. "Part III: Showing, in Many Instances, Wherein the Subjects, or Zealous Promoters, of This Work, Have Been Injuriously Blamed." In *The Works of Jonathan Edwards, A.M.,* 1:390–97. Revised by Edward Hickman. London: William Ball, 1839.

———. "Sinners in the Hands of an Angry God. A Sermon Preached at Enfield, July 8th, 1741." Edited by Reiner Smolinski. Electronic Texts in American Studies 54. http://digitalcommons.unl.edu/etas/54.

Eidam, Klaus. *The True Life of Johann Sebastian Bach.* Translated by Hoyt Rogers. New York: Basic Books, 2001.

Evans, Tony. *Tony Evans' Book of Illustrations.* Chicago: Moody, 2009.

Fee, Gordon D. *Listening to the Spirit in the Text.* Grand Rapids: Eerdmans, 2000.

Fénelon, François. "Éloquence et Critique." In *Pages Choisies des Grands Écrivains,* 97–123. Paris: Librairie Armand Colin, 1911.

Finney, Charles Grandison. *Revivals of Religion.* New York: Leavitt, Lord, 1835.

Fosdick, Harry Emerson. "What Is the Matter with Preaching?" *Harper's Magazine* 157 (July 1928): 133–41.

Franklin, Aaron, and Jordon Mackay. *Franklin Barbecue: A Meat-Smoking Manifesto.* Berkeley: Ten Speed, 2015.

Galbraith, John Kenneth. *Money: Whence It Came, Where It Went.* Princeton: Princeton University Press, 2017.

Galli, Mark, and Craig Brian Larson. *Preaching That Connects: Using the Techniques of Journalists to Add Impact to Your Sermons.* Grand Rapids: Zondervan, 1994.

General Council on Finance and Administration of the Methodist Church. "Copyright Compliance for Local Churches." 2015. http://s3.amazonaws.com/Website_GCFA /reports/legal/documents/Copyright_Compliance_for_Local_Chuches_2015.pdf.

Gerson, Michael. "Obama Speeches Gain from Teleprompter." *Washington Post,* March 27, 2009. http://www.washingtonpost.com/wp-dyn/content/article/2009 /03/26/AR2009032603114.html?hpid=opinionsbox1.

Gilbert, Josiah H. *Dictionary of Burning Words of Brilliant Writers.* New York: Wilbur B. Ketcham, 1895.

Goleman, Daniel. *Emotional Intelligence: Why It Can Matter More Than IQ.* New York: Bantam, 1995.

Greidanus, Sidney. *The Modern Preacher and the Ancient Text: Interpreting and Preaching Biblical Literature.* Grand Rapids: Eerdmans, 1988.

Heath, Chip, and Dan Heath. *Made to Stick: Why Some Ideas Survive and Others Die.* New York: Random House, 2007.

———. *Switch: How to Change Things When Change Is Hard.* New York: Broadway, 2010.

Heil, John Paul. *Ephesians: Empowerment to Walk in Love for the Unity of All in Christ.* Studies in Biblical Literature 13. Atlanta: SBL, 2007.

Henderson, David W. *Culture Shift: Communicating God's Truth to Our Changing World.* Grand Rapids: Baker, 1998.

Hennenlotter, Andreas, Ulrike Schroeder, Peter Erhard, Florian Castrop, Bernhard Haslinger, Daniela Stoecker, Klaus W. Lange, and Andres O. Ceballos-Baumann. "A Common Neural Basis for Receptive and Expressive Communication of Pleasant Facial Affect." *NeuroImage* 26 (2005): 581–91.

Hoehner, Harold. *Ephesians: An Exegetical Commentary.* Grand Rapids: Baker Academic, 2002.

Hoff, Ron. *"I Can See You Naked."* Rev. ed. Kansas City, MO: Andrews and McMeel, 1992.

Hogan, Lucy Lind, and Robert Reid. *Connecting with the Congregation: Rhetoric and the Art of Preaching.* Nashville: Abingdon, 1999.

Humbert of Romans. "Treatise on Preaching." In *Opera: De Vita Regulari.* Vol. II, 373–484. Rome: Befani, 1889.

Hutton, John S., Tzipi Horowitz-Kraus, Alan L. Mendelsohn, Tom DeWitt, and Scott K. Holland. "Home Reading Environment and Brain Activation in Preschool Children Listening to Stories." *Pediatrics* 136 (2015): 467–78.

Jacks, G. Robert. *Just Say the Word! Writing for the Ear.* Grand Rapids: Eerdmans, 1996.

Jeter, Jeremiah Bell. *The Recollections of a Long Life.* Richmond: Religious Herald, 1891.

Kaiser, Walter C. "A Principlizing Model." In *Four Views on Moving beyond the Bible to Theology,* edited by Gary T. Meadors, 19–50. Grand Rapids: Zondervan, 2009.

———. *Toward an Exegetical Theology: Biblical Exegesis for Preaching and Teaching.* Grand Rapids: Baker, 1981.

Kaufman, Gordon D. *An Essay on Theological Method.* 3rd ed. Atlanta: American Academy of Religion, 1995.

Keillor, Garrison. "Pontoon Boat." In *Life among the Lutherans*, 15–20. Edited by Holly Harden. Minneapolis: Augsburg, 2010.

Kelley, Tom, and Jonathan Littman. *The Art of Innovation: Lessons in Creativity from IDEO, America's Leading Design Firm*. New York: Random House, 2001.

Kemper, Deane A. *Effective Preaching: A Manual for Students and Pastors*. Philadelphia: Westminster, 1985.

Klass, Perri. "Bedtime Stories for Young Brains." *New York Times*, August 17, 2015. https://well.blogs.nytimes.com/2015/08/17/bedtime-stories-for-young-brains/?_r=0.

Koren, Leonard. *Wabi-Sabi for Artists, Designers, Poets, and Philosophers*. Point Reyes, CA: Imperfect Publishing, 2008.

Kuruvilla, Abraham. "Applicational Preaching." *Bibliotheca Sacra* 173 (2016): 387–400.

———. "Christiconic Interpretation." *Bibliotheca Sacra* 173 (2016): 131–46.

———. "Christiconic View" (and responses to other contributors). In *Homiletics and Hermeneutics: Four Views on Preaching Today*, edited by Scott M. Gibson and Matthew D. Kim, 43–70 (30–34, 111–12, 150–53). Grand Rapids: Baker Academic, 2018.

———. *Ephesians: A Theological Commentary for Preachers*. Eugene, OR: Cascade, 2015.

———. *Genesis: A Theological Commentary for Preachers*. Eugene, OR: Resource, 2014.

———. *Judges: A Theological Commentary for Preachers*. Eugene, OR: Cascade, 2017.

———. *Mark: A Theological Commentary for Preachers*. Eugene, OR: Cascade: 2012.

———. "Pericopal Theology." *Bibliotheca Sacra* 173 (2016): 3–17.

———. *Privilege the Text! A Theological Hermeneutic for Preaching*. Chicago: Moody, 2013.

———. "Theological Exegesis." *Bibliotheca Sacra* 173 (2016): 259–72.

———. "Time to Kill the Big Idea? A Fresh Look at Preaching." *Journal of the Evangelical Theological Society* 61, no. 4 (2018): 825–46. Also available at http://homiletix.com/kill-the-big-idea.

———. *A Vision for Preaching: Understanding the Heart of Pastoral Ministry*. Grand Rapids: Baker Academic, 2015.

———. "'What Is the Author *Doing* with What He Is *Saying*?' Pragmatics and Preaching—An Appeal!" *Journal of the Evangelical Theological Society* 60 (2017): 557–80. Also available at http://www.homiletix.com/KuruvillaJETS2017.

Kushner, Malcolm. *Public Speaking for Dummies*. Foster City, CA: IDG, 1999.

Langer, Susanne K. *Feeling and Form: A Theory of Art*. New York: Charles Scribner's Sons, 1953.

Larsen, David L. *Telling the Old, Old Story: The Art of Narrative Preaching*. Grand Rapids: Kregel, 1995.

Larson, Craig Brian, and *Leadership Journal*. *750 Engaging Illustrations for Preachers, Teachers, and Writers*. Grand Rapids: Baker Books, 2007.

Levelt, William J. M. "Accessing Words in Speech Production: Stages, Processes and Representations." *Cognition* 42 (1992): 1–22.

Lewis, C. S. *God in the Dock: Essays on Theology and Ethics*. Edited by Walter Hooper. Grand Rapids: Eerdmans, 2014.

Lewis, C. S., and E. M. Tillyard. *The Personal Heresy in Criticism*. London: Oxford University Press, 1939.

Litfin, Duane. *Public Speaking: A Handbook for Christians*. 2nd ed. Grand Rapids: Baker, 1992.

Long, Thomas G. "The Distance We Have Traveled: Changing Trends in Preaching." In *A Reader on Preaching: Making Connections*, edited by David Day, Jeff Astley, and Leslie J. Francis, 11–16. Aldershot, UK: Ashgate, 2005.

———. "Stolen Goods: Tempted to Plagiarize." *Christian Century* 124, no. 8 (2007): 18–21.

———. "The Use of Scripture in Contemporary Preaching." *Interpretation* 44 (1990): 341–52.

———. *The Witness of Preaching*. 3rd ed. Louisville: Westminster John Knox, 2016.

Lowry, Eugene L. *Doing Time in the Pulpit*. Nashville: Abingdon, 1985.

———. *How to Preach a Parable: Designs for Narrative Sermons*. Nashville: Abingdon, 1989.

———. *The Sermon: Dancing the Edge of Mystery*. Nashville: Abingdon, 1997.

Lucado, Max. *In the Eye of the Storm: Jesus Knows How You Feel*. Nashville: Thomas Nelson, 2012.

Luther, Martin. "Preface to Johann Spangenberg." In *Luther's Works, Vol. 60: Prefaces II*, edited by Christopher Boyd Brown, 281–85. Translated by Mickey L. Mattox. St. Louis: Concordia, 2011.

———. "Psalm 101." In *Luther's Works, Vol. 13: Selected Psalms II*, edited by Jaroslav Pelikan, 143–224. Translated by Alfred von Rohr Sauer. St. Louis: Concordia, 1956.

MacArthur, John F. "Frequently Asked Questions about Expository Preaching." In *Rediscovering Expository Preaching*, edited by John F. MacArthur, Richard L. Mayhue, and Robert L. Thomas, 334–49. Dallas: Word, 1992.

Mackay, Jordon. "Coauthor's Note." In *Franklin Barbecue: A Meat-Smoking Manifesto*, by Aaron Franklin and Jordon Mackay, viii–ix. Berkeley: Ten Speed, 2015.

Makary, M. A., and M. Daniel. "Medical Error—The Third Leading Cause of Death in the US." *British Medical Journal* 353 (2016): i2139.

Manchester, William. *The Last Lion: Winston Spencer Churchill Alone, 1932–1940*. New York: Bantam, 1988.

Marshall, John. *McCulloch v. Maryland*. 17 U.S. 316 (1819).

Mathews, Alice P. *Preaching That Speaks to Women*. Grand Rapids: Baker Academic, 2003.

Medawar, Peter B. *Induction and Intuition in Scientific Thought*. Philadelphia: American Philosophical Society, 1969.

Mehrabian, Albert. "Inference of Attitudes from Nonverbal Communication in Two Channels." *Journal of Consulting Psychology* 31, no. 3 (1967): 248–52.

———. *Silent Messages*. Belmont, CA: Wadsworth, 1971.

Mitchell, Henry H. *Black Preaching: The Recovery of a Powerful Art*. Nashville: Abingdon, 1990.

———. "Preaching on the Patriarchs." In *Biblical Preaching: An Expositor's Treasury*, edited by James W. Cox, 36–52. Philadelphia: Westminster, 1983.

Moberly, R. W. L. *The Bible, Theology, and Faith: A Study of Abraham and Jesus*. Cambridge: Cambridge University Press, 2000.

Newton, Elizabeth Louise. "The Rocky Road from Actions to Intentions." PhD diss., Stanford University, 1990.

Nichols, J. Randall. *Building the Word: The Dynamics of Communication and Preaching*. San Francisco: Harper & Row, 1980.

O'Connor, Flannery. *Mystery and Manners*. Edited by Sally and Robert Fitzgerald. New York: Farrar, Straus & Giroux, 1957.

Olford, Stephen F., and David L. Olford. *Anointed Expository Preaching*. Nashville: Broadman & Holman, 1998.

Osborne, Grant R. *The Hermeneutical Spiral: A Comprehensive Introduction to Biblical Interpretation*. Downers Grove, IL: InterVarsity, 1991.

Pascal, Blaise. *Pascal's Pensées*. Translated by W. F. Trotter. New York: E. P. Dutton, 1958.

Pashler, Harold, Mark McDaniel, Doug Rohrer, and Robert Bjork. "Learning Styles: Concepts and Evidence." *Psychological Science in the Public Interest* 9, no. 3 (2008): 105–19.

Philo. *The Works of Philo Judaeus*. Translated by C. D. Yonge. London: Henry G. Bohn, 1855.

Pinker, Stephen. *The Sense of Style: The Thinking Person's Guide to Writing in the 21st Century*. New York: Penguin, 2015.

Plato. *Euthyphro. Apology. Crito. Phaedo. Phaedrus*. Translated by Harold North Fowler. Loeb Classical Library 36. Cambridge, MA: Harvard University Press, 1914.

Pliny the Younger. "To Maecilius Nepos." In *Letters, Vol. I: Books 1–7*, 85–98. Translated by Betty Radice. Loeb Classical Library 55. Cambridge, MA: Harvard University Press, 1969.

Plutarch. *Lives, Volume VII: Demosthenes and Cicero. Alexander and Caesar*. Translated by Bernadotte Perrin. Loeb Classical Library 99. Cambridge, MA: Harvard University Press, 1919.

Pomerance, Laura, Julie Greenberg, and Kate Walsh. *Learning about Learning: What Every New Teacher Needs to Know*. New York: National Council on Teacher Quality, 2016.

Pope, Alexander. *An Essay on Criticism*. Poetry Foundation, October 13, 2009. https://www.poetryfoundation.org/articles/69379/an-essay-on-criticism.

Quintilian. *The Orator's Education, Vol. I: Books 1–2*. Edited and translated by Donald A. Russell. Loeb Classical Library 124. Cambridge, MA: Harvard University Press, 2002.

———. *The Orator's Education, Vol. III: Books 6–9*. Edited and translated by Donald A. Russell. Loeb Classical Library 126. Cambridge, MA: Harvard University Press, 2002.

———. *The Orator's Education, Vol. V: Books 11–12*. Edited and translated by Donald A. Russell. Loeb Classical Library 494. Cambridge, MA: Harvard University Press, 2002.

Rice, Wayne. *Hot Illustrations for Youth Talks: 100 Attention-Getting Stories, Parables, and Anecdotes*. Grand Rapids: Zondervan, 1994.

Ricoeur, Paul. *Hermeneutics and the Human Sciences: Essays on Language, Action and Interpretation*. Edited and translated by John B. Thompson. Cambridge: Cambridge University Press, 1981.

Rizzolatti, Giacomo. "The Mirror Neuron System and Its Function in Humans." *Anatomy and Embryology* 210 (2005): 419–21.

Robert of Basevorn. *The Form of Preaching*. Translated by Leopold Krul. In *Three Medieval Rhetorical Arts*, edited by James J. Murphy, 109–216. Berkeley: University of California Press, 1971.

Robinson, Haddon W. "Better Big Ideas: Five Qualities of the Strongest Preaching Ideas." In *The Art and Craft of Biblical Preaching: A Comprehensive Resource for Today's Communicators*, edited by Haddon W. Robinson and Craig Brian Larson, 353–57. Grand Rapids: Zondervan, 2005.

———. *Biblical Preaching: The Development and Delivery of Expository Messages*. Grand Rapids: Baker, 1980.

———. *Biblical Preaching: The Development and Delivery of Expository Messages*. 3rd ed. Grand Rapids: Baker Academic, 2014.

Rummage, Stephen Nelson. *Planning Your Preaching: A Step-by-Step Guide for Developing a One-Year Preaching Calendar*. Grand Rapids: Kregel, 2002.

Schreiner, Thomas R. *Paul, Apostle of God's Glory in Christ: A Pauline Theology*. Downers Grove, IL: InterVarsity, 2001.

Selby, Gary S. *Not with Wisdom of Words: Nonrational Persuasion in the New Testament*. Grand Rapids: Eerdmans, 2016.

Shakespeare, William. *The Merchant of Venice*. http://shakespeare.mit.edu/merchant/full.html.

Sjogren, Steve. "Don't Be Original, Be Effective!" Pastors.com, 2006. http://web
.archive.org/web/20060318020013/http://www.pastors.com/article.asp?ArtID=92
30.

Sleeth, Ronald E. *God's Word and Our Words: Basic Homiletics.* Atlanta: John Knox,
1986.

Smith, James K. A. *Desiring the Kingdom: Worship, Worldview, and Cultural Formation.* Cultural Liturgies 1. Grand Rapids: Baker Academic, 2009.

Spurgeon, Charles Haddon. *Lectures to My Students.* Rev. ed. Grand Rapids: Zondervan, 1954.

Stephens, Greg J., Lauren J. Silbert, and Uri Hasson. "Speaker-Listener Neural Coupling Underlies Successful Communication." *Proceedings of the National Academy of Sciences* 107 (2010): 14,425–30.

Stewart-Sykes, Alistair. *From Prophecy to Preaching: A Search for the Origins of
the Christian Homily.* Supplement to *Vigiliae Christianae* 59. Leiden: Brill, 2001.

Stott, John R. W. *Between Two Worlds: The Art of Preaching in the Twentieth Century.* Grand Rapids: Eerdmans, 1982.

Student Handbook 2016–18. Dallas: Dallas Theological Seminary.

Sunukjian, Donald R. *Invitation to Biblical Preaching: Proclaiming Truth with Clarity
and Relevance.* Grand Rapids: Kregel, 2007.

Swindoll, Charles. *Swindoll's Ultimate Book of Illustrations & Quotes.* Nashville:
Thomas Nelson, 1998.

Thoreau, Henry D. *Walden: A Fully Annotated Edition.* Edited by Jeffrey S. Cramer.
New Haven: Yale University Press, 2004.

Turabian, Kate L. *A Manual for Writers of Research Papers, Theses, and Dissertations.*
9th ed. Chicago: University of Chicago Press, 2018.

Twain, Mark. "Chapters from My Autobiography: XX." *North American Review*
185 (July 1907): 465–74.

Vanhoozer, Kevin J. "Putting on Christ: Spiritual Formation and the Drama of Discipleship." *Journal of Spiritual Formation & Soul Care* 8, no. 2 (2015): 147–71.

Warner, Jack L., and Dean Jennings. *My First Hundred Years in Hollywood.* New
York: Random House, 1965.

Warren, Max. *Crowded Canvas: Some Experiences of a Life-Time.* Kent, UK: Hod-
der & Stoughton, 1974.

Warren, Timothy S. "Definition, Purpose, and Process." In *PM103 Class Notes*, 1–38.
Dallas: Dallas Theological Seminary, 2003.

———. "The Developmental Questions (DQs I & II)." In *PM103 Class Notes*, 80–86.
Dallas: Dallas Theological Seminary, 2003.

———. "A Paradigm for Preaching." *Bibliotheca Sacra* 148 (1991): 463–86.

———. "Purpose, Proposition, and Structures." In *PM103 Class Notes*, 93–105.
Dallas: Dallas Theological Seminary, 2003.

————. "Supporting Materials." In *PM103 Class Notes*, 106–10. Dallas: Dallas Theological Seminary, 2003.

————. "The Theological Process in Sermon Preparation." *Bibliotheca Sacra* 156 (1999): 336–56.

————. "Topical Expository Preaching." In *PM201 Class Notes*, 1–25. Dallas: Dallas Theological Seminary, 2006.

Watson, Duane F. "Why We Need Socio-Rhetorical Commentary and What It Might Look Like." In *Rhetorical Criticism and the Bible*, edited by Stanley E. Porter and Dennis L. Stamps, 129–57. Journal for the Study of the New Testament Supplement Series 195. Sheffield: Sheffield Academic Press, 2002.

Wegeler, Franz, and Ferdinand Ries. *Biographische Notizen über Ludwig van Beethoven*. 2nd ed. Leipzig: Schuster and Loeffler, 1906.

Wiesel, Elie. *Night*. Translated by Marion Wiesel. New York: Hill and Wang, 2006.

Willimon, William H. *Preaching and Leading Worship*. Philadelphia: Westminster, 1984.

Willingham, Daniel T., Elizabeth M. Hughes, and David G. Dobolyi. "The Scientific Status of Learning Styles Theories." *Teaching of Psychology* 42, no. 3 (2015): 266–71.

Wingfield, Arthur. "Cognitive Factors in Auditory Performance: Context, Speed of Processing, and Constraints of Memory." *Journal of the American Academy of Audiology* 7 (1996): 175–82.

Wooden, John, and Steve Jamison. *Wooden: A Lifetime of Observations and Reflections on and off the Court*. New York: McGraw-Hill, 1997.

Wright, N. T. *After You Believe: Why Christian Character Matters*. New York: HarperOne, 2012.

Zadbood, Asieh, Janice Chen, Yuan Chang Leong, Kenneth A. Norman, and Uri Hasson. "How We Transit Memories to Other Brains: Constructing Shared Neural Representations via Communication." *Cerebral Cortex* 27 (2017): 4988–5000.

Index